HITCH
HOCKEY'S UNSUNG HERO

HITCH
HOCKEY'S UNSUNG HERO

The Story of Boston Bruin
Lionel Hitchman

PAM COBURN

Pamdre Publishing Inc, Manotick, ON

Copyright © 2019 by Pam Coburn

All rights reserved. No part of this book may be used or reproduced in any manner whatsoever without written permission, except in the case of brief quotations in critical articles and reviews. For more information, contact Pamdre Publishing Inc., info@pamdre.com

Published 2019
Printed in the United States of America

ISBN-978-1-9990297-2-2 (paperback)
ISBN-978-1-9990297-1-5 (ebook)

To the memory of Hitch, Tops, Gloria and Claude, you have inspired and left an indelible mark on those who came after you.

Table of Contents

INTRODUCTION: THREE TRIES FOR NO. 3 1
1. TORONTO, BY WAY OF ENGLAND 15
2. THE WAR YEARS 23
3. GETTING ON WITH LIFE 31
4. THE CAPITAL OF HOCKEY 43
5. TURNING? 57
6. 32 DAYS TO THE STANLEY CUP 67
7. THE OTTAWA ADONIS 97
8. IN TRANSITION 125
9. RAMPING UP 143
10. STANLEY CUP CHAMPS 185
11. GREATEST TEAM, GREATEST DEFENSEMAN 207
12. WANING 245
13. THE COACHING YEARS 279
14. LIFE WITHOUT HOCKEY 295
15. LAST WORD ON HITCH 303
Appendix 313
Acknowledgments 317
Chapter Notes 319
Bibliography 343
Index 345

INTRODUCTION: THREE TRIES FOR NO. 3

The first time a player's number was retired and never worn again in the National Hockey League was on February 22, 1934, in a ceremony just before a Boston Bruins home game.[1] The Great Depression was in full view, and the Bruins were in last place in their division. Crowds for the previous three home games averaged 4,300, in an arena that held 15,000. Boston was playing the Ottawa Senators, the "tailender" in the other NHL division.

That night, 9,000 fans came to the Boston Garden to say goodbye to their beloved "Hitch." They watched Art Ross, manager of the Boston Bruins, hand him a No. 3 Boston sweater as announcer Frank Ryan declared that Hitch's number would be forever retired.

Frederick Lionel Hitchman, or Hitch as he was usually known, played hockey in the NHL for 12 seasons. He broke into the league with the Ottawa Senators in 1923, helping them to a Stanley Cup championship that year. Hitch went to the Boston Bruins in their first season (1924-25) and stayed for the balance of his playing career. He was the team captain when Boston won its first Stanley Cup and when the team set the record the following season for highest winning percentage (.875), which still stands today.

Hitch was my grandfather, my mother's dad. As a child, I didn't know much about him, other than his hockey number was retired, and he had been captain of the Boston team. And that he and my grandmother, Tops, divorced, and he remarried, lived in Indian Lake, New York and was a forest ranger. Family trips from our home in Ottawa, Ontario, to visit Hitch and his second wife, Edna, were fun. Their property was large with rental cabins and a pond. They didn't fuss over little things and were very kind to us. After all, we were Hitch's only grandchildren: my oldest sister Claudia, brother John, sister Leslie and me.

When Hitch died, I was 12, and my mother, Gloria, was devastated. I had never seen her in that state before. He died on December 5, 1968, and she wasn't notified until just before Christmas.

She spent weeks trying to find out more about his death. The local funeral director finally wrote back to her in January, only to say that Hitch's funeral was attended at the most by three people and his wife paid the funeral expenses.

It wasn't the information Gloria wanted. It hadn't been that long since she last saw her father. If he'd been sick why hadn't anyone contacted her? Why couldn't she get a hold of Edna? What did he die of and where? Had an autopsy been performed? Where were all her father's papers, his Stanley Cup diamond ring, and watches, the rest of his worldly goods? She went into stealth mode to learn more and retrieve what she could.

Gloria, my mother, our world, was heartbroken, driven to distraction, and her grief hung over our family. While she was able to collect many of Hitch's personal effects, she agonized over what little information she had about his death. As the years marched on, the angrier Gloria got over the mystery of his death and his "secret" funeral with virtually no mourners. She wanted her father's hockey legacy preserved. Gloria contacted some hockey people she knew to help get Hitch inducted into the Hockey Hall of Fame (HHOF). It wasn't a mystery to her why he wasn't on the list, but that was water under the bridge, and it was time to right that wrong.

As I arrived home from school one day in June of 1973, Maurice "Lefty" Reid, curator and secretary of the HHOF was sitting in our living room chatting with Mom. In anticipation of her father's induction, Gloria donated two hockey sweaters to the Hall, and Mr. Reid left with "one worn by Lionel Hitchman after Boston Bruins won their first Stanley Cup, the other presented to Mr. Hitchman upon his retirement as a player."[2]

Gloria was disheartened to learn that Hitch was not on that year's list of inductees. I'm not certain what other actions she took before her death in 1984, but it continued to be unfinished business between our family and the HHOF.

In September 1995, our family received a lovely invitation from the Boston Bruins to the closing of the Boston Garden. And to participate in the ceremonies to transfer the retired player numbers from the soon-to-be-razed old rink to the new Fleet Center (now TD Garden). Dubbed the "Last Hurrah," the club paid for a couple of airline tickets and hotel rooms for our family to attend. Our dad, Claude Coburn didn't want to go. He wasn't one for spectacles generally. Plus, our extended family had just suffered a tragic loss a month earlier when former NHL player and broadcaster Brian Smith was the random victim of a gun shooting at his place of work. Emotions were already raw, and knowing how Dad felt about Hitch, it would have been too much excitement for him.

John decided to stay home with Dad and let the sisters go. With six of Hitch's great grandchildren in tow, we headed for Boston—two flew, and the rest piled into my vehicle. I don't think the club expected such a large and youthful contingent from the Hitchman clan, but they were very gracious just the same, letting the kids go to the special receptions to meet the stars such as Bobby Orr. Claudia was our representative for the retired numbers ceremony; she went on the ice to receive Hitch's No. 3 when it was lowered from the Garden rafters and put up in the new building.

The highlight for me was meeting some of the old-timers who spoke so highly of Hitch and our grandmother, Tops. Milt Schmidt, a former player on Boston's "Kraut" line, and, coach and general manager of the club, told us lots of stories. He insisted that Hitch was instrumental in signing and developing all three members of that famous forward line.He also told us that when he first arrived in Boston, he lived with Hitch and Tops, as did some of the other new players.

Four years after the Last Hurrah and just before our Dad died in 1999, he handed John and me some unique artifacts from Hitch's hockey career. John got his medals and a statue of his likeness, and I received the plaque given to Hitch from the Boston fans the night of his retirement ceremony in 1934. Dad's only request: that we continue the family effort to get Hitch into the HHOF.

I was surprised that Dad had given me the plaque and wanted me to help with this quest. He knew my interest in hockey was less than lukewarm, stemming from the fights at my brother's amateur hockey games and turning into a full-fledged aversion just before my 13th birthday. Boston had been in town to play a preseason game against St. Louis. Milt Schmidt, Boston's GM, gave Tops two tickets, and she gave them to John and me, hoping to ignite my interest in the sport. That was September 21, 1969, not a year since Hitch's death.

At the game, an incident happened that remains with me today. "Anybody close to the scene had to be chilled by the grotesque look from the fallen Green's eyes, one of them cocked crazily in a sickening stare."[3]

Seasoned tough guy Ted Green of Boston had been sparring all night with rookie Wayne Maki of St. Louis. In the act of retaliation or frustration by Maki for some jabs he'd received earlier from Green, he swung his stick wildly and hit Green over the head, in an era when no one wore helmets. As medical staff tried to get Green off the ice, he hung onto the wired mesh protector at the end of the rink, like a caged animal. After they got him freed of the wire and off the ice, the Boston team went after Maki. The whole event sickened me. I wasn't the only one who felt that way. Veteran sportscaster Dan Kelly, who was there, later told sports historian Brian McFarlane, "I could see right away that Green was badly hurt. When he tried to get up, his face was contorted, and his legs began to buckle under him. It was dreadful. I almost became physically ill watching him struggle because I knew this was very, very serious. I remember it like it happened yesterday."[4]

Green had a fractured skull that required four hours on the operating table and a metal plate. The NHL levied fines on both players and instructed the league's head referee, Scotty Morrison, to lay down the law on game violence. The Ottawa police charged both players and later they were exonerated. Green was out of hockey for a year, and there was talk he would never play again. But he did. Ironically, it was Maki who died just five years later of an unrelated brain tumor.

Even with this horrific introduction to the NHL, of course, I wanted to see Hitch in the HHOF. I think Dad included me in this quest because at the time, I was Skate Canada's executive director, and maybe he thought I could be useful in some way. But I doubted Hitch's eligibility. To someone like me, who had been peripherally around hockey most of my life, Hitch's stats didn't look remarkable. John forged ahead without me, likely sensing my (uninformed) skepticism, and I, in turn, felt relieved.

John was the right person to take up the challenge. He had played hockey at the Junior A level, then went to university. As a former All-American honors defenseman, he was invited to three NHL training camps as an undrafted player in the late '70s. Slated for a Midwest U.S. farm team, John decided to hang up his skates.

John nobly fulfilled our father's request for a second try at the HHOF for our grandfather. He spent countless hours poring over old newspaper clippings from scrapbooks our grandmother had meticulously kept on Hitch's hockey career. When John's submission was ready in 2006, he sent it to Harry Sinden, then president of the Boston Bruins, hoping the club would submit it to the HHOF.

Mr. Sinden responded on January 23, 2006, that he had read John's material and found it "very informative, educational and persuasive." However, he had already prepared a submission for another player, "which would limit the effectiveness of [him] submitting on behalf of Mr. Hitchman." Instead, Mr. Sinden spoke with and forwarded John's work to the head of the HHOF selection committee, requesting it be included in the "public submission" process, and adding that "there is no doubt Mr. Hitchman's career makes him worthy of consideration for this honor."

Unfortunately, John's submission went unanswered (the committee contacts a submitter only if successful). It seems Mr. Sinden's wasn't successful either, as no Boston player was inducted in 2006.

I still hadn't caught the HHOF submission bug, but after the Last Hurrah and my conversation with Milt Schmidt, who later made his way to Ottawa to deliver some items he had of Hitch's, I started to become very interested in my grandparents' life together. In the '30s Hitch and Tops owned a lodge in Maine that they operated as a small inn, called Koanneeta. Our parents took us there on vacation back in the '60s, long after Hitch and Tops had owned it. Mom spent most of her childhood in Boston and Maine and loved sharing with us her memories of what was a magical time for her.

For my 50th birthday, I invited my two sisters on an excursion to find Koanneeta. We knew the name of the lake it had been on, close to Kennebunkport, but that's all we knew. John gave me a gift for the trip to only be opened after we arrived at our hotel, a 10 mm film from the 1930s transferred onto DVD of Hitch and Tops at Koanneeta. It was shocking to see those two young people, our grandparents, right before our eyes.

This film stiffened our resolve to find Koanneeta. We left our hotel at Kennebunkport early on September 24, 2006, and traveled to Shapleigh, Maine, using our printed MapQuest directions. We made several stops, including the general store in that town, which doubled as the local diner, asking if anyone had ever heard of Koanneeta. No one had. The waitress there suggested we go to the craft shop, as the owner was a history buff and might have some information. We took her advice, but unfortunately, as it was Sunday, the shop owner wasn't working. We drove around some more, stopped a man at a marina and asked him. He didn't know but suggested we make our way back to the general store as church was just out and the locals would be gathered there for lunch. It had now been a few hours since we first started our journey, and we were hungry anyway, so we headed back to the diner for lunch.

When we arrived, we told the same waitress that we'd struck out and could not find any information on Koanneeta. She put down the coffee pot she was holding and turned to address the 20-some patrons, telling them that these "nice Canadians" had come to find Koanneeta, and asked if anyone had heard of it. A frail elderly woman raised her hand and said she had heard of the Fourth of July parties there with all the hockey players. A few others nodded as well. This lady, her husband, and another man pieced together where they thought Koanneeta might have been and drew us a map. We thanked them and headed off. As we left the main road and took a dirt one toward the lake, "Hitchman Road" popped up on our vehicle's GPS. If only we had known there was a road named after Hitch, it wouldn't have been such a big adventure!

Our optimism was a bit premature; as we drove along Hitchman Road, nothing looked familiar. We thought maybe one place looked like it, but no one was home, so I left a note. We drove around some more, and Les thought she spotted the location of the old dance hall we had heard so much about from our mother. I stopped our SUV, and we got out and carefully traversed a very steep hill down toward the lake, but nothing was there. We slowly walked back up to our vehicle, happy to have found Hitchman Road, but sad that nothing in the vicinity matched our childhood memories.

It was raining, and as we reached the road, a car was stopped facing our SUV. I realized in my haste to find the dance hall that I had parked in the middle of the road, blocking all traffic coming and going. I rushed over to the miffed driver in the waiting car, making my apologies, hoping he hadn't waited too long, and offering my excuse that we were trying to find our grandfather's lodge, Koanneeta, to which he responded, "I own Koanneeta. Tell me, are the stories about the bear true?"

We made our introductions. He was John Chamberlain from Marblehead, Massachusetts, and had owned Koanneeta for 16 years. John invited us to follow him there for a tour, and we became instant friends. (By the way, the place where I left the note was not Koanneeta.)

Later that year, Claudia and I went back to Koanneeta with brother John and our partners to introduce everyone and to meet John Chamberlain's wife, Nancy. Chamberlain introduced us to Inez Snowden, who had property on a nearby lake. As we discovered, her maiden name was Giafranchi, and she was the daughter of Ferdinand (Ferd) and Lul, our grandparents' close friends. Inez was seven years older than our mother, but they spent summers together and attended those July 4th parties at Koanneeta. Inez's father was an importer when Hitch and Tops first arrived in Boston. He later became vice president of Pastene wines and spirits. Ferd was also a trustee of the Boston Garden and good friends of Boston Bruins manager, Art Ross. Our connections and collective memory of a time long ago were building with the help of our new acquaintances. But our family's HHOF efforts would lay dormant for the next 10 years.

While enjoying a memorable July 1 dinner at my house with my siblings in 2016, we got around to talking about Hitch and the HHOF. John led the discussion, insisting that Hitch was the greatest defensive defenseman of his generation, overshadowed by Eddie Shore, his defense partner, and so on. John's passion for Hitch's hockey career was infectious, but I always worried it was rooted more in family folklore and bias than in fact. When sister Les asked if we'd seen the article by Dave Stubbs on Hitch, and we hadn't, we pulled it up on my laptop. The headline and byline read:

BRUINS LEGEND HITCHMAN DESERVES HALL RECOGNITION
Unsung great was dependable leader who excelled in the shadows
by Dave Stubbs @dave_stubbs / NHL.com Columnist / Historian, February 22, 2016

Those of us who did not follow hockey the way John did were blown away. Eighty-two years after Hitch had retired, others were writing about him and considered him worthy of the HHOF. I decided at that dinner to take a closer look at Hitch's life and career, and after a preliminary review, I began to see what my brother was going on about.

Stubbs' article made a general reference to Hitch being an "unsung hero." When I tracked down an earlier source, I learned that Stubbs was likely quoting the preeminent sports editor of Hitch's day, Elmer Ferguson, who has an award named after him and given by the HHOF, "in recognition of distinguished members of the newspaper profession whose words have brought honour to journalism and to hockey."[5]

Ferguson wrote a very lengthy article on February 20, 1930, for the *Montreal Herald*, setting out the reasons he was casting his Hart Trophy ballot for Hitch, some of which is repeated below:

> If Mr. Hitchman were with any other club than Boston, he would be acclaimed a super-star, for he is one of those unsung heroes of the whirl-wind ice game. . . . It was really Hitchman who beat the Canadiens in the play-offs last spring. His crashing body-checks early in the play broke the Canadiens attack, and his magnificent defensive completed what he started. It was the tearing play of Shore that brought Bruins from behind in the final game of that series, but it was the sound play of the battle-scarred fighting Hitchman, his face covered with plaster, but his heart still full of fight and courage that really swung the issue. Shore may be the dynamo of the Boston club, but Hitchman is the balance-wheel, and its steadying, sound influence—plus being the greatest defensive defence player in the game today.

In 1942, future HHOF inductee Cooper Smeaton, who served as the NHL's referee-in-chief from 1917 until 1937 and later as Stanley

Cup trustee from 1946 until his death in 1978, claimed Hitch was one of the best defensemen of his era. Here is an excerpt from an interview he gave that year to Bill Westwick of the *Ottawa Journal* on November 14:

> SMEATON'S ALL-STAR SELECTIONS
> "Of the players I've watched in the early part of my refereeing career I'll name:
> "Goal, Georges Vezina; defence, Lionel Hitchman and Sprague Cleghorn; center, Joe Malone; left wing, Aurel Joliat, and right wing, Harry Broadbent."
> What, no Eddie Shore?
> "No, no Eddie Shore this time," says Coop. "I'm naming defence players and Shore, good as he was, never would have been the player he's rated if it wasn't for Lionel Hitchman.
> "'Hitch,' to my mind, was one of the most under-rated players of all time as a defenceman.
> "Eddie drew a lot of the credit, but you ask any of those who played against them who they'd want out there if it was a one-man defence. They'd say Shore because they could get around him. None of them ever relished the task of getting by Hitchman."

Ching Johnson, a New York Rangers defenseman who was inducted into the HHOF in 1958, was asked by John Kieran of the *New York Times* on February 4, 1930, to name his NHL all-star team picks (excluding his teammates): "I'd pick Hitchman first. You notice that Boston defence. Hitchman is the boy out in front who takes 'em first as you come in. He's the shock absorber. If he doesn't stop 'em, Shore gets 'em, but usually Hitchman has thrown them off balance, and that makes Eddie's work a lot easier."

The top brass of opposing clubs also sang Hitch's praises. For instance, the president of the Rangers, Colonel John Hammond, in an interview with syndicated writer Walter Trumbull, stated on

December 19, 1929, that "Hitchman is the hardest man to get around, the greatest checker, and the greatest blocker in the game." I also found it striking that for Tommy Gorman's HHOF biography, alongside describing how he managed three different clubs to Stanley Cup championships, someone felt it noteworthy to mention that Gorman was "personally responsible" for Hitch's joining the Ottawa Senators.[6]

With endorsements like these, it became clear that some sort of disconnect was at play as to why Hitch was not in the HHOF, and I wanted to know more.

In the summer of 2017, I mentioned to my brother that I wanted to write Hitch's life story, and since John had done so much work to date, I felt I owed it to him to ask for his blessing, which was freely given. He seemed confident that I would get the help I needed on the technical stuff and would handle all content with care.

John also knew I intended to write the story with the theme of "Hitch, the greatest player NOT in the HHOF" and suggested we make one more submission attempt. This time I led the document production and wrote the submission, and like my mother and brother before me, my attempt, our third in total, was met with silence from the Hall.

Three tries at the HHOF have failed for the only player to have worn No. 3 for the Boston Bruins in the past 90-plus years. Is there any hope that a fourth submission might catch the interest of the selection committee? Well, we are a resilient and optimistic family, so we shall see. In the meantime, I have written this book to ensure Hitch's legacy lives on.

As I continued to dive deeper into the subject matter for this book, I found others who questioned Hitch's absence from the HHOF. Eric Zweig, who wrote *Art Ross: The Hockey Legend Who Built the Bruins*, used the exact words as the theme of this book when describing Hitch—mind you, he did put the word *probably* in front. Certainly, some will disagree with the premise that Hitch is the greatest unsung hero of the NHL. There are likely many worthy players who for some reason or another have been left off the HHOF list. It just seems that the last original Boston Bruin, a player who captained his team to their first Stanley Cup championship and who, according to Elmer Ferguson, "swung the issue" for Boston in the playoffs, deserves his place in hockey's shrine.

In his 1999 book *The Bruins*, hockey historian Brian McFarlane posed the question of whether Hitch deserves to be in the HHOF in a section titled "Hitchman an Unsung Hero." McFarlane answered his own question with this: "Many oldtimers firmly believe he does."[7]

To tell Hitch's story, it was necessary to find out what those "oldtimers" thought. Television was nonexistent, and radio was in its infancy when he played. But sportswriters were abundant, and they wrote profusely about hockey. And our grandmother it seems kept virtually every article that was ever written about Hitch's professional hockey career, and before her, his mother did the same of his amateur career, in their neatly organized scrapbooks, some of which were sent off to Library and Archives Canada, and some kept just for our family. They were a good starting place to find out what seems to have been forgotten.

Hitch, Hockey's Unsung Hero, presents the words of those sportswriters in their original form wrapped in quotations or shown in block quotations, with only corrections to [names] and [dates] as necessary. Sources are in the chapter notes at the back of the book.

In writing this book, it was gratifying to learn about Hitch's English roots and his time in Toronto. To dig deeper into his life in Ottawa, Boston, and Koanneeta. And while disturbing but somewhat cathartic, to learn of his unraveling at the end of his coaching career and to know more about what happened up until and including his death.

This is the story of Hitch's life, the times he lived through and the fascinating people who helped shape his character and life choices. I hope you enjoy reading it as much I did writing it.

Pam Coburn

*Hitch, Gloria and Tops, circa 1927.
(Photo courtesy of Hitchman private collection)*

HITCH'S ENGLISH ROOTS BACK TO HIS GREAT GRANDPARENTS

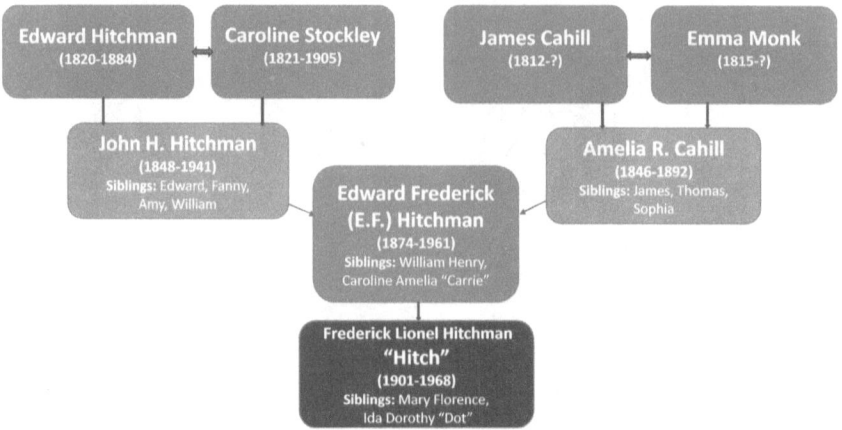

Chapter One

TORONTO, BY WAY OF ENGLAND

Hitch's English Roots

Hitch's paternal grandfather, John Hitchman, was born in England in 1848, the oldest of five children born to Edward and Caroline (*née* Stockley). The family lived in Wellesbourne Mountford, a village of about 700 people in Warwickshire county, in England's West Midlands region. It consisted mainly of laborers who worked the nearby farms. Tradesmen and their families also lived in the village and provided goods and services to those farms and workers.[1]

Today, Wellesbourne Mountford is merged with another village, Wellesbourne Hasting, and is known merely as Wellesbourne. It has a population of about 5,900 and serves as a commuter village to larger centers, the closest being Stratford-upon-Avon, five miles to the east and the birthplace of William Shakespeare.[2]

John's father, Edward (Hitch's great grandfather), was a "brazier," a person who made and repaired brass objects, and later became an "Ironmongery Grocer," an old English term for a supplier of iron and other metal goods for domestic purposes.[3]

At a time when school was not yet mandatory for children in England and only about 50 percent attended, John's parents ensured that all five of their children did.[4] From census data it is known that John attended school from the time he was three until at least 13.

The 1871 England census indicates that Hitch's grandfather John was in his 23rd year and living at home in Wellesbourne Mountford. It doesn't state his employment status, but his father, Edward, age 51, was now the ironmongery grocer and his mother, Caroline, was 50. John's siblings were listed as Edward, age 20, apprentice butcher; Fanny, age 18, dressmaker; Amy, age 14, nursemaid; and youngest brother, William, age 12, "scholar."

By October 1872, John had met and married a servant woman two years his senior, Amelia Rachel Cahill, of East Ham, Essex (part of London). They resided in Camberwell, now a district of south London and about 100 miles from his childhood village of Wellesbourne Mountford, where John worked as a gas fitter. He and Amelia had their first child, Edward Frederick (E.F.), Hitch's father, in 1874. Upon the arrival of their third and final child, daughter Caroline Amelia (Carrie) in 1881, they were still living in London with their new baby and middle child, William Henry. And, John was out of work. That same year, Hitch's father, then seven, was living with his grandparents in Wellesbourne Mountford.

It's not known for how long little E.F. was separated from his father, mother, and siblings, or for how long his father, John, was without work. The 1880s in London were an exceedingly hostile place for unskilled laborers, semi-skilled tradesmen, and their families. The "second industrial revolution" was in full swing throughout England, providing far-reaching technological advances and business system improvements, resulting in widespread access to telegraph communication, rail transportation, electricity, clean water, and sanitary conditions.[5] It also resulted in massive job losses for workers at the lower rungs of the economic ladder. The unemployed from all over the country moved to the larger centers in search of jobs, resulting in "dreadful city slums that came to characterize Victorian England."[6]

By the late 1880s, John and Amelia had made the decision to immigrate to Canada. They were likely in Wellesbourne Mountford before leaving, as John's father had died there in 1884. And they likely received monetary assistance to leave England from the National Agricultural Labourers Union, which was founded in that village in 1872.[7] Most unions in England at the time were supporting workers wishing to immigrate to Canada and elsewhere, rationalizing that this would lead to fewer workers in England and drive up wages. John and Amelia may also have received support from the Church of England or the government, as both were offering various incentives for people to leave.[8]

The English did not view Canada as the premier immigration destination in the 1880s. Although Canada saw accelerated prosperity after Confederation in 1867, it had steep competition from the United States for persons emigrating from England. But with England's high unemployment in the cities and the agricultural downturn in rural areas, enough people came to Canada, especially Ontario, that "by 1890, just under 40 percent of Ontario's population claimed to have some English ancestry."[9] By then many seeking to emigrate from England were living in cities, and fast-growing centers like Toronto held great appeal.

Noted immigration historian Lucille Campey, commenting on the late 19th-century immigration to Canada by the English, observed: "Meanwhile, a silent and largely unrecorded success story was about to unfold. The humble labourers, servants, tradesmen, and small farmers who had arrived with little apart from a determination to succeed would suddenly find themselves becoming respectable. This, in itself, was an amazing achievement."[10]

John and Amelia Hitchman, with their three children in tow, arrived in Toronto, Ontario, Canada, in 1888.

Toronto, the First Two Decades

On September 20, 1888, the SS *Parisian* of the Allan Line Steamship Co. departed Liverpool, England. The vessel made a stop in Londonderry, Ireland, and arrived in Montreal, Quebec, on September 30 carrying 102 cabin and 563 steerage passengers. John Hitchman was listed on the manifest as 40 years old, a laborer and with a final destination of Toronto. It is likely he was accompanied by his wife, Amelia, and their three children, E.F. (Hitch's dad), William and Carrie, as it was common at the time that ship lists omitted the names of wives and children, especially of "lowly" laborers.[11]

The first evidence of John and his family living in Toronto is found in the Toronto city directory of 1890, which has them residing at 344 Dovercourt. John was listed as a laborer and Amelia a nurse.

The city directory, published yearly by R.L. Polk & Co, compiled a wealth of information about Toronto and its citizens. The publisher estimated the population of Toronto in 1890 to be 216,066, a 15 percent increase over the previous year, making it one of the fastest-growing cities in North America.

In 1891, the Hitchman household moved to 162 Dundas Street and resided there for five years. The children attended Gladstone Public School. John held various jobs in Toronto, first as a laborer, then in 1892 as a gas stove maker. In the 1901 Canada Census, he was listed as a tinsmith earning $300 per year. Later he became an insurance agent with Met Life. He would continue working well into his twilight years, holding an administrative position with Prospect Cemetery on St. Clair St. W.

While living at 162 Dundas, John's life was forever altered by the death of his wife in 1892, just four years after arriving in Canada. Amelia died of peritonitis at the age of 46. The following year, John married another English woman, Edith Jane Death, 20 years his junior, who had also arrived in Canada in the 1880s with her family. The daughter of a bricklayer, Edith was the oldest of eight children and worked in manufacturing. John and Edith likely met at the now-defunct Anglican church, St. Barnabas, where John was sexton. They had a daughter, Elizabeth Fanny, in September 1895.

E.F. first appeared in the Toronto directory in 1891, at 17, as a barber. He would stay in that profession for the next 24 years, first working for J.W. Houston at 23 Simcoe Street and later employing barbers in his own shop on Dundas. In 1895, the same month E.F.'s half-sister, Fanny, was born, he traveled to Clinton, Iowa, and married Ida May Thuresson, a girl he knew from Toronto. E.F. was 21 and Ida seven months older.

Ida was the youngest of nine children. Her father, Thomas Thuresson, a carpenter, was born in England and her mother, Mary Ann, in Ancaster, Ontario, of Irish descent. Both parents belonged to the Church of England. Ida was also born in Ancaster, and the family lived there and then north of Toronto in Tecumseth, Simcoe South, before moving to Toronto. In 1890 the Thuresson's lived near the Hitchmans, and this is likely where Ida and E.F. met. The Thuresson family had left Toronto for the United States in 1894.

When E.F. returned to Toronto with his new bride in the fall of 1895, the Hitchman household at 162 Dundas became quite crowded. John and his new family, plus his older children, William and Carrie, moved out and went to what was then the west end of Toronto and eventually to 60 McRoberts Avenue in the Parkdale area.

Hitch's parents, E.F. and Ida, in Toronto, circa 1895. (Photo courtesy of Tammy McLaughlin)

E.F. and Ida remained at 162 Dundas Street for a year. They stayed on Dundas until 1909, moving a few times on the street. Ida's parents and sister Susan returned to Toronto in 1897 and moved in with them two years later, just before Ida's father died at age 78 in

1900. Her mother and sister continued living with them until 1906. Three years later they all went farther west to the neighborhood of Parkdale for their remaining years in Toronto.

While still on Dundas St., all three of E.F. and Ida's children were born: Mary Florence in 1897; Frederick Lionel ("Hitch") in 1901; and their youngest, Ida Dorothy ("Dot"), in 1909.

Favorite Pastimes at the Turn of the Century

By 1905, John Hitchman was 57 years old, his son E.F., 31. Both had worked hard to provide for their families, adjusted nicely to their new country and now enjoyed more time for leisurely pursuits and activities.

John was deeply involved with the Sons of England Benevolent Society, first established in Toronto in 1874. It was an Englishman's fraternity with the aim of providing social activities and discount life insurance to its members, and of raising funds and providing temporary financial support and funeral benefits to its members and their dependents.

John also enjoyed the game of cricket. First introduced to Canada by the military before 1800, it continually grew in popularity, particularly in Toronto. It's not known if John played while living in England, but his name shows up in the Toronto newspapers as having played well into his 50s.

He was also very musical and played in the Home Guard band.

E.F. excelled at social, musical and sporting activities. He not only joined in but also was instrumental in forming clubs and organizing leagues, demonstrating a strong sense of public service.

Both E.F. and his wife, Ida, were deeply involved in various activities at their church, St. Anne's, which today is a national historic site of Canada. Founded in 1863, this Anglican church in the Parkdale neighborhood of Toronto was replaced in 1907-08 on the same grounds as the original church by a more substantial structure in the Byzantine Revival style and is adorned with paintings and murals by three of Canada's Group of Seven artists.

E.F. and Ida sang in the church choir. Ida was involved in the women's auxiliary of St. Anne's, and the parish bestowed upon her a lifetime membership. E.F. was instrumental in the development and growth of the men's association of the church. He held various positions during his 30-plus years in Toronto and was the president of that association for 10 years. During E.F's tenure as president, the club had 550 members.

The men's club held meetings with guest speakers, organized sports leagues and raised funds for sports equipment and facilities. Among the sports offered were archery, cricket, football (rugby), lawn bowling, quoits (horseshoes), sharpshooting and hockey. Leagues were organized by age and marital status.

E.F. was the driving force behind the formation of a federation of men's associations "irrespective of Church" and "for the purpose of mutually assisting in movements for the public good."[12] It was the beginning of organized church sports leagues in Toronto.

Like his father, E.F. excelled at cricket and played well into his retirement years. He also became one of Canada's leading authorities on the sport. E.F. first played on the Grace Church cricket team and then the Parkdale team. He also did stints on other teams in and around Toronto.

While with Grace Church, E.F. played with a man who became instrumental in his son's athletic development, William "Bill" Marsden, a fellow Englishman and noted cricket and rugby player. Bill managed the famed Toronto Aura Lee junior hockey team, coaching Hitch and other renowned hockey players, including Lionel Conacher, voted Canada's top athlete of the first half of the 20th century.

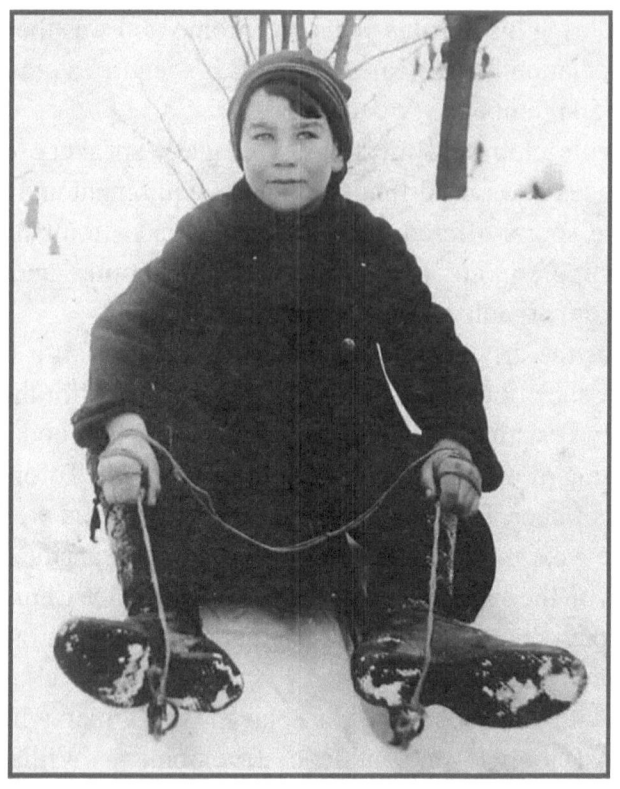

Hitch, age nine, enjoying Toronto's winter in 1911, a few years before the war broke out. (Photo courtesy of Hitchman private collection)

Chapter Two

THE WAR YEARS

Canada Becomes Involved in WWI

In 1914, tensions in Europe were at the boiling point between two feuding alliances: the Central Powers, including Germany and the Austro-Hungarian and Ottoman (Turkey) Empires, and the Triple Entente, or Allies, including France, Russia, and Great Britain. At issue were trade and land disputes and the stockpiling of military weapons.

On August 3, 1914, Germany invaded the neutral country of Belgium. This provocation was rooted in the assassination of the Austrian archduke, Franz Ferdinand, in late June by a Serbian rogue faction looking to break up the Austro-Hungarian Empire. The Empire retaliated in late July by attacking Serbia, a Russian ally, resulting in Russia's becoming involved in that conflict. Knowing France was bound to Russia by a war treaty, Germany made the miscalculation that in support of its ally, the Austro-Hungarian Empire, it would be more expedient to declare war on France than to join them in the Russian conflict. Its strategy was to take Paris by moving through neutral countries, including Belgium. Belgium refused to grant Germany free passage through its territory, and Germany declared war on Belgium.

What Germany had not counted on was that Great Britain had an agreement with Belgium dating back to 1839 to protect that country's long-standing neutrality. Great Britain fulfilled its obligation to Belgium on August 4 by demanding that Germany withdraw its troops from Belgium or be at war with Great Britain. Germany did not back down.

This was the beginning of the First World War. Few countries remained on the sidelines. Smaller European countries aligned with either the Central Powers or the Allies, and dominions and colonies added manpower and other resources to their motherlands. Later, Japan and the United States joined the Allied forces. The war lasted more than four years, killing an estimated nine million soldiers.

Canada, as part of the British Empire, was a self-governing dominion but did not control its own foreign affairs. Legally, once Great Britain was at war, so was Canada, although it did control how and to what extent it participated. So, on August 4, 1914, Canada was at war with Germany.[1]

Sparsely populated Canada committed nearly 7 percent of its population to uniform for its wartime effort. In 1915, some 330,000 Canadians volunteered for service, mostly immigrants from Great Britain.[2] By 1917, the volunteer pool had dried up, and the government passed legislation imposing mandatory military service of all men aged 20 to 45. This resulted in a deep rift between the French and English and between nationalists and imperialists. Canada at 50 was a divided country, many feeling this was not their war or that this tiny and distant dominion had done more than its fair share.

By the time the war ended in November 1918, more than 619,000 had enlisted in Canada's war effort, the Canadian Expeditionary Force (CEF), and 424,000 served overseas. Nearly 61,000 Canadians died in the war, 172,000 were wounded, and 9,000 were reported to have "shell shock."[3]

Toronto and E.F.'s Part in the War

For Toronto's part, 65,000 served overseas, representing 12 percent of the city's population at the end of the war; 5,000 soldiers died, and 25,000 were wounded.[4]

Although 80 percent of enlistees were bachelors with an average age of 26, Hitch's dad, E.F., at 41 and a father of three, volunteered on March 31, 1915. Like so many, E.F. likely felt he had a patriotic duty to his home country, England. Plus, there was a concerted campaign by the newspapers, politicians and fellow compatriots to pressure Canadian men to sign up for the war.

Most newspapers reporting on daily domestic activities infused their articles with praise for those who had enlisted and scoffed at those who did not answer the call of their country. Headlines included:

- Insurance Riflemen Get Ready for Work;
- Bride and Bridegroom Will Serve the King;
- Three Hundred from The Beaches League: Splendid Record of Enlistments;
- Of the 250 Odd Toronto Cricketers Enlisted Many Have Acquired Promotion;
- The number of Toronto cricketers who have joined the colors for overseas service goes to prove that the men who engage in England's national game cannot be classed with the 'shirkers.'

E.F. volunteered with the University of Toronto hospital, which had been approved by the War Office in March 1915 to provide, staff and equip a 1,040-bed field facility. At the onset of the war, the University of Toronto had the second largest medical school in the British Empire, second only to Edinburgh, but it offered no advance training. Involvement in the war effort led to increased knowledge and enhanced medical programming at the school.[5]

The University war facility became known as the "No. 4 Canadian General Hospital." Most of the costs relating to the hospital were borne by the Dominion Government; however, laboratory equipment was funded through donations from the likes of the Eaton family, the Rockefeller Foundation and everyday Torontonians. The university also advertised for volunteers. In addition to doctors and nurses, they required "two hundred and eighty-four non-commissioned officers and men" to assist with the day-to-day running of the hospital.

Shortly before E.F.'s departure with the hospital, the leading newspapers in Toronto reported that E.F. was honored by his church with a purse of gold in recognition of his enlistment: "Mr. E.F.

Hitchman, a former president of the Men's Association of St. Anne's Church was last night presented with a purse of gold by the members. He will leave shortly for the front with the University of Toronto Hospital."⁶

No. 4 Canadian General Hospital set sail in May 1915 for England and then to Salonika [now Thessaloniki], Greece, where the Allied forces of France, Russia, Serbia, Britain, and Italy fought mostly Bulgarian troops of the Central Powers. On Christmas Day, 1915, the *Toronto Globe* published a letter from Colonel J.A. Roberts, the officer commanding the Toronto hospital at Salonika: "At present the hospital is handling 450 to 600 patients daily, but doing little operative surgery owing to the extreme cold weather and the difficulty in raising the temperature of the tents above 35 degrees."⁷ The Allied troops would grow in number to 150,000 at the Salonika front, and into the summer months "malaria, endemic in northern Greece caused ten casualties for every one inflicted by the enemy."⁸

Despite the hardships of his surroundings, E.F. put his natural resourcefulness to good effect for the hospital, and his efforts were rewarded as reported on January 18, 1916, by the *Toronto Star*: "Another man to leave Toronto as a private was Fred Hitchman of Parkdale Club. He went away with the Hospital Base Battalion, and now fills an important staff position, and his further promotion will not be a surprise to anyone who knows him."⁹ Indeed, by the time he returned to Toronto from the war in November 1919, a full year after it had ended, he carried the title of SQMS or staff quartermaster sergeant.

On August 13, 1918, E.F. received recognition in a "Mentions in Dispatch" (MID). He was "brought to the notice of the Secretary of State for valuable services rendered in connection with the War." MIDs were considered significant citations that originated in WWI. Soldiers earning one were distinguished with a medal of victory adorned with a small fig spray. Of Canada's 424,000 active soldiers in WWI, only 5,467 were awarded a MID. Canada continued this award for WWII and the Korean War and re-introduced it in 1990.¹⁰

Hitch's father, E.F. Hitchman, entered WWI on March 31, 1915, at age 41, as a private with the University of Toronto Hospital (No. 4 Canadian General Hospital), serving in England and Greece. He was stationed overseas until November 1919, completing his service with the rank of staff quartermaster sergeant. (Photo courtesy of Tammy McLaughlin)

While E.F. served his country overseas, his wife and oldest daughter, Mary, went to work in support of the war effort as operators in a munitions factory. With the passing of the Wartime Elections Act of 1917, Ida and Mary, as the wife and daughter of a soldier serving overseas, for the first time ever, were granted the right to vote in a federal election.[11]

Hitch, Hockey and Other Pursuits During the War

At the onset of war, Hitch was 12 and his younger sister, Dorothy, only five. Their mother, Ida, had help raising these two from her father-in-law, John, and her mother, Mary Ann, both of whom lived nearby. Hitch and Dorothy were fortunate to have side-stepped most of the ill effects of the war and enjoyed a carefree childhood full of literature, music, and sports. Dorothy's daughter, Tammy McLaughlin, remarked that her mother "idolized her brother and wanted to be as good at hockey as he was."

Hitch got his start in hockey playing on his neighborhood team, Wychwood. The team initially played in the league Hitch's father founded for the Anglican Church. The team joined the Beaches

Hockey League in 1916 in the juvenile division shortly after Hitch turned 15.

The Beaches Hockey League was the forerunner of the current-day Greater Toronto Hockey League. It was founded in 1911 by 17-year-old Frank Donald Smith, who was looking for a place to play hockey. Smith began with a junior division (under 20) serving the Beaches area of Toronto. By 1915, the league also included senior and intermediate with no age limits and juvenile for boys under 18. Teams from all over Toronto now played in the league. It was touted as the world's largest outdoor hockey league and the primary feeder system for the elite Ontario Hockey Association (OHA), which had been in existence since 1891. During the war, the OHA operated with three divisions—senior, intermediate and junior—and played a six-man game.

This was a new way of playing the game. Most leagues played seven-man hockey with positions consisting of goal, point and cover point (defensemen lined up one in front of the other), rover, center, and right and left wing. Shortly after the National Hockey Association (NHA), the predecessor to the NHL was formed in 1910, it dropped the rover position.

"Well over half of the players who played in the Beaches Hockey League in 1915 had enlisted and left the city."[12] For the next season, wanting to encourage younger players not eligible for war service, the Beaches executive added a midget division for boys under 16 as of January 1 of the playing year. In 1916, the league grew to 37 teams, 11 more than in 1915.

During wartime, the Beaches league also instituted restrictions on who could play, barring senior OHA players but allowing OHA junior and intermediate players in the Beaches senior division. The purpose was to make room for soldiers stationed in the city and encourage soldier teams to enter the league. By the end of the 1916 hockey season, more than 330 active league players had enlisted in the war.

At the Beaches general meeting before the start of the 1917 hockey season, delegates voted on several rule changes, one of which affected the midget and juvenile divisions, giving teams the "privilege at half-time only of substituting one or more players, the players substituted not being allowed to return to the game under any conditions, even if overtime is played."[13] Before then, and still in effect for the upper divisions, no substitutes were permitted, and if a player had to go off because of illness or injury, the opposing team dropped a player to equalize the teams.

Another rule change was considered for the 1917 hockey season. After a very heated debate and by a close margin, the delegates voted to play six-man hockey in the senior, intermediate and junior division, while retaining seven-man hockey for juvenile and midget. Overall, the league grew to 53 teams in 1918, the year the war ended. Hitch's juvenile division had 19 teams.

Rugby was another sport that Hitch enjoyed. He attended Oakwood Collegiate in Toronto's west end and played on both the junior (1916-1918) and senior (1919) teams. In normal times Hitch would have played two years junior and two years senior, but during the war, schools were depleted of their senior boys who had enlisted and had difficulty fielding teams at that level. Still, Oakwood was a powerhouse in the sport. The senior team won the city championship in 1917, and with Hitch and his school chum and future NHL rival Charles Dinsmore on the senior team, they won again in 1919.

A year earlier, when Hitch and Charles were still juniors, their rugby team was on its way to the city championships, having just won their section on October 11, 1918, by defeating Humberside 8-5, when a new enemy emerged at home and elsewhere.

Another Enemy Emerges

Two days earlier on October 9, "forty-four Spanish 'flu' cases were admitted to the different hospitals"; the death toll in Toronto to that point was 16 as reported by the *Toronto Globe* on October 10, 1918. As the virus spread through the city, nurses were hard hit, children were kept home from school, and sports leagues were canceled, including the high school city rugby championships. Young adults were especially targeted by the pathogen. Hotels doubled as emergency hospitals, gathering places such as theaters were closed, and volunteers dug mass graves in Prospect Cemetery, where Hitch's grandfather worked. Before it was over, more than 1,750 Torontonians died. The pandemic claimed about 50,000 Canadians and globally, nearly 40 million.[14]

The only saving grace was that as the flu began to recede, so did the war, resulting in an armistice on November 11, 1918. The world had forever changed. So many dead from battle and disease; so many maimed and scarred, both inwardly and outwardly. Country boundaries were redrawn, and old socio-economic orders disbanded or rearranged.

As the dead were buried and the soldiers worked their way home, it was time for the clouds to disperse and for the sun to shine down on a weary country and its people.

Chapter Three

GETTING ON WITH LIFE

With the war finally over and the flu in retreat, soldiers started coming home, most women left their jobs, and children went back to school. People began the arduous task of rebuilding their lives, some without loved ones who would never return from the war. The healing process was in full view. Gradually, daily life returned to "normal," and people happily engaged in lighter issues and pursuits.

It was disappointing that the 1918 high school rugby season was cut short because of the Spanish flu and the Oakwood junior and senior teams didn't get the opportunity to prove their mettle at the citywide championships after winning their sections. But the juniors did get great satisfaction and acclaim for beating the University of Toronto second team 9-3 in an exhibition game on November 20, 1918, with "sensational runs by Abbey and Hitchman" for the winners.[1]

This helped cheer up a school that lost 29 students out of 160 who served overseas in the war. Oakwood was determined to honor its fallen heroes. The school launched a subscription in their names to raise funds for a commemorative "tablet" and scholarship for deserving students. They raised well over $10,000 in the first month. The tablet still graces the main hall of that sturdy and storied school.[2]

In January of 1919, Hitch turned his interest to hockey, playing for Wychwood once more in the Beaches league. His team won the juvenile title, beating the Beaches team 3-2.[3]

The war had been "officially" over for eight months, but the Hitchman household was still without its head, Hitch's father, E.F. The *Toronto Daily Star* reported on June 18, 1919, that:

The Star cricket representative has just received a letter from Fred Hitchman, a former member of old Parkdale Cricket Club, who is now in England. Fred, who has Q.M.S. in front of his name, says he has been playing lots of cricket, and that the game is now being taken up all over the country more enthusiastically than it ever was before. Q.M.S. Hitchman is widely known as the late president of St. Anne's Men's Association.

A few weeks later, the newspapers reported that E.F.'s No. 4 Canadian General Hospital, was returning to the city. On July 11, hospital personnel returned on the troop train from the British transatlantic ocean liner, the *Olympic*, to a warm reception of family and friends. They had been absent from Toronto for more than four years, first going to England and then serving at the Greece front for two years and then back to England in September 1917, where they were stationed near Basingstoke, Kent, for the remainder of the war.[4]

Unlike most of the hospital staff, E.F. was not discharged in July, and he remained on active duty in England. The Hitchman household was happy for the families whose soldiers were now home and thankful that the war was over and that E.F. was out of harm's way, but they longed to have him back.

E.F. missed both the first successes of his son's new hockey career and the wedding of his half-sister, Elizabeth Fanny, in October 1919.

He was discharged from active duty on October 15, 1919, and on November 5 sailed from London on the *Tunisian*, arriving on Canadian soil 12 days later. E.F. arrived in Toronto just in time to see his son play rugby for Oakwood, this time on the senior team. On November 21, 1919, Oakwood defeated Riverdale 35-1 to win the city championship.[5]

Less than a week after Oakwood won the rugby title, Hitch was presented with a new opportunity on the hockey front by Bill Marsden, revered coach of the OHA junior league team the Toronto Aura Lee and cricket teammate of Hitch's father.

Bill Marsden was a gardener by profession and looked after and lived on the grounds of the Avenue Road Aura Lee club. He played competitive cricket and rugby and refereed rugby at the high school level. He never played hockey but became a legendary coach in that sport.

Marsden was on the executive of the Beaches Hockey League right from the start and fielded teams in most divisions, giving a great many players the opportunity to learn the sport. Aura Lee also fielded two elite teams: senior and junior in the OHA. By Hitch's first tryout with the OHA junior team, the Aura Lee had already won two provincial championships. They would go on to win two more times and twice were runners-up in the Memorial Cup (donated in 1919 by the OHA, named for those who lost their lives in WWI, and awarded to the national junior hockey champions of Canada). "Part of his success was his belief that every physically fit youngster was a potential star if given the right encouragement and was often more a father to his players than a coach."[6]

The junior Aura Lee team folded after 12 seasons in 1925. Marsden turned down a coaching offer from Yale University and moved to London, Ontario, where he took a job with the University of Western Ontario as grounds supervisor and coached the hockey team. In his later years after his first wife died, he remarried and moved to Ottawa, just across from our grandmother Tops and near his old cricket friend E.F. Hitchman, who had moved there nearly 40 years earlier. Bill stayed in Ottawa until his death in 1960 at age 82.

Bill Marsden was known throughout Canada as a "maker of champions." He developed "dozens of professional stars" over the years including Lionel Conacher, Babe Dye, Vern Forbes, Lionel Hitchman, John Ross Roach, and Harry Watson. His teams were raided continuously by senior OHA and NHL teams. His greatest legacy was developing raw talent and steering it into a cohesive unit.[7]

At the start of the 1919-20 season, Bill Marsden was once again on the hunt for some new players. Last season the Aura Lee juniors won the Sportsmen's Patriotic Association (SPA) Championship, a preseason tournament that involved most top-tier talent in Ontario and whose proceeds went to worthy causes. In postseason play, they were eliminated in the OHA quarterfinals.

Marsden lost most of his players, including his stars, Lionel Conacher and Eddie Rodden, from the 1918-19 season. War's end fueled a resurgence in hockey, resulting in an expanded OHA senior and junior circuit. He now had some openings on his team because of a "burst up" of last year's club.[8] Hitch and two high school mates—Deacoff, who also played on Hitch's Wychwood team, and Charles Dinsmore, his high school rugby quarterback—showed up for tryouts and made the team. They had big skates to fill.

Hitch at 18, wearing his Aura Lee sweater, in his backyard at 91 Wychwood Avenue. (Photo courtesy of Hitchman private collection)

Writing for the *Toronto Daily Star* on January 16, 1920, Lou Marsh made his first reference to Hitch in the Aura Lee win over the Varsity juniors. "Beatty, the burly big defence boy, again starred for Aura Lee and he was well backed up by Roach in goal and Hitchman, his side partner on defence." Cliff Beatty would play only one season with Aura Lee and then finish his hockey career with two seasons on the University of Toronto Varsity Blues.

The careers of Lou Marsh and Hitch would intertwine over the next 10 years. Marsh had been a competitive rugby player, sprinter, and yachtsman, and he enjoyed all sports generally. He was a referee in boxing, wrestling, and hockey, becoming one of the top NHL officials of his era. His sportswriting career spanned four decades, and he rose to sports editor after the retirement of the legendary William Hewitt, father of radio and television broadcast pioneer Foster Hewitt. Marsh in his own right was considered a "pioneer of sports journalism in Canada." He held the sports editor position at the *Star* up until his death in 1936, at age 57. Shortly after, the Lou Marsh Trophy was created, honoring his legacy of sport excellence. The trophy continues to be awarded annually to Canada's top athlete.[9]

In Hitch's first season with the Aura Lee, one that Marsden considered a rebuilding year, it was the first year of OHA action for all 10 players on the team. They finished a respectable second in their group but didn't qualify for the playoffs. Of those 10 players, seven reached the height of their career as OHA amateurs and three went on to play in the NHL. Hitch's high school chum, Charles Dinsmore, entered the NHL a year after him and played four years with the Montreal Maroons, winning the Stanley Cup in 1927. Goalie John Ross Roach entered the NHL a year before Hitch and played 14 seasons with four different teams, winning the Stanley Cup in his rookie year.

Hitch finished high school in late spring 1920 and went to work with the Royal Bank of Canada as a clerk. As summer turned to fall, he continued his rugby career in the city league with Riverdale. With winter approaching, the 1920-21 hockey season began. Aura Lee tryouts got underway, with team selections made in early December. "Applegath, last year with T.C.C.; Moore and Denard of Maitlands, and Hitchman, Young, and Dinsmore of the 1919-20 Aura Lee team. Nearly all of these players were on hand last night, and showed to good advantage."[10]

Motormouth Gets His Comeuppance

The team was set, and it was time for the preseason SPA tournament. Aura Lee faced Varsity III on December 15, 1920 and lost 6-4 in overtime (no sudden death). Lou Marsh had a ball writing this story for the *Toronto Daily Star*, at the expense of Hitch, who learned a valuable lesson that night:

It was a funny game, and as usual the stay-at-home missed a real treat. . . .

Aura Lee's unexpected exhibition of combination and ginger yielded them two goals in quick succession, and they added another eight minutes later, and looked all over easy winners, with the score standing 4 to 2 when Hitchman, Applegath's defence partner, started to act like Peck's bad boy. He raced into two or three opponents because they were pestering his nets a bit too assiduously, and then penalized by Referee Vair for driving the shoulder into Plaxton, was foolish enough to start an argument with the busy official. Hitchman lost that argument before he started. He yapped and Steve's fingers telegraphed "double up the penalty." Hitchie handed out some more chin music and Vair added his thumbs to the array of digits. It's a good thing for Young Mister Hitchman of the Wychwood Wonders that Vair wasn't Six-fingered Ike. The other hand was full of bell so he let Hitchy go with a five-minute penalty.

That five-minute penalty and a two-minute one the same lad got a few minutes later lost the game for Aura Lee. The Marsden youngsters were well on top of the heap and "Judge" Jones was wandering up and down the aisles so full of milk of human kindness that he had determined to sentence a couple of pickpockets to a week in Eaton's store when Hitchman's brains addled. The boy had been playing a smart game on the defense, and the critics had him tabbed as a coming star when he was chased to the guardhouse. While he was away Varsity came on with everything they had. Aura Lee's four loose men skated themselves dizzy holding back the attack of five determined youngsters, and even though Aura Lees were still one goal up when Hitchman did get back his team mates were all in and Walters tied it up with two minutes to go.[11]

This cartoon was featured on page 27 of the Toronto Daily Star *on December 16, 1920, beside Lou Marsh's article, "Varsity Beat Aura Lee in Overtime." Marsh's article and this cartoon (bottom right sketch) likely inflicted some amount of humiliation on Hitch, contributing to his career-saving attitude adjustment.*

Hitch learned at least two valuable lessons that night. First, he needed to improve his blocking and checking skills to avoid getting penalties. And second, he learned about the absolute power a referee has in disciplining a mouthy player at the expense of a team result.

It seems he learned well. Hitch would be known as the toughest blocker in the NHL in his day. And he garnered some high praise from the person who schooled him first. On February 2, 1927, Lou Marsh wrote in his "With Pick and Shovel" column for the *Toronto Daily Star* (page 10):

> You never hear Dave Gill or Lester Patrick roaring about referees. Good hockey teams need no alibis. Neither do good hockey players. Do you ever see smart players like

[MacKay] of Chicago, Foyston of Detroit, Carson of Toronto, Clancy of Ottawa, Lepine of Montreal Canadiens, Munro of Montreal Maroons, Hitchman of Boston, Boucher of New York Rangers, Holmes of New York Americans, or Milks of [Pittsburgh] . . . arguing or protesting to the referees. They do not need any alibis because they are out there giving the best they have and playing clean hockey.

The Aura Lee juniors opened their 1920-21 season with a 3-2 loss to the Parkdale Canoe Club, but the game was replayed because three of the Parkdale players were overage and Aura Lee won 6-2. One Parkdale player of appropriate age, two years younger than Hitch, was Reginald "Hooley" Smith. Hooley played just one year with Parkdale and then went senior with the Toronto Granites for five years, winning two Allan Cups (awarded annually to the national senior amateur men's hockey champions of Canada) and a gold medal at the 1924 Olympics. He started in the NHL with the Ottawa Senators in Hitch's third season there, after which he and Hitch played against each other for 10 years, with tremendous acrimony. Hooley continued his career for another seven years after Hitch retired, one year coming to Boston when Hitch was coaching.

Between working and playing for Aura Lee, Hitch fit in time to play hockey in the Bank League. Toronto had nine major banks that employed over 7,000 people. Although the level of play was not of OHA caliber, it did include several of its players, which amplified the games. Lou Marsh also added his officiating talents to the league. The league opened on Monday, January 3, 1921, to a crowd of over 1,500 "enthusiastic supporters." In that game Hitch's Royal beat Commerce 3-2. "Hitchman, the big defense man of the Aura Lee junior team, was the outstanding player of the contest."[12]

Aura Lee played Moose Athletic Club on January 28 and beat them 5-1. Dinsmore was considered the outstanding player of the game by the *Toronto Globe*. Hitch started at wing but replaced an injured Robert McKay on defense in the second period and "turned in a credible game."[13] That same day, the OHA removed another

Parkdale win against Aura Lee from the group standings after a second violation of overage players.

The two teams played one more time before the season was over, and the *Toronto Globe* stated that an "intense rivalry" was created over the OHA's overage ruling, with Parkdale determined to prove themselves. However, Aura Lee handed them a resounding defeat of 6-0 on the afternoon of Saturday, February 5, 1921. Once more the *Globe* deemed Dinsmore the most prominent player but also gave high praise to the defense: "In Applegath and Hitchman Aura Lee have a heavy defense, and with experience and checking ability thrown in, they should be able to keep opposing teams guessing to land the puck in the net. That the defense is strong is shown by the fact that in the three games Aura Lee played only two goals were scored by their opponents."[14]

Although both Parkdale and Aura Lee had played five games that season, three against each other—two that Parkdale won but were tossed out for overage players and one as a do-over for Parkdale's first infraction—the hockey standings showed that they each played three games while Moose AC played four. In the official record book, Aura Lee had one win over Parkdale and two over Moose to win the group championship and moved on to the second round of the provincial playoffs in a home-and-home series with Bowmanville.

The first game in Bowmanville was a 3-3 tie. Hitch played right defense, and Applegath left. Bowmanville scored early in the first period, and Aura Lee got all its goals later in that period. In the second period, the tables turned on Aura Lee when two of its players were in the penalty box for tripping and Bowmanville scored. "In the final period the greater part of the play was around Aura Lee's goal, but the stonewall defense of the young giants kept the little fellows shooting at long distance."[15] Bowmanville got their final goal on a side shot. Then Aura Lee's goalie was sent to the penalty box for hooking (yes, they did that back then), but Bowmanville couldn't get past the Aura Lee defense.

The town of Bowmanville was ecstatic at the result, having tied the all-powerful, twice OHA champs, Aura Lee. A special train was arranged for February 13 to bring several hundred fans to the big city to support their local boys in the second of the home-and-home series. At the train station in Bowmanville the day before, the players received a large and loud send-off from local well-wishers. Only three of their 10 players had ever been to Toronto, and it was arranged to show them some of the sights and to take in the senior OHA game at the Arena between Aura Lee and Kitchener. They would practice at the Arena the morning of their game.[16]

Aura Lee defeated Bowmanville 9-1. "Hitchman and Dinsmore were the most effective for the winners, and they were responsible for the majority of the goals."[17] Aura Lee would now take on Cornwall in the quarterfinals of the OHA junior playoffs.

They left the morning of February 16 for Cornwall and got "trounced" there that night. "Cornwall juniors completely outclassed the much heralded Aura Lee hockey team here to-night in the first of a home-and-home game in the O.H.A championship series and won by 8 to 0." It was a clean game, "only two penalties were inflicted, Hitchman being benched twice." Cornwall had the largest crowd at a hockey game since 1903 when their team played for the senior OHA championship.[18]

Cornwall came to Toronto to play Aura Lee on February 18 and lost 4-1. Hitch was credited with getting the team on track in the second period after a shaky start in the first. In the third period, Aura Lee moved ahead by three goals, and Hitch and right winger Denard were the stars in that session. Unfortunately, Aura Lee's efforts were not good enough to win the round (total goals over the two games), and Cornwall advanced to the OHA semifinals against the winner of Hamilton and Toronto's De La Salle.[19]

Wait, It's Not Over

De La Salle prevailed in its game with Hamilton and was slated to play Cornwall on February 24. However, the OHA received complaints that three Cornwall players, two of the Contant brothers and Tilton, were ineligible because of residency rules. The OHA looked into the issue with the Contant brothers and ruled that they were in violation of those rules; they were suspended from playing any further games in the playoffs. The club wasn't to blame in the view of the OHA, and the team was permitted to advance; however, the teams that were beaten by Cornwall in the playoffs with the Contant brothers in the lineup would participate in a sudden-death runoff, namely Queen's University, Belleville and Aura Lee. The winner would play off with the winner of the De La Salle–Cornwall series.[20]

The other side of the semifinal series was dealing with its own eligibility issues. The two remaining teams in the playoffs were Stratford and Collingwood, and before that series got underway, Stratford player John Cook was expelled for falsifying his age. The team was exonerated and permitted to stay in the playoff. The teams of Preston, Kitchener, Owen Sound, and Seaforth were given another chance by way of sudden-death rounds.[21]

In Aura Lee's first sudden-death game, they beat Belleville 6-5 on neutral ice in Whitby, Ontario, on February 26. "It was the most exciting game of the season. Moore, Aura Lee's regular goaler, was unable to play owing to having sprained his wrist."[22] Two days later in Trenton, Moore was back in the game for Aura Lee, but they couldn't overcome a 2-0 lead by the Queen's University juniors, who would next take on the winners of the Cornwall–De La Salle game.

Cornwall beat De La Salle, who lodged a complaint against Cornwall alleging that they were using three overage players. The OHA set a hearing for March 4, which was held over for a day so the boys could produce their identification. They were deemed eligible, and Cornwall played Queen's in a sudden-death game, losing 6-1. Queen's University went on to play Stratford for the 1921 OHA championship, losing 7-3.

This was a season of cheaters in the junior leagues vying for the Memorial Cup. Not only were players on three OHA teams suspended for breaking the rules (Parkdale, Cornwall and the championship team, Stratford), the North Ontario Hockey Association was dealing with its own issues.

In North Bay, Ontario, on March 20 a meeting of the NOHA executive was called to decide the fate of A. Joliat and R.E.

Campbell of the Iroquois Falls team and manager J. McGrath and R. Worters of the Timmins team over a game-fixing allegation. The investigation determined that only one game had been affected and that no other players or team officials were involved. The NOHA expelled the players and men in question.[23]

In the end, the Winnipeg Falcons split games with the Stratford Midgets for the Memorial Cup, winning the round 11-9.

The 1920-21 OHA season had just finished, and the Aura Lee team was already planning for 1921-22. They were looking at several promising youngsters from the Toronto Hockey League (formerly the Beaches Hockey League) and would have all their past season players back, except Hitch.

On Monday, April 25, 1921, his father moved the family to Ottawa where he would be working for the Director General of Medical Services in the federal government Department of Soldiers' Civil Re-establishment. Hitch at 19 and younger sister Dorothy, 11, went with their parents. Three days earlier, older sister Mary had wed Charles Rogerson and remained in Toronto. The day before they left, "the men's association of St. Anne's Church presented Mr. Fred Hitchman with an illuminated address to mark their appreciation of his services to the association. Prior to going overseas Mr. Hitchman was for ten years president of the organization, and was the pioneer of the church men's association movement in Toronto."[24]

This was the end of Hitch's OHA career. He had some of the best encouragement and coaching available at that level. He played with and against some of the brightest and talented players, and he was a star of that league. It was there that Hitch's reputation as a clutch player was formed.

Before Hitch would reach the NHL, where he would once again encounter some of these players, he would go to the "capital" of hockey to further refine his skills.

Chapter Four

THE CAPITAL OF HOCKEY

The Hitchmans arrived in Ottawa, Ontario, the capital of Canada in late April 1921. They lived at 22 Cayuga Street (now Grosvenor Street), which E.F. bought for $7,200 in the neighborhood of Ottawa South, a lovely new suburb nestled between the historic Rideau Canal and the banks of the Rideau River, just two miles south of Canada's Parliament buildings.

Ottawa and Toronto were very dissimilar. With its population of 94,000, Ottawa was one-fifth the size of Toronto in 1921. In both cities, about 65 percent of the population was from or descended from Great Britain, but the mix was different. Hitchman's Toronto West community was dominated by persons of English origin. In Ottawa, there were many more Irish. But the biggest contrast between the two cities was the French influence. In Toronto West, only 1 percent of the population identified as French. In Ottawa, it was 27 percent, the largest single group, followed closely by the Irish at 26 percent and the English at 24 percent.

There were fewer Anglicans and a lot more Roman Catholics (45 percent compared with Toronto West at 13 percent). Plus, the types of jobs available in Ottawa were very different, especially in the manufacturing and service industries.

In Ottawa, only 13 percent of all occupations were in manufacturing compared with Toronto at 30 percent. The wood and paper industry made up 41 percent of all manufacturing jobs in Ottawa. Toronto had a more diverse sector, with textiles at 22 percent being most prominent.

The service industry in Ottawa accounted for 48 percent of all jobs, compared with 23 percent in Toronto. Ottawa had nearly three times the number of public administration jobs. And Toronto had many more domestic and professional service jobs than Ottawa.

Also, in Ottawa, there were 2 percent more women in the adult population, and 4 percent more worked outside the home than in Toronto.

Despite all these differences, the Hitchman clan settled in nicely. The family became members of the Anglican Christ Church Cathedral where Hitch's parents, E.F. and Ida, assumed leadership roles in various activities. E.F. could walk about 15 minutes from his home to his new job, starting at $1,700 per year. He quickly established himself within the local cricket community, founding a new council and shaping the governance of that sport for decades to come. Dorothy attended Hopewell Public School, and Hitch, now 19 years old, quickly went to work as a clerk earning $300 per year.[1]

It was another seven months before Hitch entered the very robust hockey scene in Ottawa. In the meantime, he set his sights on a new career, joining the Royal Canadian Mounted Police in August. He served with the Force as a constable at N Division stationed at Ottawa's Lansdowne Park, a short walk from his home.[2]

Hitch in his RCMP uniform, August 1921, Ottawa. (Photo courtesy of Hitchman private collection)

One of Hitch's first duties was to greet the new Governor General of Canada, the "Victor of Vimy," Lord Byng and his wife, Lady Byng. The people of Ottawa were given a half-day holiday on the afternoon of Friday, August 12, 1921, in honor of their arrival from England. Thousands went to the train station and lined the streets to welcome them and cheer the military parade in full regalia. The *Ottawa Journal* declared it was the largest greeting ever for a new Governor General, owing to Lord Byng's role in leading the Canadian troops to victory at Vimy Ridge during WWI. Hitch's RCMP detachment escorted the viceregal party from Union Station and along the parade route up Wellington street to Parliament Hill, where Prime Minister Arthur Meighen officially welcomed them to Canada.[3]

Lord Byng was already popular with Canadians because of his role in WWI. His wife, Lady Evelyn Byng, would become one of the best known and beloved patrons of Canada's national sport when in 1925 she devised and donated the Lady Byng Trophy honoring "clean play" in professional hockey, which is still awarded annually in the NHL.

A month later, Hitch responded to this newspaper article in the *Ottawa Citizen* on Saturday, September 10: "City Rugby Teams Are Hard At Work. . . . Any other person who wishes to try out will be welcome." Hitch found a spot on the Rideaus, a team that finished at the bottom of the heap the previous season. He quickly gained credit for his playing ability, helping the Rideaus in mid-November vie for the city championship against the New Edinburghs. "The Burghs" beat the Rideaus 8-7 after 20 minutes of overtime, and Hitch's "remarkable playing" earned him the "individual star" of the game. "The big fellow played a super game and in spite of a badly cut head he continued after being advised to lay off. He played in the battle till in the final overtime period he was forced to be led off through sheer exhaustion. It was one of the gamest exhibitions witnessed in a long while and 'Hitch' was given a big hand when he staggered in to the stand."[4]

Everyone now turned their sights to hockey. Ottawans affectionately referred to their home as the "capital" of hockey. As of 1921, Ottawa teams had produced 17 Stanley Cup challenge wins, and in the "modern" era with the formation of the NHL in the 1917-18 season, Ottawa won the Cup twice (the first season, it went to the Toronto Arenas, the next season the playoffs were canceled because of the Spanish flu, and Ottawa won the Stanley Cup in 1920 and 1921). Even more significant, Ottawa and surrounding towns produced so many high-quality players that at one time 50 percent of all professional players came from the area.

To say Ottawa was the capital of hockey was an understatement. For a city of less than 100,000, it had no less than 10 high-caliber senior amateur teams. By way of contrast, Toronto, five times larger, had seven senior teams.[5] Ottawa also operated a league of six intermediate teams. It had an enthusiastic civil service league where many of the seniors and intermediates also played. In addition, the city had strong school and church leagues and some independent teams that played exhibition games against league teams.

All the senior teams and leagues in the city were under the jurisdiction of the Ottawa and District Amateur Hockey Association, a member of the Canadian Amateur Hockey Association. The district also included leagues operating in the valley towns near Ottawa. For the current season, it had seven leagues and about 550 hockey players under its umbrella organization.

1921-22 marked the second and final season of the Capital Senior Hockey League. It was an offshoot of an earlier league that continued as the Ottawa Amateur City Hockey League. After much finagling, each league was comprised of five teams. The City League, better known as Group 1, included the Knights of Columbus, Montagnards, Munitions, Ottawa University, and Victorias and played out of the Rideau Rink on Waller Street. The newest league, the Capital or Group 2, included the Gunners, New Edinburghs, Royal Canadiens, St. Brigids and St. Patricks and played out of the Dey Arena on Laurier Avenue.

To determine the Ottawa and District senior amateur hockey champion, the winners of each league played off, including those in the Ottawa Valley. The ultimate winner entered the elimination rounds of the eastern Allan Cup finals. The winner then played the western Canada champ for the Allan Cup and was crowned the national senior amateur men's hockey champion of Canada, a title and trophy still awarded today.

On November 18, 1921, the *Ottawa Citizen* declared that "Ottawa Has New Athletic Star" touting him "as the greatest rugbist of the season." The article on Hitch continued:

> Hitchman is a member of the Royal Canadian Mounted Police and is at present stationed in the Capital, which accounts for his presence on the Rideau dozen. He commenced his athletic career as a member of the Wychwood juveniles, who were Toronto champions in 1917-18-19, and graduated to the Aura Lee juniors in 1919, continuing with this club till the close of last season. He was the chief performer for the Rideaus in the fight for city rugby honors, and his brilliant and game exhibition in the final against New Edinburghs will not soon be forgotten.
>
> He is only a youngster and will not attain his twentieth birthday till the latter part of the present month. He should be in for a brilliant athletic career and will take an active part in Ottawa hockey during the coming season. His name has already been connected with several City League clubs, but he has not decided yet with whom he will cast in his lot, though New Edinburghs claim to have first call on his services.

This picture of Hitch accompanied the above article from the Ottawa Citizen, November 18, 1921, page 10.

(The adjacent newspaper column reported on the November 17 finals of School League Basketball, with Hitch's sister, Dot playing for the runner-up, the Hopewell junior girls team.)

On November 22, the *Ottawa Journal* reported that "New Edinburghs are the 'mystery team' of the loop. They are said to have signed Hitchman a good player from Aura Lee juniors." A few weeks later, the same newspaper added: "New Edinburghs have landed Hitchman the big boy of the 'mounties' who starred with the Rideaus in football this fall. From all reports Hitchman is some 'pumpkins' in hockey as well as football."[6]

While the teams sorted out their players and began practices, the city went all out organizing the first ever five-day bazaar in support of amateur hockey. Captain Ed Archibald, associate sports editor of the *Ottawa Journal*, and an "energetic committee" made all the arrangements. Lumber and railway baron J.R. Booth lent his new Jackson building at Bank and Slater streets for the festivities. These included a midway with booths manned by the teams, offering gifts and food for purchase, and a dance hall with an orchestra each night sponsored by the Young Men's Hebrew Association. The bazaar was a resounding success and provided much-needed cash for the amateur teams.

Ottawa newspapers extensively followed senior league hockey practices and reported heavily on Hitch, the new mystery player from Toronto:

- "New Edinburgh, with big Lionel Hitchman in tow showed a vast improvement over their previous work and Dave Gill's men were going like a house on fire."
- "Lionel Hitchman, the long striding defence man of New Edinburghs knocked his opposition dizzy last night in the Burghs' practice. The tall brunette looked like a million yen tearing up and down the ice."
- "Round Lionel Hitchman, the Burghs have built a squad of unselfish players and with the lanky defence man doing the main individual work they should go like a well oiled machine."
- "In Lionel Hitchman they have undoubtedly uncovered the real find of the season. The football star was with Aura Lee juniors last year and he is sure to be a sensation on his practice form."[7]

On December 22, the six-team Civil Service League opened to much fanfare with a doubleheader, in which Hitch's RCMP team played in the first game against Interior. The incoming prime minister, Mackenzie King, was named the honorary president of the league, and the new Governor General "consented to extend his patronage to the league."[8] He and his wife participated in the opening ceremonies and watched their first amateur hockey game in Canada that night. This was the RCMP's first year in the league. Hitch played on the forward line, not his usual position, and played very well. But unfortunately, the highly favored Interior team won. The RCMP were much better at "getting their man" than at hockey, and they lost all their games that season.

Soon after the Civil Service League extended an invitation to the Governor General, the city's NHL team, the Ottawa Senators, made him their honorary president. Throughout the season the team went to great lengths to involve Lord and Lady Byng in game ceremonies and social gatherings. "Their Excellencies" were a huge draw and added a touch of refinement to the outings.[9]

The Capital Senior Hockey League got underway the same week as the Ottawa Senators and the Civil Service League. Hitch played with the Burghs the night after the grand opening of the Civic Service League. His senior team lost to the Royal Canadiens that night, but again Hitch was declared the "big noise" of his team.

Hitch also starred in the Burghs' next two games, one win, and one loss. Just prior, he was spotted in Toronto taking in an Aura Lee game. Back in Ottawa, it was rumored that Toronto's NHL team, the St. Patricks, was scouting him. "Hitchman is a Mountie, and the Saints would probably have to pay for his release if he turned."[10]

Due to work commitments, Hitch missed the fourth game, and on the fifth, he had an off night. That was Friday, January 13, 1922. After the game, he rushed off to catch the end of the military ball hosted by his RCMP regiment. More than 400 people attended, including former prime minister the Right Honourable Arthur Meighen and his wife, other political types, officers of the other RCMP divisions and so forth. "Arrangements were Splendid – A

Social Triumph for 'N' Division," and it was an evening that would change the course of Hitch's life.

It was there that he met a young debutante, Miss Florence Myers, the daughter of Willis Ford Myers, a teacher at Muchmore Public School and later principal of Lady Evelyn Public School. Her mother, Lillie May (*née* McRae) was a direct descendant of the Honorable William Henry Steeves, Father of Confederation from New Brunswick. Florence, who since childhood was known as Tops (or Topsy), was at business college learning the secretarial skills of shorthand and typing. Tops also took bookkeeping; she had a "head for figures," as her parents often commented. Her only sibling, older brother Warren, became a successful chartered accountant, and Tops found her way into the Department of National Revenue as a clerk. But in January 1922, Hitch and Tops fell head over heels in love.

Florence Myers, the debutante from the RCMP ball, January 13, 1922. (Photo courtesy of Hitchman private collection)

Again, due to work commitments, Hitch missed the next three games and then starred in a hard-fought game that ended in a 1-0 loss for the Burghs. In all, Hitch played eight games and was declared the "sensation of the season" and the "hardest working player in the circuit."[11] Unfortunately, mainly because Hitch missed so many games, the Burghs ended up in second last place in their league and out of the playoffs.

By mid-February with the Burghs out of the playoffs, Hitch had more time to spend with Tops. Although her parents liked Hitch, they didn't approve of the relationship because of the age difference—he was now 20, and she wouldn't be 16 until the end of March. Tops was not allowed to be alone with Hitch, and he found himself spending a lot of time with two females: Tops and her mother, Lillie.

Hitch and Tops (and Lillie) watched as his rival, the Gunners, won the Capital League and then, in the finals of the Ottawa and District senior amateur hockey championship, lost to the Montagnards of the City League. The Montagnards then beat the Quebec senior champions, the Sons of Ireland, before losing a hard-fought 8-7 round in the Allan Cup semifinal to the Toronto Granites. The Granites, representing the east, went on to beat the Regina Victorias 13-2 to capture the Allan Cup.

While the afterglow of the RCMP's glorious ball continued for Hitch and Tops, by April 1922 the organization itself was under attack on the political front. Its role was being debated in Parliament, and it was left out of the newly formed department of national defense. "Many members were of the opinion that the mounted police force should be greatly decreased and confined to the unorganized territories."[12] Hitch kept his head down, did his work, enjoyed his new romance and played cricket for the RCMP.

Hitch found himself on the opposing team of his father's militia cricket team. As reported by the *Toronto Daily Star*: "Sergt. Hitchman's son, known to many of the younger fry of Toronto, has put on the R.C.M.P. uniform, and in the game referred to gave promise of becoming a good wicket-keeper, and hit up the same number of runs, 13 as did his dad on the opposing side."[13]

During June, the hammer came down on the RCMP. The strength of the force across Canada was reduced from 1,600 to 1,200. N Division in Ottawa lost 100 of its 150 positions. The reduction was achieved through voluntary discharges, and Hitch was granted a "free" discharge on June 5, 1922.[14]

With time to spare that summer, Hitch continued to play cricket for the RCMP and took up a new interest, lacrosse. Although he never played before, he worked his way onto the Gunners team, Ottawa's entry in the Eastern Canada Lacrosse League. The league consisted of two teams from Montreal, one from Cornwall and the Gunners of Ottawa. The Gunners had won the league the past two years. At the beginning of the season Hitch served as spare, but as the season wore on, he earned a defensive position on the starting lineup. He was getting enough good press that his home town newspaper, the *Toronto Star* made this comment on July 20:

> Lionel Hitchman, the former Aura Lee junior O.H.A. player, is playing lacrosse with the Ottawa Gunners in the Eastern Canada Lacrosse League. This is his first year at the game and after playing the match at Cornwall on Saturday the critics of the Factory Town said he was the most effective man on the field. Hitchman, they said, worked like a beaver from end to end and never stopped trying. He has developed into a fine, big, strong athlete, 6 feet 1 inch in height and weighting 175 lbs. He is a high-class hockey and rugby player and even now considered the best all-round athlete in Ottawa.[15]

Before the last game against Cornwall, the *Ottawa Journal* also commented on August 5 about Hitch's progress in the sport: "Fred Hitchman, the tall defence player of the Gunner team, is playing wonderful lacrosse for a beginner. This is Hitchman's first year as a lacrosse player, and his stellar work has already earned him a regular berth on the team."[16] The Gunners played for the Eastern Canada amateur lacrosse championship on September 2, losing to the Montreal Shamrocks by a score of 13-6.

Before the end of the summer in 1922, Hitch was introduced to another new experience and one that would stay with him all his life. Tops' parents had built a log cabin on the shore of the Madawaska River just above Rock Lake in Algonquin Park. They traveled there by train, getting off at the Rock Lake Station. A city boy, Hitch hadn't any experience with the wilderness or living off the land. Tops' parents were great outdoors people, and Hitch learned to hunt and fish and also honed his archery skills first acquired in Toronto at his church club. He was at peace in the woods, and for the rest of his life he would seek out its quiet solace.

Hitch working on his archery skills at the Myers property on the Madawaska River near Rock Lake in Algonquin Park. (Photo courtesy of Hitchman private collection)

As summer came to a close, and shortly after the Gunners lost in the lacrosse championship, Hitch began weighing his options for the future. With seemingly no job prospects in Ottawa, his parents encouraged him to continue his studies, and Queen's University wanted him for its rugby team. That year Queen's won its first Grey Cup against the Toronto Argonauts. He was also asked to play senior rugby for the Toronto Parkdale Canoe Club of the Ontario Rugby Football Union. That year they won their league again and lost in the Grey Cup east semifinal to the Argonauts. "Parkdale seniors had a real turnout last night at Varsity Campus and Coach 'Mike' Rodden put them through their paces. Walter Parnell and Lionel Hitchman reported. Parnell, a St. Kitt's product, was Parkdale's best line plunger last year. Hitchman played in Ottawa last year. Queen's claimed him, but it looks as if Parkdale has the edge."[17]

New faces on Parkdale senior rugby team, senior champions O. R. F. U. From left to right: J. C. Solway, formerly Ridley and Oklahoma; Holmes, Torontos; Hitchman, Rideau, Ottawa; Parnell, St. Catharines.

"The Paddlers claim Lionel Hitchman, the former Aura Lee junior hockey defense star of two winters ago, who has been stationed in Ottawa with the Mounted Police." (Toronto Star, September 8, 1922, page 12)

On September 12, reporting on the Parkdales, the *Toronto Star* noted: "Hitchman, the long-legged Aura Lee junior hockey player, was out for a while, but he was compelled to retire when he turned his ankle. He has lots of natural ability and showed some excellent drop kicking."[18] With this injury, Hitch's hopes of a Grey Cup–worthy football career came to an end. As his ankle healed, he got a second opportunity in policing and was hired on by the Ontario Provincial Police force.

In October, Hitch was sent to Northern Ontario to assist with relief work after winds freakishly kicked up to hurricane strength. Farmers had been clearing their land with the use of controlled burns, and the storm caused a blazing inferno. On October 4, "the Great Fire of 1922" burned through 18 townships, destroying the communities of North Cobalt, Charlton, Thornloe and Heaslip, while Englehart and New Liskeard were partly consumed; 90 percent of the town of Haileybury was razed. Then on the night of October 5, the winds suddenly stopped, and it began to snow, snuffing out the fires. In total 43 people were killed and 6,366 displaced, and 414,720 acres of woodland were lost.[19]

The local newspapers expected Hitch to show up in Ottawa with Toronto's Parkdales rugby team when they rolled into town to play the St. Brigids. When he was a no-show, the *Ottawa Citizen* reported on October 20, 1922, that:

> One of Ottawa's coming football luminaries is now up in the fire-stricken zone of Northern Ontario on relief work for the Provincial Government. Lionel Hitchman, who had been out with Parkdales of the O.R.F.U., and is a member of the Provincial Police, was among those detailed to the north country. This excursion will probably curtail his football activities of the season, but he will be back here for hockey, and next fall may find him helping the Capital land a championship.[20]

Chapter Five

TURNING?

December 1922—Hitch was 21, and his relief work in Northern Ontario had just finished. Now in Ottawa with the Ontario Provincial Police, he was ready to play some hockey.

But first, he had to decide which team to play for. His Gunners lacrosse coach, Alf Smith, also coached that club's hockey team and wanted Hitch. The Gunners won the senior hockey Capital League the previous season, and Coach Smith was a legend in hockey. As player-coach, he led the Ottawa Silver Seven to four consecutive Stanley Cups. The Gunners had two strong defensemen in Rodger Smith and Tom O'Neil, and Hitch likely wondered how much playing time he would see. He practiced with the Gunners a few times but ultimately decided to stay with the New Edinburghs, who placed fourth out of five teams the season before.

(Hitch's future son-in-law's first cousin, Eileen Carroll, married Rodger Smith's younger brother Des, who played for the Boston Bruins between 1939 and 1942. Two sons of Eileen and Des Smith also played in the NHL, Gary "Suitcase" co-winner of the Vezina Trophy in 1972, and Brian, who later became a sportscaster.)

The Burghs were also legendary. The hockey club had operated for at least 12 seasons, and 17 of its past players were now in or had played professional hockey. Six would be inducted into the Hockey Hall of Fame. And four of those future Hall of Famers were currently playing for the NHL's Ottawa Senators: two defensemen, captain Eddie Gerard and George "Buck" Boucher; goaltender Clint Benedict; and right winger Harry Broadbent.

After those four players turned pro, the Burghs lost their winning ways. By re-signing Hitch, the team's pilot, Dave Gill, the all-around sportsman, and football star, was hopeful the Burghs would return to their glory days. "The defence last year was a pretty strong affair with Hitchman and Schroeder. Both have improved immensely. Hitchman who was always a strong puck carrier, has learned how to block more effectively and should be in for a big season."[1]

For the 1922-23 hockey season, the Capital League, now known as Group 2 of the Ottawa City League, was split into two halves, each with seven games. If a team finished first in both halves, it took the league title. If each half was won by a different team, those teams played off for the league title. The titleholder then represented the league in the Allan Cup playoffs.

The Burghs got off to a shaky start, losing 3-2 to the St. Pats. Hitch played up to expectation: "the big boy spilled them right and left and was the main works in front of Miller." They won their next game against the St. Brigids, but the "big boy" was not up to the task in the following game against the Gunners, and the Burghs got walloped 6-2. "Hitchman and Schroeder on the defence were not up to their usual game and were responsible for a lot of shots that may have got through."[2]

The team won their next three games, beating the Royal Canadiens, St. Pats and St. Brigids, with Hitch playing strong offense and defense, scoring critical goals in each game. Then came the Gunners and once again the Burghs lost miserably to them: "Hitchman was not up to his usual game and seemed unable to get going." With this loss, the Burghs handed the St. Pats first-half honors in the Group 2 League. The St. Pats won six of their first-half games, and the Burghs were second with four wins.[3]

The Burghs were three games into Group 2's second half (posting a win, loss, and tie) when the big-league Ottawa Senators were having issues with their center, Frank Nighbor, another future Hall of Famer and the "poke-check" king of the NHL. He had a leg injury and was refusing to play. Nighbor was one who carefully nursed his injuries, in an era when self-preservation wasn't valued. Without

Nighbor, the Senators were down to eight skaters, a vulnerable situation, especially as they were in a dead heat for first place with the previous year's league and Stanley Cup winner, the Toronto St. Patricks.

The *Ottawa Citizen* reported on January 30, 1923, that Nighbor would likely not play in the next day's game against the St. Patricks and that the team would use its sophomore spare and future Hall of Famer Frank "King" Clancy as a regular on defense and move George Boucher to center:

> The Ottawa management admitted yesterday that they were angling for new players. They are determined to annex the championship, and feel that they ought to have a couple of players added to their present squad to cinch the title. Harold Darragh, Jack's younger brother, is one of the amateurs they are after and they are also said to have opened negotiations with [Rodger] Smith of the Gunners and Lionel Hitchman, the cover point of the New Edinburgh team. If another defence man is signed, Boucher will be used regularly on the line, where his boring in powers are of great effect. Smith and Hitchman have been starring in the Ottawa City League games and Coach Green believes they would make good in the senior company. Darragh is ineligible for the city league, but had played most of the season at Pittsburgh.[4]

Frank Nighbor did not practice with the Senators on January 30, but Gunners defenseman Rodger Smith was there. According to the *Ottawa Citizen,* he had a contract from the Senators and was weighing his options. Both Harold Darragh and Hitch were out of town that night. The newspaper added that the Ottawa Senators' part-owner and secretary-general Tommy Gorman was prepared to make "good offers to both Hitchman and Darragh."[5]

By turning pro, a player forfeited the right to play not only amateur hockey but all amateur sports. It was an open secret that amateur teams paid players under the table, in one form or another, with many athletes securing well-paying jobs through their amateur connections. In addition, many of the good amateur hockey players also played other amateur sports, notably football (rugby), baseball or lacrosse, which had similar monetary or in-kind arrangements. Salaries in this era of hockey were not the great incentives of today—most players made the same as or less than a clerk in the government. But with the formation of the NHL five years earlier, players were jumping at the chance to play against the most elite in the game, and well-rounded athletes began forfeiting their amateur status to specialize in hockey.

On January 31, the Senators defeated the St. Patricks and retained their lead in the NHL. They started without Nighbor, but by the middle of the first period he went into the game and proceeded to "turn in a great game in return for a rousing ovation from the assemblage."[6] The three amateurs rumored to be under consideration by the Ottawa Senators, Darragh, Hitchman, and Smith, were not on the Senators' roster for this game.

In the Senators' next game on February 5 at Montreal, the Canadiens beat them badly, both on the scoreboard and physically. A last-minute substitution of an inexperienced referee saw the game spiral out of control, with Ottawa's Eddie Gerard badly cut by Canadiens player Sprague Cleghorn, the notorious bad man of the league. The only official on the ice didn't see the action, and Cleghorn stayed in the game. The Canadiens moved into the league lead, and with Nighbor and now Gerard injured, the Senators' need for more players became even more pressing.[7]

Two days later, the Canadiens were coming to Ottawa to play the Senators. Tickets for the game were in high demand, and there was chatter that some of Ottawa's followers were out to get Cleghorn. The NHL, not wanting a repeat of the chaos of the previous game in Montreal, was very aware of the pent-up animosity of the Ottawa crowd. League president Frank Calder took the unusual step of appointing two referees for the match: Cooper Smeaton and Harvey Pulford. Both were experienced and future Hockey Hall of Famers. Smeaton was the league's first referee-in-chief, holding that position for 20 years before becoming the Stanley Cup trustee for over 30 years. Pulford, the most decorated athlete of his time, was one of the original nine inductees into the Hockey Hall of Fame.

The Senators were hopeful that Eddie Gerard would be well enough to play. The team was expecting the largest home crowd so far that season, including Their Excellencies Lord and Lady Byng. The Ottawa police chief wasn't taking any chances. He planned to station a large number of constables at the arena and on the streets nearby to handle the crowd, further suggesting that "rough-house players will come in for a lot of attention from the Ottawa blue coats."[8]

In front of nearly 7,000, Ottawa reclaimed its lead in the NHL by defeating the Canadiens 3-0 in a thrilling game, with all goals coming in the last half of the third period. Defenseman George Boucher got the first two goals and assisted on the last. Early in the first period Eddie Gerard was injured again and taken out of play, this time when the stick of Montreal's Billy Coutu accidentally hit him in the mouth. As for Cleghorn, the Montreal player who cut Gerard down the previous game, his play was outstanding. "Clean, fast and courageous, he stood out all the way. Time after time he engineered rushes on Benedict and his great work silenced the roar of criticism that was directed against him in the first period. Cleghorn stood up under a verbal barrage without letting his temper get the best of him and while lemons and coppers were showered at him he merely smiled and played on."[9]

On Friday, February 9, two nights after the big Ottawa Senators–Montreal Canadiens game, Hitch's Burghs battled for the lead in the City Group 2 League, beating St. Pats 4-2. Hitch got the second goal, and he and Bertie Burke were considered best for the winners. "Hitchman was very effective on the defence and used his body a lot."[10]

On Saturday evening, the Hamilton Tigers roared into town, beating the Ottawa Senators 8-3. The following Tuesday, February 13, the Ottawas, as the Ottawa Senators were often called, lost 6-4 in Toronto to the St. Patricks but still retained their lead in the NHL.

That same day the *Ottawa Citizen* dropped two tidbits of information: An imminent shake-up was in store for the Hamilton

Tigers, and it was rumored that the NHL was "willing to affiliate with US clubs."[11] The *Citizen* seemingly had an inside track on the affairs of the Ottawa Senators and the NHL. It helped that Tommy Gorman, part-owner of the Senators and a former Olympic lacrosse player, used to be that paper's sports editor. As it turned out this information was on the money. At the end of the season, Art Ross, the coach of the Hamilton Tigers, was cut loose by the team's owners. Ross would referee in the NHL the following season and then sign on as manager of the Boston Bruins for the 1924-25 season, the first American team to join the NHL.

Back in the City League, on February 14, Hitch continued playing well and starred in the Burghs' overtime loss to the Gunners. The Burghs launched a protest against the Gunners for improper use of a player signed to another league. On February 16, the Burghs faced off with the Royal Canadiens, winning 2-1.

The Montreal Canadiens were headed back to Ottawa on February 17 for the last time on the season schedule: "Play will take place in the presence of Their Excellencies Lord and Lady Byng and in view of the cold weather, the Arena management promises another perfect sheet of ice."[12] Ottawa shut out Montreal 2-0 and kept their lead in the NHL. Montreal, by virtue of this loss and Toronto's win over Hamilton, dropped to third, and Toronto leaped into second place in the standings.

The City League meeting to hear the Burghs' protest against the Gunners was February 17, the same day Montreal was in town to play Ottawa:

> Stung by the attitude of the Burghs? [Rodger] Smith, representing the Gunners threw a bombshell into the meeting, by protesting the standing of Lionel Hitchman of the Red White and Black team. The constitution says that a player must be a resident of the city two weeks before the first game, whereas they claimed Hitchman arrived here two days prior to his first match. Consternation was written all over the faces of those present, and after an argument

the matter was referred to the registration committee of the C.A.H.A. and they will adjudicate upon the case.[13]

Despite the unfounded allegations about Hitch, the Burghs prevailed in their protest against the Gunners. The game was replayed on February 19, with the Burghs beating the Gunners 4-1. "[Rodger] Smith got a stiff check from Hitchman in the early stages that split his nose and the Gunner star came back with a lusty jam into the fence on Hitchman in the final period that earned him a five-minute penalty."[14] Hard to know what this do-si-do was about between Smith and Hitch. Maybe the protest, or that both boys were competing for a coveted spot on the Ottawa Senators or both!

Two nights later, the Burghs took on the St. Brigids; both teams were tied for second in the league. The game location shifted to the Rideau rink because the North American Figure Skating Championships were being staged at Dey Arena. A big crowd was on hand to see the Burghs win 1-0, after 10 minutes of "gruelling" overtime play. "Hitchman stood out head and shoulders over the others with his effective defence work."[15] With this win, the Burghs were now tied for first place with St. Pats and played them Saturday, February 24, the last game on the league schedule.

It was a do or die game for the Burghs. If St. Pats won, they would take the second half. Since they'd already won the first half, that would give them the City Group 2 League title, advancing to the eastern Allan Cup playoffs. The teams played 90 minutes of scoreless hockey and by the rules had to call it a draw and replay the game another day. "Schroeder was the star of the Burgh team, with Burke and Hitchman running close seconds."[16]

In the NHL, the Ottawa Senators had to "nail" two more games to guarantee a playoff spot. They left for Hamilton at 11:00 p.m. on Friday, February 23, to play the Tigers the following evening. Traveling by train on the Canadian Pacific Railway, they stopped in Toronto early the next morning, reaching Hamilton at 10:30 a.m. "The Senators journeyed in a private Pullman in command of Samuel 'Horseshoes' Webber, their official mascot, and will not return until [Sunday] night."[17] Their youngest player, King Clancy, celebrated his 21st birthday in Hamilton, issuing "embossed invitations" to his party in the café of the Royal Connaught Hotel. The Senators won that game 5-1. They had three games remaining in the regular season, next playing Hamilton again, this time in Ottawa on February 28.

Just after the Senators returned home, the Burghs and St. Pats played their rematch on Monday, February 26, to settle the second-half title, with the Burghs winning 3-2 in overtime: "In the third period both teams went all out and play flashed from end to end, but the efforts were for the most part individual and both defences had the forwards well in hand nearly all the time. Near the end of the period the Burghs seemed to be tiring and only Hitchman's brilliant performance kept the team in the race."[18] The Burghs now prepared to play St. Pats in sudden death for the City Group 2 League title.

They met on February 27 in a hard-fought, ruckus-filled game, where 12 penalties were handed out. Bertie Burke of the Burghs and Willis Touhey for St. Pats were thrown out of the game for rough play. St. Pats won 1-0 on a goal in the third period by Grey Burnett. The *Ottawa Journal* commented: "Hitchman scintillated with magnificent defensive play and broke up innumerable rushes with his sweeping poke check. . . . Outside of Miller in goal, their best man was big Lionel Hitchman. Offensively and defensively, he was the best man on either side, except the goalers, and but for his stellar play, his team would have been hard put."[19]

On February 28, 1923, the *Ottawa Citizen* added:

Following the game played at the Arena last night when the St Patricks team won the Group honors from the New Edinburghs, it was learned on good authority that the management of the Ottawa Hockey Club was out with a handsome offer to Fred Hitchman, the Burgh defence man and star of the game.

The Senators could use a good defence prospect, and Hitchman on the form he has displayed recently, looks the best of the flock of local talent that has passed the inspection test of the N.H.L. moguls. In last night's contest he stood out as the most valuable man on the team and his ruggedness carried him through a grueling game with flying colors.

While Hitchman is a bit green to step out in the big time, the Ottawa management might do worse and it would not be at all surprising if the big fellow would be wearing a Senator sweater when the locals skate out against the Tigers at the Arena tonight.[20]

Chapter Six

32 DAYS TO THE STANLEY CUP

1922-23 was the sixth season of the National Hockey League. For the past three seasons, the same four teams made up the league: Hamilton Tigers, Montreal Canadiens, Ottawa Senators, and Toronto St. Patricks. Each team carried seven to nine skaters, plus a goalie, and played 24 regular games. At the end of the season, the top two teams played off in a home-and-home, total-point series for the NHL title and the league trophy, the O'Brien Cup.

The Stanley Cup was not yet the exclusive domain of the NHL. Two other professional leagues, the three-team Pacific Coast Hockey Association (coast) and the four-team Western Canada Hockey League (prairie), also competed. This season the playoffs were in Vancouver, British Columbia. Starting with a best-of-five series between the NHL and the coast league champs, the winner played the prairie league champs in a best-of-three series for the Stanley Cup and world title.

Ottawa led the NHL with 27 points (13-7-1) before their home game against Hamilton on February 28. Toronto was in second place with 23, followed by Montreal at 22 and Hamilton with 12 points. Ottawa had to win at least one of its remaining three games to secure an NHL playoff position.

Senior amateur hockey was now over for Hitch, with his Burghs losing on February 27 in the City Group 2 playoffs. He had played five games in the past eight days, and he was not finished yet.

The *Ottawa Citizen* did indeed have the story right! After Hitch's final amateur game, Ottawa GM Tommy Gorman went to Hitch's home with a contract in hand for him. Hitch debuted with the

Senators as a substitute player the next evening in Ottawa against Art Ross' Hamilton Tigers.

At the time, the NHL had 40 skaters in total; the average player was 27 years old, five feet nine inches tall and 171 pounds. Hitch at 21 was one of the youngest, but at six-foot-one, he was the tallest, and at 167 pounds, a little lighter than most players.[1]

Manager Gorman was looking for a fierce competitor who could withstand the thrashing of other teams and push his weight around. Watching Hitch in the amateurs, Gorman saw a player with above-average hockey skills, but more importantly, he recognized a player with steely nerve, tremendous stamina and a champion's desire to win.

As the latest recruit of the Senators, Hitch would now suit up with Ottawa's multiple Stanley Cup winners: Clint Benedict, George Boucher, Harry Broadbent, Jack Darragh, Cy Denneny, captain Eddie Gerard and Frank Nighbor. An inspiring yet intimidating experience for a young, unproven player who was pushed onto center stage as the curtain was falling on a hotly contested season. Frank Clancy, a few months younger than Hitch, joined the Senators the season before, coming from the Ottawa senior amateur team, the St. Brigids. He, Harry Helman and now Hitch were the spares. Only Helman and Hitch of that fabled team were not inducted into the HHOF. Helman was also a rookie that season. Seven years older than Hitch, he too came from the Ottawa senior amateur league. (Decades later, Helman's great-grandnephew would marry Hitch's great-granddaughter and name their first child Hitchman Fitzgerald Helman.)

In that game against Hamilton, Ottawa's Eddie Gerard was ill and couldn't play. Hitch saw a lot of ice time subbing for George Boucher and Frank Clancy on defense. When he got in the game in the first period, "he was given a great hand." From the start of Hitch's pro career, hockey fans were with him. "He made a great impression with the fans, and when he worked a double pass with Boucher and the latter scored they almost raised the roof. Hitchman will be a decided acquisition to the Ottawas."[2]

Not everyone was for Hitch turning pro, however. In a letter to Brian Devlin's "From Another Angle" column in the *Ottawa Citizen*, a football fan asked: "What about the Ottawa Football Club, who thought to have him as a great halfback? Just as soon as they get a good one, the Ottawa Hockey Club makes him a pro. What a half-back line Boucher, Gerard and Hitchman would have made." To which Devlin responded:

We are forced to admit that the point is well taken. No athletic organization which had counted on landing an athlete of Hitchman's type could figure that it was in line for anything but commiseration; and we see now that our inclusion of 'everybody' may have appeared somewhat sweeping . . .

It does seem too bad, as our contributor intimates that professional hockey in the last ten years should have taken the three outstanding back-division men from the football club; but to us the shame seems that men of the Gerard-Boucher-Hitchman type should be barred from amateur football because they happen to be professionals in another sport.[3]

The football community wasn't the only group concerned about Hitch turning pro. His employer, the Ontario Provincial Police, told Hitch that if he signed a contract with the Ottawa Senators, it would violate police rules. Tommy Gorman did a bit of backpedaling, telling the *Ottawa Citizen* that Hitch had not signed a contract with the hockey team, "though he consented to jump into the game the other night and help out the red, white and black when they were in desperate straits." Gorman was making efforts to get permission from the police force for Hitch to continue with the team. "The Senators need Hitchman for the playoff, and have made special representations to his department. Hitchman himself is ready to help the Ottawas for the balance of the season, but must, of course obey orders. He is in grand shape, and he made such a big hit in

Wednesday's game against Hamilton that his loss now would be serious."[4]

Ottawa beat the Tigers 6-3 that night, securing their playoff position and affording the team's management the opportunity to give their newest recruit some needed experience.

Just before leaving for Montreal on March 3 to play the Canadiens, Hitch resigned from the Ontario Provincial Police. General Victor Williams, the commissioner of the provincial force, spoke to the issue by saying "he would encourage his officers engaging in amateur sport but the police regulations held that as a business officers must engage in police work and no other."[5] This ended Hitch's career in law enforcement.

The Senators left for Montreal on the 3:30 p.m. Grand Trunk train via the Canadian National Railway. Two days earlier, the team announced they had a block of tickets for purchase and made special arrangements with the train to bring their followers to Montreal. In addition, about 100 Ottawa Rotarians were in Montreal for their national meeting and would be attending the game.

Although the Senators had secured their spot for the playoffs, the second team was still up in the air. With Montreal's win over Toronto on February 28, the two teams were still separated by 1 point but switched positions in the standings, with Montreal now in second and Toronto in third place. This game with Ottawa was crucial for Montreal to get that last spot in the playoffs. Toronto was also playing that night in Hamilton and had to win if they were going to upend Montreal for the spot.

On March 3, in front of 6,500 spectators at the Mount Royal Arena, on natural ice that had not been flooded before the game because of the warmer than usual weather, Montreal beat Ottawa 1-0 to maintain second place in the league. Eddie Gerard did not play, and Hitch lined up with George Boucher on defense. Six penalties were handed out, three to Hitch. Cooper Smeaton refereed, and Harvey Pulford was the judge of play. Montreal newspapers took notice of Ottawa's newest acquisition. The *Montreal Gazette* commented that Hitch "created a good impression with the local public. He is a big husky fellow, a smart stick handler, and above all has plenty of courage. He showed a willingness to use his body, and took his bumps with a smile. With the exception of the time he spent in the penalty box he played throughout the game."[6]

Acclaimed sports editor Elmer Ferguson of the *Montreal Herald* added:

> It is usual in professional hockey to give every newcomer a test for gameness, and Hitchman, the big Ottawa recruit, was put over the hurdles Saturday night.
>
> 'They won't find Hitchman lacking in anything,' said Secretary Tommy Gorman, of the Ottawa Club, before the game. 'A few days ago, while he was connected with the Provincial Police, he had occasion to visit a boot-legging dive harboring some pretty tough characters. Hitchman didn't even have a gun, and was outnumbered, but when he was dared to enter, he piled in and cleaned up the joint with his bare hands. Any one who thinks that he'll quit is making a big mistake.'
>
> And so it proved. All hands stepped into the lanky ex-policeman—for he quit policing on Saturday because it would interfere with his hockey—but he took his bumps and came up smiling. He went down occasionally from hard clean checks, but got up laughing and came back for more. His good nature was unfailing.[7]

The *Ottawa Citizen* reported that after the game, NHL president Frank Calder went to the Ottawa dressing room "to congratulate the newcomer on his brilliant playing and good sportsmanship he showed after a terrific ride. Mr. Calder stated that Hitchman would become one of the greatest hockey players in the National League." The Montreal papers hadn't fully explained that the Montreal fans were trying to "rattle" Hitch, shouting "police" at him throughout the game. "But the big fellow took it all with a smile that won the hearts of all the spectators. He was repeatedly cheered in the closing stages of the match. He gave Sprague and Odie Cleghorn, [Billy Coutu] and Billy Boucher some staggering body-checks and waded through the slush at top speed throughout. He is certain to be of great assistance to Ottawa in the playoff games."[8]

His third and final regular-season game was in Toronto on Monday, March 5, 1923, against the St. Pats. Gerard was back in his starting position on Ottawa's defense for this game, but Frank Nighbor was absent, and Frank Clancy replaced him at center. Hitch saw plenty of action as a spare for the two starting defensemen. The general view was that Ottawa was taking it easy in this game, having already secured their playoff position. Toronto went hard at Ottawa, needing the win to keep their playoff hopes alive. They won 2-0 but also needed Montreal to lose against Hamilton that night, but Montreal dominated with a 4-1 score and advanced to the playoffs against Ottawa.

The two main newspapers from Toronto were judicial with their comments on Hitch's first appearance in his hometown as a professional hockey player. From the *Globe*: "Lionel Hitchman former Aura Lee player made his initial appearance in professional hockey here and did good work. He is not a finished performer, but has ability and courage and should improve. . . . Hitchman is big and does not lack speed or stickhandling ability." And the *Toronto Star*: ". . . he is certainly fearless. He waded in on the Irish goal and gave the defense more real trouble than all the rest put together."[9]

NHL Playoffs

The home-and-home, total-point series between the Senators and the Canadiens began in Montreal on March 7, with the next game in Ottawa two nights later. Hitch's first teacher on penalty etiquette from his days with the Aura Lee, Lou Marsh, was picked by the NHL to referee the series along with Cooper Smeaton.

In the NHL's short history, the Canadiens had won the league championship once in 1919, but that season the Stanley Cup playoffs were canceled because of the pandemic. They were runners-up in the NHL finals to Ottawa the next season but were kept out of the playoffs the following two seasons when Ottawa and Toronto dominated the league.

For the opening game of this season's NHL playoffs, Montreal was expecting its biggest crowd in league history. People queued hours before the box office opened, the line stretching a half mile in length. The weather had turned colder, allowing for the rink to be flooded the day of the game and ensuring high-caliber hockey. Those making wagers on the game had the Canadiens at 6-to-5 favorites.[10]

Hitch had been a Senator for all of three games and was on his way to the NHL playoffs. He had garnered a lot of attention owing in part to the controversy over his police employment, the tales of his actions on the force, and his high profile in both Toronto and Ottawa as a rugby football star. His "gameness," talent and good nature shone through, even with fans of opposing teams and with the media: "The addition of Lionel Hitchman to the Ottawa defence has given the Ottawas one of the brightest stars that the National League has ever produced, and the defence is therefore a mighty one for the Canadien sharpshooters to tackle."[11]

Also, after only one week in the NHL, in the first playoff game in Montreal on March 7, won by Ottawa 2-0, Hitch became the target of one of the most ruthless attacks in hockey history and suffered his first of many concussions.

The Mount Royal Arena was jammed to the rafters with 7,000 Montreal fans. The first period did not go well for the Canadiens, with Aurel Joliat getting three penalties. The penalties kept coming for Montreal, causing them to play one or two men short for two-thirds of the game. Partly in efforts by Montreal to kill penalties by "ragging the puck," and other tactics like kicking the puck, the game was stopped 39 times, adding to the frustration of the hometown players and fans. The largely partisan crowd was enraged by the ref's decisions and hurled insults, paper, fruit and then glass bottles in the direction of the Ottawa team and Lou Marsh, who handed out most of the penalties. The game had to be stopped several times to clear debris, and Cooper Smeaton took to a megaphone to warn the fans.

The first period went scoreless. Ottawa took the lead in the second on Cy Denneny's goal off a pass from George Boucher with the Canadiens down two players. Rounding the net after scoring, Denneny was deliberately hit on the head from behind by Billy Coutu, "which caused him to roll several times on the ice and lie bleeding from a cut on the head." Needing medical attention, Denneny was helped off the ice. Several stitches were used to close the gash, and he didn't return to the game. Coutu received a match penalty and was banished from the ice. Montreal was already down one player owing to a previous penalty and would now play with only three skaters on the ice.

In the third period, while the Canadiens were still down a player because of Coutu's match penalty, Jack Darragh scored for Ottawa. After the penalty had run 20 minutes, the Canadiens were permitted by NHL rules to substitute for Coutu and were briefly at full strength. Hitch came into the game for the first time, replacing Darragh. Hitch went back on defense with Eddie Gerard, and George Boucher was moved to left wing to cover his younger brother, Montreal's Billy Boucher. With five minutes remaining, a glass bottle was hurled at Marsh, causing another delay. When play resumed:

> Hitchman immediately made his presence felt and the first man he sent sprawling with a terrific bodycheck was Odie Cleghorn, whom he spilled head over heels. Sprague Cleghorn, bad man of the N.H.L. then went to his brother's assistance and attempted to crosscheck Hitchman at the Ottawa nets. Hitchman met Sprague with a bodycheck that also sent him spinning and Sprague skated back to the Canadiens defence, evidently in distress. Two minutes later Hitchman rushed and as he shot, Cleghorn charged over and knocked him down with a terrific blow across the head. As Hitchman fell Cleghorn stabbed him again and the officials jumped into it and sent Cleghorn to the dressing room, while five thousand people, seeing the championship slipping out of the hands of their idols, roared their approval of the attack on the newest star in professional company. Hitchman arose to his feet with blood streaming

from his face. "Hitch" still had his smile and he went back to the Ottawa defence, determined to continue. He was in no condition to do so, however, and the Ottawa management pulled him out of the game and sent Frank Clancy in to replace him. Hitchman was cut on the back of the head, his right ear was painfully bruised and his lips were split. Dr. Hand rushed to his assistance and put several stitches in his head. Hitchman stood it all with a smile and sat back grinning while the surgeons patched him up.[12]

The *Montreal Gazette* reported that Hitchman "later collapsed and had to be carried from the rink." They further stated: "The general disgraceful episodes that occurred during the game culminated in a small-sized riot at the finish, when a spectator attacked Referee Lou Marsh, several others tried to get at Ottawa players and other fights between spectators and the police added to the general pandemonium which took 20 policemen 15 minutes to quieten."[13]

The *Ottawa Citizen* recounted the scene at the end of the game more vividly:

The crowd immediately broke across the ice and made for the Ottawa players, Boucher, Broadbent and Clancy being jostled about. The Ottawa players and their officials backed up against their bench and the players had their sticks swinging when the police broke in and pulled their batons. Cooper Smeaton protected the Ottawa players and Capt. Savard threw a cordon of police around the Senators until they got Benedict and Gerard off the ice and then rushed for the shelter of their dressing room, where Hitchman and Denneny lay under the care of surgeons. Cooper Smeaton used his fists freely in the battle and the police grabbed two or three of the ringleaders. For half an hour the crowd surged and shouted while the police were powerless to prevent their demonstrations. Meanwhile the Ottawa players barricaded their dressing room door and began to shout and sing in the delight of their hard fought victory. None of the Senators were hurt in the scuffle but it was due to Capt. Savard and his sturdy policemen that some were not badly injured as the fans were infuriated. It was said that several arrests had been made. Lou Marsh was not hurt and Cooper Smeaton came out of it with a couple of slight bruises.

President Frank Calder, of the N.H.L. helped preserve the Ottawans, while Charlie Querrie and Percy Hambly, of the Toronto St. Pats, fought their way into the Ottawa dressing room and assisted in patching up the injured players. Querrie said that the Ottawas gave the gamest exhibition he had ever witnessed, and declared that both [Coutu] and Cleghorn should be barred from hockey for their attacks on Denneny and Hitchman, respectively."[14]

After the game, the Ottawa team made its way to the Windsor Hotel to spend the night. Tommy Gorman announced that Hitch was under the care of the hotel's Dr. Wesley and a nurse. By the next morning, if Hitch's condition hadn't improved, he would be admitted to hospital.

The Montreal Canadiens were swift to head off the likely actions of the NHL governors by immediately suspending Billy Coutu and Sprague Cleghorn. But their managing director, Leo Dandurand, in a statement featured on page one of all major newspapers across Canada, lay the blame for the game's violence and mayhem at the feet of Lou Marsh:

> There is nothing in the rule book to prevent ragging, nothing at all. The Ottawa players stood right inside the blue line and permitted our players to rag and made no attempt to get at them.
>
> Then when Sprague Cleghorn called Marsh's attention to it he said he did not like ragging; it was not allowed in the O.H.A. What our players are kicking at and what makes

them mad, is that the last time Marsh came to Montreal, he went back to Toronto and wrote in his paper that there had been missiles thrown and I was responsible for it, . . . while in Ottawa for the last two years, they have been throwing lemons, pipes and rubber boots and nothing has been said, . . . while here he struck a spectator and threw the officials' bell at a spectator in Toronto. The players knowing this, naturally lost their heads.

To show that I do not approve of rough play, I have suspended Sprague Cleghorn and fined him $200 and he will not participate in next Friday's game. I have also suspended [Coutu] and fined him the same amount; and another judge of play will have to be found or I will not go to Ottawa to play.[15]

NHL president Calder responded publicly to Dandurand's demand to remove Marsh for the next game: "Canadiens will play all right under Marsh at Ottawa. As a matter of fact, the appointment of Marsh was moved by Canadiens, so that the joke is really on them. I think that Marsh was probably a trifle over-zealous, and that he had a chip on his shoulder, but he's the appointment." Calder further stated that Montreal had disciplined their two players as effectively as the NHL would have but added: "I believe Sprague Cleghorn made a great mistake in attacking Hitchman. The latter is a big, good-natured chap, of undoubted courage, and there was nothing to gain by such an action."[16]

"Nothing to gain" other than to ensure he couldn't play in the next game. When Hitch didn't arrive in Ottawa with the team, rumors abounded that he had died of his injuries. Both Ottawa newspapers searched for his whereabouts. He stopped by the offices of the *Ottawa Citizen* on March 9 to dispel these stories:

With his usual offhand manner stated that he would be in uniform this evening if that were at all possible. The big fellow looked rather shaken up and exhibited a dressing over his left temple, that had three stitches under the bandages. Such a blow would undoubtedly take the pep out of most men, but Hitchman has the physical and moral attributes that cause such incidents to be made light of. However, one inch lower down would have certainly proved very dangerous if not fatal as the cut is directly above the temple. A lacerated right ear and puffed lips were other evidences of the attention paid to the Ottawa player by Sprague Cleghorn.[17]

Their Excellencies Lord and Lady Byng and another 8,000 "orderly" fans watched on Friday, March 9, as the Senators lost 2-1 to the Canadiens but won the round by two points, winning the NHL championship and O'Brien Cup.

Sprague Cleghorn was nowhere to be seen, but Billy Coutu did make the trip with the Montreal team and about 100 supporters. Both Denneny and Hitchman dressed for the game; Denneny was placed in reserve while Jack Darragh filled his usual spot at right wing. Montreal got both goals in the first period, both from Ottawa boys: Aurel Joliat, his first of the season, and Billy Boucher. The Senators struggled to get going; five minutes into the third period, badly bandaged Cy Denneny got his team's lone point. Later that period Hitch was sent in to show the crowd that he was okay, and he received a thunderous ovation.

Before the game, four members of Hitch's New Edinburghs hockey club presented him with a club bag: Dave Gill, Archie Atkinson, Bertie Burke, and Joe Miller. After the game, Tommy Gorman gathered up his newly minted NHL champions and presented them to Lord and Lady Byng in the viceregal box at the arena. Ottawa mayor Plant and other civic officials visited the team's dressing room to extend congratulations, as did the NHL directors on hand for the game.[18]

To Vancouver

In the earliest hours of Sunday, March 11, the Senators were greeted at Union Station by hundreds of cheering fans. Just after 1:00 a.m. they boarded their private train car, the Neptune, for their long trip to Vancouver, where they would play the coast league champs starting on March 16. Their trusted mascot and porter, Sam Webber, had everything ready for the journey. Jack Darragh wasn't able to get away, and the Ottawa team made a request to the coast league to substitute Billy Boucher of the Canadiens for Darragh. Boucher was put on a train at Montreal and would meet the team in Calgary en route to Vancouver. Coach Green also was not available for the trip, and Tommy Gorman would make all the coaching decisions.

All the other players made the trip to Vancouver, including the injured Hitch and Denneny. The party also included club president Ted Dey, Tommy Gorman, trainer Cosy Dolan and sports editors for both the *Ottawa Citizen* and *Ottawa Journal*, Ed Baker and Basil O'Meara, respectively. Sammy arranged for all the comforts, including musical instruments in the lounge. Prohibition was still in effect in many of the provinces in 1923, including Ontario, and team management was very strict about no alcohol on the train or elsewhere.

Before leaving, Tommy Gorman handed the *Ottawa Journal* a long letter that they printed the following day. He thanked Ottawa's loyal followers and assured them his team would represent the city "as true sportsmen and to bring back when they return victorious or defeated, Ottawa's remarkable reputation just as clean and untarnished as it now exists."[19]

The two newspaper scribes cabled reports of the journey back to Ottawa. Ed Baker commented on the camaraderie of the Ottawa party: "Right from the time the train pulled out the harmony boys have been whacking away at a piano, and an assorted orchestra has been outdoing a Victrola on the near symphony stuff. Lionel Hitchman created a sensation with the musical renditions on the violin and 'Mischa' will be a special feature from now on. Cosy Dolan and Ed. Gerard have been handling the music box, and they have their orchestra which held its first recital Sunday. The general result was fine. Tommy Gorman and Frank Nighbor sang 'Adeline' like its author never intended it to be sung."[20]

At various stops along the journey, Denneny and Hitchman were attended by doctors. Denneny's condition seemed to be worsening during the long train ride. Hitch was in great spirits and kept the team entertained with his musical talents.

At all the train stops, people came out to greet the players and wish them well. In Winnipeg, the team watched part of an amateur hockey game and mingled with some "old boys" from Ottawa. Hitch and Denneny were seen by Dr. Laidlaw, who redressed their wounds and reported that they were coming along, although he instructed that both not play in the exhibition game arranged for in Calgary. The team also got word that Frank Patrick, head of the coast league and manager of the Vancouver Maroons, had denied their request to use Billy Boucher.[21]

They received a rousing welcome in Regina, and at the Swift Current stop, Hitch was greeted by Corporal Crockhit of the RCMP. He and Hitch had been stationed in Ottawa back in 1922 and played together on the force's hockey team.

Hitch with RCMP Corporal Crockhit in Swift Current, March 13, 1923. (Photo courtesy of Tammy McLaughlin)

The Senators arrived in Calgary on March 15 and settled in at the Pallister Hotel for a few hours before playing the Calgary Tigers of the prairie league in an exhibition game in front of 2,500 spectators, losing 4-0. Every player was used in the game, and it was viewed by the team as an opportunity to work out the kinks (but the Calgary team, who placed third in the prairie league, now had bragging rights of beating the NHL champs). After the game, the Senators were feted at a banquet at the Plaza before saying their goodbyes. Billy Boucher met up with the team's car at midnight. The Senators protested Frank Patrick's decision not to let them use Boucher as a replacement player, hoping a favorable decision would ensue.

Their Neptune car pulled out of Calgary at 4:40 a.m. on March 16, arriving in Vancouver with enough time for the players to settle into the Hotel Vancouver Annex and dress for their first playoff game that night.

Once in Vancouver, Tommy Gorman was told of Frank Patrick's decision, and his hopefulness was soon replaced with anger. Patrick not only refused once more to let Boucher play, but he was also now insisting that Denneny not play in the opening game because of his "fractured skull" without being seen and given the okay by his Vancouver team doctor. Hard to know if this concern was for Denneny or to bolster his team's chances of winning over the Senators. Also, Patrick was questioning Hitchman's eligibility to play because of his length of time in the pro ranks.[22]

Stanley Cup Elimination Round

The night of their arrival in Vancouver, after six nights on the train, the Ottawa Senators stepped onto the ice in front of 9,000 spectators to play the winner of the coast league, the Vancouver Maroons, in the first of a best-of-five series. The playoff games alternated between western- and eastern-league rules, starting with western rules in the first game. These allowed kicking the puck except into the goal and awarding a 30-foot penalty shot when a player is tripped while in possession of the puck with a clear shot on net.

The Senators and Maroons played 55 minutes of scoreless hockey before Ottawa's Harry Broadbent's goal beat Vancouver 1-0. At the time of the goal each team was down two players, and Hitch was on the ice. Both "Clancy and Hitchman were given several opportunities to show their wares, and both showed up well."[23] During this game, Senators goalie Benedict received a gash to his head and needed four stitches. The game featured two sets of brothers playing against each other: Cy and Corbett Denneny of Cornwall, Ontario, and Ottawa's George Boucher and another brother Frank.

Tommy Gorman, incensed by the tactics of Frank Patrick, took to his old ways, writing a special opinion piece for page one of the *Ottawa Citizen* on March 17. It was a brilliant rebuke of Patrick's heavy-handedness, not allowing Ottawa to use Billy Boucher as a replacement player, interfering in Ottawa's decisions about the fitness of their players and protesting Hitch's eligibility. He also gave a play-by-play of the game, stating that Benedict and Nighbor stood out and that "Hitchman and Clancy got into the thick of it and both played superbly on the defence."[24]

The same night the champion of the prairie league was decided, with the Edmonton Eskimos defeating the Regina Capitals, after two overtime periods and on a penalty shot.

Also on March 17, Tommy Gorman and two other Irishmen, Frank Clancy and Basil O'Meara of the *Ottawa Journal*, walked in a St. Patrick's Day parade. The team also had a car tour of Vancouver, visiting Shaughnessy Heights, Stanley Park, and other parts.

The second game was played on March 19 in front of another crowd of 9,000. Vancouver scored early in the first period. Ottawa couldn't penetrate Vancouver's defense, and on a return attack by Vancouver, Benedict was hit in the face by the puck off a hard drive by Mickey MacKay. Play was stopped while Ottawa's goalie received medical attention. Frank Boucher scored Vancouver's second goal about two minutes after the first goal and then again with five minutes remaining in the period. Their fourth goal came in the second period and Ottawa got its only goal in the third. Basil

O'Meara commented: "Just when Ottawas were apparently hitting full stride in the second period Gerard had his leg cut by a skate, and had to retire for 15 minutes. Ottawas were weakened by his loss, and though Hitchman, who replaced him, did well, considerable of the Senatorial punch was taken out by the loss of the skipper."[25]

More injuries were reported on March 20, Cy Denneny this time, with a badly swollen elbow. In between games, practices, and misfortune, the team was fully feted by the people of Vancouver. They had a tour and attended a banquet in their honor aboard the *Empress of Russia*, a Canadian Pacific steamship. "Vancouver residents with Ottawa hockey sympathies have been round looking after the players. King Clancy, Hitchman and Helman, the Broadway trio, are the most sought after for their dancing technique, and the senoritas at the Orpheum Grill are strong for this triumvirate. Ottawas are very popular wherever they go and are a credit on and off the ice to the Capital."[26]

"Ed. Baker, 'the camera king,' took some wonderful pictures. Ed has shot a thousand feet of film and is leading the Kodak league with Hitchman a strong second." Basil O'Meara, Ottawa Journal, *March 21, 1923, page 14. This picture was taken from Hitch's camera. (Photo courtesy of Hitchman private collection)*

Ottawa's management began to wonder if their team was being "killed with kindness" and decided they needed to focus solely on their mission, to win the Stanley Cup. All further outings and banquets were curtailed.[27]

Then on March 21 in practice, Harry Helman fell as he was rounding the net and slid into Frank Nighbor's skate blade. He was cut on the face near his nose and lip and was rushed to the hospital, where he received seven stitches to close his wound. Helman would be out for the rest of the series. The team was now down to eight players, of which four had varying degrees of injuries, and with no real wing substitute. After practice, the team relaxed in the hotel lobby, where they were in big demand for pictures and autographs.

Tommy Gorman stayed in his room and once again took to his typewriter for the *Ottawa Citizen* to air his grievance against Frank Patrick's punitive stance on not letting his team use a replacement player. He cited all the examples of replacement players permitted to play in past championships, and itemized the list of injuries to the Ottawa team:

> Cy Denneny and Lionel Hitchman are still showing the effects of injuries sustained in the Eastern play off, and neither have been of much use to the team. Denneny, our scoring ace, has not registered a goal in our last three games. Hitchman's head bothers him greatly and it is unfair to put him into the games. Today Harry Helman, our ninth player, was so badly cut at practice that he is up in St. Paul's hospital, and out of hockey for the season. Clint Benedict has been put out of business twice in the world's series so far and is carrying cuts on his head and face.

Gorman further maintained that he cabled Stanley Cup trustee William Foran for a decision, stating he was "elected to arbitrate in disputes between the East and the West." Unfortunately for Gorman, Mr. Foran was of little help in the matter. When the *Ottawa Citizen* reached out to him, he responded: "Billy Boucher, under the rules, is not eligible to play with the Ottawas. However, the trustees, as last year when Gerard was allowed to play with St. Patrick's will not stand in the way of any agreement between the opposing teams." Thus, ended the Billy Boucher replacement player saga.[28]

But fortunate for Gorman, Patrick didn't see Hitch as a threat and didn't put up a stink over his eligibility. Patrick could have removed Hitch from the series, as the memorandum between the leagues for the Stanley Cup championship stipulated that the cutoff date for adding new players was February 15th. And, Ottawa had already publicly stated that Hitch hadn't signed until the end of that month.[29]

The next game against Frank Patrick's Maroons was March 22. Harry Helman was still in the hospital, and Cy Denneny's swollen elbow was giving him more trouble than his "slightly" fractured skull. This game would be played under western rules.

The Senators' hopes of winning anymore games against Vancouver were all but written off by their most loyal followers. Reporters back home prepared their readership that it was inevitable the Senators would lose: "While our wishes are all with the crippled but game Senators, we hardly expect their quest to be met with success. Ottawa may rest assured that it is represented by a collection of athletes which would bring credit to this city . . . for as great as they are as hockey players, they are greater as representative of clean fair sport."[30] Even their president, Ted Dey, was resigned and busied himself organizing a fishing trip for the lads. However, Gorman was relentless. He continued his appeal to Patrick, to no avail, and put his team through intense practices, forgoing any further social activities (including fishing).

At practice the day before the third game on Friday, March 23, "Hitchman worked out with tube skates and he showed better form. He found the ice a trifle heavy for his automobile runners but with the tubes he is able to turn much faster."[31] The plan was to get him into the game often, and even Tommy Gorman was practicing in case he needed to suit up as the ninth player with Helman still in the hospital. Vancouver was the heavy favorite for the game. Edmonton had just arrived and would take in the game to see how their prospective opponents looked.

"Crippled Ottawas Battle to Great Victory Over Vancouver Maroons and Now Lead in Worlds Hockey Series." The Senators played the entire game with just one spare, King Clancy, who played all positions except goal, winning 3-2. Vancouver scored first, and then the Senators evened it up and scored again in the first period. Vancouver scored again, tying it up late in the second period. In the third period, the Senators scored at 2:13 and played defensive hockey until the clock ran out. "King it might be remarked, played the game of his life. Had he been less courageous the Senators would probably not have been in the lead as they are now in the present series, and Tommy Gorman attributes tonight's victory to this good son of a famous father."[32] (His father was Tom, the original King Clancy, a baseball and rugby star, and former president of the Canadian Rugby Football Union.)

After the final and deciding game of the Ottawa–Vancouver series, the headline in the *Ottawa Journal* read "Go into Finals with a Badly Crippled Team." Ottawa won 5-1, eliminating Vancouver from the Stanley Cup final, but in the process, their captain suffered a knee and shoulder injury, with fears that he would be sidelined for the balance of the championship. Gerard was playing in his best form, scoring the team's second goal. After colliding with Vancouver's Corbett Denneny early in the second period, he was replaced by Hitchman, who, "getting his first real chance in the series, showed to advantage. Hitch played a defensive game to orders, and played it well." The other spare, King Clancy, got his first goal in the playoffs in this game. Corbett Denneny, the unintentional reason Ottawa lost its captain, summed up Ottawa's win: "That's a great money team. When they seem to be at their worst they usually come out at their best."[33]

Stanley Cup and World Championship Finals

With Eddie Gerard now injured and Harry Helman still recovering from his face wound, King Clancy moved up to the starting line, and Hitch was the only sub for the first game against Edmonton in the Stanley Cup final, a best-of-three series. The first game took place on March 29. Now that Vancouver was eliminated, the crowds had fallen off to 7,000 for this opening game. Ottawa took it 2-1, with the two original gimps, Cy Denneny and Hitch, the "heroes."

The game went goalless in the first period, and Edmonton scored in the second. They dominated play and were clearly the freshest and sturdiest team on the ice. Then in the third period, "Hitchman stopped Trapp in a rush toward the Ottawa goal and carried the puck the entire length of the ice driving the rubber past Winkler for the tying goal in 13:06." In overtime, Denneny got the winning goal. "But it was Lionel Hitchman, recruit, whose tying goal in the third period gave the faltering Senators the punch that transformed them from an apparently beaten team to a winning combination."[34]

After the big win, Tommy Gorman was at his typewriter again, and the topic of Hitch took up two long paragraphs:

With only a short time to go, 'Punch' Broadbent, who had gone the route at full speed waved signals of distress and motioned for relief. We had only Lionel Hitchman in reserve as it was out of the question to attempt to play Eddie Gerard, so Hitchman got the call, and Frank Clancy, champion all-round substitute of professional hockey, moved up to the attack. 'Get us a goal,' we begged of Hitchman. 'Here's your chance to hang your picture in the Hall of Fame.' And as Clancy had done in the previous struggles, 'Fairy' Hitchman arose to the occasion. 'Duke' Keats, skated and played to a frazzle by merciless Frank Nighbor, staggered off the ice and almost collapsed beside Manager MacKenzie so fierce had been the pace. Joe Simpson had cracked under the strain and it was evident that the Ottawa machine had gotten in its work.

'A three-man rush,' we shouted from the bench. 'Carry it to them Ottawa.' Hitchman suddenly broke away near the Ottawa nets and with him out from a mass of flying forms shot young King Clancy. Cleverly, Hitchman, the latest acquisition to the Ottawa squad, dodged from side to side in on the defence, while the big rink was in an uproar.

Clancy's cry of 'Shoot Hitch shoot,' could be heard above the din. Hitchman let it drive and the puck landed behind Winkler, for as pretty a goal as was ever scored. Ottawa players—those that were left of them—threw their arms around Hitchman. Then the 'Eskimo Pies' wilted before the attack of the Ottawa team.[35]

And Basil O'Meara with a little more distance had this to add about Hitch's play that game: "Edmonton had nine men in uniform, all seasoned players, and they used 'em all. Ottawas had one, Hitchman, and his game up to tonight had not been anything to write home about. How that baby did ramble through when he got steamed up. It was his effective and crashing body checking that did as much to slow up the green and white as anything. Once he looked Duke Keats in the eye and sent him tumbling into a corner, and Duke was forced to take the count."[36]

And he played with a broken nose. "The big fellow was only on for a few minutes in the last game of the Vancouver series when he received a bad crack on the bridge of the nose which broke a small bone.... Tonight Hitchman, instilled with that fighting spirit which permeates the Ottawa camp, dug in determinedly and used his body with telling effect on the Eskimo forward line."[37]

Seven thousand cheering fans, many for Ottawa, showed up for game two of the final on March 31. It would be the last game of the series, with Ottawa winning 1-0, the goal coming at 11:23 in the first period from Harry Broadbent off a pass from Frank Nighbor. Ottawa had 21 shots in the first period and 14 and 13, respectively, in the second and third periods on Edmonton's goalie, Hal Winkler. Edmonton shot 15, 18 and 15 respectively on Ottawa's Clint Benedict. Edmonton considered one of the fastest teams in professional hockey that season, if not the fastest, could not break through Ottawa's systematic defense.

Eddie Gerard, with his sprained knee and dislocated shoulder, and George Boucher, with his badly cut foot from the first Edmonton game, started on defense but came off the ice often and retired early. The team relied heavily on the "kiddie defence" of

Hitch and King. "It was thought when the series opened that Ottawa was weak in spares. The work of Clancy and Hitchman, throughout the series belied this report. . . . With two subs acting as Ottawa's defence, the Eskimos made desperate efforts to break through but found themselves stopped very effectively."[38]

In this game, Clancy made his mark being the first (and only) player ever to play every position in a game. When Ottawa goalie Benedict was given a penalty for roughing, Clancy was sent in to mind the nets for two minutes, although Edmonton was not able to take advantage of the weakened Ottawa team. The game overall was clean, with each team being assessed four penalties.

After the win, Tommy Gorman was quoted in the *Ottawa Journal*:

> "Harmony has been another great factor in the success of the Ottawas and in our triumphant march to the Stanley Cup, our players have been like one big happy family. Then the old Ottawa grit was there. Injuries shattered our team but they couldn't break our spirit. There will never be another team like that of today, when people thought we were weaker than two years ago, whereas we were much stronger. Clancy and Hitchman pulled us out of very tight corners. . . .
>
> "They're the greatest and gamest bunch of athletes I have ever met. They have shown rare pluck in the face of heartbreaking adversity; their speed and their strategy has been marvelous, but I attribute their triumph chiefly to their discipline and their adherence to training rules. Their conduct has been wonderful. Good, clean living enabled them to survive."[39]

Basil O'Meara of the *Ottawa Journal* added:

> For 50 minutes Ottawas played defensive hockey and gave an exhibition that thrilled and astonished the 7,000 fans in the rink. The Edmonton players desperately tried to break

their way through, but were met with a masterly defensive game that balked all their efforts.

When Gerard's shoulder went bad, [Gorman] shot Hitchman into action, and the Adonis of Granville street threw some of those heartfelt body checks of his into the oncoming forwards and made them make a wide detour when they came his way.

[In the final session] the speed increased as time went on. Hitchman shot on goal one instant, and in a trice was making a headlong dive that alone prevented the tricky Keats from evening the score.[40]

More commentary came in touting this Stanley Cup winner as the greatest team to have won the championship:

Canadian Press: "Everyone agreed that the Senators played and won under very exceptional handicaps. They are a great team, one of the greatest ever seen in action in the West. Western teams undoubtedly could learn something from them in the matter of team work. Individually, the Vancouver team are quite as brilliant. But, welded into a whole and working as a team the Senators are probably without peers in Canada today."[41]

Coach Pete Green stated, "I have handled a lot of hockey teams but the 1923 team is the greatest hockey machine that has ever gone on ice."[42]

Andy Lytle, sports editor, *Vancouver Province*: "If I were asked for an analysis of the Ottawa Hockey Club, my answer would be based on the assumption that I was dealing with super strategists. I doubt very much if their coast record in the series just closed will be achieved by any other puck chasing aggregation in a generation."[43]

Ed Baker, sports editor, *Ottawa Citizen*: "They are fitting representatives of the Capital of this great Dominion, and while Ottawa in years past has honored some great teams, rugby, lacrosse and hockey, the Senators, world's hockey champions of 1923, will go down in history of sport as one of the greatest, if not actually the greatest, band of athletes ever assembled." Baker also noted that

"Harry Helman, who had been seriously injured in practice ten days ago, was on for a short time relieving Broadbent."[44]

And the final quote goes to Frank Patrick, president of the coast league and manager of the Vancouver Maroons: "That's a great team; I never saw one better."[45]

For their accomplishments, the Ottawa Senators each received $700 as their share of the gate receipts, the largest amount awarded thus far to a championship team. Edmonton received $319 and Vancouver players $116.[46]

Ottawa Journal, *April 2, 1923, page 14. This was Hitch's first NHL picture, taken in Vancouver.*

And before leaving Vancouver, president Ted Dey got his wish: His team won the Stanley Cup, and he got to do a little fishing for big salmon.

Ted Dey fishing in B.C. Photograph taken by Hitch, late March 1923. (Photo courtesy of Hitchman private collection)

And, so did Hitch!

Hitch went on that excursion with Ted Dey and had his first taste of fishing for salmon. It would become a passion of his, and he enjoyed years of recreational and tournament fishing. (Photo courtesy of Hitchman private collection)

Send-off

The Ottawa Senators received a large send-off from Vancouver the night of Sunday, April 1. For entertainment, "the jazz band started early and played often. Cy Denneny was doing duty on the drums by seven o'clock, and Lionel Hitchman tore off 'souvenir' on the violin somewhere about dawn." Basil O'Meara of the *Ottawa Journal* would later say of Hitch that he "does a lot of things musically, and handles a violin like a virtuoso."[47]

As they rolled east in the comfort of their private train car, the Ottawa club was showered with "congratulatory messages." By

Regina, the players' jazz band was at full pitch and running pranks on Tommy Gorman, "aided and abetted by the genial Sammy Webber."[48] The team stopped in Winnipeg for only an hour and were greeted in near-freezing temperature by a group of Ottawa fans. The Senators were to play an exhibition game there against the Victoria Cougars, but because of all their injuries, they canceled, much to the disappointment of the Cougars and Winnipeg fans. The Senators' revised arrival time in Ottawa was late morning on Friday, April 6, and the locals were busy planning a homecoming parade and banquet. As the train moved into Ontario, the boys worked on a skit fashioned after the vaudeville comedic duo Gallagher and Shean, led by their trusted captain, Eddie Gerard. They also concerned themselves with rumors that Tommy Gorman was going west to work with Frank and Lester Patrick on a new professional hockey league. The newspapers reported that Gorman had admitted as much but that he was not in a position to talk about his plans. Next, the team was greeted in Fort William (now Thunder Bay).

At Pembroke, the Senators' private car, the Neptune, was unhitched from the Imperial Limited and attached to the Pembroke local train for the last 90 miles to Ottawa. The team had breakfast at Hotel Pembroke, "with band accompaniment." "Headed by the Board of Trade band, members of the athletic clubs, the heroes 'fell in' and marched via Pembroke and Mackay streets to the C.P.R. station."[49] The procession of marchers extended over two blocks, and when they reached the station at 7:30 a.m., 500 strong cheered and congratulated the world champs, going wild for their hometown boy, the Pembroke Peach, Frank Nighbor. By 8:00 a.m. the team was back on their train car waiting to travel the last leg of their triumphant trip.

Homecoming

Their train arrived at Union Station in Ottawa at 11:40 a.m. on Friday, April 6, 1923, to the largest homecoming for any athletes in city history. The police were unable to hold back the thousands of well-wishers who stormed the station as the train rolled in, "while the Ottawa Silver Band attacked 'Home, Sweet Home.'"

"The reception given at noon today to the members of the Ottawa hockey team, World Champions and Stanley Cup holders, on their return home, surpassed any similar demonstration ever held in the Capital. Thousands of cheering citizens gathered at Union Station, blocked the approaches, crowded on the Plaza and lined-up along the route of the parade and cheered the superb constellation of hockey stars who have brought such notable honor to Ottawa."[50]

Tommy Gorman, the team strategist of the championship Senators, was the first off the train, followed by Ted Dey, the club president and captain Eddie Gerard, George Boucher, Cy Denneny, Harry Broadbent, Clint Benedict, Frank "King" Clancy, Frank Nighbor, Lionel Hitchman, and Harry Helman. The two scribes were next: the *Ottawa Journal*'s Basil O'Meara and the *Ottawa Citizen*'s Ed Baker. Bringing up the rear were trainer Cosy Dolan and Sammy Webber, team porter and friend. Billy Boucher of the Montreal Canadiens was also with the team, returning to his hometown with brother George.

Greeting the team at the station were Mayor Frank Plant, members of city council, service clubs, the board of trade, the organizing committee, and family and friends. Police led the team to cars waiting at Besserer and Little Sussex streets.

> The crowd cheered and applauded enthusiastically as the parade of automobiles started down Besserer Street. All along the route of the parade, from Besserer Street to Mosgrove, Rideau Street, Sparks Street, Bank Street, Laurier Avenue West, Metcalfe Street, Wellington Street to the Plaza, thousands of citizens had gathered to greet the triumphant players and give them a warm welcome home. The parade was led by the Ottawa Silver Band, under Mr. J. Fanlayson. Police officers on foot cleared the way in advance of the parade. The automobiles, gaily adorned with flags and the Ottawa colors, were the cynosure of all eyes as the crowd watched to catch a glimpse of the players.

There were some 33 cars altogether in the parade. A number of these were splendidly decorated with flags, bunting and wreaths. Some of the cars bore in large letters the names of the players who were to ride in them. . . . a feature during the parade was the number of buildings from which flags had been hung and in which bunting had been placed. All the windows along the route were crowded, all office work and shop work stopping while the victors were passing by. Each car carried one member of the team and his family.

At the Chateau Laurier the parade broke up. There the players were given another informal reception and assured that Ottawa was proud of them. They were then driven to their homes. . . . Moving picture men from the big American news feature syndicates were present and took pictures in the station and along the route of the parade."[51]

The day after the homecoming, team captain Eddie Gerard, in an interview with the *Ottawa Citizen*, "was very emphatic in his statement that the greetings yesterday was the finest event of its kind he had ever seen." He further stated, "I rate the Senators as the greatest hockey team I have ever had the honor to play with, and at full strength it would have been a more decisive win." Gerard also added that Hitch "was a real surprise and his work was a treat throughout."[52]

Banquet

The organizing committee, consisting of the who's who in Ottawa business and sporting circles, arranged both the homecoming and a formal banquet to honor the Ottawa Senators. Four hundred of Ottawa's most prominent gathered at the Chateau Laurier on the evening of April 9 to pay tribute to the world champions. The Stanley Cup and O'Brien Cup, overflowing with red roses, were positioned on the tables of the guests of honor. Members of the Silver Seven hockey team were present, as was Chauncy Kirby, who played with Harvey Pulford for Ottawa, the runners-up to Montreal in the first Stanley Cup challenge in 1894. The players were led into the grand ballroom by two pipers. After all the festivities and speeches, city controller Joe McGuire and Harvey Pulford presented gold watches to the players.

In appreciation, Eddie Gerald on behalf of the team thanked the city for its support, summing up that "our success was due to harmony on the team."

In closing, Tommy Gorman gets the last word on his 1923 world champions and Stanley Cup winners: "They represent all that is clean, honorable and successful in the wide wide world of sport."[53]

OTTAWA, N.H.L. AND STANLEY CUP CHAMPIONS, 1923.

Top row, left to right—B. O'Meara, E. Baker, G. Boucher, Defence; L. Hitchman, Defence; F. Dolan, Trainer; F. Nighbor, Centre; B. Pringle. Middle row—F. Clancy, Forward; E. P. Dey, President; H. Helman; T. Gorman, Secretary; C. Benedict, Goal; E. Gerard, Defence. Bottom row—Cy. Dennenay, Forward; H. Broadbent, Forward.

The above photo is of the party that traveled from Ottawa to Vancouver for the 1923 Stanley Cup and World championship, including the Ottawa club players, staff and executive; and the two Ottawa sports editors. Source: Hockey Year Book 1923, *(Toronto: George King, 1923).*

Chapter Seven

THE OTTAWA ADONIS

Unlike the western leagues, which played 30 games and started mid-November, the NHL for the 1923-24 hockey season again played 24 games, beginning December 15 with Ottawa in Hamilton and Montreal in Toronto. The reason: artificial ice, or lack thereof in Montreal. This season, Ottawa moved to a new building with piped-in refrigerated ice, joining the ranks of Toronto and Hamilton for a truly modern indoor skating experience. The 10,000-person capacity (seated and standing) Ottawa Auditorium (Aud) was being rushed to completion for the December 1 opening featuring an exhibition game between the Ottawa Senators and the Stanley Cup finalists, the Edmonton Eskimos.

While their new home received its finishing touches, the Senators took to the trains for an exhibition series in Winnipeg against Calgary, Edmonton, and Regina. Ottawa was to play Regina in two games for total points. The other two teams did the same, and the winners of each series played in a final game.

Ottawa's team heading west consisted of the same group of players that Hitch first took to the ice with on February 28, 1923, except Eddie Gerard. He had an undisclosed illness that ended his playing career. Years later it would be revealed that he had a nonmalignant growth in his throat, caused by a hockey stick accident. For the current season, Gerard would remain with the team, receive his full salary and help coach the club.

They left for Winnipeg in the early morning of November 16. "The Senators reorganized their famous jazz band last night, and are scheduled to give their performance when their train reaches Pembroke to pick up Frank Nighbor. Lionel Hitchman, 'King'

Clancy, George Boucher, and other well known musicians will be found at their best."[1]

Hitch's Worlds Pendant

The Senators arrived in Winnipeg on November 17 and had a few practices before the first game. Their brand-new uniforms featured a small crest sewn on the upper left side of their sweaters bearing the words "World's Champions, 1923."

For the first game on November 19, the Senators started Clint Benedict in goal, George Boucher and Frank Clancy on defense, and Frank Nighbor, Punch Broadbent and Cy Denneny on the forward line. Jack Darragh, Harry Helman, and Hitch were the spares.

The Regina Capitals won 5-2 in the opening game. The sports editor of the *Winnipeg Free Press*, W.J. Findlay, singled out Frank Nighbor as the "bright star" for Ottawa, and "Darragh and Hitchman proved very capable subs." The game was tied 1-1 after two periods, but Ottawa petered out in the third period, probably because of lack of on-ice conditioning, as they hadn't stepped on the ice until they arrived in Winnipeg. Findlay also took note of Ottawa's "brilliant defensive system. For two periods the Regina team invariably found a six man defense to beat."[2]

Ottawa's famous defense system, known as "kitty-bar-the-door," was devised by their longtime coach Peter B. Green. After the Senators won the Stanley Cup the previous March, Green commented: "The Ottawa defensive system is no puzzle, the usual practice has been to send down two forwards, the odd man playing back with the defence. When the opponents rush practically every man towards the Ottawa goal, then the [Senators] would change their system and uncork a three-man rush."[3]

Ottawa won the second game against Regina by a score of 2-1. Findlay again commented on Ottawa's defense and noted that "Hitchman, who likes to rough things was not used much but put a lot of life into the play when he was on the ice while Jack Darragh gave a glimpse of his old form when he scored Ottawa's second counter."[4] Regina won the round 6-4 and would next beat Edmonton 7-4, the winners on the other side of the tournament. Ottawa rushed home to get ready for a two-game, total-point exhibition series against Edmonton for the opening of the "Aud."

While the team was in Winnipeg, Tommy Gorman was making arrangements to purchase Earl "Spiff" Campbell from the Edmonton Eskimos. Spiff was a year older than Hitch, a boy from nearby Buckingham, Quebec, and another protégé of the Ottawa New Edinburghs. A defenseman, he had been with Edmonton for part of the last season, brought over from the Saskatoon Crescents, both of the prairie league.

Campbell was in practice with the Senators before they opened at the Aud against Edmonton, but he would temporarily remain with Edmonton.

The official opening of the Ottawa Auditorium was a regal affair. His Excellency the Governor General, Lord Byng, declared the new building opened and "faced" (dropped) the puck, while members of the Cabinet, Senate and House of Commons looked on. Ottawa mayor Frank Plant and NHL president Frank Calder were also in attendance. Lou Marsh was tasked as the sole referee for the two-game series.

In the opening game, Ottawa started the same team it opened with against Regina. Edmonton's lineup included Spiff Campbell as a spare. In front of 7,000 spectators, Edmonton beat Ottawa 3-1, with Campbell getting their second and third goals. George Boucher was out of the game for 15 minutes for rough play, and Hitch was singled out as the weak link on the team: "Frank Clancy had his usual burst of speed but too much work took its toll. Hitchman showed more speed than usual, but his blocking was nothing to rave over. With Boucher off the Clancy-Hitchman combination did not hit things off as smoothly as the Gerard-Boucher combination or the Boucher-Clancy tandem."[5]

This criticism seemed to give Hitch a jolt. He may have seen Clancy as the heir apparent to Gerard's defense position but Hitch sure as hell wasn't going to let Campbell step over him should he end up with the Senators for the regular season.

The next game against Edmonton was played on December 3, with the Senators winning 2-1. One headline declared: "Hitchman Hero of Game with Winning Goal in Third Period." Hitch finally got in the game, replacing Boucher with two minutes left in the second period. "He broke Trapp's rush and raced down centre and passed to Denneny who made sure of his shot sending a hot waist high drive smoking into the left hand corner of the net." Again, replacing Boucher in the third period, "he went down the right side shot and took his own rebound from a scramble and pushed the puck into the nets."

The Ottawa Journal, *December 4, 1923, page 14, about Ottawa's second game against Edmonton.*

It was also noted that "Hitchman was the darling of the gods after his goal was scored. The big fellow was given an outburst of applause every move he made."

With the series split between Ottawa and Edmonton, the total score was 4-3 in favor of Edmonton, and they won the exhibition series.[6]

The Ottawa players took their tournament receipts and put them toward shares in the Ottawa Auditorium Company on December 6, 1923, becoming bit owners in this new venture.[7]

What made the defense seem so weak during these two games, something no one knew prior, was that Boucher had the flu and Clancy was injured. And with the loss of Gerard, the local critics put much of the blame on Hitch. Despite his great plays in the second game, he was struggling, but it wasn't for lack of conditioning, skill or effort—he was having trouble with his skates. When the team got their new gear, they changed the players' skates, and Hitch was not adjusting to the change.

But he played well enough to get noticed by Edmonton's manager, Kenny MacKenzie, who just before leaving town stated: "Hitchman is the most improved hockey player in the professional league. He will be a superstar this season and should develop into one of the greatest in the game."[8]

Ottawa decided to take a chance on Hitch:

> Fred Hitchman known in the family circle by the more euphonious name of Lionel, will now step up while the spotlight plays on him. "Hitch" has been selected as running mate on the defence for George Boucher, and for the time being he will hold forth there. Frank Clancy who can do a little bit of everything in a hockey way, is first relief for Senators and will alternate as defensive and forward substitute with strong possibility of doing a 40 minute shift in every game.
>
> It took Tom Gorman considerable deep thinking to work out a scheme to fill the shoes left by Eddie Gerard. He has finally decided that the improvement shown by Hitchman is sufficient and in Hamilton the defence Adonis will hold forth for the first time and Tommy is betting a new chapeau that he makes good all the way.
>
> Ottawas worked out that combination last night and it looked very good. Hitchman is showing good ability at blocking now and there never was anything particularly lacking in a puck carrying way on his part.[9]

The season opener for the Ottawa Senators took place in Hamilton with a win of 3-2. "Ottawa also trotted out a newcomer in Hitchman, a sturdy defence man who showed puck carrying ability and a style all his own in breaking up a rush."[10]

> After last night's struggle, Hamilton critics are convinced that the Senators are the team to beat. If anything they are more formidable than in previous seasons. True they are without the services of Eddie Gerard, but Gerard sat on the Ottawa bench and assisted Manager Gorman in directing the play of his team mates. In Hitchman, a lanky youngster, who took Gerard's place on the defence, the Ottawas produced another bright star, who fitted in perfectly. Hitchman turned in a beautiful game from start to finish and will, no doubt, prove a worthy successor to the one and only Gerard. And in addition, the Ottawas also showed the greatest comeback artist of recent years—Jack Darragh. The veteran played with a snap and a dash that was not to be denied. He had speed to burn and to his trusty stick fell the honor of notching the goal that decided the spoils.[11]

The next game was at home on December 19, the first of the season in the new Auditorium. It had almost all the fanfare of the opening against Edmonton, with Lord and Lady Byng in attendance and the Governor General's Foot Guards Band playing between periods. Sammy Webber, the C.P.R. porter, and friend of the Senators sat on their bench, "decked out in a world's champion sweater." Art Ross, the former manager of the Hamilton Tigers, was now refereeing in the league and handled the game, the only official on the ice. Six thousand fans saw Ottawa win decidedly against Toronto in a 5-2 victory. Hitch started on defense with George Boucher but saw only about eight minutes of play, the balance going to Frank Clancy. He had trouble with his skates again.[12]

Ottawa was to travel to Montreal for game three on December 22, but it was canceled because of mild weather, Montreal not having artificial ice. The game would be fit into the schedule at a later date. In the meantime, management of the Ottawa Auditorium was busy retrofitting their new rink to accommodate another 800 seats in the "rush end." With the Montreal Canadiens, Ottawa's "ancient hockey rival," coming to town in a few days, they wanted to sell as many tickets as possible.

A crowd of 8,300 showed up for the game on December 26 against the Canadiens, the largest ever to see a game in Ottawa. Art Ross again refereed, and Ottawa beat Montreal 3-2 in overtime. Hitch lost his place on the starting lineup to Clancy, who played a "remarkable" game, though it was noted that while on the ice, Hitch was "prominent." The newspapers also noted that Tommy Gorman and Eddie Gerard were on the hunt for more amateurs, with an eye on right winger Frank Finnigan. They had already brought in Leth Graham, a former Burgh and Senator left winger who had played with the Hamilton Tigers the previous season. Graham would play in only the first three games. In addition, the Senators were still holding out for Spiff Campbell.[13]

The next game was also at home, this time against Hamilton, who had also picked up some new players in Billy Burch, Jesse Spring, and Redvers (Red) Green. Ottawa's Jack Darragh took a bad fall, cracking his kneecap, and would be out of commission for a month. And George Boucher suffered an ankle injury. Ottawa lost in overtime, 3-2.

The Senators were criticized for not playing their subs. Hitch got in the game for only a few minutes, and his performance wasn't considered helpful, getting a penalty at the wrong time in overtime play. Helman and Graham saw no time. The *Ottawa Journal* reported that management argued that their system of play relied on a precise and delicate balance, and it was better to play a tired regular than a fresh sub not fully immersed in the system's intricacies. Clancy, with two more years of experience, was fitting in nicely. "Hitchman, if he has the goods, is bound to show, and at times has shown some very good hockey, though he cannot be rated a really finished player yet."[14]

It appears some of this criticism did not fall on deaf ears. Surely they needed to sub players more frequently to avoid overtiring their star players, which could only lead to poor results and injuries. It seemed to be more a question of the right subs. With Darragh and Nighbor both injured, Hitch and Helman were to get a thorough workout in the upcoming game in Toronto, and the team had just acquired Rod Smylie from the Toronto St. Pats.

On January 2, 1924, Ottawa stormed into Toronto and came away with a 4-3 victory. The newest sub and "discarded" player of the St. Pats, Dr. Rod Smylie, got the first goal of the night. Hitch started on defense with Boucher, and "Tommy Gorman said after the game that Hitchman was the best man on the ice. The big fellow showed a lot more than in previous starts. . . . Hitchman used his weight to advantage. St. Pats slammed him hard, and the big fellow came right back." The *Toronto Daily Mail* commented that "Lionel Hitchman, a former Aura Lee player, was another who took a prominent part in the defeat of the locals. He checked well, and mixed matters right merrily, with the Irish heavyweights. Hitchman is an accurate marksman, and he kept Roach constantly on the alert lest he slip one past him." And "Billy Hewitt [sports editor, the *Toronto Daily Star*] predicts that 'Hitch' will be one of the brightest stars of the N.H.L. season."[15]

Ottawa played Toronto again on Saturday, January 5, at the Aud, fortified by Spiff Campbell. It was announced before the game that Hitch would again start on defense with Boucher. With 6,000 spectators watching, Denneny and Boucher ran up the score with four goals in the first period. The score was 6-0 for Ottawa by the end of the second period and ended 7-3 for Ottawa. "Hitchman started out on the defence and his play was a revelation to those who saw him sprawl all over the ice in former games. . . . Hitchman played a real good game, and it must be said he is a very unselfish player and knows when to pass the puck." He "shot and scored on his own rebound."[16]

Ottawa prepared for their next game against Montreal and for the time being decided on Hitch over Clancy to start with Boucher on defense. "Senators will start the same team that sent St. Pats tumbling. Hitchman showed such prowess that he can be depended on from now on. Boucher of course, is a certainty, and Clancy will be main relief. The regular forwards start out, with Smylie, Campbell and Helman in reserve."[17]

Ottawa's mayor-elect Henry Watters, in his first official appearance, dropped the puck in front of 8,000 spectators. Lou Marsh took charge of the game as referee, and Ottawa won 2-1 with a goal from Broadbent in the dying minute of the third period. Hitchman "played a strong game." Clancy was hurt in the opening period by Sprague Cleghorn's stick to his head. He was able to return later in the game and was the only sub used that evening. "Every player on the Ottawa team was at his best from Benedict out. George Boucher and Hitchman, who started on the defence end, both turned in splendid games and Clancy, who relieved Hitchman at times, was also brilliant."[18] After seven games, Ottawa was ahead of the other three teams by six points.

However, Ottawa's toughest part of the schedule was yet to be played, with five of the next six games on the road. Because of the canceled game in Montreal on December 22, Ottawa's next three games against Montreal would all take place in that city, a home advantage if ever there was one.

First up, Ottawa went to Hamilton, and with four minutes left in the third period came from behind to tie the score at 2-2, sending the game into overtime. After nearly 15 minutes, Broadbent scored to save the game for Ottawa, disappointing the 6,300 Hamilton fans.[19]

Ottawa went to Montreal and in front of 7,000 lost 2-1 after four minutes of overtime, with Sprague Cleghorn getting the winning goal. Cy Denneny was injured early in the first period when his arm was cut in a bumping incident with Sprague Cleghorn. Clancy and Smylie alternated in his left wing position. The ice conditions were deplorable if not dangerous, with soft, slushy ice and deep grooves. Frank Nighbor did not have a good game. "Hitchman played a very sound game and his unique way of stopping Odie Cleghorn by giving him a flying mare when he came down was effective if somewhat awkward. Hitchman used his body generously and didn't spare either of the Cleghorns with his weight. Boucher, too, used his body with telling effect and Broadbent and Clancy handled themselves well in the going."[20] Mike Rodden of Toronto made his refereeing debut. Ottawa was now four points ahead of Toronto. Montreal was in third and Hamilton in last place.

In another overtime game, Ottawa beat Hamilton 2-1 at home in front of 6,000. Denneny played but suffered another injury to his arm and would be out for the upcoming game with Montreal. "Hitchman is going ahead in every game. Tommy Gorman had great faith in this boy and stuck to him when Hitchman was going rocky."[21]

The makeup game in Montreal took place on January 21 in front of 6,000 very partisan fans. Art Ross was the sole referee. Jack Darragh returned to the lineup after suffering his split kneecap a few weeks earlier but saw only a few minutes of play. Without Denneny, Clancy filled the void wonderfully, getting the first goal and the winning one, making the score 3-2 for Ottawa. Broadbent was injured in the second period, needing stitches to his forehead. Hitch and Clancy were singled out as the stars for Ottawa, while Sprague Cleghorn and Howie Morenz were the picks for Montreal. Hitch was noted for the speed of his rushes and his blocking of incoming opponents:

> *Montreal Gazette:* Howie Morenz suffered a severe jolt when he was heavily, though fairly, bodied by Hitchman in the second period. Morenz bounded off Hitchman and hit the boards, remaining prone on the ice. He soon revived. But in the meantime an ardent Canadien supporter had attempted to jump over a group of spectators in the front of the promenade, bent on getting at the big Ottawa defence man. He found himself blocked by justly wrathful spectators [including Cooper Smeaton] and was soon hustled from the rink. In the meantime Bedlam was loose, the crowd yelling till the referee's whistle could hardly be heard above the din.[22]

> *Ottawa Citizen:* Though Canadien officers wanted Hitchman penalized after Morenz had been laid out in the third period, Referee Art Ross declared that the check was

fair in every way. Morenz afterwards admitted that it was a straight body check, but added it was the worst he had ever received. Hitchman gave [Billy] Boucher and Joliat some terrific tumbles, but did it all in a legitimate manner. He has gone through six games without getting a penalty, and is the most improved player in the league. Every critic on the circuit has been singing his praises. 'Hitch' turned in a really marvelous game at Montreal and deserves great credit for his rapid rise. He is playing the game as it should be played and should get every possible protection from the officials.[23]

At this point in the season, with both Broadbent and Denneny injured in games at Montreal, Ottawa's management raised concerns of intentional rough play by Canadiens players. Ottawa's new president, Frank Ahearn, put forth an official complaint to Frank Calder, president of the NHL, and Tommy Gorman aired their grievances in the Ottawa newspapers; this article is from the January 23, 1924, *Ottawa Citizen*:

"It is time that the National Hockey League stepped in and put a stop to this butchery at the Mount Royal Arena," said Manager Gorman in discussing incidents of Monday's battle. "Eddie Gerard and Frank Nighbor were badly hurt there in the early stages of last season and in the playoff Hitchman and Denneny were nearly killed by foul blows from Cleghorn and Coutu. In our first game there last week, Cy Denneny was put out of commission. Harry Broadbent was deliberately jabbed last night and is also out of hockey. Who will be next?

"We are not blaming Referee Art Ross. Ross is a square shooter and he did the best he could under the circumstances. We will insist hence-forth, however, on having two referees for our matches at Montreal. It is impossible for one man to follow all the play. Sprague Cleghorn slashed and chopped every time our players carried the puck in. He repeatedly threatened to get young Clancy and after Broadbent returned to the game he told him he would 'open him up more' if he tried to go in again. Hitchman took more abuse than any man has ever had to stand up under and it is a wonder that more of our players were not seriously injured.

"Cleghorn knocked some of [Hamilton's] Ken Randall's teeth out in a recent game at Montreal. Then he opened a vicious wound in Cy Denneny's arm, and then cut down Bill Stuart in a match at Toronto. Billy Boucher smashed Frank Nighbor here and then attacked Broadbent at Montreal. Joliat's work was also disgraceful. He didn't attempt to play hockey. Our players have put up clean hockey all through the season. They have played to capacity crowds in all their games away from home and it seems a great pity that they should have to stand the stuff that Canadiens are repeatedly handing out. Our games against Toronto and Hamilton are keenly contested and are strenuous, but neither the Hamilton nor Toronto players would descend to such tactics as are employed at the Mount Royal Arena. Leo Dandurand ought to realize that these rowdy players are killing his team's chances and disgracing hockey. The time has come for a showdown and the National Hockey League should take action at once.

"The Canadien management could remedy the evil if it desired, but apparently Cleghorn, Boucher, and others are being encouraged to cut down their opponents. Now it is up to the National Hockey League. President Frank Calder has the full authority and should act immediately."[24]

Going into the next game in Toronto on January 23, the Senators increased their lead over the St. Pats to six points. They would be without Broadbent and Denneny for the game, relying on Clancy and Campbell. Ottawa employed its famous "kitty-bar-the-door" defense, and the two subs responded beautifully—as the defense broke up incoming attacks, they transitioned with bursts of speed for one- and two-man rushes on Toronto. Ottawa won 5-1, with Boucher and Nighbor each getting two goals; with four minutes remaining in the game, Hitch got the fifth on a backhand shot. "Hitchman showed further improvement and on his playing graduates from the recruits' class."[25]

The season was at the halfway mark, with the Senators eight points ahead of the St. Pats and both the Canadiens and Tigers trailing the leader by 12 points. Ottawa had just set a new NHL record, winning 10 of 12 games in the first half, beating their previous record of three seasons before by one win. The top three goal scorers in the league were Ottawa's Denneny (10), Boucher (9) and Nighbor (8), and in 11th pace was Broadbent with five goals. With the loss of Gerard and the serious injuries to Darragh, Broadbent, and Denneny, no one expected the Senators to keep pace with the leaders and certainly not to be setting new records. This new record was built on the play of their newest and youngest players, Clancy, Hitch, and Campbell. When Broadbent and Denneny were injured, Clancy and Campbell gallantly stepped into the breach. Hitch, by definition still a rookie who hadn't yet played a full NHL season, proved his mettle by earning Gerard's position. "Lionel Hitchman is now hailed as one of the finest defence men in the game."[26]

Ottawa's next game was on Saturday, January 26, in Hamilton, but first Ottawa management was summoned by Frank Calder to a special meeting of the NHL heads in Toronto to discuss their rough play allegations against Montreal. "The Montreal papers state that the prexy is going to demand an apology from Secretary Gorman for his charges as outlined in the papers and they claim that the other teams will stick with Canadiens."[27]

It seems Montreal whipped Toronto and Hamilton to line up with them against Ottawa, who had diligently laid out their complaint in a lawyerly manner, with witness statements all duly notarized. Montreal brought Sprague Cleghorn to the meeting. Not much more was immediately known of the proceedings or outcome of the meeting other than the passing of a resolution "empowering President Calder to impose a fine of $500, or more, should he see fit, for any club sending out propaganda about rough play."[28] The message was received loud and clear: Rough play will continue, and the NHL will not tolerate airing of differences in public. The other item of business at the meeting was to accept a new award for the league, the Hart Trophy recognizing the most valuable player to a team.

That day, Ottawa lost not only in the boardroom but on the ice as well. In front of Hamilton's crowd of 6,000 in a game refereed by Art Ross, Ottawa was outplayed 5-1. It was the second time this year that Ottawa lost to Hamilton. P.J. Jones, sports editor for the *Hamilton Herald*, made these observations about the Ottawa players:

> The Ottawa forward line played like Hamilton teams of other years. They skated themselves into a state of exhaustion, yet got nowhere. And the Hamilton team played as the Senators do when at full strength.
>
> George Boucher and Lionel Hitchman were Ottawa's star performers, the defence men worked hard every minute. Defensively they had more to do than usual because of the three-man attacks launched by their opponents, and on the attack they were far more dangerous than their forwards. Boucher's stick handling was a bright feature of the game. He could not get through the Prodgers–Randall defence however. Hitchman rushed even more often than Boucher and the big fellow didn't stop trying at any time.[29]

The following Wednesday Ottawa played Toronto, with Art Ross refereeing. Toronto was still in second place behind Ottawa. It was the Senators' first home game in two weeks, and for the first time in four games, the team would have its full complement of players. "Manager Gorman stated last night that he would start out Ottawa's 'Super-Six,' Benedict, [George] Boucher, Hitchman, Nighbor, Broadbent and Denneny, keeping in reserve Darragh, Clancy, Campbell, Smylie and Helman."[30]

A crowd of 5,000 showed up to see Ottawa beat Toronto 7-2. Toronto pulled out in front by two goals in the first period. Shortly after the second period started, Hitch passed to Nighbor to put Ottawa on the scoreboard. Then in the third period, Hitch passed to Denneny for the goal that put Ottawa ahead in the game. In total, Hitch got four assists (in an era when only the pass closest to the goal, commonly referred to today as the primary assist, counted as an assist). Denneny got three goals that night, all off combination plays with Hitch. "Lionel Hitchman is one of the most unselfish players in the league. He gave four perfect passes for goals in the last game which certainly entitles the big fellow to just as much applause as those who scored the goals." Hitch was the ultimate player's player and likely very happy that the quiet and committed spare, Harry Helman, got into the game toward the end of the third period and "scored on a splendid bit of stickhandling in half a minute and the crowd gave him an extended cheer."[31]

Ottawa left for Montreal at 3:30 p.m. on Saturday, February 2, for the game that night at the Mount Royal Arena. Frank Nighbor didn't travel with the team, owing to injuries to both wrists. Ottawa lost 1-0 but would have won if all the goals scored had been allowed. Campbell, Broadbent, and Hitch all had goals overturned for one reason or another. Hard to know if referee Art Ross was overcompensating for the public criticism levied at him from Charlie Querrie of Toronto over the previous game in Ottawa. Querrie alleged that Ross and umpire Ernie Butterworth were not impartial in the game, plus Boucher, Broadbent, and Clancy were allowed to get away with rough play. The Ottawa Club launched a complaint with the NHL against Toronto and Querrie for breaking the new antipropaganda rule and for making false charges. Gorman's letter of complaint was published in the *Ottawa Citizen*, where he also stated: "And if we don't back up our referees, we might as well close the rinks."[32] A special meeting was called in Montreal by Frank Calder that weekend to deal with this latest spat between clubs.

The Montreal game was played to a capacity crowd that included NHL president Frank Calder and several journalists from the United

States. Rumors were swirling about the possibility of one or more U.S. teams joining the league the next season. In the game, George Boucher was taken out by what was deemed an accidental collision with Sprague Cleghorn. "Cleghorn, however, was blamed for putting Hitchman down for the count in the final period and was given a major penalty by Art Ross. The offence occurred when Cleghorn, coming down center ice, passed the puck between Hitchman and Clancy, who had closed in, and in jumping between the Ottawa defence players, jabbed Hitchman near his right eye. As Hitchman writhed in agony, the crowd, or the majority of those nearest the play, jeered the offender." The *Ottawa Citizen* also reported that Hitch "played the cleanest possible brand of hockey and was always effective. He had the puck all through and played his eighth game without a penalty of any kind."[33]

After the game Frank Calder issued two rulings: that Charlie Querrie of the Toronto St. Patricks be fined $200 for disparaging referee Art Ross after the Ottawa–Toronto game early in the week; the other, "Sprague Cleghorn, for carrying his stick in such a manner as to endanger opposing players after having been warned against so doing, is suspended from taking part in any game until further notice." President Calder said: "This high carrying of sticks, and checking around the head and neck must stop. The next offence will not find the player suspended, but expelled outright from organized professional hockey."

Leo Dandurand, manager of the Montreal Canadiens, said they would appeal the decision, citing that Ottawa's statement that "Hitchman finished the match, but was delirious after it, and required medical attention on Sunday as he suffered from intense pains in the head," was an exaggeration. Dandurand stated he had seen Hitchman in the hotel restaurant after the game and he looked fine. "Our players never indulge in puerile complaints. The many thousands who attended the game on Saturday saw Hitchman continue to play without even leaving the ice after the collision with Cleghorn. To my consternation President Calder overrules Referee Ross by imposing a suspension on Cleghorn."[34]

The controversy raged on for several days, with the story being rewritten by sportswriters in Montreal. "Montreal papers say that Cleghorn was going through fast and that Clancy and Hitchman tried to sandwich him and Cleghorn put up his stick to protect himself." Leo Dandurand, as quoted in the *Montreal Star*, added: "I certainly think the Cleghorn–Hitchman incident was a trifling affair. I had promised President Calder that there would be no foul play, but I did not promise that we would play ping pong hockey. I have no ping pong players on my team and leave it to the public to say whether Ottawa has Sprague ran up against the two Ottawa defence men who placed themselves in his path before he knew it, and he merely tried to get through. Considering the terrific speed of the match I do not think it was extraordinarily rough."[35]

Philip McCann of the *Ottawa Citizen* reported that on Tuesday, President Calder called on Gorman and Dandurand to "drop the nonsense which was fast making the league a laughing stock," further offering that if the two hockey clubs "cut out the 'pernicious propaganda' and unnecessary 'rough stuff,' a very large majority of hockey supporters will be pleased beyond measure."[36]

Helping to turn the focus away from the intrigue of the hockey magnates and to start a whole other line of speculation was the *Ottawa Journal*'s decision to print the musing of a smitten young lady. Her target was also Hitch. Surely he received some razing from his teammates and probably more than that from his girlfriend, Tops:

OH YOU LIONEL
"Would you please publish this?"
 A young lady stood at our desk and proffered a letter which contained the following feminine tribute to Lionel Hitchman. The Ottawa "Adonis" has a lot to answer for. It is as follows:

"Each time I go to see Ottawas play I see 'Hitch' improving in every way.
He knows how to pass and he knows how to shoot.

When he starts to play hockey his opponents all scoot.
He is a boy that works with a will,
His checking fills many a fan with a thrill.
His attractive appearance and play give him fame
And to me he is always the star of the game."

L.B.[37]

Montreal was en route to the capital to play Ottawa. Both teams were absent their veteran defense leaders: Sprague Cleghorn still tied up by the indefinite suspension for his jab to Hitch's right eye, and Boucher still suffering from the effects of his injury in Montreal the game before. Also, Ottawa would be absent Spiff Campbell because of the death of his father.

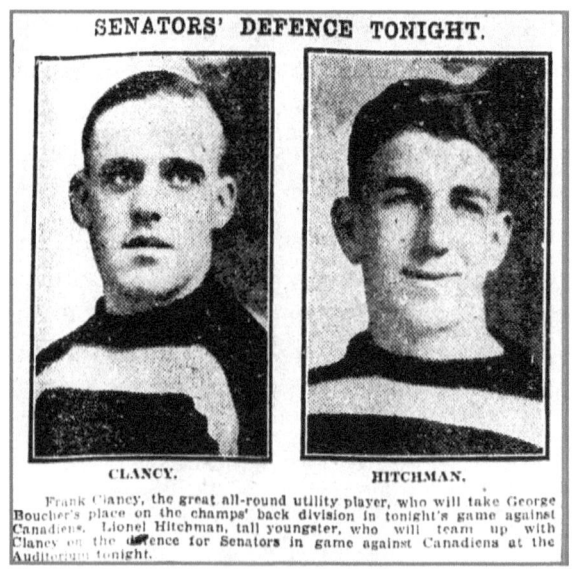

Ottawa Citizen, *Wednesday, February 6, 1924, page 10.*

Before the game started, Frank Ahearn and Tommy Gorman escorted members of the royal family of Denmark to the viceregal box in the arena. His Royal Highness Prince Erik of Denmark was in town to marry Lois Booth, the granddaughter of Ottawa's lumber and rail tycoon, John R. Booth. Prince Erik was invited to drop the puck, assisted by his father Prince Valdemar, brother Prince Viggo and Admiral Juhnke of the Danish Navy. Miss Booth was presented with a floral arrangement by captain Frank Nighbor.[38]

About 10 percent of Ottawa's population came to the Auditorium, a record-breaking crowd of nearly 10,000, to watch as the "kiddie defense" came through for Ottawa. Goalie Clint Benedict had only half a dozen shots to contend with as Ottawa won 4-0, with two goals from Denneny and one each from Nighbor and Hitch. The *Montreal Gazette* wrote that "Hitchman played a phenomenal game, and absorbed considerable punishment, and handed out the body generously. His puck control was marvellous. His goal was a beauty. Clancy was another who caught the eye of the fans, and his good blocking and clever puck carrying earned him much well deserved applause." Hitch was also injured in the last minute of play by a jab to the right eye from Billy Boucher, which laid him out flat on the ice. The incident was not seen by either referee Art Ross or judge of play Jerry Laflamme, nor deemed intentional. This was Ottawa's 16th game, and they now led the league by 10 points over both Toronto and Hamilton and were 12 points ahead of Montreal.[39]

Ottawa continued its winning ways with a one-goal shutout against Hamilton in Ottawa in front of about 6,000 spectators. Nighbor scored the single tally. "It was the second game that the kid defence came through without being scored on. In both these games the lean Ottawa goal-keeper has had quite an easy time, and has seldom had to resort to going to his knees. . . . Hitchman, with his long poke check adding insult to the injury already done by Nighbor, played a very effective game." Ottawa set two season records that night: "In addition to going through without a penalty, they went through the entire game with their original six players." In the other game on Saturday, February 10, Montreal fought its way back into contention, beating Toronto 4-3 with Sprague Cleghorn back in the lineup.[40]

On learning of Cleghorn's return to play, Frank Ahearn, president of the Ottawa Hockey Club announced his intention to resign from hockey with the following statement:

"At the N.H.L. meeting at Toronto, I presented a sworn affidavit charging Sprague Cleghorn with numerous attacks on and threats to Ottawa players, which I informed the president of the league, and the delegates present would be backed up by the Ottawa players mentioned in it. This affidavit was read to the meeting and a little later Sprague Cleghorn was called in and it was read to him, clause by clause. He denied every charge made in it.

"When he left the meeting I asked, and Mr. Gorman and Major MacDowell asked repeatedly that arrangements be made to have our players examined by President Calder. Mr. Calder seemed agreeable to this and even suggested that he should come to Ottawa to do so. For a time everyone understood this would be done. However, near the end of the meeting, it was suddenly moved by Mr. Percy Thompson of Hamilton and seconded by Mr. Querrie of Toronto, that the Ottawa charges be not sustained. This was carried by a vote of three to one.

"I was placed in the position of having my sworn affidavit thrown to one side and not even examined, while Cleghorn's unsworn and unsupported statements were accepted. Since then Cleghorn has again attacked an Ottawa player and has been disciplined for it, but not, in my opinion, to the extent that he deserved, in view of all that had gone before.

"I made these charges because we wanted to put an end to Cleghorn's continued attacks on Ottawa players. I thought that this would meet with the support of the league owners, who should, in my opinion, be glad to stop dirty play. I have every reason to believe that my opinion is shared by the vast majority of those who attend the N.H.L. matches.

"F. Ahearn, president Ottawa Hockey Association."[41]

The Senators played the St. Pats in back-to-back games, first in Toronto and then Ottawa, losing both games. Hitch played well in both. The first game was rough, with Clancy getting a tooth knocked out. "Hitchman wasn't feeling very good going into the [second] game. He played well but has had a lot of hockey and a rest up wouldn't hurt him any. Boucher was in the game for a short time but his knee wouldn't stand the pressure and when he fell while skating hurt it some more and the fatigued Hitchman had to go back on."[42] Toronto and Montreal were now tied for second and within eight points of Ottawa.

On February 20, the *Montreal Gazette* wrote a lengthy editorial in response to learning of Ahearn's pending resignation, some of which is repeated below:

> Mr. Ahearn has been fighting to keep the sport clean and according to his statement he has not had the cooperation from the National Hockey League that he ought to have had. In consequence, and as a protest, he goes out, and the conditions which he sought to remedy are presumably, to continue....
>
> Deliberate brutality has no place in any well-directed or well-played game, and the few conspicuous habitual offenders against the rules of hockey should get over the notion that they are great players because they succeed in maiming individual opponents. That kind of thing never was and never will be reconcilable with good sportsmanship, and the player who cannot make good without it ought to go out of the game....
>
> If rough play is being encouraged with the idea of swelling gate receipts, those who are responsible will find that they have sadly misjudged their public. Lacrosse went down in this way, and baseball—professional baseball—would have gone in like manner but that those in authority in baseball were shrewd enough to see that only a clean game could survive....[43]

The Senators won the next game against Montreal, 1-0 on Broadbent's "blazing" shot from the blue line. A crowd of 8,500 watched the game in Ottawa, and a new spare arrived during the first period for the home team: Frank Finnigan from nearby Shawville, Quebec. "Hitchman played a clever rushing game on the defence, used his body legitimately and with telling effect and his puck carrying was three star stuff." That was until he was knocked out in a collision with Billy Coutu in the third period. Before that Aurel Joliat butt-ended Hitch after he had checked him cleanly into the boards, for which Joliat was penalized. He would repeat the same action with the same effect. "Broadbent and Hitchman played great hockey. Broadbent was very effective and Hitchman did a tremendous amount of rushing till he was hurt." With this win, Ottawa secured a playoff position.[44]

On February 27, a year minus a day since Hitch started with the Senators, they played the Hamilton Tigers in Ottawa and won 7-4. "Hitchman was at his best and his work was always good."[45] Boucher was also back to his champion form, but unfortunately, goalie Benedict was severely injured by a flying puck.

Ottawa traveled to Hamilton minus Nighbor, who was resting up for the playoffs. Benedict was out for a week after his injury the previous game, and Sammy Hebert was brought in to take his place. Denneny and Broadbent traveled with the team but would be used sparingly. Like Hitch the year before, Finnigan would see plenty of ice time in the lead-up to the playoffs. Four thousand cheering fans saw Hamilton win 5-2. Manager Percy LeSueur of the Hamilton Tigers commented to the *Hamilton Spectator* that "Hitch is improving in his play every time out and with another year's experience under his belt should just about be the class of the league."[46]

Ottawa returned home after the game minus Hitch and Clancy, who went directly to Toronto and likely stayed with Hitch's grandfather until the game in Toronto four days later. By now it had been decided that Ottawa and Montreal would be in the finals. Ottawa had accumulated 30 points in 23 games, and Toronto was four points behind Montreal with no time left to make up the difference.

Ottawa wrapped up the regular season with an 8-4 win over Toronto, with Cy Denneny getting four of those goals and reinforcing his position at the top of the league scoring list. Hitch and Clancy tied for first in league assists. And Ottawa achieved a winning percentage of .667, an improvement over the previous year and their second-best season in total points since the NHL started.[47]

The NHL Playoffs

In the first game of the playoffs in Montreal, Ottawa lost 1-0. Referee Mike Rodden injured himself on the treacherous and slushy ice surface, catching his skate blade in a hole. "The work of George Boucher and Hitchman on the champs' defence was all that could be desired. They played their positions perfectly."[48] It was announced just before the start of the game that Frank Nighbor had won the first-ever Hart Trophy for most valuable player.

Ottawa Citizen, *Friday, March 7, 1924, page 10.*

With over 2,000 people lined up to grab the few hundred non-season-ticket-holder seats available for game two of the playoffs, another NHL record-breaking crowd in Ottawa, counted as 11,650 (9,972 official paid admissions according to the Canadian Press), watched as their team succumbed to Montreal 4-2, losing the round 5-3. Hitch figured in the play that got Ottawa's first goal to tie the game. The *Ottawa Citizen* reported that "only Hitchman and George Boucher were up to form on the Ottawa team. Denneny and Broadbent did not seem to get going at their best, although Cy did account for the exchamps' two goals. The left winger received a bad shaking up in the opening period when he fell heavily against the boards and that apparently slowed him down somewhat, but he kept trying. Benedict and Nighbor were both below their usual good form." The *Ottawa Journal* had a different take, suggesting that Hitch was more of a detrimental factor in the outcome, "time after time Ottawa players failed to get the pass to Denneny, but tried to storm through on their own. This was noticeable in the case of Hitchman." But the Canadian Press in the *Montreal Gazette* stated that "on the Ottawa team, Denneny and Hitchman stood out. The latter worked at top speed throughout and was in the play all the way. George Boucher was strong, but not brilliant, while Nighbor and Broadbent were very closely watched all evening." All seemed to agree that the two-time scorer Howie Morenz, in his first year with the Canadiens, was outstanding.[49]

After the game, Tommy Gorman stated: "We had the hardest kind of luck. We have played under a terrific handicap all season due to injuries and illness among our players, and the team has done remarkably well to finish where they did. We have established an N.H.L. record of 16 wins and 8 defeats, we have the leading scorer in Cy Denneny and the best all round man in Frank Nighbor. Hence there is no disgrace attached to our defeat by Canadiens."[50]

One thing was for sure: The fans in Ottawa didn't like to lose. As the letters to the editors showed, they were on the verge of eating up and spitting out their players, in particular, goalie Clint Benedict and Hart Trophy–winner Frank Nighbor. The *Ottawa Journal* put out an editorial on March 13 in an attempt to remove the venom of its readers: "The Senators quit themselves like men. They were perhaps not the mighty machine that has carried Ottawa to victory in many a memorable fight, but they 'played up and played the game' to the bitter end. Nor is there need for excuses, or fault-finding or recriminations: the team that has brought Ottawa three championships in four years is deserving of better than that. After all, the thing in sport is not whether one wins, but how one plays the game, and the splendid sportsmen who have made the name of Ottawa synonymous with clean hockey have no need to feel ashamed."[51]

Days later Tommy Gorman still felt compelled to defend his players. Here is the part relating to Hitch from the *Ottawa Citizen* on March 15:

The loss of Eddie Gerard, right on the eve of the start of the season was a staggering blow. It was enough to take the heart out of anyone. Yet, we rallied under it and called on Lionel Hitchman, a youngster, raw from the City League, to fill the shoes of our captain, one of the most brilliant players that has ever worn the blades. And Hitchman more than made good. Thrown into the breach when our hopes seemed very slim, he held down the position with remarkable style. Hitchman has really been the most consistent man on our team. He has played more hockey than any man in the squad. Cecil Hart told me after Tuesday's game that he considered Hitchman a super-star and the most improved player in the game. Ask players of the Hamilton and Toronto teams and they will tell you something similar. We wouldn't trade Lionel Hitchman for any other defence man in the game.[52]

A report out of Montreal on March 18 stated: "Although not confirmed it is understood that Tom Duggan, who has been the prime mover in the international scheme and who holds the option on franchises for United States clubs in the N.H.L. has disposed of one franchise to the Boston syndicate."[53]

The Montreal Canadiens went on to win the Stanley Cup final against the Calgary Tigers.

After the Season

Hitch and Frank Finnigan were the first players to sign their new contracts for the 1924-25 season, followed by George Boucher and Frank Clancy. In early April, Ottawa signed a new goalie from Sudbury, Joe Ironstone, and announced they would place three of their veteran players on waivers, names not disclosed.

As the season wound down and players dispersed to their other jobs and families, a great tragedy befell the team with the unexpected death of Jack Darragh. At age 33, he had played with the Ottawa Senators for 13 years and won the Stanley Cup four times. He was a popular player and well known around Ottawa as the chief cashier of the Ottawa Dairy, Limited. His death occurred on Saturday, June 28. He had been sick only a few days, the diagnosis peritonitis, the same illness that killed Hitch's grandmother. (An inflammation of the peritoneum—a silk-like membrane that lines the inner abdominal wall and covers the organs within the abdomen—usually due to a bacterial or fungal infection but also possibly from an abdominal injury.)[54]

On Dominion Day, July 1, Jack Darragh lay in state at Stewarton Presbyterian Church while members of the Ottawa Senators team, two at a time, kept a guard of honor over his casket as the public paid their respects. Pallbearers were Clint Benedict, George Boucher, Lionel Hitchman, Harry Broadbent, Cy Denneny, Frank Nighbor, Frank Clancy, Harry Helman, Tommy Gorman, and Frank Ahearn, and they carried the casket out of the church to the waiting hearse completely adorned in flowers. As the hearse slowly made its way past the new Auditorium and over to Beechwood Cemetery some three and a half miles away, the pallbearers plus others from the Ottawa team walked alongside it. Hundreds fell in behind the cortege, and thousands looked on.[55]

Jack Darragh played for the Ottawa Senators for 13 years and died at the age of 33. (Photo courtesy of Hitchman private collection, circa 1923)

Three days later, Hitch at 22 and Tops at 18 were married in a quiet ceremony at her parents' home at 207 Sunnyside Avenue. They left the next morning by train for Rock Lake, where they honeymooned at her parents' cabin.

Chapter Eight

IN TRANSITION

Losing to the Montreal Canadiens in the 1924 NHL playoffs was the beginning of the end of the Ottawa Senators lineup of the previous few years. Manager Tommy Gorman "lashed back" at criticism of his players, providing glowing commentary on most and recounting the hardships in which some, including Nighbor, were playing. The only one who received a lukewarm review by Gorman was goalie Benedict: "Clint Benedict's illness last week forced us to call on Sammy Hebert, and though Benedict recovered, he was far from himself in the play-off series."[1]

With the signing of new goalie Ironstone in March for the upcoming season, gossip had it that Benedict was finished in Ottawa. By early June, "former" goalie Benedict sued the Ottawa Senators for $800 in back pay, claiming his salary for the season was $2,300, and he received only $1,500. The hockey club countered, stating that Benedict was fined for "repeated breaches of training rules, and after frequent promises on his part to mend his ways."[2] The team further disclosed that they were forced to add another $300 to Benedict's contract on the eve of the first NHL game otherwise he refused to play.

On September 25, 1924, the *Ottawa Citizen* printed the club's statement of defense and counterclaim to the legal action brought by Clint Benedict. At a time when alcohol was prohibited in Ontario, the club alleged that Benedict was drunk many times on or near the days of practices and games, rendering him incapable of discharging his duties under his contract. The statement also claimed Benedict gave liquor to players and incited some to hold up the club for more money. The following day both the *Ottawa Citizen* and *Ottawa*

Journal dedicated their front page lead to Benedict's denial of any misconduct.[3]

The night before the lawsuit was to be heard in court in early October 1924, Benedict settled with Ottawa for $350. Lucky for the club that this was over, because two days later their former team doctor wrote to Benedict saying, "I am of course, aware that you are not a total abstainer but in fairness to you, I must say that I have never had reason to believe that your use of alcohol in any way prejudicially affected your health." Mind you the good doctor was not in Montreal the night of the first playoff game when Hitch and Frank Finnigan were awoken at 2:30 a.m. to fetch and put Benedict to bed after a heavy night of drinking.[4]

While this unfortunate public airing of Ottawa's dirty laundry was playing out, team management was dealing with the real need to restock its stable of players after the tragic death of Jack Darragh. Also, without explanation, Harry Broadbent was put on waivers. Rumors were rampant about who was coming to Ottawa. In August the name of Reginald "Hooley" Smith came up. Most recently with the amateur Toronto Granites, Smith was Hitch's Aura Lee competition during his days with the Toronto Parkdales.

It was a season of change all around. After 12 years of operation, Frank Patrick's coast league folded into the prairie league, or Western Canada Hockey League. Six teams would compete, all Canadian: Calgary, Edmonton, Regina, Saskatoon, Vancouver, and Victoria.

For months there had been talk of the NHL adding two more teams, making it a six-team league as well. It was thought they would both be in the United States. Rumor was Art Ross would manage a Boston team and pick up players from the now-defunct Seattle team of the late coast league. A team in New York was expected but didn't materialize. Instead, a group in Montreal who owned a new rink (soon to be called the Montreal Forum) started a second team in the city, considered the English Montreal team, and applied for an NHL franchise. Cecil Hart left the Canadiens and became part of this new team, which would become known as the

Maroons. Rumor had it they were after Ottawa's Eddie Gerard to coach and also wanted Benedict and Broadbent.

The league was to start in mid-November, adding six more games to the schedule, and by early October there was still no official word on the approval of these new teams. Meanwhile, the four original clubs were busy cementing their player picks for the season. The group fronting the new Montreal team wasn't having any part of it: "It is plain that the league intends to hold us up until near the opening of the season, then wish a few castoffs on us and turn our team into a joke. We are not going to be caught this way, and unless there is immediate and definite action you can look for fireworks and the biggest hockey battle ever staged in Canada."[5]

Finally, on October 12, the NHL governors met and confirmed the acceptance of a Boston team to be known as the Boston Bruins and a second Montreal club, each paying a $15,000 franchise fee. New York "would be a certain entry next year, and another United States city might also be represented." The season opener would be pushed back to December 1. "President Frank Calder and the club owners were reticent regarding possible player shifts, but it is regarded as certain that some of the regulars of the four teams that formerly comprised the league will be found on different teams this season."[6]

At the annual general meeting of the NHL on November 2, the schedule was finalized, and the playoff structure decided. The team that finished first would get a bye into the finals, and the second and third teams would play in a preliminary round. Both series would be decided in a home-and-home, total-point format. The other feature of the season was that kicking the puck would be allowed in the center ice area.

Shortly after, Ottawa announced that Ed Gorman (no relation to Tommy) was turning pro and joining the Senators with a three-year contract. At 32 and fresh off an Allan Cup win for the Ottawa Montagnards, Ed was considered the preeminent amateur in Ottawa senior hockey circles. A left-shooting defenseman, he was nearly as tall as Hitch, with a larger frame. Hooley Smith was now in the fold playing wing, Frank Nighbor had settled his contract issues with management and was back at center, and the club also signed newcomer Alex Connell, a goalie Hitch played against in the Ottawa senior league.

Ottawa would warm up with a two-game exhibition series against the Stanley Cup finalist, the Calgary Tigers, on November 24 and 26, with the winner taking 60 percent of the net gate receipts and the loser the balance. About 4,500 came to each game. For Ottawa, the new recruits saw a lot of action, except Smith, who had injured his foot. Ed Gorman started on defense, while Boucher and Hitch saw little time. The first game ended in a tie and the second game was won by Ottawa, 5-1. "The insertion of Hitchman into the play from time to time stiffened up the defence, and he gave a good exhibition of blocking and was of considerable aid in the verdict."[7]

The new Boston team also played an exhibition series, and the *Ottawa Journal*'s Basil O'Meara had a little fun at the expense of the Boston press:

> BUNKER HILL OVER AGAIN.
> Boston made the grade in attendance anyway in its first professional engagement. Five thousand fans saw what must have been a very satisfactory game, according to press reports. For an exhibition feature that isn't too bad. Bruins have been given tons of space in the Boston press. Most of the writeups are apparently written by "experts," to whom some of the finer points of hockey are as foreign as a pair of skates to an Arab, but quantity makes up for quality. Reading some of the excerpts one would think the Boston Bruins were about to leave their families to go over the top at five o'clock in the morning. They mean well, however, and they leave no stone unturned to impress the merits of the game as it appeals to them on the public.[8]

Ottawa opened the new NHL season in Hamilton against a vastly improved team. In front of nearly 6,000 spectators, the Senators lost 5-3. Ottawa started out with Connell in goal; Clancy and Boucher on defense; Nighbor at center; and Smith and Denneny on the wings.

Spares included Hitch, Gorman, Campbell and Finnigan. George Boucher and Frank Clancy looked best for Ottawa, and Alex Connell was "beaten on some easy shots and needs more polish."[9]

The next game was the home opener for Ottawa on December 3 against the Montreal Canadiens. Lou Marsh refereed, and 7,500 watched as Ottawa beat the Stanley Cup champs 2-1 in overtime on a sweet piece of work by Denneny, Smith, and Gorman, with the latter scoring the final tally. Early in the first period after Hitch came in to relieve Clancy, he collided with Howie Morenz of Montreal, falling hard to the ice and sustaining a "slight" concussion. "Hitchman tried to rise to his feet, but crumpled in a heap and had to be carried off. The injured player was given immediate attention and apparently recovered sufficiently to take his place on the Ottawa bench. He was however, unable to resume playing. Hitchman suffered considerable pain after the game and until 3 o'clock this morning, when he got some relief." Later the next day, Hitch was "still in a daze and does not yet remember clearly the circumstances of the accident."[10]

Ottawa met the Maroons in Montreal three days later, playing against Benedict in goal and Broadbent at right wing, with Eddie Gerard as coach. Also signed to this new team was Hitch's high school friend and former Aura Lee teammate Charles Dinsmore. In front of 8,000 fans, the Montreal Maroons won 3-1, off two goals by Punch Broadbent. Ed Gorman got the Senators' only goal. Ottawa was without the services of George Boucher, who was home nursing a boil on each of his hands. "Lionel Hitchman, who was painfully injured in the game in Ottawa Wednesday night came over with the team, and was sent out in the final period, although plainly in no condition to play. Coach Green was almost forced to use him owing to the absence of Boucher and penalties to his other defence players."[11]

After losing two of their three first games, the Senators next nine resulted in five wins, three losses, and one tie. Hitch saw little playing time before and after his head injury. After starring on the defense in his first full season the year before, it appeared he was destined to warm the bench this season.

It didn't break until early December, but all of that fall the Senators' two principal owners, president Frank Ahearn, and secretary general Tommy Gorman, had been in a raging battle over philosophical direction and on-ice management of the team. In Hitch's first two seasons with Ottawa, Tommy Gorman was the de facto coach. Pete Green, who had been with the Senators for most of two decades, was the official coach, but he did not travel with the 1923 team to the Stanley Cup final, and for much of the 1923-24 season, Tommy Gorman made the game decisions, aided by Eddie Gerard.

As stipulated in the legal proceedings between the two owners, Tommy Gorman was not permitted to coach or manage the team, and as the 1924-25 season began, Green's role grew in prominence. Tommy Gorman was Hitch's most ardent supporter on the club, and under Green's direction, Hitch was demoted to defensive substitute. Ed Gorman, the celebrated and very talented amateur, initially took Hitch's spot on the "super six," but he was not quite ready for prime time, and Frank Clancy took his place.[12]

In the midst of the Gorman–Ahearn ownership dispute, Tommy Gorman offered to loan Lionel Hitchman to the Boston Bruins for the rest of the season so Hitch could get more playing time. "Tommy would not discuss any developments in the controversy between he and Frank Ahearn and referred interviewers to his solicitor, Mr. Hal Burns. He stated that there was a possibility that Lionel Hitchman would be loaned to Boston for the rest of the season. He did not state, however, whether this would go through or not. Frank Ahearn had nothing to say regarding the controversy. He is still 'watchfully waiting.'"[13]

On January 9, 1925, the newspapers reported that Hitch was going to Boston for the balance of the season, on loan from Ottawa. "Lionel Hitchman will go to Boston today. He is entirely agreeable to the change which will only be for the winter. Hitchman who is anxious to play more hockey than he has shown this winter is being loaned to Bruins and is subject to recall."[14]

LIONEL HITCHMAN GOES TO BRUINS FOR REMAINDER OF N.H.L. SEASON

It was announced last night that Lionel Hitchman, substitute defence man of the Ottawa N.H.L. hockey team, has been loaned to Boston for the remainder of the season. The deal is dependent on Hitchman coming to terms with Manager Art. Ross, of the Bruins, to whom he is to report in Montreal on Saturday.

With Boucher and Clancy playing so effectively on the Senators' defence, and Gorman and Hitchman in reserve, there is not much opportunity for the subs to get into action. Hitchman has advanced the request that he be sent to the Bruins and the Ottawa officials have acceded, on the understanding that any deal put through will be for this season only.

Hitchman has had a meteoric career in Ottawa hockey. Coming from the Aura Lee Juniors of the O.H.A. in Toronto, he immediately jumped into the senior City League here with New Edinburghs, and the R.C.M.P. team in the Civil Service League. He remained with the Burghs for two seasons, turning professional just before the close of the regular N.H.L. schedule in the spring of 1923.

At this time, Burghs had an outside chance for the title, and Hitchman stuck with them until they had been definitely eliminated. He then signed with Ottawas, took an active part in the hectic playoff series with Canadiens, and went west with the team in quest of the Stanley Cup. It was in the memorable series with Edmonton that he came into great prominence.

Senators were one goal down in the first game with minutes to go, when Hitchman broke through and tied the score. A second Ottawa goal following shortly after gave the Senators the verdict.

At the start of last season he alternated on the defence with Clancy, teaming up with Boucher. About the first of the year, he was playing regular and then when Boucher was forced out of action with a bad

LIONEL HITCHMAN.

knee, he and Clancy formed the famous "kid defence," for a number of games.

As stated in previous paragraphs an abundance of defence men has kept him out of the majority of Ottawas' starts this season. The change to Boston and more work will undoubtedly be to his advantage, and he should be a decided acquisition to the Bruins.

"Hitch" was one of the most popular of local players with the fans, the rush end "millionaires" especially applauding his every move. He is a good stickhandler and shot, a deceptive skater and a fearless blocker. His many friends in Ottawa will wish him all kinds of good luck in his new field.

Ottawa Citizen, *January 9, 1925, page 11.*

BOSTON REFUSES TO ACCEPT OFFER OF HITCHMAN ON LOAN

President Adams of Bruins Declares Club Will Not Borrow Players

SHAY DEAL JUSTIFIED

Will Stand by Agreement Not to Raid Ranks of Amateurs During This Season

---

(Special to The Gazette.)

Boston, Mass., January 9.—Failing evidently to appreciate the sportsman-like spirit which prompted the offer, owner Charles F. Adams, of the Boston Bruins has declined with some bitterness the proffered loan to the Bruins of Lionel Hitchman, the rangy substitute defense man of the Ottawa Senators. Owner Thomas Gorman of the Ottawa aggregation expressed his willingness to turn Hitchman over to the Bruins for the remainder of the season, to bolster up the team and help it make a better showing in Boston's first year of professional league hockey.

"I cannot accept charity from the Ottawa club or any other club for that matter, and furthermore I do not intend to," declared President Adams this afternoon. "I appreciate Gorman's offer but we would a great deal rather lose with our own men than win with players borrowed from other clubs. We will stand or fall upon merits of the team of our own that we can put on the ice standing ready at all times to pay a fair price for any man who, in our estimation, might strengthen the team. Our aim is to build up a team

Montreal Gazette, January 10, 1925, page 18.

Then on January 10, 1925, newspaper coverage had Hitch staying in Ottawa. They reported that Charles F. Adams, owner of the Boston Bruins, was emphatic that his club does not borrow players. He gave a long dissertation on the pitfalls of this practice and hoped the Ottawa club would "consider an outright sale of Hitchman's services to the Boston club if it can spare him."[15]

The only press outlet to not report on the loan caper was Gorman's old newspaper, the *Ottawa Citizen*. And unlike the *Ottawa Journal*, they didn't show Hitch in the lineup with Ottawa for their home game that night against the Montreal Maroons.

Clearly, the negotiations were unfolding in public, as Hitch showed up that same night in Montreal to play against that city's other team, the Canadiens, wearing a Boston Bruins uniform.

Before Hitch went to Boston, the Bruins had won only one game, their first at home against the Montreal Maroons to a cheering crowd of 5,000. They lost the next 11 games and the interest of the Boston public. On January 10, the night Hitch started with Boston, they played the Stanley Cup champs, who were currently tied with Hamilton for first place in the league. The last time Boston played the Canadiens in Montreal, they lost 5-0.

The next day, the *Montreal Gazette*'s headline read "Boston Surprised Canadiens, Taking Overtime Tilt 3-2." Further down it read "Hitchman Bought by Boston and Starred." The article continued:

> Art Ross gambled heavily in the game. He started a sextette against the champions that was changed over any former Boston line-up, with the exception that Charlie Stewart was in his regular place in the nets. Lionel Hitchman, former Ottawa defence man, who was offered to the Bruins on loan, but who was actually secured Saturday morning on option, teamed with Bobby Benson, former Calgary player, on the defence. "Sailor" Herberts was moved up to right wing; Bernie Morris started at centre, and Shay, a former United States amateur, was at left wing. . . . Lionel Hitchman and Herberts were the bright stars of the Boston team. Hitchman proved a most effective defence man, despite the fact that he was playing under a severe handicap with a badly swollen ear—which, incidentally, was the target for considerable attention by the opposition—and he was also a little lacking in condition, not having been used to any extent by Ottawa this year. He demonstrated that all he needed was a chance to get going steadily to show his wares and this he did with a smile, despite a rough trip whenever he was on the ice."[16]

The Gorman–Ahearn legal dispute raged on for two more weeks after Hitch was presumably "bought" by the Bruins. On January 24, 1925, the sale went through of Tommy Gorman's interest in the Ottawa Hockey Club, making Frank Ahearn its sole owner. Gorman received "$20,000 in cash, one half of the Ottawa Hockey Association profits for the current season, his salary for the remainder of the year as manager and secretary; 50 per cent of the

Ottawa Hockey Association's split from National Hockey league revenue for this year, and a percentage of Ottawa's share of the admission fees of Boston, New York, and Montreal."[17] Ahearn named Green as coach and brought in Hitch's old coach Dave Gill from the Burghs as team manager.

The next day at the NHL Board of Governors meeting in Toronto, "a difference of opinion between the Ottawa and Boston clubs over the transfer of the contract of L. Hitchman from Ottawa to Boston was ordered left in the hands of the President." Then in December 1925, Gorman sued Ahearn for an additional $5,000, stating the club's profit for the 1924-25 season, of which he was to receive half, didn't reflect the sale of Hitchman to Boston, among other things. The *Ottawa Journal* reported that Ahearn was prepared to defend the club's accounting if "Mr. Gorman persists with his action."[18] The veiled threat might have meant that Gorman, while under orders not to conduct club business during his legal dispute with Ahearn, had no right to sell Hitchman, and he sure as hell wasn't going to profit from it.

During the week of Boston's big win in Montreal against the Canadiens, the league standings shifted slightly. The Canadiens still remained tied for first place with Hamilton, but Ottawa moved up to third place on their win against the Maroons, who dropped to fourth. Behind them were the St. Pats, then the Bruins.

Hitch traveled to Boston for the next game, where he appeared in his first home game as a Bruin. Founded in 1630, Boston in 1925 was the seventh largest city in the United States, with a population of about 750,000. It was at the height of its expansion and was seven times larger than Ottawa and about the same size as Toronto. "The Hub," as it continues to be known, remains the center of New England activity—transportation, manufacturing, financial, academic, sports, cultural and so on.

The Boston Bruins played at the Boston Arena, first built in 1910 and still in use today as the Matthews Arena and owned by Northwestern University. It is the oldest arena in the United States. In 1925, the Boston Arena had a seating capacity of 4,700 for hockey.

Art Ross frequently referred to Hitch as his first "money player," and the term originated from his first two games with Boston, where he showed championship determination at every turn. From these games, the Bruins' defense began to crystallize.

The Boston Bruins had been averaging 2,000 spectators at their home games. But after their spectacular win in Montreal, a near-capacity crowd came out to watch them play the Hamilton Tigers on January 12.

Mutt and Jeff Defense Pair Instantaneous Hit
Lionel Hitchman and Bobbie Benson, the former long and the other short in stature, made an instantaneous hit with the big crowd that sat in.

Truly, despite the defeat, professional hockey arrived last night. The crowd that turned out to see a local tailender play a leader was enthusiastic and demonstrative. Its magnitude showed just how popular the pro game is destined to be here when the newly-built team gets into stride and its color and aggressiveness becomes known.

Hitchman scored the first goal on one of the prettiest pieces of work seen at the Arena this year. Burch bore down on the Bruin defenses with the puck on his stick. Hitchman timed his poke just right and jabbed the puck out of Burch's possession, pursued it, out-skated the Hamilton forwards and himself came against the defense. He shot low and hard from outside and the puck landed in the netting.

Stanley Woodward, Boston Herald, *January 13, 1925, page 15*

Boston Globe, *January 13, 1925, page 11. Hitch wearing No. 15 scores his first goal in Boston. In the cartoon, bottom left, Hitch and Benson became known as the "Mutt and Jeff" defense, from the popular comic strip. Hitch at almost six-foot-two was Mutt and Benson at only five-foot-three, Jeff.*

In 1925, there were no fewer than eight well-read daily or weekly newspapers in Boston and surrounding areas, all of varying editorial persuasions, reporting on local, national and international news. The Boston Bruins, anxious to get a toehold in the city, systematically and strategically worked the papers for press coverage. With the Bruins losing 11 straight games, interest quickly faded. While Boston was a refined and cultured city and supported its prestigious schools, it wasn't keen on backing another loser (the Boston Red Sox just finished their 24th pro baseball season in second last place, their sixth year below .500). The Bruins also had to compete with amateur hockey, which was well supported both at the club and scholastic levels.

The papers followed the interest of the people, and maybe the people followed the interest of the papers. The Bruins likely hoped both were at work and made sure each sportswriter and editor in the city had what they needed to cover this new sport.

From the Boston Bruins' 1929-30 season program, page 11.

The Boston Post *was the largest newspaper, reaching across New England, its paid circulation about 700,000. The* Boston Globe *followed with* 600,000, Daily Advertiser *500,000,* Boston Herald *400,000,* Boston American *245,000 and* Boston Transcript *80,000.*

Art Ross and Bruins owner Charles F. Adams were keen to feed stories to the sports editors at these papers. Also included on their list were sports editors from smaller but influential papers such as the Boston Traveler *and the* Christian Science Monitor.

The Bruins lost that home game, Hitch's first, against Hamilton on January 12, 1925, in front of 5,000. Boston reached the halfway mark of the season in the next game in Ottawa, where Hitch received a hearty homecoming from local fans. Ottawa, still third in the standings, narrowly beat Boston 3-2. "The revamped Bruins chased the Senators right to the wire and the crowd was on its feet at the finish. . . . Both teams applied the body unsparingly with the visitors excelling at this game. . . . Boston surprised the fans with its display and is a vastly improved team over its last appearance here."[19]

The Bruins lost their next two games—to the Montreal Maroons, 2-0, and to the Toronto St. Pats, 4-3. Hitch set up his teammates for goals, but they couldn't finish. In Toronto on January 24: "Hitchman was the only Boston player to show very much, the former Ottawa man blocking and rushing well. He pulled many a dangerous rush in the last period, leading all of the Boston attacks."[20]

The same night Boston played Toronto, the Canadiens were in Ottawa where all-out fisticuffs broke out after Sprague Cleghorn allegedly attempted to maim George Boucher, which the ref did not see. Both fighting principals were suspended from play. Calls came from across the league to use two referees in all games and to institute more severe penalties for fighting. League owners didn't address the number of refs, but at their January 25 meeting, in an attempt to tamp down rough play, they adopted a new rule that would start the following Wednesday: "if a player draws three major penalties during a season he will be automatically suspended. A player getting one match penalty will be suspended as usual."[21]

The Canadiens traveled to Boston for their next game, minus Sprague Cleghorn. The Bruins hoped to repeat their winning performance of January 10 and rearranged their lines by moving Red Stuart up to left wing and Herb Mitchell back on defense with Hitchman. The Canadiens scored in the first period and fell back into a defensive game to run out the clock. Boston had its largest crowd ever at this game, but the spectators went away dismayed not only by the loss but also by the style of hockey that was employed. This was Boston's 16th loss out of 18 league games, with 12 games left to go in the season.

Boston would see the Canadiens five games later in Montreal on February 14 and lose 5-1. "Hitchman, for Boston, played a great game, being the outstanding player of the visitors. . . . Hitchman poked the puck from Joliat's stick twice in succession when nearly through."[22]

It was hoped that in the next game against Hamilton in Boston, the return of right winger Carson Cooper, who had been off most of the season with an injury, would help turn things around. But Boston would lose again, with Hitch providing the only goal for the team. "Big Lionel Hitchman had a regular hockey carnival all evening. Seldom has a player worked so hard to win as this former member of the Northwest Mounted Police. He was here, there, and everywhere, snatching the rubber or stiff checking his opponents. It was his vigorous work that enabled Boston to score in the third period. . . . Hitchman took a pass out from Stan Jackson and drove for Forbes. The Tiger goalie parried it, but it bounced out front. Hitch was in fast and scored."[23]

Boston would again lose to Ottawa on the road in the next game. By now the Boston papers had left little room on their pages for the Bruins. It was a deflated experience all around for fans, reporters, players and the club owner. Only Bruins manager Art Ross wasn't fazed. He had gone through a roster of 22 players (other teams averaged 14) and now centered the team around Hitch, and he was methodically moving players and introducing new plays, which finally started to pay off in fits and starts. In game 21, Boston defeated the Montreal Maroons in the first overtime game played on home ice by a score of 2-1. Hitch got the tying goal, and Red Stuart finished it off with the winning goal. For only the second time in 13 home games, the Bruins had won, both against the same team.

It would take another five games before Boston won again, their second consecutive win at home, again beating the Maroons 2-1 on February 24.

After one more loss, they won two games back to back for the first and only time that season. Their reputation for beating the best was mounting for they defeated the Canadiens once more by a score of 3-2 for their third consecutive win at home, and then they traveled to Hamilton to beat the top-ranked Tigers in a 2-0 shutout. "Every member of the Bruin team turned in a smart performance. Stewart's work in goal for Boston was sensational. . . . Mitchell and Hitchman resembled the proverbial stone wall and turned back many a Hamilton attack. Both men made good use of their bodies and by constantly stepping in, took much speed out of the local front line."[24]

Boston beat the Maroons three times and the Canadiens twice, knocking both out of playoff contention. And after just beating the league-leading Hamilton Tigers 2-0, they were now cast as giant killers and league spoilers. Boston's final game of the season was on home ice against Ottawa. With Boston's unexpected wins messing with the natural order of the higher-ranked teams, this game for Ottawa against bottom-rung Boston held new importance.

The Boston Bruins, the team that started the season as the football of the Professional Hockey league, having cast off all traces of their losing habit and having defeated the world champion Canadiens and the league-leading Hamilton Tigers in successive games, tonight will make their last appearance of the season at the Arena. Strangely enough, our Bruins, having complicated the league standing abominably by that victory over the Canadiens, now are playing the title role in the National league. For their opponents tonight are the Ottawa Senators, to whom victory might mean a chance to play for the eastern championship.[25]

The Senators beat Boston 4-1, but with the Canadiens' win over Hamilton that same night, Ottawa was kept out of the playoffs (and Montreal claimed the final postseason spot). This game sparked a turning point for Hitch.

He had suffered four serious head injuries in the past two years, the latest a concussion earlier that season from an elbow to the head. In this last game of the season, for the first time ever, Hitch started a fight with another player, Ottawa's Hooley Smith. The rookie Smith had already gained a reputation for dirty, sneaky play. After the first Ottawa Senators game against the Montreal Canadiens on December 3, 1924, Canadiens manager Leo Dandurand complained in the *Montreal Herald* of Smith's tactics: "Smith kneed, butt ended, and cross checked, but he won't always get away with it. If the officials don't catch him at it, some irate player will take him sure."[26]

In Boston's final game of the season, Ottawa took an early lead in the first period, with Clancy and Denneny each scoring. Both scored again in the final period, followed by Cooper for Boston. With the score 4-1 and only 30 seconds remaining in the game, Ottawa's Hooley Smith, who had been roughing up Boston players all night, elbowed Hitch in the head near the Boston net. Hitch went after Smith; they both dropped their sticks and went at it. "It was no stage play, and when Referee Jerry LaFlamme went to break them he found Hitchman pounding wicked rights on Smith's midriff." Both were sent off for fighting.[27]

Hitch had served notice that he would no longer tolerate any dirty play by other players and, if provoked, would protect himself.

Lady Byng also stepped in to offer an incentive for the league to deal with rough play. In a letter to President Calder she wrote:

> Feeling a great desire to help your effort to clean up hockey and eliminate the needless rough play that at present is a threat to the national game, and also to leave a tangible record of the enjoyment I personally have had from the game during our sojourn in Canada. I am writing to ask if you will let me offer a challenge cup for the man on any team in the National Hockey League who, while being thoroughly effective is also a thoroughly clean player.
>
> I am convinced that the public desires good sport, not the injuring of players and if, by donating this challenge cup, I can in any way help towards this end, it will give me a great deal of pleasure.
>
> Evelyn Byng of Vimy.[28]

Her offer was accepted, and the same jury of sportswriters who voted for the Hart Trophy would also vote for the Lady Byng Trophy. Frank Nighbor won the inaugural award, as he had with the Hart Trophy the year before.

The Canadiens ended up winning the NHL championship and O'Brien Cup but in the most unusual way. The NHL season ended with the Hamilton Tigers in first place, the Toronto St. Pats in second and the Canadiens third. The Canadiens beat Toronto in the semifinals for the honor of playing Hamilton for the NHL championship and O'Brien Cup.

However, the Hamilton players threatened to boycott the NHL championship unless their club paid each player an additional $200 as compensation for the extra games in the schedule. Hamilton refused and further threatened its players with forfeiture of monies still owed if they didn't play in the championship. The club and players did not resolve their differences, and NHL president Calder awarded the title to the Montreal Canadiens, who traveled west to represent the NHL in the world championship, losing to the Victoria Cougars three games to one in a five-game series.

It was later reported that the Hamilton club paid its players their back pay, but that each player would be sold to other teams. It was also reported that of the six teams, only Boston lost money that year ($20,000). In this first season, Boston struck its first record, their worst winning percentage in franchise history (.200).[29]

What began as a season of uncertainty for the NHL also ended that way, with the Hamilton team up in the air and the possibility of two new teams. For Boston, Hitch's new team, even with the reported financial loss and the humiliating record, owner Charles Adams was upbeat: "watch us next season."

(Also in 1925, Hitch's younger sister, Dorothy, at age 15, made her debut as a spare on the Ottawa Alerts, who won the Ladies Ontario Hockey Association championship the previous two years and were runners-up that season.)

The artist gave Hitch this original cartoon, circa 1925. It accompanied an article on Hitch, titled: "Royal 'Mounties' Sometimes Lose Their Man." (Source unknown)

Chapter Nine

RAMPING UP

1925-26: CLUTCH PLAYER

The next season got under way on November 26, 1925. Each team played six more games than the last season, bringing the total to 36 games. Two more teams joined the NHL, as speculated, but it would not be an eight-team league. The first-place Hamilton Tigers folded after their player uprising; the players were sold off to the New York Americans, one of the new franchises. The Pittsburgh Pirates also came on board, initially comprised of the recently disbanded Pittsburgh Yellow Jackets, who had won the 1924 and 1925 U.S. Amateur Hockey Association championship. Three U.S. teams now played in the seven-team NHL, which now included the Boston Bruins, Montreal Canadiens, Montreal Maroons, New York Americans, Ottawa Senators, Pittsburgh Pirates, and Toronto St. Patricks.

The NHL introduced several rule changes for this season including:
- Only two players on defense were permitted inside their own blue line when the puck left the defensive zone.
- A face-off would be called for "ragging the puck" unless the team was playing shorthanded.
- Only team captains could talk to referees.
- Timekeepers were to signal the end of a period with a gong instead of the referee's whistle.
- Goalkeeper pads were limited to 12 inches wide.
- Player rosters were limited to 14, with only 12 dressing for any one game.
- A team salary cap of $35,000 was put in place.[1]

The NHL playoff format remained unchanged, and the champion traveled west to face the winner of the six-team Western Hockey League in a best-of-five series. (The WHL was the renamed Western Canada Hockey League of the previous season.)

The Ottawa Senators placed first in the 1925-26 NHL season. The Montreal Maroons and Pittsburgh Pirates came second and third, respectively. The Maroons won the NHL championship, O'Brien Cup and Prince of Wales Trophy (the latter introduced that season for the winner of the inaugural game at Madison Square Garden, and then awarded to the NHL playoff champion). The Maroons went on to beat the WHL's Victoria Cougars, defending Stanley Cup winners, three games to one, for the 1926 world championship and Stanley Cup.

The Boston Bruins finished one point out of playoff contention, in fourth place behind the Pittsburgh Pirates. It was the "only season in NHL history where the number of playoff berths was less than half of the number of teams in the league."[2] Boston improved its winning percentage over the previous season by .328, an NHL record at the time, and it remains the third best single-season improvement ever.

Boston's most notable player acquisition in 1925-26 was defenseman Sprague Cleghorn from the Montreal Canadiens, Hitch's sparring partner of the past three NHL seasons. Cleghorn was twice suspended for attacking Hitch, first during the 1923 NHL playoffs and again in Hitch's second season. Cleghorn grew up in the same Montreal neighborhood as Art Ross. He was five years younger and, as a teenager, worked for Ross' Montreal sporting goods store. They played together for three years on the Montreal Wanderers of the National Hockey Association, the forerunner to the NHL. Sprague was 11 years older than Hitch, and during this season he became a great mentor to the young defenseman.

Hitch's style of play and personality contributed significantly to the development and popularity of the game in Boston. The *Boston Globe* featured him in more pictures, stories, and reports than any other player on the team. Ross used Hitch's backstory as a former police officer and his unique relationship with Sprague Cleghorn to pump the press. The December 6, 1925, feature in the *Boston Herald* is one such example. The illustration shows Hitch and Cleghorn battling for the puck. Over 1,300 words in this article were devoted to Hitch and Cleghorn. The part relating to Hitch began:

> Just then another husky with that slight accent which stamped him as a Maple Leafer came in, asked a question and went out again.
>
> "Hitchman," the manager indicated. "He is the vice-captain. Friend of Cleghorn. There's a yarn, too. You newspaper men ought to grab on to it."
>
> It was a yarn, and a very remarkable one. To begin it right, it is necessary to double on Mr. Hitchman's life trail and follow it back to the beginnings.

Boston Herald, *December 6, 1925, page 57.*

Also contributing to the growth in the Bruins' popularity was the introduction of radio broadcasts starting in their inaugural season. Owner Charles F. Adams and Boston Arena manager George V. Brown were instrumental in putting the Bruins' 15 home games on the air that first year through Westinghouse Station WBZ and rebroadcast by CKAC of Montreal. Listeners from across Canada, the United States, Mexico, England, and Ireland heard the play-by-play commentary of *Boston Traveler* sportswriter Frank Ryan. Home games would again be broadcast this season. Also, when the Bruins were in Pittsburgh on March 12, playing for that final playoff spot, the game was "direct wired" from the Duquesne Garden into the Boston Arena. Play-by-play of the game was announced from the Arena bandstand during the "international match" between Boston College and the Ottawa Burghs (Hitch's old team). "This is the first time any rink has ever offered a direct service of an out-of-town game, with every play of the game clearly depicted."[3]

Of course, winning helped too. After an abysmal first season, the Bruins' popularity at home grew exponentially in their second season. Virtually every home game was sold out. The Boston Arena held only 4,700 seated spectators, and upwards of an additional 2,000 standing-room tickets were sold, while thousands were turned away for each home game. On March 6, 1926, in the fourth remaining game of the season and the third last at home, the Bruins were fighting for a playoff berth and defeated the top-ranked Ottawa Senators 1-0 before an estimated 7,000 fans. "During the progress of the first period three of the windows behind the standing room customers were pushed out, sash and all. The crowd behind the seats was packed in so tightly that late-comers, who held seats, had difficulty reaching them. Nearly 2000 standing room admissions had been sold, and three hours before the game several thousand fans were lined up in the snow waiting to buy them. It is estimated that 12,000 or 15,000 persons were turned away."[4]

Also in this season, the Bruins' "Royal Rooters" were formed—a revival of the original fan club of 1903 that cheered on their baseball team, the Boston Americans, to the World Series. This new one was organized by A. Vernon Adams, the brother of the Bruins' owner. They traveled to out-of-town games, first to New York in January, followed by Montreal in February and Pittsburgh in March. What started as a group of about 100 fans steadily grew into the high hundreds as they became well known, organizing excursions to all cities in the NHL to cheer on the Boston Bruins.

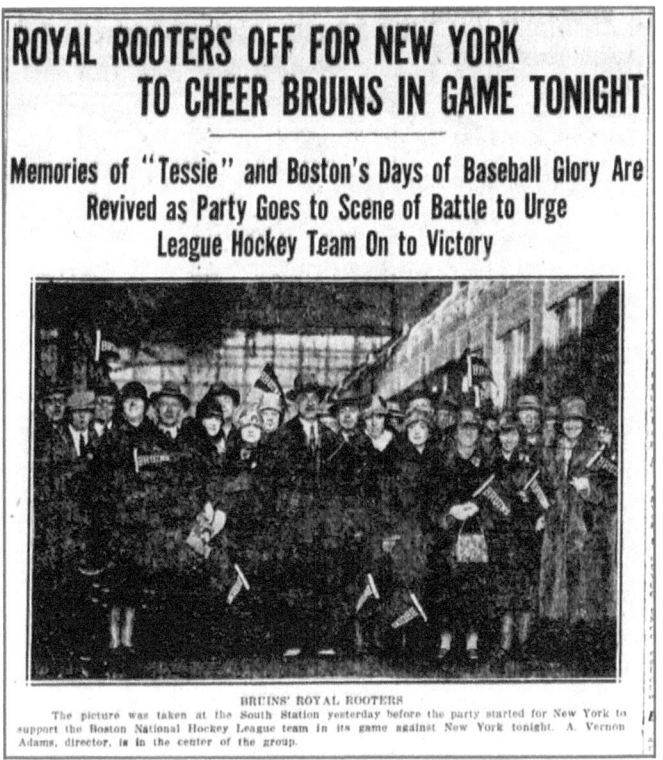

Boston Globe, *Saturday, January 23, 1926, page 8.*

Hitch played in all 36 league games. Early in the season, "the startling work of Lionel Hitchman [was] the outstanding feature of the Bruins' work. 'Hitch' is the talk of the pro game."[5] This was especially important as Boston had sustained several injuries, causing most of the regular defensive line (Cleghorn, left defense; Stuart, defense alternate; and Stewart, goalie) except Hitch to miss all or some of the first 12 games. Hitch was also injured, suffering a broken rib in game six, which the Bruins won 3-2 over the Montreal Maroons in Boston on December 8, 1925. He would continue to play injured. Boston would win four games and lose eight of their first 12.

Boston's management recognized Hitch's leadership qualities by naming him vice-captain to Sprague Cleghorn. This role became more vital this year with the new rule that only captains could address referees on the ice, and Sprague was not present for the first 10 games because of injury.

Before the eighth game, and fourth at home, against the Ottawa Senators, on December 13, the *Boston Post* ran a feature story on Hitch's background. The full article is reprinted here:

HITCHMAN BUMPING HIS WAY TO FAME
Bruin Star Found Mounted Police Too Dull --- He's Best 100 Proof Stuff From Across Border
By Fred Hoey
When a young man quits the Royal Canadian Mounted Police force because it is too dull, that person craves action. This is the precise situation in which Lionel Hitchman found himself in 1921.

Chasing a million miles, more or less, through snow and subsiding on a diet of icicle lolypops and snowball sundaes as fiction sometimes tells us are among the hardships endured by the mounted force, had no appeal to Hitch. He wanted action and he got it. Hockey was his salvation.

ONE OF THE GAMEST
So when Boston hockey fans watch No. 2 of the Boston Bruins, tall, fearless and reckless, crashing the enemy to the ice they will appreciate that Hitch is right in his element. He loves bodily contact. Hitch is the most daring hockey player ever seen in this city. Fear and timidity are foreign to this young man's makeup. "The bigger they are the harder they fall," is the axiom handed down by Bob Fitzsimmons to athletes of Lionel Hitchman's type.

An idea of Hitch's gameness was best illustrated in the game between the Bruins and the Montreal Maroons played here last Tuesday. The score was deadlocked 2-2. Young Roberts was in goal for Boston, filling his first pro assignment. A Boston puck foul five feet in front of the Boston net called for a face off. Ordinarily defensive players make a wild dash to hook opponents' sticks and prevent a shot from face off. Hitch had another plan. When Referee Lou Marsh dropped the puck at the face off Hitch plunged head first to smother Nels Stewart's shot. He had blocked the drive at the unseasoned young goalie and probably saved the game for Boston.

Hockey makes strange team-mates. Hitch and Sprague Cleghorn once were avowed enemies. When Hitch wore Ottawa regalia and Sprague played with the Canadiens, pro hockey's richest and wildest feud was born. These defence men crashed each other at every opportunity. The climax came when Cleghorn's stick bounced off Hitch's head.

After Hitchman was discharged from the hospital he went gunning, or rather slashing, for Sprague. This feud had its happy climax here this fall when Cleghorn was purchased by the Boston Bruins.

BEST OF FRIENDS NOW

Sprague reported to Coach Art Ross at the Bruin dressing room. "Sprague, I want you to meet Hitch," chirped Ross. "Put it there, old-timer," replied Hitchman, as he extended his duke to his old enemy.

"I believe, Sprague, if we can team up on defence with as much vigor, dirt and energy as we showed against each other, we ought to keep those other league birds away from our net," declared Hitch.

"You said it, Hitch," said Cleghorn and up to the time Cleghorn was hurt no foe very often ventured within the zone occupied by this pair, preferring long shots.

Hitchman's career has been short, sweet and hectic. His face is constantly covered with gauze cocoon. Hitch regards this as a badge of honor. This young man earned his amateur senior spurs with the Aura Lees of Toronto in 1921. New Edinborough of the Ottawa claimed him the following season.

HARDENS UP IN WOODS

Then came the call from the Royal Canadian Mounted Police, its subsequent dullness, as Hitch describe it and his resignation.

In [1923] he joined the Ottawa Senators for his professional baptism. Then Hitch took a flier at the

Provincial police, which corresponds with our State constabulary. Again he found this service too quiet.

Coach Ross purchased Hitchman last year and here he is in Boston crashing his way to fame, regardless of who is in his path.

In the off season Hitchman is a guide in the Ontario backwoods. Bruin opponents declare he goes into the sticks to bump bears. He comes out as hard as nails, weighing 170 pounds over his 6 ft. 1 inch frame, which is a pretty fine build for a man 24 years old.

Hitch is the best 100 proof hard stuff that ever came out of Canada.

In game nine on December 19 in Montreal against the Canadiens, Boston put up a mighty fight but lost 6-5 in overtime, and Hitch's popularity was sorely tested as reported by the *Montreal Gazette*. "Hitchman came in for attention from a spectator of the so-called weaker sex, who leaned over from a promenade seat and cracked him over the head as he brought up suddenly against the promenade boards after a body check. Hitchman did not know exactly what had happened, but when he got to his feet started gunning with his stick until he discovered who had hit him; then with true gallantry he smilingly retired to his position."[6]

"The Boston Bruins came into their own at the Arena" on January 5, 1926, in game 12. "They outskated, outplayed and, above all, outscored the Pittsburgh Pirates thereby lifting themselves out of the league cellar. They gave as nifty an exhibition in all departments as anyone would want to see. The score was 3 to 0. More than 7000, the largest crowd that ever saw a professional hockey game in Boston, were in at the Pirate death." This was Boston's second shutout of the season, two in a row. "Naturally the tendency is to talk about offense, without a thought for the boys who undermined the Pirate attack during those first two periods, but let us say that Hitchman and Cleghorn were great back on defense, and that Hitch's poke-checking, never better, was the particular thorn in the Pirate side."[7]

Boston had pulled themselves out of last place, only to find themselves there again. Once more, goalie Stewart was injured during the next game in New York, which lasted two overtimes and resulted in a tie. After a 5-1 trouncing in game 16 at Pittsburgh, the Bruins were "firmly in the cellar" and made some personnel changes. It would take two more tied overtime games and an 8-2 morale-destroying defeat by Ottawa before Boston would start their ascent up the standings ladder. They then went on to beat the top two teams, including the first-ranked Senators in game 22 in Ottawa on Hitch's winning goal. The *Ottawa Journal* commented: "the laurels of the evening should rest on the brows of Lionel Hitchman, the Ottawa boy, and Dr. Charlie Stewart. 'Hitch' is a wonderfully improved player and has outgrown the awkwardness that characterized his play when with Ottawas. He was great defensively and offensively."[8]

Boston had finally beaten every team in the league, and in game 26 they won their first overtime game. This took place at home against their archrival the Pittsburgh Pirates. In overtime:

Lionel Hitchman poke checked the rubber away from Dune McCurry, the disk skimming to the center of the ice, in the hockey game at the Arena last night, this paving the way for a Boston triumph. Then Rodger Smith, the Pittsburgh defense player, tried to beat the tall Boston man to the object, in the race that ensued Hitchman was the winner, and he picked it away and his speed carried him to the left side of the rink close to the boards. There another Lionel, Conacher, the ace of the Pirates tried to stop Hitch. There was no stopping the Boston man, however. He whipped off a shot. The puck went low and by Roy Worters, the guardian of the Pittsburgh cage, and Boston won the first overtime game played in the NHL series, 3 to 2.[9]

Hitch's poke check was gaining notice around the league. After sportswriters in Ottawa, Montreal and Toronto had commented on the vast improvement of Hitch's play, the *Boston Globe* followed suit with this commentary by John J. Hallahan on February 17, 1925:

> Hitchman is the outstanding feature of the Boston team's play. He has mastered the poke check as well, with the aid of a longer stick than he used earlier in the season, that he has become a new player. 'Hitch' was hit hard many times last night, especially by Conacher and while he was knocked down he came up and played throughout the game. It was his masterly poke checking that brought victory to the Bruins in the first overtime game play by the team in Boston this winter. His exhibition in scoring the winning goal was a masterpiece. His fast skating carried him by Rodger Smith, who thought he had the necessary speed to beat 'Hitch.' Then the tall Bruin outguessed a tired Conacher by whipping the puck past him into the net.[10]

Boston would finally put more games in the win column in game 29 against the Toronto St. Pats. For the second straight time at home, Boston won in overtime on a goal by Hitch.

> Lionel Hitchman, the big Boston defense man, pulled another game out of the fire last night at the Arena. In the third minute of overtime play he carried the puck the length of the ice and scored the deciding goal from outside the defense of the green-clad St. Pats of Toronto. The shot gave the Bruins their sixth straight victory and their ninth victory in the past 10 games and sent the biggest hockey crowd that ever sat in the Arena home completely at peace with the world. It was the second time in a week that Hitch has come through with a scoring shot in overtime play. Last Tuesday night he performed the same feat in the first minute of extra time against the Pittsburgh Pirates.[11]

This win put Boston firmly in third place with a five-point lead over Pittsburgh.

(That same week, Dot Hitchman, Hitch's 16-year-old sister, playing center for the Ottawa Rowing Club, beat her old team the Alerts by 3-1 in the first game of the Ottawa and District Ladies' Hockey Association championship.)

By game 33, Boston was still in third place, but the margin had narrowed to three points. In the game, where at least 12,000 people were turned away, Boston beat Ottawa 1-0. "Hitchman poke-checked Denneny at the Boston defence, retained the puck and skated up the ice on a sortie which produced the first Boston goal. He carried to the Ottawa points and fed Carson Cooper a beautiful pass. Cooper cut loose a vicious shot. Connell saved brilliantly, but Cooper followed in and lifted the puck over his prostrate body and into the net."[12]

Boston lost games 34 and 35 to New York and Pittsburgh, respectively, with a team full of injured and sick players, ultimately halting their run for the playoffs. In Pittsburgh, the Pirates scored first. Hitch got the tying goal, sending the game into overtime. Boston ended on a good note by beating the Montreal Maroons, who went on to win the Stanley Cup that season. Boston's record for its second year of operation stood at 17 wins, 15 losses and four ties, a quantum improvement of points percentage over the previous year by .328, for a total of .528.

For Boston, Hitch tied for third in points with Cleghorn, behind right winger Carson Cooper and center James Herbert. Cooper and Herbert were second and third, respectively, in total scoring for the league. Hitch's reputation as a clutch player had been formed in his first season on the coast for the Stanley Cup championship. This season that reputation was reinforced, with three game-winning goals, two in overtime, and new and improved defensive skills. He perfected his poke-check, something he learned from Ottawa's Frank Nighbor. "Lionel Hitchman gave one of the most remarkable exhibitions of poke-checking since Frank Nighbor's last appearance." In later years, Hitch would take the baton from Nighbor as the preeminent master of this skill.[13]

(Sister Dot's Ottawa Rowing Club won the Ottawa and District Ladies' Hockey Association championship in front of 600 fans.

"Dot Hitchman went well at centre and was a constant back checker." Her team then lost to the Toronto Pats in the semifinals of the Ladies Ontario Hockey Association championship. Dot was injured in the first game with Toronto but played just the same in the second game.)

Sprague Cleghorn and Hitch, Boston Post, *November 25, 1925.*

Boston Globe, *March 9, 1926, page 23.*

Boston Advertiser *Photo, March 12, 1926. Caption: "Bruin brides see their hockey husbands off to Pittsburgh at Back Bay station. Left to right, Mrs. Harrington, Mrs. Stewart, Mrs. Hitchman, Mrs. Cleghorn, Mrs. Stevens. Much depends on tonight's game with the Pirates."*

1926-27: THE GANG'S MOSTLY HERE

The Evolving League

In this 10th season, the NHL saw its largest expansion yet, adding the Chicago Black Hawks, Detroit Cougars, and New York Rangers. For the first time, the league split into two divisions:
- American: Boston Bruins, Chicago Black Hawks, Detroit Cougars, New York Rangers, Pittsburgh Pirates
- Canadian: Montreal Canadiens, Montreal Maroons, New York Americans, Ottawa Senators, Toronto St. Patricks

It also expanded to 44 games from 36 the previous season.

The WHL folded in May 1926, and its player contracts were sold to NHL team owners. Boston Bruins owner Charles F. Adams purchased a significant number of contracts, keeping Frank

Fredrickson (but lending him to Detroit), Eddie Shore, and Duke Keats and reselling the balance to other NHL and AHA teams.

The Toronto St. Patricks were sold midseason to a syndicate headed by Conn Smythe. They continued to use their current name until the next season when they became the Toronto Maple Leafs.

The Stanley Cup now belonged exclusively to the NHL, and the two new divisions played for its honor. Each division had its own semifinal and final playoff, with second- and third-placed teams competing to take on the leader for the division final. Both series followed a total-point, home-and-home format. The two division champs then vied for the Stanley Cup in a best-of-five series.

A new league award was added that season in memory of Montreal Canadiens goalie Georges Vezina, who had played with that team for 16 seasons (seven in the NHA and nine in the NHL). He started to play the previous year before being diagnosed with tuberculosis; he died in March 1926. The Vezina Trophy was donated by the Montreal Canadiens' owners and presented to the league's goalie with the "best average," which was won by George Hainsworth of the Canadiens.

Boston's Breakout Season

After last season's success at the gate, the Boston Arena was refurbished. A balcony level was added to accommodate more spectators. The Boston Bruins continued to break new attendance records, with several games surpassing 10,000 fans. As in the previous year, crowds lined up for hours to get standing-room-only tickets for some of the regular games and the playoff games.

Boston began its training season on October 20, 1926. Hitch was absent from practice for nearly two weeks because of the birth of his first child, daughter Gloria, in Ottawa. He arrived November 2, and by then manager Art Ross had 15 men in training: left wingers Percy Galbraith, Archie Briden and Hago Harrington; centers Jim Herbert (also known as Herberts), Duke Keats and Bill Stuart; right wingers Carson Cooper, Harry Oliver and Charles Cahill; defensemen Sprague Cleghorn, Lionel Hitchman, Bill Coutu and Eddie Shore; and goaltenders Charles Stewart and Mauri Roberts.

There was much anticipation and speculation as to how future Hall of Famer Eddie Shore would rank among the other defensemen. "Eddie Shore, the 23-year old youth from the Far West, who is hailed as a super star in the making, recently started one of his wild rushes for the opposing defense. His forwards were checked and he tried to split Bill Coutu and Lionel Hitchman. The pair stepped into him, and Shore crashed to the ice badly shaken up."[1]

At the beginning of the season, sportswriters reported that Shore was a hit with the fans for his great speed, aggressiveness, and rough play. As the season wore on, Shore cost the team some critical games with his excessive penalties and three major misconducts, leading to a game misconduct and suspension. His mad rushes resulted more in off-balance shots and a weakened defense. For a time, the writers turned on him and his style of play.

The team was whittled down to 12 players by the opening game on November 16. Hitch and Shore were both slotted for right defense, with Sprague Cleghorn and Billy Coutu on left defense. Throughout the year this order would change, and eventually, Eddie Shore would start on right defense with Hitch on the left.

Hitch proved once again to be a valuable "money player" for Boston. His poke-checking, body checking, puck-advancing skills, aggressive play without fouling, ability to draw penalties and cool-headed demeanor were instrumental in Boston winning the American Division and reaching the Stanley Cup final for the first time in their franchise history.

He played all 44 regular-season games except two, on account of multiple injuries. He was 14th among all defensemen in total points, accumulating nine (according to newspaper reports his points were higher). His penalties also placed him in 14th spot among all defensemen, with 72 minutes in regular play. The famed referee and *Toronto Star* writer Lou Marsh, in his February 16, 1927, article, singled out one player from each team whom he considered "are out there giving the best they have and playing clean hockey." He chose Hitch from Boston.

In the lead-up to the first postseason game against Chicago, John J. Hallahan of the *Boston Globe* wrote about the four Boston defensemen, Cleghorn, Coutu, Hitchman, and Shore: "They are tough, and use their bodies very effectively. Of the four, Hitchman is considered by the writer to be the most effective. He is not as fast as Shore, but with his poke check will stop more attacks than will Shore."[2]

Hitch played in all eight playoff games and starred in six of them. He was considered the best defenseman on the team, in a group of very impressive players, both by the observers of the day and by team management. Hitch was awarded the second highest playoff bonus by Boston owner Charles Adams, next only to Percy Galbraith, the NHL playoff points leader. $10,000 was divided on the basis of "value to the club and good behaviour." Galbraith received $1,600 and Hitch $1,400, and the next level of players including Shore and Cleghorn received $1,000.[3]

Hitch's Season in More Detail

The Bruins won their season opener, defeating the Canadiens 4-1 in front of 8,000 Boston fans. With the new recruits, it was already apparent that Boston could be a contender. "The Boston team is as powerful defensively—judging by last night's game—as ever, and what it lacked in scoring strength last Winter has been added by the new men whom Owner Adams picked up at the close of the Western League last year."[4]

Hitch sprained his knee in game three and was put in the hospital after getting a charley horse in his left leg during game four in Boston against last season's Stanley Cup champions, the Montreal Maroons. It was a rough game; Hitch also suffered "bruised ribs, lacerated eye and cut mouth." He missed the next game against the Pittsburgh Pirates to rest his leg and didn't play much in the next two losses against the New York Rangers.[5]

After four straight losses at home, for game nine against the Detroit Cougars, "Manager Art Ross made a new but not entirely unexpected move by starting Lionel Hitchman at centre, and the big boy from Toronto showed the crowd the defensive value of a good poke check. Also, he teamed up well with Carson Cooper on several occasions, and the pair came pretty near poking a couple more goals into the strings after Stuart came back from the detention cell."[6] Boston "walloped" Detroit 7-2, a needed home win to stoke the fan base.

Boston met the Maroons for a second time in game 13 on December 23 in Montreal, beating them 2-1 and propelling Boston into a tie for second with Chicago in the American Division, behind the New York Rangers. Hitch played right defense for this game. Shore received his first of three major penalties and a fine. "Shore struck the Maroon [Nels Stewart] with his stick three times while he lay on the ice. . . . Herberts, Cleghorn and Hitchman were outstanding for the winners while Siebert and Stewart played good hockey for Montreal."[7]

It was at this point that the *Boston Globe*'s John J. Hallahan called for a change in conduct at professional hockey games, both by the audience and the players. Not until the NHL arrived in Boston had fans gotten out of hand with throwing items on the ice. "Boohing and the like is all right, but throwing of things because something has gone against a favorite team is something that must be stopped." As for player conduct, regarding this episode with Shore and an earlier one with Cleghorn where he punched a player because of a decision by the referee, Hallahan further commented:

> There are certain players on the Bruins squad who seem to delight in being unnecessarily rough in their efforts to win. Such tactics hurt the game. Hockey, seemingly had developed into a series of brawls. Players are being injured, some being forced to stay out of the game for several weeks. When keen sportsmen decry the actions of Boston players as has Commander J.K.L. Ross, well-known horseman, and others, referring to the game played last Thursday night at Montreal, it is time for action.[8]

With their 2-1 win at home against the Americans on December 28, the Bruins momentarily tied for first in the division with the Black Hawks and the Rangers. In that game, Hitch cleanly "handed

[Lionel Conacher] a body-check which lost him his wind and necessitated temporary retirement."[9]

After losing the next two games on the road, the Bruins were back in Boston to play the Ottawa Senators in the first home game of 1927. More than 10,000, the largest crowd so far in Boston Arena history, watched the Bruins beat the Senators 2-1 in overtime. Boston was once again tied for first with Chicago and the Rangers. Right after this game, Art Ross announced a shake-up of the team's forward line. Although he had tried Hitch at center and Shore up on wing, he preferred to use them back on defense. Center Frank Fredrickson and left winger Harry Meeking of Detroit were swapped for Boston's Keats and Briden.

Boston met the Montreal Maroons for the third time at home in the next game, losing 3-0 in front of yet another record crowd. "The players carried high sticks and Hitchman, in thwarting Dutton received a gash on the head, which drew blood."[10]

Game 19, on January 11, was the third home game in a row. Boston beat Chicago and set a different Arena record: scoring four goals in one minute, 25 seconds. The Bruins lost the next two games, including game 21 in Ottawa to the Senators by 5-4. "The first real threat of the contest came when Hitchman raced close in to pass in front of the goalmouth, but Shore fumbled the combination."[11] The Rangers widened their lead in the division, leaving Boston and Chicago again tied for second.

Next up the Rangers came to Boston to play the Bruins on January 18 for game 22, the halfway mark of the season. "There will be two new players in the Bruin's garb tonight. Billy Boucher, obtained in a trade that sent Carson Cooper to the Canadiens, and Hal Winkler, formerly of the Rangers. . . . Stewart is to be given a rest. This he needs, as he has been greatly handicapped by poor health." The reorganized starting line-up included Jim Herbert at right wing, Frank Fredrickson at center and Percy Galbraith at left wing, with Eddie Shore and Lionel Hitchman on defense and Hal Winkler in nets (the former Edmonton goalie whom Hitch scored on during the 1923 Stanley Cup final). Boston beat the division leaders 7-3, setting a total-goals record at the Boston Arena. "Lionel

Hitchman was as valuable as ever in the Boston defense. His poke-checking broke up any number of promising Ranger attacks."[12]

By beating Pittsburgh on January 25, the Bruins moved firmly and solely into second place. While playing with a persistent and severe charley horse, Hitch scored his first goal of the year. "He skated the length of the ice, whirled around the Pirate net and crammed the puck under Worters. It was Hitcher's first goal of the season and it was a dandy, for he made his run with every member of the Pirate clan chopping at him and trying to step into him."[13]

Hitch was still "nursing a charley horse" in game 27, when Boston beat Toronto for the first time on February 1 in a 1-0 shutout. It was a hard-fought game with a bit of levity and humanity sprinkled in. A young boy had been in the upper tier of the arena providing entertainment to the "gallery gods," when somehow, he made his way onto the ice surface between the second and third period of the game. In front of the large crowd, he "danced the Charleston and Black Bottom, causing a shower of coin to be thrown on the ice, making it necessary to hold up the contest before the teams resumed their battle in the third period." Players from both teams dug and picked at the ice with their skates to free the coins from the frozen surface. They were collected and placed in the boy's hat, and Captain Cleghorn handed it back to him "amid a tremendous ovation from the crowd."[14] When the game resumed, Boston played defensively to protect their lead.

After this game, Hitch needed an operation on his left leg to deal with a blood clot that had formed from his unhealed charley horse. He stayed back as the team traveled to Toronto for the next game. The Bruins lost 1-0, with both Shore and Cleghorn receiving major penalties. This was Shore's third major; he was suspended and at a minimum would miss the next game. Hallahan of the *Boston Globe* again called for the game to be cleaned up: "Hockey, is a he-man's sport. At its best, it is a rough game. Therefore, if it is going to hold the public which has made it possible for the players to get high salaries, it must be played fairly. Cutting men down and fights have no place in the game, and Boston's fair name for sportsmanship should not be tarnished."[15]

Boston then beat Detroit 2-0 with Hitch and Cleghorn on defense. Next up in game 30 were the Montreal Maroons on their home ice. This was the fourth time the Bruins played the Maroons that season. Each team had now won twice, with Boston taking this game, 3-2. "Galbraith missed a seemingly sure goal after a rush by Hitchman gave him a close in shot. . . . Hitchman was boring in fast for rebounds and Dutton was forced to trip him to save a goal on one quick thrust by the big Boston defense man. Boston's sturdy defense was cracking the Maroon rushes and the champions could not get close. . . . Hitchman's long stick was unbeatable."[16]

The Bruins shut out the Black Hawks 3-0 on February 15 in Boston. "The playing of Dick Irvin, McVeigh and Hay was brilliant, but they had little chance of breaking through the defense of Hitchman and Coutu, and later of Cleghorn and Hitchman."[17]

Boston Globe, *February, 16, 1927, page 21.*

After losing to the Americans in New York in game 32, Boston met them at home, winning 5-0. "The popular Hitchman skated slowly past [Conacher and Reise], his smart stick-handling more than compensating for his lack of speed and making the goal was a formality. Billy Coutu who started the game with Hitchman, played his best game of the year."[18]

Hitch's second goal was in Boston's 5-2 win against the Pittsburgh Pirates in game 37. In the Bruins' 2-1 win against the Black Hawks in Chicago on March 15, Hitchman provided assists for both goals, one in overtime. "Herberts got back into the game in time to take a pass from Hitchman and beat Lehman for the first score of the evening. His time was 19:15."[19]

Hitch scored the final goal in the 3-1 victory over Detroit on March 19. In the second last game of the season, the Bruins won 4-3 in Pittsburgh. Boston was down 1-0, and Herbert scored twice to give Boston the win, first on an assist by Billy Boucher and then from Hitch, who was cut in the game, needing three stitches. Boston beat the division-leading Rangers 4-3 in overtime at the Boston Arena in the final game of the season. With this result, the Rangers finished 11 points ahead of Boston and awaited the result of the playoff between them and third place Chicago.

Division Semifinal Against the Chicago Black Hawks

On March 29, 1927, Boston started Cleghorn on left defense and Hitch on the right for the first playoff game in Chicago, winning 6-1 against the Black Hawks. "Lionel Hitchman and the other Boston defense men were a little too tough for the Hawk attack and Hal Winkler in the net played a consistently cool and capable game." Five Boston players contributed to the scoring, with Fredrickson getting two goals.

The second game on March 31 in Boston in front of yet another record-setting crowd of over 10,000 saw the home team battle Chicago to a 4-4 tie.

Boston won the total-goals series 10-5 and advanced to the division final.[20]

Division Final Against the New York Rangers

Boston played the Rangers at home in the first game, ending in a scoreless tie. Stanley Woodward of the *Boston Herald* offered this assessment of Hitch:

> HITCHMAN BEST BRUIN ON ICE
> Lionel Hitchman, best when the going is toughest and undismayed by anything short of a 16-inch shell, was by all odds the outstanding player in a good Boston team. He did more than his share of the attacking and on numerous occasions drilled shots at Chabot that were right on the net work. He was great as a defensive cog, and his sweep checks broke up several of the dangerous and infrequent New York attacks.
>
> Once Hitch was left alone on the defensive by accident and when Murray Murdock got a clean jump and bore down on the Boston cage it looked curtains for the Bruins. But Hitch played him perfectly. He bent over as is his custom, with his stick almost flat on the ice and neatly snitched the puck.
>
> Fred Cook was caught cross-checking and sent to the pen and while he was off the Bruins attacked dangerously with Lionel Hitchman leading the way. He carried the puck the length of the ice and tried to poke it in from the side. Johnson bodies him out of the picture. Hitch almost beat Chabot with a wicked shot from the left a minute later.
>
> The crowd roared as Hitchman catapulted into Johnson and knocked him flat. Hitch was playing the most prominent part in the Boston attack, drilling shots at the net from all angles.[21]

While attendance numbers for this game varied by newspaper report, all agreed it was the largest crowd to date to watch a hockey game in Boston. "Fans went begging for tickets, and just before game time they were bidding as high as $30 for a pair of tickets."[22]

In the next game on April 4, Boston beat the Rangers in New York 3-1 in front of 16,000. Twenty-seven penalties in total were handed out, only one to Hitch. He scored the second goal to put Boston in the lead. Harry Oliver scored the final goal, and with that, in their third NHL season, the Bruins became the first American team in the NHL to advance to the Stanley Cup final. How fitting for Hitch that the team he played for in his first Stanley Cup championship, the Ottawa Senators, was the team he would now face.

(The Ottawa Rowing Club girls' hockey team defeated the Ottawa Alerts after 20 minutes of overtime, with Shirley Moulds scoring the only goal of the game "on a pass from Dot Hitchman." They advanced to the Ladies Ontario Hockey Association championship and won the opening game against the Toronto Pats. "Dot Hitchman was also very good and was conspicuous with her play." The Ottawa Rowing Club sewed up the championship on April 4 at Varsity Arena in Toronto in front of 500 to 600 fans.)

Stanley Cup Final

The series with the Rangers was grueling, and the day before the first Stanley Cup game, Hitch was treated by the team doctor. "He is covered with cuts and bruises, but he maintains that he is all right. What can you do with a guy like that?"[23]

The NHL governors decided to lift the prevailing $25,000 player pool limit for the title series: "the two contending teams will get 45 percent of the net gate receipts for the first three games of the five-game series, this to be divided on the basis of 60 percent to the winners and 40 percent to the losers." The governors estimated that under this new arrangement, the "cut" promises to double any previous year's pool.[24]

The first two games were played in Boston. For game one on April 7, thousands stood in line all day to buy tickets. Ottawa and Boston battled for three periods, but after 20 minutes of overtime neither had scored, and the game was called because of bad ice. NHL president Calder declared that despite the tie, there would be only four more games in the series. A total of six penalties were handed out in this first game, none to Hitch. "The Bruins outplayed the Senators. Harry Oliver, Eddie Shore and Hitchman being the men who stood out in the efforts of the Bruins to score."[25]

In the second Cup game on April 9, the Senators won 3-1. Thirteen penalties were handed out, none to Hitch but five to Shore. John J. Hallahan of the *Boston Globe* observed: "Boston's outstanding players Saturday night were Lionel Hitchman and Harry Oliver. The former, a great money player, was in the game, working like a trojan all the time." He further commented: "It is general belief that Sprague Cleghorn's days with the Bruins are about over. It further is generally believed he has not been used much for fear he might be chased for roughness, but after what Shore has shown, the team would not be any worse off with Cleghorn in the game more."[26]

Bob Coyne, Boston Sunday Post, *April 10, 1927.*

The third game was April 11 in Ottawa, ending in another tie after 20 minutes of overtime with a score of 1-1. It was the first time in Stanley Cup history that two games ended in ties. Sixteen penalties were handed out, one to Hitch. Stanley Woodward of the *Boston Herald* commented: "Eddie Shore was off when Ottawa scored, serving his third penalty of the period and his fifth of the game.... Lionel Hitchman, being an Ottawa boy has plenty of friends here. He was the most effective of the Boston defense men. His sweep check broke many of a sortie." And the *Toronto Star* added: "Lionel Hitchman, a former Senator, was one of the stars of the Boston aggregation. 'Hitchie' played like one possessed in battling his former team-mates and stood out with Frank Clancy for aggressiveness."[27]

The fourth and final game of the series was in Ottawa on April 13. The Senators won 3-1, giving them the world championship and Stanley Cup. It was a rough game resulting in major penalties and two fights at the end of the third period, one with Hitch battling both Ottawa's Hooley Smith and George Boucher. Hitch and Boucher were ousted with just over four minutes of play remaining in the game. This was Hitch's only penalty in a game of 12 penalties. Shore got his only penalty in the game shortly after by starting a fight with Hooley Smith. Woodward of the *Boston Herald* explained the events leading up to and including these fights:

> It was a fitting climax to a vicious hockey game and there are hard feelings on all sides. Third period was nasty beyond all description, with Hooley Smith, the Ottawa winger, doing his worst.
>
> First he butt-ended Lionel Hitchman in the mouth and a general battle started. George Boucher of the Ottawa defense was looking for Hitch to get even for a hard body check which the latter had handed out. He pitched into it and got a smash in the eye that turned blue before he could get off the ice.
>
> He and Hitchman were sent to the coop for the rest of the game, but wonder of wonders, LaFlamme [the ref], in whose premise the fight took place, allowed Smith to remain on the ice.
>
> He stayed long enough to smash little Harry Oliver in the mouth with a nasty cross check. Eddie Shore came up to avenge Oliver, who was lying flat on the ice, and when he swung his stick at Smith, LaFlamme sent them both off.
>
> The fight under the stand developed out of a heated argument between President Charles F. Adams and Manager Art Ross of the Bruins [and LaFlamme] into which some of the players thrust themselves. Words

became heated and some one cracked LaFlamme. They say it was Coutu.

Numerous Boston sympathizers who were at the game were agreed that the Bruins did not benefit in the least from the refereeing. LaFlamme gave Herberts a major [for hooking and protesting] in the second period that practically ruined the Boston cause. At the time Ottawa was leading, 1 to 0. The Senators profited by the short-handedness of the Boston team to score their second goal and practically sew up the game.[28]

Hitch, Herbert and George Boucher were levied $50 fines for fighting, taken out of their "world series" receipts and given to charities in Ottawa and Boston. Later that night, Hitch "chased Hooley out of a restaurant down the streets of Ottawa." It's not known if Hitch caught up to him, but the NHL did, and for Hooley Smith's vicious attack on Oliver he was later fined $100 and received a month's suspension to commence at the beginning of the next season. LaFlamme identified Billy Coutu as the person who hit him, and Coutu was expelled from the league.[29]

1927-28: PRINCE OF WALES

The 1927-28 NHL season and playoff format remained unchanged. But the O'Brien Cup and Prince of Wales Trophy were repurposed as awards to the teams in the Canadian and American divisions, respectively, that finished first in the regular season. The Montreal Canadiens won the O'Brien Cup, and the Boston Bruins won the Prince of Wales Trophy.

In the Canadian Division playoffs, the top-ranked Canadiens lost to the Maroons in the final. Boston followed suit, losing to the second-ranked New York Rangers in the American final. The Rangers won the Stanley Cup in three straight games to become the second American team to win the trophy (the Seattle Metropolitans were first in 1917).

This was the second year this playoff structure was in place, and the second time the leaders of each division were knocked out of the race for the Stanley Cup. At the end of the season, Art Ross campaigned for changes. He thought the division winner's bye, resulting in a prolonged layoff, created a disadvantage for them.

In 1927-28, 1,350,000 spectators watched NHL regular-season hockey, an increase of about 20 percent over the previous season. Some of this increase was attributed to the availability of larger venues for teams to play in, including Detroit's new stadium. The Canadiens had been in their Montreal Forum for two full seasons and led attendance records, averaging 10,400 spectators per game, a 9 percent increase over the previous season.[1]

A few notable rules were added this season in efforts to speed up play and increase scoring. Forward passing was permitted in the defensive zone, and goaltenders' stick blades were limited to 14 inches and their leg pads reduced in width by two inches to 10. Despite these changes, scoring actually dropped (the league total was 837 compared with 879 the previous season).[2]

Boston began the season with the same starting lineup as it finished with the season before: Percy Galbraith, left wing; Frank Fredrickson, center; Harry Oliver, right wing; Hitch, left defense; Eddie Shore, right defense; Hal Winkler, goal. The only other holdovers were Jimmy Herbert and Sprague Cleghorn.

Cleghorn remained team captain, although he played very little and partway through the season was called on to coach the team when Art Ross became ill. Once Ross returned, Cleghorn was sent on a scouting expedition to the U.S. Midwest and signed Ralph "Cooney" Weiland, center of the AHA Minneapolis team, for the next season.

New players for this season included Aubrey "Dit" Clapper, star of the Boston Tigers from the Can-Am Hockey League (forerunner of the professional American Hockey Association), Norman "Dutch" Gainor from Calgary, Nobby Clark from Minneapolis, Martin Lauder from the Owen Sound amateurs, Harry Connor from the Saskatoon professionals (an Ottawa boy) and Fred Gordon from the Detroit Cougars.

Partway through the season, Boston sold top-scoring Jimmy Herbert to the Toronto Maple Leafs and called up Hago Harrington from New Haven. With Herbert's departure, Hitch was the last remaining original Bruin.

Hal Winkler led the league in shutouts, tying Alex Connell of Ottawa with 15. Winkler's shutout mark remains a Boston record today. None of the Boston players reached the top 10 in points this season. Herbert, Oliver and Shore came in at 18-20 on the league points list with 19, 18, and 17 points respectively. This season, the Bruins were noted more for their strong defensive tactics and fluid teamwork.

Boston fans showed tremendous interest in the Bruins' season. Management added new features to the entertainment, including a popular jazz band that played before the start of each game and during intermissions. Building code enforcement for this season imposed limits on attendance, and there were no more 10,000-plus attendance records as in the previous season. However, the Bruins consistently had capacity or near-capacity crowds for all regular-season games, peaking in game 23.

Hitch was named vice-captain for a third year. When Art Ross became ill, and Captain Cleghorn handled the coaching duties in his absence, Hitch was made acting captain. He had a great rapport with all his teammates and generously encouraged "second string" players. Decades later Dit Clapper recounted his first goal with Boston and being "on the receiving end of a massive celebratory handshake from Hitchman."[3]

With Boston finishing first in the American Division in a hotly contested race, Hitch had the honor of accepting the Prince of Wales Trophy on behalf of the Bruins. He played all 44 regular-season games. The team had a complete second forward line, but only Hitch and Shore played regular defense. Cleghorn played very few minutes in this season, and Clapper played forward mostly but subbed for defense on penalties. Shore led the NHL in penalties for the second year. He had 165 penalty minutes in 43 games to Hitch's 87. The next 10 skaters to Shore in penalties averaged 107 minutes (in 42 games). With Shore spending so much time in the penalty box, Hitch saw more time on the ice than any other player on his team.

The defensive team of Hitch and Shore jelled this year. They were opposites in most respects but complemented each other. Shore was an explosive player, known for his fast rushes and quick temper. Hitch was not slow at all as some later reporting suggested. Shore had exceptional speed compared with anyone, and often the comparison was made with his defense partner. Hitch had a calm demeanor, and it took a lot to get him riled. Together their blocking was impenetrable. With Hitch's sturdy defense, Shore was free to leave his defensive post for the offensive frontier, which he frequently did. Maybe too frequently at times.

Boston suffered their first loss in game four on November 26 at home against the New York Americans, putting them in second place in the division by one point in front of the Detroit Cougars and one point behind the New York Rangers. The next evening in New York, Boston played the Rangers in front of more than 17,000 spectators. After 10 minutes of overtime, neither team could break through, resulting in a 1-1 tie, their league standings unchanged. Boston's goal came in the second period off the stick of Jimmy Herbert. He also went to the penalty box for five minutes, three for mouthing off to the referee. The Rangers scored in the third period to tie the score. Hitch was singled out as "a shining star" of the game.[4]

The first time Boston saw the reigning Stanley Cup champions, the Ottawa Senators, this season was in game eight in Ottawa on December 3. Boston lost 3-2 in front of a crowd of 7,000. Hitch got the assist on both of Boston's goals. Ottawa came from behind in the third period to win the game while Eddie Shore and Harry Connor consecutively sat in the penalty box. "Buck [Boucher] made the play all the way alone and warped his stick around Shore's legs as he drove from fifteen feet out." Toward the end of the overtime period, "Hitchman broke up another Ottawa attack when his long stick intercepted Clancy's pass to Kilrea. It would likely have been another counter if Hitch had missed this as Kilrea had a clear run to the net. The game ended a little later with Ottawa winners by 3 to 2."[5] After this game, Ottawa moved into third position in the

Canadian Division, and Boston remained in second in the American Division.

As the Bruins prepared for their first game against the Montreal Canadiens in game nine on December 6 in Boston, John J. Hallahan of the *Boston Globe* (page 20) observed that Hitch "had been doing two men's work" thus far in the schedule, and if Shore "can avoid penalties his value to the Bruins would be greatly increased." Some have argued that Shore was unjustly targeted by the referees, but if so, he made it easy for them, as he often injected himself into the fray when other players were sizing each other up. As in game four against the New York Americans when referee Bell "stepped in just in time to stop a promising brawl" between Hitch and Red Green, and "Bell had a hard time stopping a ruckus between Red and Eddie Shore, who sprang forward to revenge his co-defense man."[6]

"Among the 'bad men,' Eddie Shore of the Bruins is the leader. He has spent 48 minutes of the 11 games played by the Boston team in the 'cooler.'" This is "20 minutes more in penalties than the leading 'villain' in the Canadian division, King Clancy of the Ottawa Senators, who has had 23 minutes off in 10 games."[7]

Game 11 was the sixth overtime game played by Boston. They won 2-1 in Detroit on December 11. Young Gainor scored both goals, the first on an assist from Hitch and the latter on one from Percy Galbraith. This win put Boston in first place in their division. But they didn't stay there after losing to the Rangers the following game in Boston on December 13. There were no Boston heroes in that game. "Boston can attribute its defeat to the failure of its men to play hockey and keep in the game, for after gaining a lead of 2 to 0, the team was weakened when two men were chased by the officials." A total of 38 penalty minutes were handed out, 20 to Boston. This was not atypical, especially against the Rangers. But they came two players at a time for Boston, severely handicapping the team. Herbert and Fredrickson were both doing time in the penalty box, and Hitch was sent up to the forward line when one goal against Boston was scored. Then Hitch and Shore were sent off for penalties when the game was tied. "Hitchman was still in the box, and the game ended when Shore attempted to carry the puck out from one side of his net, only for Bill Cook to take it away from the Boston star and snap it by Winkler for the winning goal."[8] The Rangers leaped over Boston by one point to gain the division lead. Detroit trailed Boston by three points. Soon after Jimmy Herbert was sold to Toronto.

Hitch might have felt the need to redeem himself after the Rangers fiasco and the subsequent 5-1 loss in Montreal to the Canadiens, sending Boston into third place. In the next game (14) against the Senators in Boston, the Bruins won 1-0, moving into a tie for second place with Detroit. It was a nail-biter of a game; Boston's Harry Oliver scored off Frank Fredrickson's pass with only three minutes remaining. The *Boston Herald* declared "Hitchman skating in tip-top form."[9]

Boston met the Rangers for the third time on December 27 in game 15 of the season. "With a fiery attack that would not be denied and a sturdy defense that withstood the efforts of the New York Rangers, Boston Bruins scored a 2 to 0 victory over Ching Johnson and his mates at the Arena last night before a crowd that filled every nook and cranny in the spacious auditorium." Shore got the first goal off a rebound in the second period, and Harry Connor got the second counter in the final period, bringing Boston to within one point of the Rangers in the division standings. Hitch was lauded for his "stick-checking." He continually broke up the Rangers' incoming combinations and forced them to take long, easy-to-defend shots on Winkler's net. "Shore was good. The newcomers were good. Oliver and Galbraith were always dangerous. Winkler was steady and dependable in the net, but head and shoulders over every other member of the team stood Hitchman, as valuable a player as Boston has had since professional hockey came into being here."[10]

The headlines stayed on Hitch for game 17 in New York against the Americans. "Hitchman Shines as Bruins Win, 3-2" And "Hitchman Hero of Great Game." In a game that attracted 10,000 spectators, the Associated Press summarized Hitch's contribution: "Lionel Hitchman, Bruin defense star, was the hero of the game. He scored two goals unassisted and engineered the goal which gave his team victory. The Bruins by virtue of their success went into a tie with the New York Rangers for first place in the American group of the NHL."[11]

At the midpoint of the season, Boston went to Ottawa to play the Senators. For days before the game, the *Ottawa Journal* built up the spectacle, rating Boston as the "heaviest checkers" in the league. In one of several articles, they stoked and helped create Shore's 'bad man' reputation. "[Boston seems] to have one championship nailed down now, and that is an undisputed claim to the 'bad man' title held by the erratic though often brilliant Eddie Shore." The headlines raged for days. Here is the one from January 14, 1928, on the day of the game: "Contest Teeming With Action Promised When Bruising Team From Hub Clash With Senators - Shore Wins Bad Man Title of League - Hitchman Is Star Boston Attraction." The article associated with this headline went on to state: "Hitchman is a prime favorite in Ottawa. So is Eddie Shore, leading 'bad man' of the league according to penalties. There is no discounting this twin. Hitchman always packs them in and he has a big following here. Shore has always shown that he can give and take."[12] Sadly for Ottawa, the game took place during a severe snowstorm, but at least 5,000 faithful disregarded the disruptive weather and came to the game. Boston won 4-2, sending Ottawa down the ladder to fourth place in the Canadian Division. Boston took the lead not only in the "bad man" title but also in the American Division.

After Boston's successful trip to Ottawa and just before the lead-up to game 23, J.W. Mooney of the *Boston Post* did a full-column article on Hitch on January 15, 1928. The text of the article and accompanying image are reprinted here:

Lionel Hitchman, nearly 190 pounds and over 6 feet tall.

Gosh, they make these Lionel fellows pretty big in Canada. There is Lionel Conacher, another champ who performs on skates in the National league.

And they must make them good natured for Big Hitch is as comical and as full of fun as the deuce, until somebody jams a high stick in his face on the ice and then the real fun starts.

TOWER OF STRENGTH

Hitch, who has a nifty way of breaking up attacks with either a stiff check or by dropping to one knee and laying a flat stick on the ice that seems to cover yards and yards of space around him, is a great teammate for Eddie Shore at the Bruin outer defence.

The big fellow is a great player at his position and a most valuable asset to the Bruin defence, but the thought is that if his size rated him to be a forward he would be even more sensational.

It is well known that a good defence player keeps to his position, for the most part, and after a trek down the ice hustles right back to his position. This is the hardest lesson Hitch has to learn in hockey, because his temperament is not altogether fitted for the defence.

He just can't stand waiting for things to come to him. He must go right in and meet it, get in the middle of it and forever keep dashing around where things are the liveliest. It gets on his nerves to see his forwards pressing in and bombarding a rival goalie with him down at the other end of the rink. He can't resist the temptation of moving up and playing the part of a forward. It would be disastrous to the Bruins if Hitch had the idea only, and was without the ability to play far down the ice, but luckily he has versatility and handles himself well enough among the forwards.

It is this aggressiveness that impresses Manager Art Ross with the idea that Hitch should have taken up the fight game. Always wanting to be in the thick of the scramble and taking his knocks as they come makes Ross vow that his tall defence player would go big in the squared ring.

Ross isn't encouraging Hitch to take many trips down the ice and stay there, for he would rather be certain that the defence is well protected, and further, he is not always so certain that Hitch will streak it back at top speed in checking back. When Hitch does hustle, he turns in a wonderful night's work.

The lanky one joined the Bruins the first year C. F. Adams put a pro team in Boston. He wasn't one of the first group like Jim Herberts, but came down from the Ottawa team about mid-year. However, he is the only one left of the first pro team in Boston.

Born at Toronto 26 years ago, Hitchman has had a sound foundation in hockey. He learned to skate when he was five years old and started hockey about 11 years ago with the Wychwood Club in the Toronto Hockey league. After two years he went up with the Aura Lees in the Junior O.H.A. for two years. Then he went up with the New Edinboro club in the Ottawa City league, from where he was grabbed by the Ottawa Senators. He immediately jumped into a regular berth on the defence and the next year, 1925, was sold to the Bruins. That was a lucky break for Boston.

In the off season, Hitchman is in the insurance game and with his wife and baby daughter Gloria, lives in Watertown [MA] winter and summer.

Before settling down, Hitch was aching for a taste of rough and ready life and joined up with the Royal Canadian Mounted Police, and later with the Ontario provincial police. He had 10 months of it, during which time his work took him over lonely snowbound trails, where in nights of sleet storms and blizzards he was subject to all sorts of hardships.

His troop was highly recommended for its work during the great forest fire in 1922, which covered a strip of nearly 50 miles from Haileybury to Charlton Junction. Daring deeds of heroism and sacrifice kept Hitch in continual danger, but of these he is silent.

However, he came out with a whole skin to jump right into another fearless undertaking, and the battles of many a hockey game are examples of just the kind of a time this big fellow loves.

Hitch Was Once a Royal Mountie

Aching for Excitement Led Him to Hazardous Life---Should Be Fighter, Says Ross

"HITCH"
Popular and capable defence man of the Bruins. His voting name is Lionel Hitchman, but everybody knows him as "Hitch."

In game 23, Boston lost 3-1 to the Canadiens at home on January 17, and the Canadiens retained their first-place rank in their division, a full 15 points ahead of second-place Montreal Maroons. Boston also retained their lead in their division, but by just one point.

It was estimated that 40,000 persons tried to get into the local ice-emporium. All day long the hungry ticket-hunters roamed the streets. Early in the afternoon a long queue of potential standing room customers formed a line at the side entrance. By 8 o'clock this line stretched across the Gainsborough Street Bridge and up Columbus Avenue as far as the Old Columbus Street grounds, more than half a mile. The gates were closed on thousands before the permitted number of standings had got in for the police saw threatening gestures in the crowd and were concerned that a thousand or so were about to rush the gates. The 8000 or so who did get in, representing only a scant fourth of the crowd that sought admittance, saw a game that will be remembered when most will be found only in the musty records of the NHL.

The Bruins were handicapped sorely by the fact that Lionel Hitchman, the outstanding Boston defensive player, was not himself. He was hurt at Ottawa and he could hardly move during the brief periods that he was on the ice. A severe back wrench made playing torture for him and weakened Boston a great deal more than most of the fans realized.[13]

The results of the next four games–two losses, and two overtime ties–sent Boston into second place behind the Rangers by three points. By game 28, Hitch's back spasms had subsided, and he was back to full strength. However, Art Ross was not doing so well, ailing from what was termed a stomach condition; he was sent home to Montreal for medical treatment, likely for an ulcer. Sprague Cleghorn took the reins of the team, starting with a win in game 28 against the New York Americans. They continued on the winning trail for the next game, and by game 30 in Montreal, the "Canadiens could not get past the Shore-Hitchman defense as they did on the Bruins' last appearance in Montreal and had to be content with an overtime draw, 1 goal to 1."[14]

Still, with Cleghorn at the helm of the team, Boston beat the Rangers 2-0 in New York on February 19 in front of 18,500 spectators. "The Bruins were strong as steel in every department of play. Their combinations made those of the Rangers look crude and their defensive work, punctuated by some of the most resounding body checking of the season on the part of F. Lionel Hitchman, the noted citizen of Belmont, was the tightest ever seen outside of

Pittsburgh."[15] With this win, Boston reclaimed the lead in the American Division.

The Bruins experienced their only loss under Cleghorn's management in Montreal against the Maroons, by a score of 3-1. "The Bruins finally got a goal when Hitchman drove a bullet-like drive from the defense which whistled past Benedict."[16] But they redeemed themselves at home against the same team the following game with a 2-1 win, Hitch getting the winning goal.

> It was only fitting that Hitchman should be the hero of the game and the one to score the winning goal. It came a few minutes after he had returned from the hospital section with a large cocoon on his forehead, and it was remarkable that he came back in the game at all.
>
> In the early stages of the period he and Hooley Smith, with whom he had become entangled last season in Ottawa, came together at the defence. The butt end of Hooley's stick ripped a cruel cut on Hitch's left eyelid and necessitated medical treatment.
>
> He left the ice and five stitches were taken in the cut, which was a wicked affair. But he returned to the ice with the wound sewed up and covered with plaster and broke that tight game open for the Bruins.[17]

Game 36 was the end of Cleghorn's interim coaching gig. In that game, Boston tied Toronto in overtime, giving up its exclusive hold on first place in the American Division, now sharing it with the Rangers, each with 42 points. In the nine games that Cleghorn coached, the team won six, lost one and tied two.

In the next game, Art Ross was back at the helm, and the Bruins beat Ottawa 1-0 in Boston on March 6. This gave Boston a two-point lead over the Rangers. The defense team of Hitch and Shore was "next to impossible" to get by, and Hal Winkler was "astonishing" in nets. "Hitchman, who has been taking a great many hard smacks from rival butt ends in recent games, took some more last night, but played through with wonderful effectiveness. In the first period, he refused to leave the ice when Nighbor gave him the butt-end." He received a much harder hit in the second period from George Boucher, whose "attack on Hitchman seemed to be deliberate. He skated to the defence and shot, then lifted his stick and gave it to Hitch solidly in the face. The latter went down, but was patched up on the ice and continued after half a minute's armistice. Boucher was chased and Shore, who argued with the officials, was sent off, too. The penalty epidemic, however, broke out again shortly. Alex Smith went after Hitchman and took a minor."[18]

The last time Boston saw the Rangers in the regular season was in game 38 at home, ending in an overtime score of 3-3 and preserving their two-point lead over New York. Harry Connor, Hitch and Shore played "sensational" hockey, "although the latter suffered from a major penalty."[19]

Part of a cartoon by Bob Coyne, Boston Sunday Post, *March 11, 1928.*

Boston ended the 44-game season with 20 wins, 13 losses, and 11 ties. They played 14 overtime games, winning one, losing two and tying 11. By finishing first in the division, Boston got a bye and waited for New York and Detroit to complete their preliminary playoff round before taking on the winner. The Rangers emerged victoriously, and the two-game, total-point division final with Boston began on April 1, 1928, in New York.

Playoffs

Hitch, Oliver, Shore and Fredrickson,
Boston Post, *April 2, 1928.*

Boston and New York played to a 1-1 overtime tie in game one of the playoffs in front of 17,000. "The Boston men fought desperately and Shore and Hitchman did yeoman work." Shore got four penalties to Hitch's one, leaving Hitch and Winkler with a lot more action to contend with. "Shore, on returning to play, made one of his spectacular dashes, only to be downed by Johnson. . . . Hitchman drove a wicked shot from his right, and Chabot contributed a great save, not only on the vice-captain's drive, but on the rebound on which Galbraith tried to sneak the disk past Chabot."[20]

The second game played in Boston before a crowd of 8,500 ended Boston's hopes of another Stanley Cup final berth. The

Rangers won the game 4-1 and the playoff round by 5-2. The Bruins kept the Rangers scoreless in the first period, but the Rangers were able to get one in the second period and then skated away with the game in the third, adding three more goals. Harry Oliver scored for Boston with 15 seconds remaining in the game. The *Boston Post* commented: "On the Bruin side none played a more effective or harder game than 'Big Three' Hitchman who was a tower of strength on the defense and a plugger from first to last. Eddie Shore wasn't himself. He was trying hard enough and was there a few times with his old sensational dashes but his pep lagged and was costly on the second Ranger goal when he was caught napping and was outskated trying to catch up." The *Boston Globe* reported that Shore was weakened by a "mouth ailment." Boston also made the tactical decision to play with four forwards for most of the game, trying to score. The *Globe* continued: "Hitchman starred for the Bruins, but he could not get the disk into the strings, although he threw more than one scare into the Rangers' ranks. Defensively he was there and when the tide was turning against him and his mates he labored with all his might to carry on to a successful conclusion." But it was not enough.[21]

Whether it was the week-long layoff while the second and third teams played off, or Shore's not being at full strength, or the decision to trade away the team's leading scorer, Jimmy Herbert, or all three, is just speculation. But if anything, this series revealed certain weaknesses on the team that would be addressed in the next season.

Chapter Ten

STANLEY CUP CHAMPS

At Boston's urging, the NHL playoff format was revised for the 1928-29 season, guaranteeing that at least one of the top division teams would make it through to the Stanley Cup final. The new arrangement was as follows:

- Canadian and American Division winners played a best-of-five game semifinal series.
- The other semifinal was a best-of-three series, and the finalists were determined by two interdivisional preliminary series:
  - The second-place Canadian and American Division teams played a two-game, total-point series.
  - The third-place teams did the same in the other preliminary series.
- The semifinal winners played in a best-of-three game final series for the Stanley Cup and world championship.

The American Division emerged as the strongest division in the playoffs. The Boston Bruins defeated the Montreal Canadiens in three straight games in the division-winners semifinal. The New York Rangers won the other semifinal against the Toronto Maple Leafs to play Boston for the Stanley Cup, the first time two American teams played for the championship.

Boston won the world championship and Stanley Cup in two straight games. In total playoff games, including the semifinal, Boston won five straight. It was the second time in NHL history that a team won all their playoff games (the Canadiens were first in 1924), and it would not happen again until 1952.

Building a Championship Team

Sprague Cleghorn was no longer associated with the Boston Bruins, and Hitch was named captain of the team. Building Boston's championship team began back in their inaugural season in the league with the purchase of Hitch, followed by the acquisition of players from the west, which brought Eddie Shore. Cy Denneny, Hitch's former 1923 Stanley Cup–champion teammate from the Ottawa Senators, was hired to work specifically with the team's forward lines. He also played in some games. During this season, Ralph "Cooney" Weiland, Aubrey "Dit" Clapper and Norman "Dutch" Gainor, under Cy's tutelage, played together on a forward combination that became known as the Dynamite Line.

Training camp was over by early November 1928, and manager Ross retained the following 15 players in preparation for the first game of the season: left wingers Percy Galbraith, Red Green and Cy Denneny; centers Frank Fredrickson, Cooney Weiland and Dutch Gainor; right wingers Harry Oliver, Eddie Rodden and Eric Pettinger; defensemen Eddie Shore, Lionel Hitchman, Dit Clapper and Lloyd Klein; and goaltenders Hal Winkler and Cecil "Tiny" Thompson.

The team was well supplied with two forward lines. However, it was an ongoing concern that Boston did not have strong defensive spares. "As things are now, the Bruins are none too well fortified on the defense. Capt. Lionel Hitchman and Eddie Shore will play first string, of course, but the only other actual defence man on the squad is Klein, from the Pacific Coast League. It would not be surprising if Manager Art Ross shifted both Dit Clapper and Dutch [Gainor] back to the defense." During the season this happened several times.[1]

Throughout the first part of the season, several changes to the team composition occurred. In November, Hal Winkler, goalie, was sent to the Minneapolis Millers of the American Hockey Association. On December 21, center Frank Fredrickson was traded for Duncan "Mickey" MacKay. Dit Clapper was moved up to the forward line. Harvard grad George Owen, defenseman, joined the team on January 8, 1929, sending Eric Pettinger to the Toronto

Maple Leafs on January 9 (Toronto had the rights to Owen). Defenseman Myles Lane came to Boston from the New York Rangers on January 23. Dentist Dr. Bill Carson, center, came to Boston from the Toronto Maple Leafs on January 29. And on January 30, Boston loaned Eddie Rodden to a semi-pro team in Windsor, Ontario.

By the end of the season and all through the playoffs, the team lineup was as follows: Oliver, right wing; Carson, center; Galbraith, left wing; Hitchman, left defense; Shore, right defense; Thompson, goal; Weiland, Clapper, Gainor, MacKay, Owen, Klein and Lane, spares.

Ross had assembled a remarkable team and worked them to peak at the right time.

Hitch's image spanned the length of the front page of the Boston American, *sports section, November 20, 1928, the night the Boston Garden opened. (The artist William Wood, gave Hitch the original artwork.)*

The New Boston Garden

The Bruins played for the first time in the new Boston Garden on November 20, 1928, in their first home game against the Montreal Canadiens. For hockey games, the new arena held 15,000 spectators:

14,500 seated, plus 500 standing. For that first NHL game in the Garden, all seats were presold, and people lined up for hours for the standing-room seats, which went on sale 90 minutes before the game started. When the gates opened, throngs of people stormed the doors, and it was estimated that between 16,000 and 17,500 in total attended the game. Two days later, three "speculators" were fined for selling 2,000 game tickets above face value.

> Owner Charles F. Adams of the Bruins, and Manager Sheldon Fairbanks of the Garden had a talk yesterday [November 21] concerning some way of handling the crowds at future home games. Both feel there will be no further trouble. Extra police details will be assigned to the Garden on Bruin nights and an entire system of traffic control will be worked out to make another crush impossible.
>
> The demand for seats for the season is becoming so heavy that the Bruins management is considering doing away with admissions, and may decide further to limit tickets for standing room.[2]

The Bruins played to capacity and overcapacity crowds most of the season and to overcapacity crowds for their three home playoff games.

The Regular Season (26-13-5)

The Bruins had a very successful regular season, earning 57 points, the most so far for the American Division. In total they won 26 games, lost 13, and tied five, securing the American Division championship and Prince of Wales Trophy at the end of game 41 (of their 44-game season) in New York by beating the Rangers.

Harry Oliver was the only Boston player to make the top 10 in league scoring, with 23 points. He was seventh (Ace Bailey of Toronto was first with 32 points). Tiny Thompson tied for second with Roy Worters of the New York Americans with a 1.15 goals-against average (George Hainsworth of the Canadiens was first with 0.92). Worters won the Hart Trophy that season.

A Rough Start

Before suffering a serious injury, Hitch played in the first seven games, five wins and two losses for Boston. In the first game, played in Pittsburgh against the Pirates, Boston won in overtime, 1-0. Shore spent 11 minutes in the penalty box, and the game was stopped for five minutes in the second period when the Pirates' Tex White was knocked out after colliding with Hitch. In overtime, Hitch was badly cut over one eye but continued playing until Dit Clapper got the Bruins their goal (overtime wasn't sudden death in those days).

In game four in Detroit, Hitch was again cut over the eye and left the game in the second period. Boston lost 2-0, Detroit's second goal coming from Jimmy Herbert on a pass from Carson Cooper, both former Boston Bruins originals. During the Bruins' win (2-0) on December 4, 1928, in game seven at Boston against the New York Rangers, Hitch sustained an injury to his shoulder early in the first period but continued playing. Through multiple X-rays, it was diagnosed that he had separated his shoulder. "Although Capt. Lionel Hitchman will be unable to play for the Bruins against the Montreal Maroons at the Garden tomorrow night, it is most reassuring to followers of the team to learn that Hitch will be back in there Tuesday against the Americans."[3]

The Americans won that game 3-0 in Boston. After a week's rest, Hitch started but "got a fearful bump on the bad shoulder in the closing minute of the first period and had to leave the ice," reported Stanley Woodward of the *Boston Herald*. A day later Woodward also commented: "It was too bad to see a great hockey player like Lionel Hitchman out on the ice when he obviously should have been among the spectators. We understand that he insisted on playing despite his injured shoulder. He had better listen to reason and let it get well."[4]

Hitch stayed home to rest his shoulder when Boston traveled to Toronto, where they lost 2-0. The Associated Press noted that "Hitchman's absence because of illness had a disastrous effect on the Boston team. The Leafs got through the Boston defense repeatedly for shots on Thompson."[5]

Ross used Gainor and Clapper to fill Hitch's spot for that Toronto game and in the next two, which also resulted in defeats. The newspapers were calling it a losing streak, and Art Ross attempted to calm the waters: "Did you ever see a Bruins team start at the same pace as some of our Canadian rivals?" John J. Hallahan of the *Boston Globe* offered that Shore "has been playing fine hockey with Hitchman out, seemingly realizing that he has added responsibility."[6] With these three losses, Boston was now in third place in the division behind second-place Detroit and first-place Rangers. Hitch's injury was worse than first thought, with his collarbone also out of place, and he was sidelined for two weeks.

Without their captain, Boston next played Detroit at home in front of 11,000 fans on December 18. They needed a win not only to calm the jitters of the press and public but more importantly to restore the team's confidence. Ross moved Gainor and Clapper back up to the forward line where more scoring was needed and sent left winger Percy Galbraith back on defense. He showed well enough to free Shore up to hit the offensive zone. Shore, Weiland, and Gainor scored, giving Boston its first win in four starts and lifting them into second place in the division.

After this game, Art Ross traded center Frank Fredrickson for Pittsburgh's Mickey MacKay in the hopes of getting more out of the offensive line. This move was looked upon with some skepticism by the local sportswriters, and unfortunately, the next game on Christmas Day confirmed their concerns with Boston's 2-1 defeat to the last-place Chicago Black Hawks, dropping the Bruins to third place in the division.[7] Of the top 10 scorers in the division so far, four each were from the Rangers and Detroit. Boston (Oliver in fifth) and Chicago each had one player. Former Boston players Carson Cooper (second) and Jimmy Herbert (eighth) both made the list.

During the Christmas holidays, Hitch, Shore, and Thompson made time to headline a free sports night for the children of North Cambridge. Three nights later, Hitch got back in uniform in New

York against the Rangers. Boston lost 2-0 but played much better than in the last several games.

One-third of the season had now passed, and Hitch hadn't dressed for five games and was not in any condition to help in many of the others. In these first 14 games, Boston won five, lost seven and tied two. They remained in third place in the division, but the point spread increased to nine points behind the first-place Rangers and six points behind second-place Detroit. Overall, in the NHL, Boston was seventh out of the 10 teams. To say that Hitch and the team got off to a rocky start was an understatement.

New Record

The middle part of the season was a different story. With Hitch back at left defense, Boston mounted an undefeated streak, even after Eddie Shore sprained an ankle and was out for four games. In all, they won 11 games and tied for two in a row, setting a new club record.

During game 16, in Montreal, Boston beat the Canadian Division's third-place Maroons, 1-0, on January 3 on a goal by Shore. Hitch was butt-ended by Hooley Smith and suffered a chipped hip bone. He played the following game in Boston against Pittsburgh, crashing with Frank Fredrickson and causing more damage. Hitch needed time to heal and Ross needed to shore up the defense. Not only was Hitch injured, but Dit Clapper would miss the next game to rush to Toronto to be with his fiancée, Norma Anderson, who took ill and was hospitalized there. He was absent for two more games when she tragically died of spinal meningitis three weeks later.

Worried about Hitch's health, Ross brought in amateur star George Owen, a popular choice with Boston sportswriters and fans. He was Canadian born but moved to Boston when his father became a professor of marine architecture at the Massachusetts Institute of Technology. George went to high school in the Boston area and attended Harvard, becoming a star player in football, baseball, and hockey. Carl Warton of the *Boston Herald*, commenting on the acquisition, offered: "But what commends him most to the expert eye is his ability to turn with the play and cover even after a player has passed him. Lionel Hitchman is the outstanding exponent of this most difficult of maneuvers, and it is said that none more closely approaches him in this respect than Owen."[8]

At the start of Owen's first game in a Bruins uniform on January 8, 14,000 spectators silently stood in memory of the late promoter George "Tex" Rickard, who had designed and built the Boston Garden and died two days earlier at age 59. Owen got off to a good start, with the Bruins winning 5-2 over the Toronto Maple Leafs. Harry Oliver was the outstanding star, getting three goals.

Boston tied Detroit for second place in the American Division with their 3-2 win in game 20 on January 12 at home, with Shore getting the winning goal. This brought Boston's winning streak to six consecutive games. After Hitch chipped his hip bone in game 16 against the Montreal Maroons, he played sparingly in the next four games, and Owen, the new defensive recruit, had some great successes. In fact, the whole team was rounding into top form. Shore was at his best, and the second line of MacKay, Weiland and Clapper "rose to great heights against the [Detroit] Cougars"[9] in game 20. The Bruins had won the last three games with little assistance from Hitch and Galbraith, who also suffered an injury, and they were about to be challenged by more injuries to two other players, Eddie Shore and Mickey MacKay, both receiving ankle sprains in the last game. And next up was the reigning world champs and current division leader, the New York Rangers.

In game 21 at home, Boston beat the Rangers 4-1 on January 15, 1929, with no effect on the current division standings. The *Boston Herald*'s Stanley Woodward commented: "Capt. Lionel Hitchman appeared once more on the Boston defence and was the same bulwark as before he amassed the multiplicity of injuries which has kept him out of the game much of the season. He and George Owen were rough, tough gentlemen for the Rangers to pass after they got used to each other's style. Hitch was looking for Taffy Abel all night and he handed the New York colossus a number of checks which took the fillings out of the teeth of the gallery customers." Two days after the win against the Rangers, Woodward added: "Capt. Lionel

Hitchman of the Bruins never will get the credit he deserves. His all-around defensive play for the Shoreless Bruins Tuesday night was superb, and his willingness to take punishment for the cause was magnificent."[10] In the next game without Shore, Boston played the Cougars in Detroit, in front of 13,000 fans, to an overtime 1-1 tie. Boston and Detroit retained their second and third places, respectively, in the American division.

Two more games were played without Shore, and Boston was now 10 games without a defeat. They were still in second place but narrowed the margin with the first-place Rangers to one point. Boston acquired two more players in time for the win against the Rangers in New York in game 25: local boy and defenseman Myles Lane from the Rangers and center Dr. Bill Carson from the Maple Leafs. Boston would win two more before ending their undefeated streak of 11 wins and two ties.

It Gets Worse Before It Gets Better

Game 28 was at home on February 2, with 15,000 in attendance to watch Boston lose to Toronto 3-0. Hitch was once again injured early in the first period, this time a knee, and Shore and Owen played the balance of the game. The only saving grace was that they remained in second place.

Hitch played part of the next game against the Americans but was not in top form. "The Bruins worked hard, but it was apparently a big mistake to use Hitchman, who could do little other than bump the opposition for the time he was in the game. He was relieved by George Owen, and the team then took on a new lease of life. However, Boston could not beat the defensive play of the Americans."[11] They lost 1-0.

Final Race for the Prince of Wales Cup

The Bruins lost by the same score in Montreal to the Maroons on February 9, but Hitch was in much better shape. Renowned sports editor Elmer Ferguson of the *Montreal Herald* gave a colorful description of the effects of one of Hitch's clean body checks:

The turbulent 'Hooley' Smith led the penalty parade, with five in all. Smith was a marked man by the Bruins, and finished second in the exchanges, for in the second frame the lanky Hitchman dropped him with one of the hardest checks of the season. Smith was dropped like a log, and when referee Romeril helped him up he tottered like a punch-drunk fighter, fell flat on his face again, but gamely crawled up, and started to wobble drunkenly to his post. His knees were bending, and coach Gerard called him off. Smith was shaking his head doggedly to clear the cobwebs. He could just stagger to the bench, falling again just as he reached the gate.[12]

After these three losses, Boston remained in second place in their division, but the first-place Rangers now had a six-point lead. This was narrowed to four points on Boston's win against the Black Hawks in Fort Erie, Ontario (Chicago's rink being otherwise occupied). The Associated Press reported that both Hitch and MacKay did "yeoman work on defence." Another win at Boston against the Pittsburgh Pirates and an overtime tie with Canadian Division leader the New York Americans brought Boston to within one point of the Rangers. In game 36 at home, Boston shut out the Montreal Maroons 1-0 on February 26 on Harry Oliver's goal. "Hitchman, tall, lengthy defense man of the Bruins, turned in his best game of the season. He was banging the opposition with all his power and several times was a threat to the Montrealers." Still, within one point of that elusive Prince of Wales title, the tide was about to shift for Boston.[13]

With Boston's 4-0 win over Ottawa in Game 37, they moved into a tie with the New York Rangers for the lead in the American Division. And in Game 41, Boston beat the Rangers 3-2 in New York on March 10 to move solely into first place.

For Game 42 in Boston against the Chicago Black Hawks, Ross used all his spares including Klein, Lane, Gainor, Owen, Clapper, Weiland and MacKay. The Bruins won 11-1, a record score for the team, and secured the division title and the Prince of Wales Trophy.

On March 14, in Game 43 of the 1928-29 NHL season, Hitch made his coaching debut, beating the Detroit Cougars 5-1 on the road, and without his first-line players. "Eddie Shore, Capt. Fred Hitchman, Harry Oliver and Percy Galbraith, the quartet which has seen more action than the other players on the Bruins' squad, will not play in Detroit tonight. Hitch will accompany the team in the capacity of manager as Art Ross was called to New York on other business. It has been thought best to rest the four Bruins for the playoff which starts Tuesday, although all these players will get a warming up against Pittsburgh here Saturday night."[14]

Before game 44 in Pittsburgh, "a delegation of Boston hockey fans presented wrist watches to the Bruins."[15] One was also saved for former goalie Hal Winkler. Boston beat Pittsburgh 3-1, finishing the season in first place with 26 wins, 13 losses, and five ties. They finished five points ahead of the Rangers and 10 ahead of Detroit. On the Canadian side, the Canadiens emerged on top with 59 points for the O'Brien Cup, nine points ahead of the New York Americans and 12 ahead of Toronto.

Double-digit point-getters for Boston were Harry Oliver (23), Dutch Gainor (19), Eddie Shore (19), Cooney Weiland (18), Dit Clapper (11) and Mickey MacKay (10). George Owen and Bill Carson, both with nine points, followed closely. Hitch ranked with spares Myles Lane and Lloyd Klein for one point—on the surface underwhelming, but Hitch was the one who quietly did his job so that goalie Tiny Thompson could earn the most wins in the league and Eddie Shore could become the top defensive point-getter with 12 goals and 7 assists. In Brian McFarlane's *The Bruins*, Tiny Thompson is quoted as saying, "Without Hitch it would have been a different story."[16]

Shore was fourth in the league in penalty minutes, but his total of only 98 minutes was a vast improvement over previous years. The top three "bad men" were the Maroons' Red Dutton (141 penalties in minutes), the Americans' Lionel Conacher (136 PIM) and the Maroons' Hooley Smith (124 PIM). Hitch ranked 21st with 64 PIM.

Playoffs

Hitch's value as Boston's "first money player" was cast long before the 1928-29 season, and for this playoff series, he did not disappoint. Game one of the Stanley Cup semifinal for the Boston Bruins and the Montreal Canadiens took place in Boston on March 19. The next day, the headline on page one of the *Boston Globe* read:

BRUINS CAPTURE THE FIRST GAME
Weiland's Shot from Pass By Hitchman Wins 1-0
Canadiens Outplayed Before 15,000 Shouting Fans

John J. Hallahan, the paper's sports editor, continued: "The Bruins scored first blood in the opening game of the playoff series with the Canadiens for the Stanley Cup last night at the Boston Garden. When little Cooney Weiland picked up a pass from Capt Fred Hitchman and drove home a winning shot from an angle, after the first 7 minutes 20 seconds of play. It proved to be a successful one for the Bruins and carried with it the game, score 1 to 0." Hallahan added this of Hitch on page 13: "When one speaks of stellar performances one must include Capt Hitchman. Always a great money player, he excelled in all departments of the game. He bodied with a vengeance. 'Hitch' played the best game he has shown this season."

Page one of the *Boston Herald* on March 20, 1929, carried the following headline, and Stanley Woodward's article began as follows:

BOSTON CAPTAIN ALL-AROUND STAR
15,000 CAPACITY CROWD SEES HOME TEAM TAKE LEAD IN TOP PLAY-OFF
Capt. Lionel Hitchman, always at his best when the stakes were highest and the going hardest made the scoring play, and the gigantic crowd shouted and roared with such tremendous volume, and pertinacity that the referee's whistles could not be heard for several minutes.

Hitch swooped up from his defence position to pick up the puck in the centre zone. He cut loose a burst of speed and passed to Weiland at the left at the French defence. Cooney took it on the blade, coasted in and picked the far side of the cage with a shot which left the exemplary George Hainsworth standing glued to the far post and impotent.

Every Bruin, not forgetting Cecil 'Tiny' Thompson, the goaler, played his part to the full. If however, it were necessary to pick out a man who stood out above the rest, it would have to be Hitch. He was titan of the defence and a ripper in the attack. It was he who, with well-known 'money' instincts swooped in to make the play that won the game. Likewise it was he who thumped a dozen dangerous attacks into oblivion.

Woodward's article continued on page 35:

Capt. Lionel Hitchman, one of the greatest "money" players in the history of hockey, was a giant in the attack and on defence, with the rest of the Bruin cast coming well up to standard. . . . Hitchman continued to stand out in all departments and his covering around the net and his body blocking was superb. He dumped Mantha so hard behind the net that Sylvio called for help.

THE WINNING GOAL. Boston Herald, *March 20, 1929, page 35.*

Woodward also let it be known that "Fifteen thousand persons saw Tuesday's game yet when Capt. Lionel Hitchman accidentally shot into the crowd he hit his own father on the chin, fortunately without dire results."[17]

Another writer at the *Boston Herald*, W.E. Mullins, also wrote about Hitch's money instincts: "We nominate Lionel Hitchman as one of the 'than-whomers' in the distinguished list of 'money' players. Hitch drove to the Garden in a shining new chariot painted gaily in green and yellow with wire wheels."[18] (I wonder if this writer knew that Hitch had won this car from Art Ross in a poker game.)

The newspaper with the largest circulation, the *Boston Post*, offered the following by sports editor J.W. Mooney:

[Weiland] was helped by Captain Hitchman, the well-known money player, who is all-star stock any time he fits into a World's Series. Hitch the popular, dug the disc away from Howie Morenz in the centre zone, legged it to the points and passed to Cooney steaming up on the left lane. The lad in his clever manner completed the play, swung Leduc on the defence, let go a sharp angle shot to the tight further corner and whizzed it past Hainsworth for the only score of the game. It seems the cheers for that goal are still echoing. . . .

Always in Melee

Captain Hitchman was a working wonder. He popped up everywhere, smashed up the attack and handed out a severe and bruising bumping game. Early in the period he was just nosed out of reaching his own rebound by Hainsworth himself.[19]

A. Linde Fowler, sports editor for the *Boston Evening Transcript*, added:

Hitchman, once again the "money player," as he showed all through the game, broke away down the centre lane.

Little Cooney Weiland was on the ice at this time and, never hesitant at any time as to where he belongs in a play, he quickly linked up with Hitchman, skating swiftly down the left lane, ready for a pass.

Not until he had the defense concentrated on him did Hitchman pass and then his job was perfectly done. Directly on Weiland's blade the puck landed and, unimpeded, he coasted fairly well in before he put all his power behind an angle shot that lodged the rubber in a twinkling into the right corner of the net. Even if you weren't at the game, but were anywhere this side of Providence, you must have heard the yell that this play evoked.[20]

The tone was set: Captain Lionel Hitchman was on the job and wanted another Stanley Cup. Game two went much the same as the first with a 1-0 win for Boston on the goal by Weiland, this time off of Gainor's rebound. The *Boston Herald* reported that both goaltenders "played brilliantly" and Shore and Hitch were "Boston bulwarks." Hallahan's article in the *Boston Globe* stated, "Shore was again chased for tripping Morenz, and Hitchman made a great check when he went down on one knee for Mondu's dribble, and Hitch followed it up by making a good rush down the left line and giving Hainsworth a difficult one-hand stop to make."[21]

The *Boston Post* added:

Hitchman was the man of the hour on many occasions with his long sweep checks, breaking up two and three-man combinations.

Beside that, Hitchman was getting in for dangerous close shots.

When Patterson came back the Bruins were a man shy in comparison. Patterson took the right lane and was ready to pass to Morenz in center when Hitchman snatched for a sweep check to save a delicate situation.[22]

Game three moved north to Montreal, with Boston winning 3-2 on Shore's goal. The *Montreal Herald*'s Elmer Ferguson reported that "Lionel Hitchman who, with forehead plastered to cover a long cut, played a really heroic game on the Boston defence." He further summarized the play:

> It was a herculean struggle, this final game, into which most of the thrills of hockey were written. The packed house saw Canadiens, at top speed sweep into a two-goal lead as they launched a dazzling attack in the first period. Then they saw the team weaken, stop to a walk under the sheer weight and manpower of the sturdy Boston crew, yield three goals with a suddenness that stunned the crowd, and through the last period, saw Boston employ a wide range of defensive tactics that included the dexterous play of Weiland in the centre ice area; the sweeping hook-checks of the rangy Hitchman; the hard body-checking and the clever stick-manipulation of Shore as he raced around in circles defying his opponents to take possession, and, finally, the ancient but effective method of tossing the puck down the length of the ice.
>
> In the first period, when Bruins were two down, they staged a desperate offensive in the closing stages, playing four men up in Canadien territory, Shore being prominent. This came near to resulting disastrously, for Mantha broke away with the puck and had only Hitchman to beat. Hitchman timed the rush nicely, threw himself flat and hooked the puck away with a long poke-check, this averting a third Canadien goal.[23]

To put the enormity of this feat of making it to the Stanley Cup final in terms that Bostonians would understand, the *Boston Globe* (March 25, 1929) offered: "Boston's honor roll in sports now contains the names of three hockey defense players—Shore, Hitchman and Thompson—to stand beside those of Hooper,

Speaker and Lewis, Red Sox immortals on the diamond, and some of the earlier outfield combinations."[24]

Boston Record sports editor Peter F. Kelley wrote from Montreal that "the Bruins slept in their special car, Bienville, at the Windsor station of the Canadian Pacific Railroad, Saturday night. Capt. Lionel Hitchman's father who was in Boston for the games and here for Saturday night's game, voiced the sentiment of all when he declared the worst is over." Kelley further reported that each player would receive a "big diamond ring" and $1,000 for beating the Canadiens and likely would receive another thousand for the Cup final as part of the league playoff pool.[25]

The Bruins arrived home from Montreal at 7:30 p.m. on Sunday, March 24, to a cheering crowd of 3,000 at the North Station. Every player was cheered, the loudest for fan favorite Shore. John J. Hallahan of the *Boston Globe* added "There was not a man who was forgotten, and Capt Hitchman, with his forehead and nose covered with plaster, also was given a reception he long will remember. He was accompanied by Mrs. Hitchman." The *Globe* further commented that "only the Olympic athletes of 1896 and World Series baseball champions have been accorded such a tribute." Stanley Woodward of the *Herald* added that the players wore "broad smiles and a few miscellaneous scars of battle. The most notable dent inflicted during the game is in the countenance of F. Lionel Hitchman of Belmont, who took the butt-end of Albert Leduc's stick over the right eye and across the bridge of his nose. It was what is known as a 'three-stitcher.'"[26]

The team now waited for either the New York Rangers or the Toronto Maple Leafs to emerge as the winner of the other semifinal. The first game of the Stanley Cup final took place on March 28 in Boston with Tiny Thompson's brother Paul at left wing, and Hitch's teammate from his Toronto Aura Lee days, John Ross Roach, in goals for the Rangers.

Ottawa boy, who teams up on the Boston defence with Eddie Shore, is playing the best game of his career this season. "Hitch" was a big factor in the Bruins' victory over Canadiens. He will be on the job against N. Y. Rangers tonight.

Boston Record, *March 28, 1929.*

And Hitch was on the job. Boston won 2-0 on goals by Clapper and Gainor. John J. Hallahan, of the *Boston Globe,* commented: "The heroes of the game were Dit Clapper, Dutch Gainor, Tiny Thompson and Hitchman. Hitchman took keen delight in bumping the 'Horsemen' almost out of the Garden. The play of the Rangers, especially their passing, was broken up, and as a result about 50 percent of their attack was smashed." George MaGuire of the Canadian Press added: "In addition to Gainor and Clapper, there were two other outstanding stars on the Bruin line-up. They were Ralph 'Cooney' Weiland and Hitchman. These two did yeoman service with their clever poke checking and a big percentage of the Ranger attacks were turned back by their timely checking."[27]

Harry Oliver scored first, and Bill Carson got the winning goal in Boston's 2-1 defeat of New York in game two, clinching the world title and Stanley Cup. The Associated Press offered: "A strong, well-balanced team with a really great defense told the tale for the Bruins against the Rangers." The Canadian Press provided further comment on the two American teams vying for the coveted "Canadian" title:

> The contest was exceptionally rugged though fairly clean. Only nine penalties were imposed for slight offences.
>
> Boston had a clear margin in territorial play and their defence also appeared stronger than that of their opponents. Roach was called upon to make 35 saves many of them from close-in shots, while Thompson at the other end played 32 safely, but many of these were from long range.
>
> The game was a fitting climax to one of the greatest, if not the greatest season the National Hockey League has had since its inauguration, and the best team in the league undoubtedly won the league championship and the Stanley Cup. Out of eight games between the two teams this season, Boston has won seven of them. The Bruins had also taken the measure of Montreal Canadiens, Canadian group winners, in three straight games in the inter-group play-off.[28]

Ed Baker, sports editor for the *Ottawa Citizen*, wrote:

> Manager Ross was in possession of one of the most powerful teams that ever went through a National Hockey League season. He had a surplus of players, any one of whom could be called a star and they worked in perfect harmony with the hockey championship of the world as their goal and they won it.
>
> Local hockey enthusiasts may, in a measure, share the joy in the Stanley Cup victory of the Boston hockey team

as Lionel Hitchman, star defence player with the Bruins and the team's captain, is an Ottawa boy and former member of the Senators, who won the Stanley Cup in 1923 in Vancouver.[29]

The official team photo of the 1929 Stanley Cup winners. (Photo courtesy of Hitchman private collection.)

A Night of "Gold and Praise"

The Bruins wrapped up their season of winning on April 2, 1929, at the Copley Plaza hotel at a banquet to celebrate the team. The Swiss room was decorated with two regulation-size hockey nets filled with flowers. Each team member, including trainer "Win" Greene, received $500 in gold for winning the Stanley Cup, in addition to the playoff splits and $35,000 team bonuses that were divvied up according to contracts. Ross spoke to team unity as the key for winning: "There has never been a professional team where there has been less bickering, fewer jealousies, and better spirit. All season long that has been the case." Historian Brian McFarlane stated that Ross gave special mention to Hitch in creating this team environment, calling him "a cornerstone of the franchise."[30]

Each player was showered with praise by Ross for their dedication and expediency in winning the Stanley Cup. President

Adams, half-joking, commented that maybe the team was too expedient winning in straight games, costing the club "perhaps $60,000." The players also offered gifts to President Adams, a bronze bruin and the winning puck of the final game, mounted on silver. Art Ross received a set of golf clubs. To close out the night, "Capt. Hitchman, the lion-hearted man of hockey, was right in his element last night, doing the honors that attached to his position. His father is as much a hockey enthusiast as son is a player and when he got the news that the Bruins had won the decisive game, father sat down and parodied William Shakespeare's Henry the Fifth, sending the result to Captain Hitchman as follows:

A Bruin:
   Oh that we now had here some of our castoffs, – Freddy, or Jimmy or Harry or –

Enter King Ross:
   What's he that wishes so.
   No, if we are marked to lose, we are enough.
   And if to win, the fewer men the greater share of honor.
   I pray thee wish not one man more.
   Rather proclaim it that he which have no stomach for the fight, let him depart. We would not lose in that man's company.
   He that outlive this game and come safe through will yearly on the vigil feast his company and show his scars and say, "These wounds I had the night we won the Stanley Cup," Old men forget; yet all shall be forgot. But he'll remember what feats he did that night.
   Then shall our names familiar in his mouth as household words – Hitch, the skipper; Eddie and Tiny, Perk, Dutch and Cooney, Doc and Mickey, Harry and Dit, George, Myles and Cy, and Baby Klein – be in their flowing cups freshly remembered.

We few, we happy few, we band of brothers, and those not with us now will be kicking themselves all over the lot.[31]

And with that the team disbanded for another season, most leaving for Canada the next day. Hitch was staying in Boston, and he, Oliver, Gainor, Owen, and Lane hightailed it over to the Keith-Albee Theatre for the midnight show.[32]

Chapter Eleven

GREATEST TEAM, GREATEST DEFENSEMAN

Structurally there were no changes to the 1929-30 NHL season over the previous one. The same 10 teams played 44 regular-season games, and the playoff scheme remained unchanged. However, some key rule changes affected the play of the game and individual player points.

If a goalie held a puck for more than three seconds, a face-off would be called for in front of that goalie's net. Forward passing, kicking and dragging the puck would be permitted in all three zones, compared with the previous season where it was allowed only in the defensive and neutral zones. Players were now permitted to enter the offensive zone ahead of the puck. This last rule was reversed in late December 1929.

The other change related to assists. Both first and second passes before a goal would now count toward a player's points, resulting in a steep increase in the number of points available compared with previous years. For example, Frank Boucher, center for the New York Rangers, led in assists in both the 1928-29 and 1929-30 seasons with 16 and 36, respectively (and he played two fewer games in 1929-30).

The Bruins' Stanley Cup team remained mostly intact. One vital addition was Martin Barry, center, drafted from New Haven of the Canadian-American League.

Boston had a record-breaking year with 38 wins, five losses, and one tie, for 77 points, a full 30 points ahead of the second-place Chicago Black Hawks in the American Division and 26 points ahead of the Canadian Division leader, the Montreal Maroons. This record earned Boston a .875 points percentage, still a record as of the 2017-18 season and likely never to be broken.

To properly compare this season's team, it should be done against those who played 44-game seasons. But to look at the profound success of the 1929-30 Boston Bruins, let's also consider all NHL seasons:[1]

1929-30 Boston Records (in 44 Games)	Previous Record by a 44-Game Team	First Team to Best the 1929-30 Boston Record
Points percentage: .875	Ottawa, .727 in 1926-27	Unbroken in 88 years (as of 2018)
Total points: 77 out of a possible 88	Ottawa, 64 points in 1926-27	Canadiens, 78 points out of a total possible 120 in 1946-47
Most wins: 38 out of a possible 44	Ottawa, 30 wins in 1926-27	Canadiens tied the record in 1943-44 in a 50-game season, then beat it with 39 wins in a 70-game season in 1958-59
Successive home victories: 20	New record	Matched by the 1975-76 Philadelphia Flyers and finally surpassed on February 14, 2012, by the 2011-12 Detroit Red Wings
Lowest number of games lost in one season: 5	Ottawa, 8 in 1926-27	Never beaten by teams that played 44 games or more; tied only once, by the Canadiens in 1943-44 in a 50-game season
Longest winning streak in one season: 14	Canadiens, 11 in 1926-27	New York Islanders, 15 wins in 1981-82 in an 80-game season
Best average goals per game: 4.07	Boston, 3.23 in 1928-29	Scoring increased during the early 1940s, widely attributed to the depleted talent during WWII. Boston's record was finally beaten in 1943-44 by four of the six league teams. That season, the center red line and passing out of the defensive zone was introduced, designed to reduce offsides and speed up play.
No losses in Canada	New record	Unbroken as of 2018

The Dynamite Line of Cooney Weiland, Dit Clapper, and Dutch Gainor had their finest season to date. Cooney was first in overall points for the league, and Dit and Dutch placed third and ninth, respectively. Cooney was first in total goals (43), followed by Dit (41) in second place. Dutch was second to Frank Boucher in league assists with 31, and Cooney tied with the Rangers' Bill Cook for third (30).

Eddie Shore scored 31 points, second place for defensemen. King Clancy of Ottawa was first with 40 points. Shore played 42 games and was second overall in penalty minutes with 109. George Owen also played 42 games and finished the season with 13 points (31 PIM); in 39 games, Hitch had nine points and 58 PIM.

Tiny Thompson ranked first for goalies with a 2.19 goals-against average and was awarded the Vezina Trophy.

After starring in the 1928-29 Stanley Cup championship, Hitch either had his best season to date in 1929-30, or else his contribution to the Boston Bruins was just now being fully realized. As one reporter noted, there were no stats kept on the things Hitch did better than anyone else in the league: He took the puck off incoming opponents with his sweep- or poke-checks and safely passed it to his forward line, he directed the play of his team from his defensive post, and he forcefully, but cleanly, body-checked opponents to destabilize their offensive plays. Colonel John Hammond, president of the New York Rangers, commented to syndicated writer Walter Trumbull in December 1929 that "Hitchman is the hardest man to get around, the greatest checker, and the greatest blocker in the game."[2]

While some pundits lauded Hitchman and Eddie Shore as the "best pair of defense men in either section" and as the main reason for Boston's "running away with the American division,"[3] others compared the relative worth of these two players when assessing Boston's success. It didn't help that Shore's behavior at times seemed unhinged and that his best self didn't show up for the Stanley Cup final.

It was a heady time for the team. They were busting through all previous records. Hitch did his best to steady the team, to keep them down to earth, while others told them the sun and moon revolved around them. The *Boston Transcript*'s A. Linde Fowler reported:

> When some of us went into their dressing room in the Montreal Forum after the game, to congratulate them on establishing a new record, they were a pleased lot of athletes without being what might be termed exultant.
>
> "Didn't you get a real thrill over winning that game, especially against the Maroons, and creating a new record?" I asked Hitchman. The elongated defense man, imperturbable off the ice as he is on it, rejoined: "Thrill? Why, man, we've only just started. Wait till we've put it up to thirty straight, then we'll have something to talk about."[4]

The Greatest Season in More Detail

Hitch got into the scoring mode in game two for Boston's 6-5 win in Toronto against the Maple Leafs on November 16, 1929. Last season this didn't happen until game 40.

In game four, the team was in Montreal to face the Maroons and came from behind twice to beat them 4-3. Both Harry Oliver and George Owen were absent: Oliver with a bad case of the "grippe" (flu) and Owen so he could provide analysis for the *Boston Globe* at the Harvard–Yale football game. Hitch played the entire game, with Baz O'Meara of the *Montreal Star* noting that "Hitchman swept the ice with his encircling stick with telling effect."[5]

Shore played an outstanding game until he received a high stick across the face from Babe Siebert and went off in the final minutes of the third period. He was replaced by Percy Galbraith, who held his own, and the Maroons did not get any more goals. It was a rough game, and Elmer Ferguson of the *Montreal Herald* described the action directed at Shore: "Maroons beaten by an even better and more powerful hockey crew than that which won the world's title last spring, hacked, battered and smashed at Shore, until he was finally forced to stagger off the ice, bathed in blood, with a two-inch gash over his left eye-brow, another rip on his right cheek-bone, a broken nose which was spouting a crimson geyser, and three teeth left on the ice in a pool of gore that had to be literally shovelled away by the ice-scrapers." Ferguson's colorful description seemed to work up the scribes of Boston and afforded Art Ross an opportunity for some great press in advance of the team's hosting the Maroons in the next game. But some staid reporters in Canada weren't buying it:

> Down in dear old Boston, where they still recall the immortal Tea Party and think that the Battle of Bunker Hill was one of the outstanding military achievements of history, they are beginning to emit the loud and raucous squawk. It all occurs over the treatment accorded Eddie Shore, the idol of the gods and more of a popular hero than Mayor Curley. Edward was treated rather roughly at Montreal on Saturday by none other than Babe Siebert....
>
> Along came Art Ross, the chief referee baiter of pro hockey, with the statement that the hockey displayed by Maroons was a crime, that Boston players were badly battered but undaunted and Bruins were ready to give Maroons a real battle in Boston tonight. All of which means that standing room will be at a premium tonight in Boston Arena.[6]

While the Boston press got all worked up over the treatment of Shore in game four, they failed to notice other parts of Ferguson's article on that game:

> Blood flowed early in this battle, the most sanguinary since the memorable March night at the Mt. Royal Arena when Sprague Cleghorn laid out Hitchman, and Billy Coutu gave "the works" to Cy Denneny, the Canadien club then taking the law into its own hands by suspending both its offending players. Oddly enough it was Hitchman again who was the first butt for attack on Saturday night. Early in the play, a

flying Maroon stick nicked Hitchman over the left eye, bringing a stream of blood, but the battle-scarred Boston captain never left his post.[7]

Shore didn't play in game five, the return game against the Maroons three days later in Boston, smartly resting after the previous battle in Montreal. The Bruins lost 6-1, and Boston reporters declared the result of this game proof of Shore's worth to the team. It should be noted that Oliver was still out with the flu and had passed it on to some of the other players, who did not play well that game. In addition, as A. Linde Fowler, *Boston Transcript*, explained, Hitch was weakened by a "cut over one eye which he sustained in Montreal and a cut on one leg, but these were not so handicapping as a blow on the ribs be received during last night's game, which was responsible for his sitting on the sidelines some of the time."[8]

The Bruins bounced back in the next game with a 6-2 win over the Pittsburgh Pirates. Harry Oliver and Cooney Weiland led the scoring with two apiece. Mickey MacKay got a major penalty for fighting. Hitch got a black eye attempting to keep the Pirates player from retaliating against Mackay and "apparently realized the wrought-up condition of the Pittsburgher and laughed it off."[9]

In game 11, American Division leader Boston met Canadian Division leader Ottawa on their home ice. The *Ottawa Journal* reported that more than 8,000 Ottawa fans watched the 2-2 deadlocked game as "Eddie Shore tossed the dynamite into Ottawas' chances in the third period when he scored on a perfectly timed pass by Hitchman . . . a well thought-out play on the part of Hitchman, who went straight for the Ottawa defence, brought over two defence men to him and whipped the disc to Shore, who sent it whizzing high into the left corner." The *Journal* also commented that Tiny Thompson was the hero of the game, stopping 42 shots compared with Ottawa goalie Alex Connell's 19 stops. The *Journal* continued, "Hitchman was very effective, in fact about the most effective man on the Boston team." Ed Baker, sports editor for the *Ottawa Citizen*, added: "From a purely defensive point of view, however, Lionel

Hitchman proved that if he is not the best in the league—he is surely the best that has shown here this season."[10]

The Bruins saw Ottawa again in Boston on December 17 for game 13, beating them soundly 6-2 with goals from Clapper (2), Barry (2), Carson and Gainor. The game was marked by some rough play and fine acting by Eddie Shore. In the second period:

> Shore was knocked cold as he mussed Clancy and landed on the ice. He was able to continue, however. This was the signal for some bumping, and war waged. Hitchman knocked down Finnigan with a hard body check.
>
> As the Ottawan lay on the ice, Weiland, picking up the puck, raced down the middle and passed to Clapper, the rush being finished as Finnigan was on the ice, Clapper scoring.
>
> Bedlam broke loose, the spectators going wild as the players used the wood. Finally Weiland and Lamb became embroiled in an argument, Lamb was chased for two minutes for tripping, and the popular "Cooney" was given a major penalty calling for five minutes. Eddie Shore jumped out of the players' box to engage in the discussion, for which he was fined $25.
>
> The Bruins showed a stubborn defense, as they were playing with men shy almost throughout.[11]

This was the last game before the new rule went into effect on December 21 "prohibiting a player from advancing into the scoring area ahead of a puck carrier who has not crossed the blue line."[12] After this game, Boston led the American Division with 22 points (11 wins and two losses). Chicago was next with 16 points and the New York Rangers with 15. In the Canadian Division, the Canadiens led with 17 points, followed closely by the Maroons with 15 and Ottawa with 14.

John J. Hallahan of the *Boston Globe* reported that Hitch "starred" in the next game against the second-place Chicago Black Hawks, with Boston winning 4-1. "He played better than at any time this season, his sweeping stick and poke-checks halting the fleet Hawks." Shore set a new record of six penalties in the game. Hallahan added the next day:

> However, the Blackhawks must be watched, for they are not afraid to tear loose. But they found the stubborn defensive tactics of the Bruins something that could not be easily overcome. And talking of defensive play, Lionel Hitchman, who captains the Bruins, when he is physically fit stands up there, takes his bumps and gives them, but his greatest assets are his sweep and poke checks.
>
> He was very close to being at his best Saturday night, and he did more to break up the speed and passing game of the Hawks than any other player.[13]

The Bruins' last game of 1929 was played on Saturday, December 28, in Montreal against the Canadiens, who were still in first place in the Canadian Division, now one point ahead of the Maroons. It was game 17, and Boston came into the game with nine consecutive wins. On Monday, the headline of Elmer Ferguson's article in the *Montreal Herald* read: "Bruin Machine Smothers Canadien Speed As Champs Win Their Tenth Straight." Boston won 3-2. Hitch assisted on the first goal, but more importantly, he kept the Canadiens out of the Boston zone. Ferguson wrote: "Hitchman carried the brunt of the defensive load, his sweeping hook-check breaking up the loosely-organized Canadien attacks, or forcing them to the corners. He gave a much better display on the night than did Shore."[14]

The Bruins rang in the new year with their 11th consecutive win, beating the New York Americans 5-1 in Boston on January 1, 1930. They equaled the record set by the Montreal Canadiens in the 1926-27 NHL season. J.W. Mooney of the *Boston Post* reported that "Hitchman broke up many attacks with his long flat stick and recovered to be a real threat in the attack."[15]

The Bruins left for Montreal on January 3rd to set new NHL record. Boston Herald, January 4, 1930, page 17.

In the next game in Montreal against the Maroons, Boston won 4-2, setting a new record of 12 consecutive wins. The *Montreal Star* reported on January 6: "The spotlight almost forgot Eddie Shore was on the ice. It shifted around the angular form of Lionel Hitchman most of the time. Hitch turned in a great effort—one of his best on Montreal ice. He seemed to anticipate every move of the Maroons and was always in the right place at the right time. No better testimonial can be given to a hockey player."[16]

The streak reached 13 wins after Boston beat the New York Rangers on January 7.

An article by Ross Cameron of the *Winnipeg Tribune* on January 9 gave an explanation for Boston's success. "Figures generally tell the tale straight. The most recent issue of the National Hockey League scoring reveals three Boston Bruins high up the list. They are Weiland, Gainor and Clapper. To this fact add that in Hitchman and Shore, Art Ross' clan has the best pair of defense men in either section, and its not difficult to understand why the Bruins are running away with the American division and are favored to win the Stanley Cup again."[17]

The streak continued. The team's 14th consecutive win came in game 21 in Pittsburgh.

Henry J. Disken, a Montrealer writing for the *Boston Advertiser*, wrote a 760-word article on Hitch's defensive skills on January 10, 1930, with quotes from Canadiens star Aurel Joliat:

> Joliat
> CANADA STAR SAYS HARD TO PASS HUB ACE
> Hitchman Enjoying Greatest Year of Career at 27 Years of Age
> MASTER OF DEFENSE
> Fans Fail to Notice Real Ability of Defensive Stars While Watching Progress of Play
>
> "When Les Canadiens play the Boston Bruins, I keep away from that fellow Hitchman," says Aurel Joliat. "That long stick of his can break up any play and I don't go down on his side if I can help it."
>
> Coming from Joliat, the brainy little "mite" who fears nothing in a game and can skate and stick-handle his way through the best in the league, this opinion of Hitchman gives us a real line on the value of the big fellow that is contributing more to the success of the Bruins than the fans are giving him credit for.
>
> Art Ross and his players realize the real worth of Hitchman. He is not spectacular, and the thrills that Shore, Mantha, Johnson and King Clancy give are missing. "Hitch" does not rank offensively with these great stars, nor has he their goal-getting ability, but he more than evens matters on the defensive play.
>
> Hitchman is the hardest man to break through in the National Hockey League. He wields a wicked stick that can stop the best stars in the game. The way he is going this season it is almost an impossibility to score on his side, and

the opposing players are beginning to give him a wide berth.

HITCHMAN A MASTER

In rating the value of a defense player, hockey records, as compiled by the league, are deceiving. We can get the number of goals scored by a player, his assists and penalties, but there is no way in which we can look back and study his effectiveness in his position.

It is only by watching his play and system, check up on his saves, noticing the dangerous formations and splendid team plays he breaks up that his real worth is brought out.

Hitchman is a master in his position and he has brains enough to stay "put." The Bruins have three great front lines and with Weiland, Barry, Oliver and practically every other forward socking in the counters, the defense players can well afford to lay back in their positions and knock off the goals that might be scored against them.

Penalties take away value. There is a mistaken idea that the players with heavy penalty records are deliberately bad men and are trying to rough up the other players and cause serious injuries.

FEW REAL BAD MEN

There are a few in the game, very few, that run amuck and don't care what injury they inflict, but the game will weed them out within the next few years.

There are other players with bad penalty records that have no deliberate motive other than to stop a player with no thought of causing him an injury. Shore, Clancy and Ching Johnson are of this type. They are tough and when they step into a player the crash looks bad, but I have failed to see any players carried off on stretcher.

Players like Hitchman and Mantha and Herb Gardiner are masters. They play their position with greater science, and the result is their penalties are not so great.

Such players have a great poke check and a wonderful sense of distance. They can lay back in their position and figure out the play as it swings toward them. A swing of the stick and they have the puck or the dangerous looking play is tucked safely away in a far corner.

DON'T STUDY SCIENCE

The science of defense is not studied by the fans as well as it might be. Much color is lost sight of in the thrills we get watching the forwards sweep down the ice. We cheer the beautiful team work and marvelous passing of the puck, then lose the play in the jumble of the defense, failing to realize that the clever, and planned play was broken by a defense that had proved that much greater.

Defensively, Hitchman is one of the great stars of hockey, rating second to no other player in the game. At 27, he is at the best years of his life and this season has reached the peak of his form.

He has many years ahead of him and will be starring when many others have passed out. The Bruins are lucky they have him and knowing his real value the Bruins and Ross will make sure that they hang onto him.[18]

The streak ended the next game with a 3-2 loss to the New York Americans. They came back strong in game 23 in Boston against the Ottawa Senators with a 5-1 victory on January 14. Ed Baker of the *Ottawa Citizen* commented on the article about Hitch by Henry Disken: "Henry may, or may not, know much about hockey players, but in the writer's opinion he hasn't overrated Hitchman. The long fellow may not score as many goals as some of the other defence stars–may not be as flashy as Shore or as good an actor, but as a guard against goals, he is a powerful aid to the Boston team."[19]

Chicago was the only team to beat Boston twice. In this third attempt in game 26 at the Boston Garden on January 21 in front of 15,000 fans, Boston defeated them 5-1 in a rousing performance, the game closer than the final score indicated. J.W. Mooney, *Boston Post*, wrote:

Any expecting to see Manager Art Ross' sensations outplayed by a group whom many considered were the Bruins jinx must have been pleasantly surprised to be on hand on a night when the Boston club was playing whirlwind hockey, when speed and aggressiveness was second nature to them, when the tremendous Eddie Shore was offering an exhibition that might recall the best he had ever given, when the sterling leader Captain Hitchman, was even craftier than usual, when all down the Bruin list, each man played as though inspired to settle once and for all the question as to whether or not the Hawks were to be the nemesis of the Bruins for the rest of the season, even perhaps through the playoffs.[20]

A. Linde Fowler, *Boston Transcript*, wrote that Hitch shined in the game against the Black Hawks:

What gave a large percentage of last night's spectators an extra "kick" out of a spirited game was the all around work of Frederick Lionel Hitchman. The tall defense man made himself solid with what Bruins fans there were from the night of his first appearance in a Boston uniform in the season of 1924-25 and in all intervening years he has had the much desired reputation of being a "money player."

He apparently decided that last night was the right time to go out and once more demonstrate that faculty, to teach the Hawks that a bear's cuff is more than a Hawk can stand. F. Lionel did about everything one man could do in one game. He was a raging lion, rather than a Bruin. He swept the puck off of opposing sticks in characteristic fashion; he dumped Hawks with stiff bodychecks that had behind them the unworded message, "when I say stop, you stop!"

Not content with slamming Hawks around in his own territory, he turned around and treated them similarly in their own back yard. He rushed much more than usual and had more speed. Once he nearly brushed off a couple of chandeliers as he climbed high on the shoulders of big Taffy Abel, trying to jump through or over the defence. His speed was such that on one occasion when he lost the puck he wheeled, chased back and stole the rubber away from the man who got it from him.

And then when he carried down for a shot, dashed in for his own rebound and slammed the disk home, what a wild burst of enthusiasm there was! The crowd simply let loose with all its batteries of approval. It was an ovation such as might be expected from a winning goal in a Stanley Cup series and it left F. Lionel in no uncertain frame of mind as to where he fits in the affection of the Boston hockey followers.[21]

The first time a writer referred to Hitch as an unsung hero seems to originate with the *Toronto Star Weekly*'s column The Falcon on January 25, 1930, about five players who didn't get the recognition they deserved, including Hitch. Elmer Ferguson picked up on the theme the next month, and for decades since, writers have used the phrase to describe Hitch's worth as a player. The Falcon wrote:

UNSUNG HEROES OF THE NATIONAL HOCKEY CIRCUIT
Better Than Shore
Passing on to Boston, we find another Toronto boy, Lionel Hitchman, playing excellent hockey in every game, although he is in a total eclipse to the highly touted Eddie Shore. Shore combines his hockey ability with extraordinary showmanship and then he is favored with being located in Boston, a city where they are given to hero worship more than in most others. Hitchman, following a knee injury, has given up most of his offensive work, specializing on keeping the puck away from his own end of the rink.

Personally I think that Boston could dispense with Shore more readily than with Hitchman. Last year Boston were hanging up a victory record going through the month of January without a defeat. When they came to Toronto Hitchman collided with Art Smith and had his knee injury aggravated, a few days later in the return game at Boston, Hitchman again tried to body check Smith but missed him with his body receiving the full weight of the Leaf behemoth across his dinky knee.

Hitchman retired to the side lines and with Owen as his partner, Shore was hard pressed to hold out the other clubs until the hard working ex-Mountie was able to return to his place on the defence.[22]

In game 28, without the services of Eddie Shore once more, this time because of an injured shoulder, Boston won 2-1 in Montreal against the Canadiens on January 25. Baz O'Meara of the *Montreal Star* wrote: "To win without Shore was a great achievement, and it will have its effect undoubtedly on that temperamental star. In his absence Hitchman rose to singular height of efficiency, and there was a spirit of co-operation that nullified the effect of the 'great ones' absence. That grin of Hitchman's is tantalizing but even his worst enemy must admit he is one of the gamest lads wielding a stick today." Elmer Ferguson of the *Montreal Herald* added: "Once while Hitchman, the Bruin defensive mainstay was off, play for the whole two minutes surged right around the Bruins nets, with only such let-ups as came when some frantic Boston player hurled the puck the length of the rink. The game proved that Bruins can win a hockey game without Eddie Shore. Hitchman performed in his usual splendid style, this long and lanky chap being one of the greatest real defence players in the game, and the sturdy Owen turned in a steady, useful game."[23]

With Shore still off in the next game in Boston against the Pittsburgh Pirates, Boston won 6-0 on January 28. Stanley Woodward, the *Boston Herald*, commented: "By this time opponents of the Bruins should be pretty tired of trying to get by F. Lionel Hitchman. It is almost as futile as throwing billiard balls at the moon. Hitch is the only player who puts his stick flat on the ice when he checks. Thus he hooks in several hundred well-meant and well-directed passes in a season. He stands out in the modern forward-passing game. If he missed with the body the opposition still has to deal with his sensitive stick."[24]

Just after Boston's 3-3 tie with the Rangers in New York, future Hall of Famer Ching Johnson of that team sat down with John Kieran of the *New York Times* for an interview. When asked if he would pick Eddie Shore first on defense for an all-star team (not including players from his own team), Johnson replied: "I'd pick Hitchman first. You notice that Boston defence. Hitchman is the boy out in front who takes 'em first as you come in. He's the shock absorber. If he doesn't stop 'em, Shore gets 'em, but usually Hitchman has thrown them off balance, and that makes Eddie's work a lot easier."[25]

Boston won game 31 at home against the Detroit Cougars 3-1. Hitch assisted on the winning goal: "Weiland had been checked several times, but with the veteran Hitchman he finally got free. Hitch took a pass from Goalie Thompson, raced down the left side, and just before reaching the defense, passed to Cooney. The latter, with his clever back-hand flip, lifted the puck over Beveridge's left arm and inside the goal posts for the second goal." Trouble started in the second period when Shore started bumping rookie Rusty Hughes away from the puck. Hughes got frustrated and hit Shore, and he went off with a five-minute misconduct. At the end of the game, this spat morphed into a "free-for-all-fight." John J. Hallahan, of the *Boston Globe*, explains:

> Shore and Hughes had a battle, but they could not have it alone. It became a general affair, as the players tried to separate the men. Goodfellow held Shore off, and they became engaged in another fight. Not to be stopped, Referee Mallinson also tried to halt this pair, with the result Shore drove a straight right to the official's jaw.
>
> It was only when Manager Ross went out on the ice that Shore was held off and quieted.

A hurried call for the police went out as the players were mixing it up. Spectators tried to get into the fight, but were finally subdued, although one patron of the game claimed he was struck in the head by [Ebbie] Goodfellow's stick.

Loose officiating was responsible for the affair, as Shore's interference of Hughes was allowed to slip by without notice.[26]

The *Boston Globe* reported that two days after the game, Art Ross was "ordered to take a two weeks' vacation by Owner C. F. Adams. Ross was told to go where he pleases but not to return until the Boston–New York Rangers game [on Feb. 23]." The *Globe* added: "The manager will start for Montreal soon. While he is not ill, he is showing the effects of the strain of the long campaign. During his absence Capt Lionel Hitchman and Mickey MacKay will be in charge of the teams. They will handle the men in the long siege of five games in eight days which starts Tuesday night when the Bruins will play Toronto at the Garden."[27]

Ross and Shore were similar in many ways and fed off each other. As hockey players they played a similar style of game. Both thrived in the limelight. Ross may have been more calculating than Shore; he certainly was more restrained, the latter giving way to his immediate impulses. All the attention that Hitch had recently received likely did not go unnoticed by Shore, especially all the comparisons between the two. Shore was having a great year, but so was Hitch. The difference was that Hitch's skills, not easily tabulated on a leaderboard and skills he did better than Shore, were getting wide appreciation. Maybe this bothered Shore, maybe not. In any event the Bruins were two-thirds through a spectacular season and their flashy defense star was acting out. The team manager, either egging him on or incapable of controlling him, was sent away on stress leave by the club president.

The third game without Art Ross at the helm started a whole new cycle of articles focused on Hitch. It was game 34 in Toronto against the Maple Leafs. Boston won 5-3 on February 15 under the guidance of Hitch, who also played, and Mickey MacKay, who didn't. The coverage went as follows:

C.W. MacQueen, *Toronto Mail and Empire*: "Hitchman and Shore played the defence positions without relief and while Shore staged a number of speedy rushes, they were not as dangerous as those of his defence partner, who was much stronger defensively than Shore. The latter halted proceedings to get his drink of water as the Leafs were making a strong effort to knot the count after Boston had taken the lead."[28]

Toronto Telegraph:
One reads much ballyhoo about the great Mr. Shore when studying the history of the championship hockey team from Boston this winter, but a howling mob of enthusiasts at Andy Taylor's Arena Gardens Saturday night were ready to pin the "spark plug" honors on Lionel Hitchman as the mighty Bruins staged a four-goal rally during the final 11 minutes of play, handing Maple Leafs a 5-3 setback.

Enjoying himself in picking little pieces of dirt off the ice for the biggest part of the game, Captain Hitchman decided, as the third period was nearing the halfway mark, that it was about time to get going and add another win to the Bruins' lengthy list. The clever Lionel stole the puck from Jackson and skated down the unprotected left side. The official scorer recorded the goal that resulted as Barry scoring from Hitchman, but to the press box aggregation it looked as if Hitchman had counted with a burning drive from the left side.

Sensational work in Boston's goal by "Tiny" Thompson and Lionel Hitchman's effective bodychecking on the defence held the battling Leafs to a single goal in the second period.

Having sent George Owen home from Fort Erie with a bad charley-horse, Lionel Hitchman and Eddie Shore did nearly 60-minute service on the local defence. On two short occasions Clapper dropped back on the defence when

Shore wanted a rest. The "Great One" pulled all his Boston tricks, stopping the game for the water act and falling with that pained look when spilled, but it went over the heads of the local following who appreciate real hockey.

Hitchman directed every play from his position and made what rushes he did execute count for goals or near-goals. Shore was easy to skate around, Jackson proving as he fooled the Bruin star with a perfect shift.[29]

Baz O'Meara, *Montreal Star* (February 17, 1930): "As the club advances along there is revision of estimates among experts regarding the worth of members of the club. It mainly revolves around the showing of Hitchman whose play is taking some of the sheen off Shore. He is being lauded as a better defence man, and his fighting qualities have been a tremendous factor in their play."[30]

Boston met the Montreal Maroons in the next game (#36) at home on February 18. Both teams were in first place in their respective divisions, Boston by 19 points and the Maroons by five. By this time Boston had already made the playoffs, the same for the Maroons, it just wasn't clear if they would retain first place, thus sidestepping two preliminary rounds before the final. Boston won 3-2, and the Maroons moved on to play the Americans in New York. And that is where Elmer Ferguson penned his 1,329-word "Mr. Hitchman, the Unsung Hero" article for the *Montreal Herald* on February 20, 1930:

MR. HITCHMAN, THE UNSUNG HERO.
NEW YORK, Feb. 20. – It is high time, it seems to your correspondent, that some one with a good strong voice did some singing on behalf of the hitherto unsung heroes of hockey.

They are a numerous race, these stars who are overlooked for many reasons. Sometimes it is because they are teamed up with colorful superstars who, while possibly less useful, have the dramatic instinct which forces them into the centre of the picture. Sometimes it is because their play is effective to a degree without being spectacular. Sometimes it is because they lack the magnetic athletic "It," and are great athletes in reality, but unnoticed.

So far as this writer is aware at the present time, his ballot this season in the voting to decide who shall win the Dr. Hart Trophy which goes to the player adjudged the most useful to his team in the National Hockey League will go to Mr. Lionel Hitchman, the long, angular and extremely efficient left defence player of the amazing Boston Bruins. Your correspondent is divided somewhat between the merits of Messrs. Hitchman and Duncan Munro, chubby pilot of the Montreal Maroons, who by the sheer force of his own fine personality, his diplomacy in the dressing room, and his sterling example on the ice, has brought the disrupted and dissension-torn team of last year into a fine, harmonious and powerful machine. But the Boston club having achieved such amazing records in the current campaign, it must be that the team possesses some amazing athletes. That is obvious, even to a hockey expert. And it seems to me that the most consistent, steady and durable Bruin performer is the cool-eyed, fearless and polished ex-Mounted Police, Mr. Hitchman.

With the discretion acquired by several years of contact with hockey, in public and private, your correspondent has carefully refrained from giving vent to these sentiments until having departed from environs of Boston. To mention any other hockey player as greater than Mr. Edward (Bam! Bam! Bammy!) Shore, in or near the City of the Sacred Codfish, would be considered as lese majeste, treason, or what have you, and the malefactor would be immediately rushed to Faneuil Hall to be condemned to death in boiling-oil, at least. The fans of Boston take their hockey very seriously indeed, and it is one of the tenets of Boston hockey fandom that the colorful Mr. Shore stands alone as a hockey player. Probably they are right, in many respects. Shore is a mighty athlete. He has everything, including color and a flaring personality, that any great athlete should possess. He is a dashing, spectacular, and glittering performer. And yet, your correspondent is of the opinion that Mr. Hitchman is even more useful, in the capacity of the steadying influence which has been a balance-wheel in the amazing successes of these amazing Bruins.

If Mr. Hitchman were with any other club than Boston, he would be acclaimed a super-star, for he is one of those unsung heroes of the whirlwind ice game. Hitchman's qualities are dimmed by the blazing light exuded from the vicinity of Mr. Shore, whose glamour, indeed, dims that of all the rest of this great crew.

The Hardest Player in the League to Pass.

But if you enquire of practically any hockey player he will tell you that the hardest player in the League to pass is not Mr. Shore, but Mr. Hitchman.

Shore may be, in fact he is, hard-hitting on defence and dynamic on the attack, but you might notice, if you happen to notice these things, that players undertaking an attack on the Boston nets generally swing to that sector of the ice guarded by Mr. Shore, in preference to that patrolled by the beetle-browed, hard-eyed Mr. Hitchman. The reason is obvious. They may pass Shore, they are unlikely to pass Hitchman. If attacking players skate too close to Mr. Hitchman, he hurls his hard, muscular and unyielding form into them with crashing and destructive force. Mr. Hitchman is built on the general lines of a string-bean, and at first glance gives the impression that in a hard collision he might possibly break in two. But contact with Mr. Hitchman's close-knit form has dispelled that idea for opposing athletes. Mr. Hitchman is not only solid, unyielding and of high courage, but he knows how to hit a fair, clean body-check with devastating force that has knocked all interest in subsequent proceedings on that night out of the body of many an ambitious athlete. Mr. Hitchman, indeed, hits a harder and more punishing body-check than does the robust Mr. Shore, and if you don't believe it, ask any of the athletes who have had a sample of both. The legality of his checking as compared to that of Mr. Shore is attested in the respective penalty-lists of the two players.

The body-check is not the only quality possessed by Mr. Hitchman. Of long and angular construction, he has developed the use of these physical assets to the highest point of efficiency. He carries a stick that comes right to the limit of the League regulations in point of length. Coasting about the blue line, able to sweep the ice with this far-reaching stick either on his right or left side, Hitchman constitutes a formidable menace to attacking forces. Fifty per cent of the attacks which veer to the left side of the Bruin defence founder on the Hitchman stick. The players sweep past the keen-eyed kneeling form, but most of the time, after the attack has torn by, Hitchman pulls his long figure out of the crouch, the puck nesting in the bend of his stick, and either passes it to one of his own teammates, or glides away on the attack himself. And Hitchman on the attack is no idle threat. He may lack the catapultic, charging and battering qualities of Shore, but he is a clever, cool stick-handler, and a menace when within range of the nets.

Hitchman's Stormy Introduction to Pro Hockey.

Hitchman broke into hockey in the most spectacular fashion. He was signed up by Ottawas in the spring of 1923, just before that team engaged in one of the most memorable of all play-offs with the Canadiens, and his introduction was a stormy one. In a stirring and rugged battle at Mount Royal Arena, Hitchman was the storm-centre of one of hockey's classic socking-sprees. The tall, black-haired gangling youngster, game in the face of a terrific ride, was finally walloped by Sprague Cleghorn, and knocked cold. Billy Coutu, enthused by the success of his team-mate thereupon walloped Cy Denneny, sniping Ottawa left wing, and wild scenes followed as the crowd rushed on the ice at the end, compelling referee Lou Marsh to fight his way off. Canadiens, in sporting fashion suspended both Cleghorn and Coutu, and went into the final game without them, practically tossing off any chance they had of winning.

Hitchman was sold by Ottawas to Boston when that team first came into hockey. Naturally, the Ottawa owners didn't think much of Hitchman's chances of ever becoming a useful player, but he fooled them. Under the tutelage of the crafty and canny Art Ross, he developed into a superstar, and one of the greatest money players in the game. It was really Hitchman who beat Canadiens in the play-offs last spring. His crashing body-checks early in the play broke the Canadien attack, and his magnificent defensive completed what he started. It was the tearing play of Shore that brought Bruins from behind in the final game of that series, but it was the sound play of the battle-scarred fighting Hitchman, his face covered with plaster, but his heart still full of fight and courage, that really swung the issue.

Shore may be the dynamo of the Boston club, but Hitchman is its balance-wheel, and its steadying, sound influence—plus being the greatest defensive defence player in the game today.[31]

During Art Ross' absence, the team played five games in eight days, three on the road, winning all five under the direction of Mickey MacKay and Hitch. As planned, Ross returned to his post behind the Bruins bench in New York on February 23 for the game against the Rangers. During his furlough, instead of resting, he took a trip to the west coast to visit his friend Frank Patrick, who was now part-owner and president of the minor hockey Pacific Coast League, with teams from Vancouver, Victoria, Portland, Seattle, and Tacoma. While there he signed an amateur from Edmonton, Guy McNeil (who played one year for Boston's farm team, the Boston Cubs).[32]

Early March 1930. Gloria with Eddie Shore, Tiny Thompson and her Dad. (Source unknown.)

(There were many photos like this of Gloria and of other Bruins children.)

Ottawa was in Boston for game 39 on Saturday, March 1. The Bruins won 2-1 on a goal from Cooney Weiland late in the third period. There was an incident at the top of the second period that only the *Boston Herald* reported on in their post play description. "Hitchman received a savage crack in the cheek as Shore lifted the puck in trying to clear."[33] Hitch remained in the game, and no one thought any more of it.

Hitch knew something was wrong but didn't want to bother the team doctor, who was busy working on Cooney Weiland's scalp wound. He went home after the game but had a restless night—Hitch couldn't eat and was in a lot of pain.

The next day Henry Disken of the *Boston Advertiser* pegged Hitch as favored for the Hart Trophy. For the past five years, he'd correctly predicted the winner for his newspaper. "Hitchman, Morenz, Nels Stewart, Joliat, Shore, Weiland, Frank Boucher, Mantha, Barry and Hec Kilrea make the lineup as I see it through this season. Hitchman is the most valuable player to his club in the National League and he stands out so far in the values on which a player is judged that it is probable he will receive the coveted Dr. Hart trophy for this year. And, he has earned it!"[34]

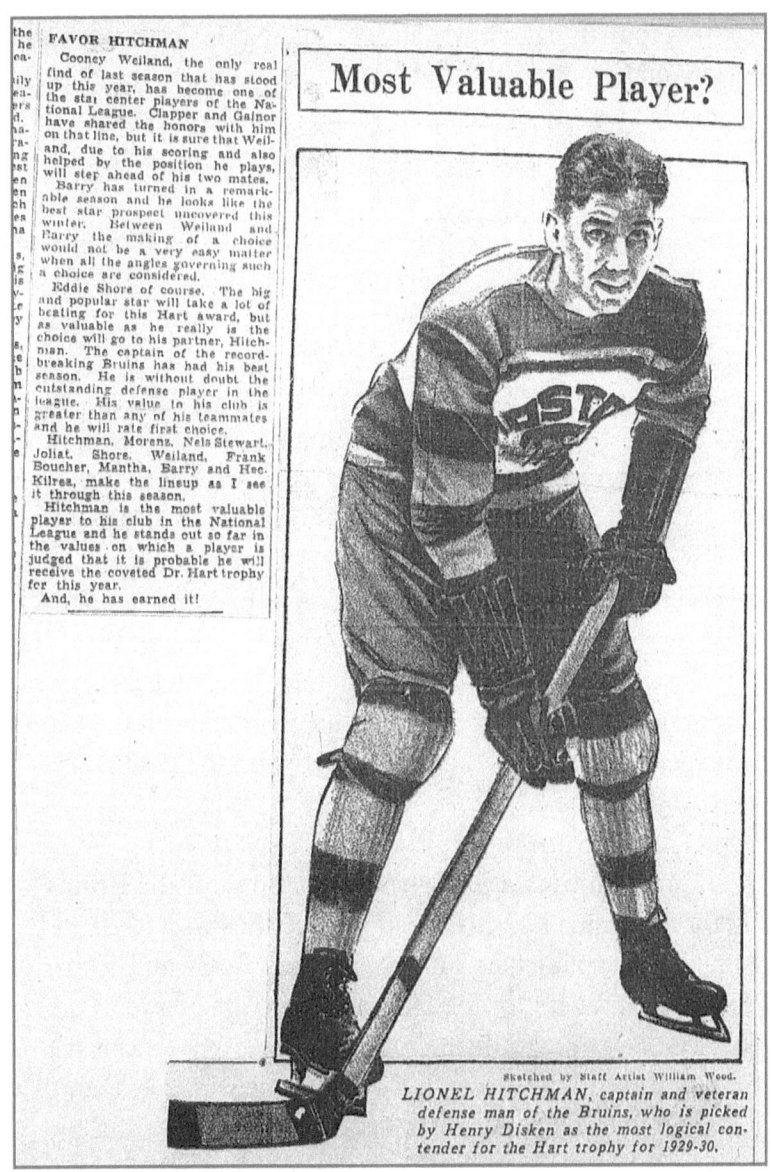

FAVOR HITCHMAN

Cooney Weiland, the only real find of last season that has stood up this year, has become one of the star center players of the National League. Clapper and Gainor have shared the honors with him on that line, but it is sure that Weiland, due to his scoring and also helped by the position he plays, will step ahead of his two mates.

Barry has turned in a remarkable season and he looks like the best star prospect uncovered this winter. Between Weiland and Barry the making of a choice would not be a very easy matter when all the angles governing such a choice are considered.

Eddie Shore of course. The big and popular star will take a lot of beating for this Hart award, but as valuable as he really is the choice will go to his partner, Hitchman. The captain of the record-breaking Bruins has had his best season. He is without doubt the outstanding defense player in the league. His value to his club is greater than any of his teammates and he will rate first choice.

Hitchman, Morenz, Nels Stewart, Joliat, Shore, Weiland, Frank Boucher, Mantha, Barry and Hec Kilrea, make the lineup as I see it through this season.

Hitchman is the most valuable player to his club in the National League and he stands out so far in the values on which a player is judged that it is probable he will receive the coveted Dr. Hart trophy for this year.

And, he has earned it!

Most Valuable Player?

Sketched by Staff Artist William Wood.

LIONEL HITCHMAN, captain and veteran defense man of the Bruins, who is picked by Henry Disken as the most logical contender for the Hart trophy for 1929-30.

Boston Advertiser, *March 2, 1930.*

That same day Hitch reported to the team doctor and had an X-ray taken. His mouth was temporarily wired shut until the film was developed on Monday. A broken jaw was diagnosed. A permanent wire was substituted for the temporary one, and Hitch was put on a liquid diet and told to rest for the next three weeks. The team had five games remaining. They had won their division over a month previously and were now ahead of the second-place Rangers by 30 points and the Canadian Division leader, the Montreal Maroons, by 22 points.

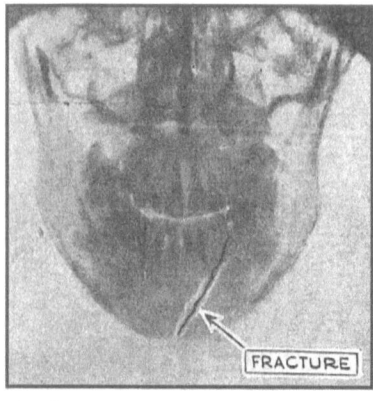

Hitch's X-ray, Boston Traveler, March 3, 1930.

As word got out, the newspaper coverage revealed a shocked and worried press corps. Here are a few excerpts:

Peter F. Kelley, *Boston Record*: "Hitchman is out for the rest of the regular season, but Dr. Joseph Shortell, the club physician and surgeon, hopes to have him in condition to play in the post-season series which will start at Montreal on March 20. Hitch is extremely popular and undoubtedly the most valuable player on the team and in the league. His loss will be a severe blow to the Bruins."[35]

Ralph Clifford, *Boston Traveler*:
The injury comes at a particularly bad time for the Bruins and for Hitchman himself. He apparently has won the favor of the writers and fans all around the circuit and is the foremost candidate for the Hart trophy, emblematic of the most valuable player in the league. His absence from the few remaining games may influence some of the selectors who rate any others near Hitchman, but judging from the comments heard in the past few weeks he has such a long lead over all others that his absence will make little difference in the nominations.

It is funny how by a mishap to one man, a team that is considered powerful in not only its first-string department, but in its substitutes can be demoralized by the loss of that man. And it was a crucial blow when "Hitch" was forced to take the count.

He is the "spark plug" of the Bruins. His fighting heart, a spirit that has been prominent in the success of the Bruins is what is needed in the final playoff. What a leader he made! And even if it is just to get out there and urge the gang to fight, that's all the Bruins' strategy board is asking.

The Bruins are clinging to that hope.

Hitchman himself scoffs at the thoughts that he will not be able to face his hockey rivals in that series. The Bruins captain simply refuses to be discouraged and is confident he will be at left defense when the playoff gets under way.

How can you check a spirit like that! How can a gang of fellows do anything but fight for a fellow like that! A fellow that has taken more than his share of the hard knocks and came up smiling all the time![36]

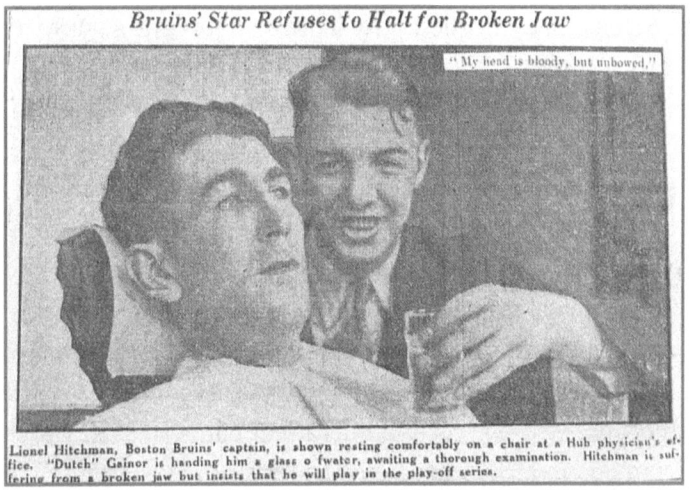

Dutch Gainor with Hitch, Boton Record, *March 4, 1930.*

John J. Hallahan, the *Boston Globe*: "Lionel Hitchman, one of the greatest defense players of all time in hockey, and largely responsible for the success of the Bruins in the National Hockey League has a broken jaw. . . . should the tall poke and sweep checking defence man not be at his best for the Stanley Cup play it would be a sad blow to the Bruins. His absence is likely to mean the

Bruins may not make any more records. . . . They have a few they are after, as they now have won nine games in a row, and have played 15 without a defeat."[37]

Just as Hallahan feared, Boston's winning streak came to a halt in game 42 in Chicago on March 13. A crowd of 14,000 packed the arena, and the game was delayed for almost 20 minutes because the lights went out—literally and figuratively for Boston. Only three teams in the league had beaten Boston: the Montreal Maroons and the New York Americans each took one victory, but the Chicago Black Hawks, with their latest 3-2 win in overtime, had beaten Boston three times in the six games they played each other. The Associated Press reported that Shore "drew a major penalty and a $25 fine for striking at the goal umpire after the second Blackhawk goal." And "the result prevented the Bruins from tying the record set by Les Canadiens in 1927-28 of playing 18 consecutive games without defeat. They needed only a draw in tonight's game to match that record."[38]

The final game of the season took place in the Boston Garden against the New York Rangers, with the Bruins winning 9-2. To the surprise of most, Hitch suited up for this game with his new football-styled headguard, complete with a steel chin plate to protect his broken jaw. J.W. Mooney of the *Boston Post* reported:

> It was a real treat to see Captain Hitchman take his place in the Bruin defence and he got a rousing reception. As the clash progressed and swung into a real battle of skill which entertained and delighted the followers, the strength of Hitchman's great stick check became more and more evident and if he stopped a Ranger attack he stopped over a half-dozen in his first siege of 15 minutes. So strong was Hitch that the Gotham crowd found difficulty getting in for close up shots, unless after rebounds.

Mooney further commented: "It was a glorious ending and the Bruins showed off in a way that it was evident they meant to put the old fear into any opponents they must yet meet this year in the play offs." He went on to say that the Bruins lost only one home game this season. "That is a record that should hang for some time." And it did, for 88 years and counting![39]

The Playoffs

Boston took on the Canadian Division leader, the Maroons, in Montreal on March 20 for the first game in the best-of-five semifinal series, winning 2-1 on a backhand shot from Harry Oliver in the 46th minute of overtime. At the time it was the longest playoff game in NHL history at 105 minutes, 35 seconds.

Elmer Ferguson of the *Montreal Herald* commented: "It was obvious that both these rugged teams would use rugged measures, and both did, from the start. The first body-check was handed out by Hitchman, when he bowled over [Hooley] Smith, and later in the game, he dropped Smith heavily with another clean hit. . . . Hitchman played a smashing hockey game. His far-reaching stick played havoc with many attacks, and he bodied clean but with crashing force."[40]

That second check to Hooley Smith came in overtime and sent Smith to his home bench for a rest, giving Boston's forwards a chance to get going without his dirty work to worry about. Stanley Woodward of the *Boston Herald* added that when Hooley returned to the game, "he dropped the puck in front of the defence and leaped straight for Hitchman's face, cracking him on the jaw with his forearm. Hitch pulled off his patent mask and went on as if nothing had happened."

Woodward also noted that: "President Frank Calder of the National league today refused to state who had won the Hart trophy, sometimes called the 'valuable player trophy.' It is said that the three leaders in the running are Capt. Lionel Hitchman of the Bruins, Cooney Weiland of the Bruins and Howie Morenz of Canadiens. The dope seems to be that Hitch will get it and that Weiland will get the Lady Byng trophy for clean play."[41]

Game two in Montreal was two nights later, and Boston beat the Maroons 4-2. John J. Hallahan of the *Boston Globe* reported:

It did not matter to the Maroons whether Lionel Hitchman had a broken jaw or wore a headgear. In fact it was lucky for Hitch that he had the protection of a stout head-piece.

Hooley Smith and Dave Trottier were the greatest offenders. Smith cracked Hitch on the helmet, rising a lump the size of an egg, and in the second period, when the Bruins were outplaying the Maroons, Trottier applied the wood to the head of the Bruins' captain. Perhaps he was trying over Hitch's broken jaw, but apparently he was attempting to wreck the gallant, courageous leader. Hitch, on leaving the ice, had to have two stitches taken over his eye.

The Maroons were desperate, realizing that the Boston machine was too much for them. They figured that by chopping, high sticking and general roughing they might out-game the Boston plays.

In this they were mistaken, for Hitch and Eddie Shore, upon whom the Montrealers directed their attacks were able to withstand the continuous hammering, and came back for more.[42]

J.W. Mooney of the *Boston Post* commented: "For what he took Shore governed himself remarkably well. Hitchman, a cooler proposition under fire, often skated close to Shore and waved his hand, as much as to warn Shore to hold his head and stay on the ice. In fact the whole Bruin team did well in this respect."[43]

Elmer Ferguson commented that "Hitchman's far-reaching poke-check was the rock on which early Maroon attacks founded, the helmeted Bruin captain playing a brilliant game all through that over-shadowed his more dynamic team-mate Shore."[44]

Boston Globe, *March 24, 1930, page 9.*

The Bruins and their 100-plus royal rooters arrived at the North Station in Boston on the evening of March 23 to thousands of well-wishers. And Hitch came home to pick up the *Sunday Globe* and read the lifestyle feature article on him, his wife Tops and daughter Gloria, titled "Tamest of Lions When at Home."[45]

Two days later on March 25 in the sports section of the same newspaper, John J. Hallahan reported that:

Manager Art Ross intends to send his team after the game from the start. And he is going to protect as much as possible the well being of his players, as he plans to have his defense men, Lionel Hitchman, Eddie Shore and George Owen use headgear tonight. The high stick carrying and stick wielding of the Maroons in Saturday's game has forced Ross to take the step. The headgear worn by Capt Hitchman was meant to act as a protection for a broken jaw, but when he was clouted on the top of the protective piece by Hooley Smith, it proved valuable as a head protector.[46]

By noon that Tuesday, the "gallery gods" had claimed their general-admission seats in the second balcony, waiting for the third game of the Bruins–Maroons playoff to start at 8:30 that night. In all, 16,000 crammed into the Garden, all that it could handle.

It was a fierce game, as Victor O. Jones, *Boston Globe* (March 26, 1930) reported:

> Boston's three defense men wore football head guards and looked queer in the rig.
>
> When Hooley Smith led the first assault on the Bruin cage a terrific boo went up, but when Hitch sent him sprawling you couldn't have heard a 10-inch salute set off under your hat. On Hooley's next dash Shore sent him kicking.
>
> You gotta have nerve to stand in the way of Dunc Munro when the Montreal heavyweight comes down the ice full speed ahead. Hitch did it once last night, broken jaw and all, and the two went down with a crash which could be heard above the general din.
>
> The hardest check of the evening was handed out by Lionel Hitchman in the third period when he sent Hooley Smith several feet into the air head over heels. The check for Hitch totalled two minutes in the cooler.[47]

And as Stanley Woodward, the *Boston Herald*, explained, "the Montrealers stuck to their hockey, took the savage body-checks of the helmeted Lionel Hitchman and Eddie Shore without extra legal comeback and stayed on the ice," and won 1-0 after two overtime periods. It was the "first defeat in 21 home games for the Boston team."[48]

Baz O'Meara of the *Montreal Star* commented that "Shore and Hitchman played great hockey along with Thompson for Bruins. Fred Hitchman gave everything he had."[49]

The next evening another crowd of more than 16,000 showed up at the Garden to cheer their team and watch as Hitch "executed one of his low sweeping checks against Nelson Stewart as the latter shot and Nelson's stick flew up and caught him over the eye. Seven stitches were taken in the cut. Hitch came out with the team at the start of the third period [to a roaring ovation] but did no more playing. Actually, he wasn't needed at this time, for George Owen, Jr., was going well on defence and the brunt of the Maroon onslaught had been absorbed." Stanley Woodward of the *Boston Herald* further explained:

> [In the first period,] Shore foolishly charged Trottier and took a penalty.
>
> The Bruins still were two men short when the second period opened and the Maroons started five forwards. Hitchman did some wonderful defence work, dropping to the ice to block shots by Smith and Phillips, and Shore came back into the game.
>
> With all hands back, the Bruins scored their second goal when Hitch and Barry capitalized on some wet backchecking by Stewart and Smith. Barry got the break and Hitch, seeing left-wing open, went along too. Barry passed at the defence and the Boston captain coasted in, coolly waited for Walsh to drop, and neatly hoisted over him.[50]

Boston Herald, *March 28, 1930, page 36.*

The Bruins remained in Boston for the opening game of the Stanley Cup final against the Montreal Canadiens on April 1, 1930. Another crowd of 16,000 watched as their beloved Bruins lost 3-0. Elmer Ferguson of the *Montreal Herald* attributed the loss as follows:

> It was a clear-cut game marred by little rough or foul play in which Canadiens blazed to victory last night. The only turbulent tendencies developed just at the end, and as usual, the Boston Bad Boy, blonde Eddie Shore, was prominent in the proceedings. Shore roused the crowd by arguing with Referee Mallinson after drawing a penalty for taking a crack at [Pit] Lepine while the latter was entangled with goaler Tiny Thompson after the two had fallen to the ice.
>
> No sooner was Shore back than he became entangled with Wildor Larochelle as the latter scurried in with no one to beat but the goaler. Shore wrapped his stick around the buoyant little habitant wrestled him and finally took a swing at him. He was chased and it took four of his team mates to keep Larochelle from going after the big blonde. Heavy body-checking was conspicuous by its absence but of what there was of this Canadiens had the shade. For big "Battleship" Leduc twice dropped Shore and earlier in the play hooked Weiland badly in the face.[51]

With idle time on the train to Montreal for the second game of the Stanley Cup final, the Boston scribes busied themselves with speculation on the winner of the Hart Trophy. It was strange that the winner had not yet been announced, as it had just prior to the end of the regular season in past years. Peter F. Kelley of the *Boston Record* explains:

> Although President Frank Calder of the NHL refuses to make any announcement about the Hart trophy or Lady Byng prize awards it is rumored that Captain Lionel Hitchman of the Bruins will receive the Hart cup.

This trophy is for the most valuable player to his team in the National League and the consensus of opinion seems to be that Hitchman deserves the honor.

"Hitch" is regarded as the most valuable man on the Bruins and other hockey magnates declare that if they were in the market for a player and they had their choice they would pick Hitchman.

If it should come to pass that Hitchman wins the Hart trophy everybody will rejoice. He has been a "money" player in the true sense of the word and has been a veritable fortress in the Bruin's outer defense.[52]

Ralph Clifford of the *Boston Traveler* put out the results of his annual managers ballot on best players for each position. (The NHL started its own all-star team balloting the following season.) "The 1930 NHL all-star team looks very much like the Boston Bruin Club of the current season. . . . When the results of the individual selections were collaborated, a Bruin player was named for every position except that of left wing, which goes to the brilliant young Hec Kilrea of Ottawa. Capt. Hitchman of the Bruins was the first choice at left defence of six managers and second choice of three. No other defence player received as many nominations as Hitch."[53]

On April 3, in Montreal, Boston battled to a 4-3 loss to the Canadiens. Elmer Ferguson explained: "Canadiens were great in victory, Bruins courageous and compelling in defeat, as, always dangerous, they went down battling stubbornly, to the last ditch, beaten 4-3 in the second and deciding game of the two-in-three final series." He added, "Hitchman gave a powerful defensive display."[54]

The *Boston Globe*'s John J. Hallahan commented: "The Canadiens not only won the Stanley Cup—the first time since 1924—but also gained the further honor of being the only team to defeat the Bruins on Canadian ice this season." He further reported that "After the final bell, the players consoled and congratulated each other. Capt Lionel Hitchman and Manager Ross raced to the Canadiens' dressing room to congratulate the victors."[55]

Baz O'Meara of the *Montreal Star*, who had traveled with the Ottawa Senators to Vancouver in their quest for the Stanley Cup in 1923 when he was sports editor of the *Ottawa Journal*, remarked, "Tommy Gorman who discovered Hitchman, would have shed tears had he seen the way in which his 'find' was battered up."[56]

It would be another four days before the NHL announced that Nels Stewart of the Montreal Maroons and Frank Boucher of the New York Rangers had been awarded the Hart Trophy (most valuable player) and Lady Byng Trophy (cleanest player), respectively. Each had previously won these awards.

The balloting went as follows for the Hart Trophy: Nels Stewart, 101; Lionel Hitchman, 94; Cooney Weiland, 79; Frank Clancy, 77; Frank Boucher, 75; Norman Himes, 70; Howie Morenz and Chuck Gardiner, 60 each. And for the Lady Byng Trophy as follows: Frank Boucher, 127; Norman Himes, 103; Ralph Weiland, 82; Harold Darragh, 81; George Hay, 73.

Some were shocked by the Hart Trophy result, while others rationalized that the vote for Hitch was split with Cooney Weiland. It's possible that Ferguson's endorsement of Hitch had an unintended consequence, as the reporter received a fair amount of backlash from the two Montreal teams and the sportswriting community in that city after his article was published.

Although Boston did not win the Stanley Cup and Hitch did not win the Hart Trophy, 1929-30 remains the Bruins' greatest season, smashing old records and skating to the most successful season of all time, not only in Boston but in the NHL. Hitch, as the Hart Trophy voting revealed, was proclaimed the best defenseman that year. And he captained this marvelous team of 1929-30.

Off to the Coast

Two days after the final Stanley Cup game, most of the Bruins took the train west to play exhibition games against the following minor professional hockey teams: Vancouver, Seattle, Portland, San Francisco, Oakland, and Hollywood. They were joined by Hec Kilrea and King Clancy of the Ottawa Senators, who were used to strengthen the local teams against the Bruins. This was a tour that

Art Ross and his buddy Frank Patrick had cooked up, and Ross also used it as a recruitment excursion.

Crowds in the 9,000 range showed up for games in Vancouver, after which Boston headed south. A change in schedule saw them play the Chicago Black Hawks in San Francisco on April 23. The Hawks were in Los Angeles for a series against the local Richfields team. Using Kilrea and Clancy, the Bruins beat the Black Hawks 4-2. They then headed to Los Angeles and beat the Richfields 8-3. Los Angeles promoter Floyd Carleton, manager of the Winter Garden Ice Palace corporation, slated Boston to play the Black Hawks two more times.

It was the first of May and Shore decided he had played enough and headed for his farm in Alberta. Owen also left and went back to Boston. With the help of the two Ottawa players, and in front of a packed house, Boston beat Chicago 4-3. Art Ross told the promoter the team wasn't going to play the next game, that the whole purpose of the tour was to play local teams and not one from their NHL division. The promoter sued Art Ross for $10,000 for breach of contract. Ross scoffed and left for Boston on May 2 along with Galbraith, Clapper, Oliver, and Weiland. In an attempt to mitigate damages, eight of the players—Thompson, Clancy, Hitchman, Lyons, Chapman, Kilrea, Gainor, and Barry—stayed on and played the second game against the Black Hawks, losing 4-3.

The *Boston Herald*'s Bob Dunbar on May 7 reported: "Manager Art Ross of the Bruins returned to Boston from the far coast yesterday, well pleased with the performance of his club against western rivals. The B's dropped the first game and then won eight in a row. They now have disbanded until Oct 5, when they will report for another season."[57]

Seven of the eight players who stayed for the second game against the Black Hawks left by train for the east shortly after. Having made friends with the movie star George Raft, Hitch stayed behind as his houseguest for two weeks. Hitch then headed back to Boston, where he played cricket for the St. George's A.A. team in the Massachusetts state league.

The 1929-30 Boston Bruins. Best winning percentage of all time!
(Photo courtesy of Hitchman private collection)

Chapter Twelve

WANING

H itch's Seventh Playoff Season

After returning home to Melrose, Massachusetts, from his whirlwind trip to the coast, Hitch maintained a busy and varied sporting life until the 1930-31 NHL season began. He was a hit with the cricket crowd not only for his superb skills but also for bringing cricket back into the limelight. He "won the hearts of all the fans by his pleasant and pleasing and unassuming manner." Hitch enjoyed tennis and played competitive golf on a pro-am circuit for his club, Bellevue. On June 10, 1930, he won best net at the fourth annual NHL Golf Tournament in Montreal.[1]

Photo is from the Boston Globe, *July 13, 1930, page 22.*

In early August he and the family headed to Ottawa and up to Tops' family camp near Rock Lake, where Dit Clapper joined them for a visit. Hitch and Dit then went on to New Brunswick for some salmon fishing at Hartt's Island pool on the Saint John River.

Although he kept himself very busy, he was not in the best of shape. His broken jaw from the errant puck off Eddie Shore's stick last March hadn't properly healed, and he had an operation to reset the bone. But he headed into the upcoming season with this injury unresolved.

The 1930-31 NHL season again included 10 teams, but for the last time during Hitch's career. The Pittsburgh Pirates moved to Philadelphia to become the Philadelphia Quakers, and the Detroit Cougars changed their name to the Falcons.

It was the last 44-game season. Only one change was introduced to the playoff structure: At the urging of Art Ross, the Stanley Cup final became a best-of-five series instead of the previous best-of-three. The Montreal Canadiens won again this season, beating the Chicago Black Hawks three games to two.

The effects of the Great Depression were beginning to be felt, with consumers unable to spend or invest as they did in the 1920s. This started to have an impact at the gate and would later affect player salaries and team operations.

Manager Art Ross and captain Lionel Hitchman led their Boston Bruins to their fourth straight division win. The team had the best overall league record for the second year in a row with 62 points (28 wins, 10 losses, and six ties). This translated into a .705 points percentage, the second best up to that point for Boston and the 10th best in franchise history (at least until 2018).

In a hard-fought battle, Boston lost to the Canadiens in the Stanley Cup semifinals, three games to two.

Several new young players were added to the Boston roster, most acquired on the team's western trip at the end of the last season. Some were tried at defense for a few games here and there, but inevitably they took their place on the second or third forward lines or were rotated out of the club.

For defense, Ross continued to rely on Hitch, Eddie Shore, and George Owen. Shore and Owen each had great seasons, leading the league in points for defensemen (Shore first with 31 and Owen second with 25). This was Shore's breakout season. He hit his all-time highest goal total (15), with five of those game-winning goals. He was less disruptive this year (though he did start two bench-clearing brawls) and was more consistent in the playoffs.

Cooney Weiland continued to lead the team in total individual points (38). He was ninth overall in the league. Marty Barry and Eddie Shore followed, each with 31 points, tying for 13th in the league. Dit Clapper and Harry Oliver were right behind with 30 points.

The comparisons between Hitch and Shore from the previous season lingered into this one. The *Detroit Free Press* wrote this on November 23, 1930: "There is not a more effective defense man in hockey than Hitchman. The lanky veteran is the hardest man in the league to swing around and most of the swings around his side wind up in the corner. Shore is not a defense man of Hitchman's ability, but he is a much better puck-carrier and one of those athletes often described as colorful. Shore, one of the highest salaried players in hockey, also is something of an actor when he wants the other fellow to draw a penalty."[2]

Hitch's surgery before the opening of the season did not properly address his broken jaw. He didn't complain and played 41 of the 44 regular-season games. But it was obvious something was wrong. After the game in Montreal on November 29 against the Canadiens, the Canadian Press reported: "Lionel Hitchman looked ill, and took long and frequent rests."[3] His playing time during the season was reduced, and not until after the playoffs and more than a year after the injury, six months since the first operation, would another attempt be made to reset the jaw.

George Owen was given more playing time on defense and excelled at the offensive end of the game. However, the new Bruins writer for the *Boston Herald*, Arthur Siegel, who took over for Stanley Woodward (credited with coining the term *Ivy League* and who moved to the *New York Herald Tribune*), reported extensively on Hitch, noting that his poke- and sweep checks were still working at high efficiency and his body checks still as devasting as ever. For the tough games against the Canadiens, Black Hawks, Rangers,

Maple Leafs and Maroons, Art Ross relied extensively on Hitch's defensive skills.

One such typical comment by Siegel appeared in the *Herald* on December 10 after Boston's 2-1 win against the Maroons the night before: "Hitchman broke up several disastrous forays and on two occasions averted disaster when he alone was the only man left in front of Thompson."[4]

John J. Hallahan, sports editor for the *Boston Globe*, also observed that Hitch was still needed for the tough games, commenting on Boston's 2-1 win over the Black Hawks in game 32 that "Hitchman, however, played a big part by stopping a threat at the points. . . . 'Old Reliable' Hitchman showing the same effectiveness as in years past, poking and sweep-checking the puck out of danger."[5]

After the next game in Montreal with the Bruins 4-2 win over the Maroons, this sketch from Hardin Burnley appeared in several newspapers on February 16, 1931. (Photo courtesy of Bristol (PA) Courier / Bucks County Courier Times)

With five games remaining in the season, Boston was in first place over the Black Hawks by a comfortable 12 points. Boston would likely face off in the semifinal series against the Montreal

Canadiens, who had a similar record in the other division. Siegel was the first to summon Hitch's monied instincts for the upcoming playoffs. "Manager Art Ross calls Hitch his 'money player,' the man who can come through in the pinch and who remains unruffled and maintains his maximum efficiency while others are likely to become panic-stricken." Always the company man and team motivator, Hitch was quoted in Siegel's 875-word article: "Our team today is composed of a wonderful bunch of players. They have the speed, both of skate and of mind. The same type of fellow plays hockey today as did 10 years ago or six years ago, but the difference is in speed. The 1925 team did not think so fast. Now they think so fast it's hard for the other team to keep up with them. They have the right spirit, they play cleaner hockey and they have everything, including an owner and manager, which goes to make up a great outfit."[6]

Hitch's wife Tops and daughter Gloria sitting at the piano, while he plays the ukulele. (Photo courtesy of Boston Herald, *March 8, 1931, page 21.)*

At the end of the season, other Boston scribes chimed in. Here are excerpts from two:

J.W. Mooney, *Boston Post*:
The National Hockey league playoffs, the great money series where the boys do their hustling on the ice with an eye on the gate "cut," starts tomorrow night at the Boston

Gardens with the two most colorful teams in the sport battling—the Bruins and Les Canadiens.

Captain Hitchman of the Bruins, the smartest defence player in the league, and who is known as a money player, if ever there was one, was considered to have slipped some, but of late has been climbing steadily in the admiration of the fans who may see him in the series as the most effective, as well as cleverest defence player, a title he rated in the last successful quest for the Stanley mug.

Hitchman has preserved himself all season for the big start tomorrow night. There isn't another Hitchman when he gets steamed up. When sore and bleeding, the lanky wonder plays with abandon, and then woe to those who cross his path.[7]

Bill Grimes, *Boston American*:
"Capt. Lionel Hitchman has not been himself all season, and although George Owen has developed noticeably, he is not up to the standard set by Hitchman during the Maroon and Les Canadiens series last spring. Hitchman is one of the greatest money players the game has ever produced. If he can offer the brand of hockey he played last year, the Bruins have an even chance of winning their way to the finals. Otherwise their chances are not bright."[8]

This was Hitch's ninth season in the NHL, his seventh time in the playoffs. For this season's playoffs, as before, and as the Boston scribes petitioned, Hitch was relied on heavily to throw off opponents, break up rushes and feed passes to Bruins forwards. But as Mr. Grimes predicted, with Hitch not at his best, Boston's "chances [were] not bright."

The first Stanley Cup semifinal game was played in Boston, and the Bruins beat the Canadiens 5-4 in overtime on March 24, 1931. J.W. Mooney, *Boston Post*, wrote: "Hitchman, who started the game presumably to give the Bruins a sturdier defense, saw the new game, liked it instantly, and proceeded to bounce Georges Mantha of the

Canadiens. After the third bounce, Mantha was out. Hitchman is not such a much during the regular season, but when the play-ons commence, he is the Rock of Gibraltar, the Bank of England and the Anti-Saloon League rolled in one."[9]

The second game was two nights later in Boston, and the Canadiens won 1-0. Arthur Siegel reported: "Through the game Shore had worked like a bulldog on offence and defence. Capt. Lionel Hitchman and Owen stood out like towers of strength."[10]

The playoffs moved to Montreal, with the Canadiens taking the third game, again by one goal, 4-3. Boston won the fourth game 3-1. Elmer Ferguson, *Montreal Herald*, remarked: "Canadiens rallied in dazzling fashion in the final frame, and with five forwards carrying the attack a full ten minutes, stormed the Bruin citadels unceasingly, only to meet an almost stone-wall defence. One goal only penetrated the net minding skill of Thompson, and the fine defensive of Shore, Hitchman and Owen."[11]

Boston lost game five and their chance to advance to the Stanley Cup final. Hitch was injured near the end of the game "as Sylvio Mantha and Hitchman became entangled in a pile-up, with both being rather severely hurt. There were no penalties on this play, but there was when [Boston's] Chapman took a swing at Morenz in a mix-up and was sent to the box for five minutes. Then came a Canadiens' attack which was maintained until the end of the game, with everyone taking a pot-shot at the goal as Bruins merely tried to protect their net. [Lepine got the winning goal.]"[12]

At the end of the playoffs, rumors swirled around the league about Hitch's status with the Bruins. Used to seeing Hitch on the ice for 60 minutes and noticing that some of his playing time had been given to George Owen, some speculated that Hitch's days in Boston were almost up. The *Boston Herald*:

SUGGESTED SALE OF HITCHMAN
Rumors are rife that Lionel Hitchman is on the auction-block. It is said that Hitchman has lost his speed and his zest for body-checking, without which no man can hope to take up space on the Bruin defence. It is sincerely hoped

that Dame Rumor in this case is the unrepenting fabricatress that she has so often proven herself in the past.

Hitchman has played splendid hockey for Boston from the time he joined them. He was a player who could both "give it and take it." Yet young, unless the seams of his frame have been loosened by his sturdy bulwark efforts in throwing back countless waves of attack, his years should still be long in the land of hockey. Mayhap he has grazed too long in the one pasture and a change of scenery is all that he requires.[13]

Stories coming out of Montreal had Hitch going to Detroit as player-manager. They were carried across the Associated and Canadian Press wires, to which Bruins owner Charles Adams responded in the *Boston Herald*:

At no time have I considered the sale or transfer of Captain Hitchman. I cannot understand from what source such an unfounded rumor has circulated. Now that the season is over, Hitchman will undergo a very thorough examination in an effort to discover what may be his trouble.

Undoubtedly it is physical. Dr. Arlie V. Bock of the Massachusetts General Hospital, my personal medical adviser will handle Hitchman's case. I am confident that when another season rolls around, Hitchman will be playing in his 1929 form for the Bruins.

In the same article, the *Boston Herald* gave the reason for Hitch's poor showing in 1930-31: "This was not due to any lackadaisical play on the part of the rangy point, but rather traces back to an injury which he sustained just prior to the 1929-30 playoffs. Eddie Shore, in clearing the puck in a regular season game, lifted it against Hitchman's face, breaking his jaw."[14] For now, the trade rumors were put to bed and Hitch needed another operation to fix his jaw, but first he had a commitment to keep.

Hitch returned from Montreal just to pack up and ship some of Dit Clapper's belongings to Vancouver, then he and Tops went to Toronto to meet up with Dit. The three of them motored cross-country to Vancouver. Hitch would be Dit's best man on April 28, 1931, as he married Lorraine "Honey" Pratt, a girl Dit met out west during the 1930 postseason exhibition series. On the newlyweds' return to Ontario, they visited Hitch and Tops at her parents' camp in Algonquin Park.[15]

"Now Is the Winter of Our Discontent"

The Great Depression was taking its toll across North America and elsewhere, and the NHL was not spared. The 1931-32 season was reduced to eight teams, with Ottawa and Philadelphia suspending operations. At the same time, the league schedule increased to 48 games, and the Maple Leaf Gardens opened in Toronto in November 1931, holding 14,550, including standing room.

The Toronto Maple Leafs swept the Stanley Cup best-of-five series against the New York Rangers, three games to none.

At the onset of the season, Ross selected the following 15 players for the Bruins' squad: right wingers Dit Clapper, Harry Oliver and Hank Boyd; centers Cooney Weiland, Marty Barry and Art Chapman; left wingers Bill Touhey, Perk Galbraith, Bud Cook and Frank Jerwa; defensemen George Owen, Eddie Shore, Hitch and Joe Jerwa; and goaltender Tiny Thompson.

The league continued to call for only 15 players on a team roster at any given time, and by February the players had to be set. Boston experimented with 25 players, while the other three teams in the division went through fewer players (Rangers, 15; Falcons, 16; Black Hawks, 21). Ross tried different forward combinations to improve scoring. He also tried a different goalie partway through the season but brought back Tiny Thompson. Hitchman and Shore were relied on extensively for defense.

George Owen took over captain duties from Hitch this season. Boston finished with 15 wins, 21 losses, and 12 ties, and sank to last place in the American Division. Only the New York Americans of the Canadian Division scored fewer points.

In league scoring, Boston's usual top guns did not show well. Dit Clapper was ninth, Marty Barry tied for 11th, Cooney Weiland tied for 22nd, Art Chapman tied for 27th, Eddie Shore and George Owen tied for 33rd, and Harry Oliver tied for 41st. Tiny Thompson was fifth out of eight goalies in goals-against average.

Rumors of a Hitch trade surfaced again just before the season started, this time to the Montreal Canadiens. Once again Bruins owner Charles Adams made a definitive statement: "It is not the policy of the Bruins to sell any player who is of value to the club." Art Ross, who was in Montreal at the time for a medical procedure, told the Associated Press that Hitch "is not for sale at any price."[16]

Hitch had a good year, with few injuries. He played all 48 games and put in a strong defensive performance with only 36 penalty minutes. He also scored more goals than usual (four, plus three assists for seven points)

Boston had just beaten second-place Toronto of the Canadian Division. There was still a chance to make the playoffs going into the third last game of the season against the Detroit Falcons, who were up two points on Boston. The Bruins started Clapper, Weiland, and Barry on the forward line, Hitch and Shore on defense, with Thompson in goal. By then Ross had settled on the following second line and spares: Yip Foster, Owen, Oliver, Galbraith, Chapman, Boyd, Frank Jerwa and Paul Runge.

The game ended in a 1-1 tie in overtime, and according to the Associated Press, it was "the greatest game of the current season on Detroit ice. . . . More than 7500 screaming fans saw the two teams, fighting desperately for play-off positions, battle through two scoreless periods, Boston scoring midway in the third session with a flashing play when Weiland passed to Clapper for the goal. With the Bruins on a firm defence, the Falcons threw five forwards in the play and less than two minutes before the end of the third session [Ebbie] Goodfellow scored the tying goal." Overtime play was mostly in the Detroit end, but Boston couldn't get past Alex Connell, the Ottawa goalie now playing for the Falcons.[17]

Boston lost their next two games, cementing their position in the basement of the division for the first time since their inaugural season, out of the playoffs for the first time in six years.

Division Winners Again

On the news that Boston's Cooney Weiland was traded to Ottawa for Joe Lamb (who had been "rented" to the New York Americans), the Ottawa Senators returned to the NHL for the 1932-33 season, once again under the ownership of Tommy Gorman and bringing the number of teams up to nine. For a second season, the league schedule called for 48 games. The Detroit Falcons were once again renamed, finally to the Detroit Red Wings.

After a summer of championship golf in many parts of Canada and taking third place in the Atlantic Salmon Class of the *New York Herald Tribune* competition for his catch of a 27-pounder in New Brunswick, Hitch was summonsed to Boston for the October 17, 1932, preseason press banquet. He was to introduce and welcome center Nels Stewart, Boston's latest acquisition from the Montreal Maroons (Stewart had beaten Hitch in the Hart Trophy balloting in 1930).

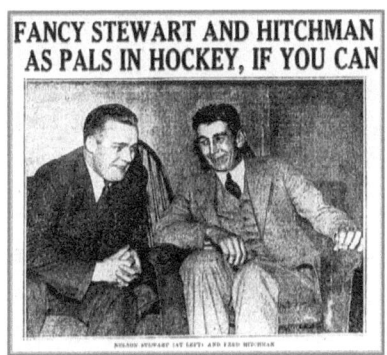

Photo Left, Boston Globe, *October 18, 1932, page 20. Caption: "Nelson Stewart (At Left) and Fred Hitchman.*

Detroit and Boston tied for first in the American Division standings with 58 points, but Boston was awarded first place based on their better head-to-head record with Detroit.

The Bruins played the Canadian Division leader, the Toronto Maple Leafs, in a best-of-five semifinal, with Toronto winning three games to two. The New York Rangers emerged the victor in the other semifinal, and for the second year in a row, they played the Toronto Maple Leafs for the Stanley Cup. This time, New York won the best-of-five series, three games to one.

A new award was introduced this season, Rookie of the Year, won by Carl Voss of Detroit. After nine years in the league with five division wins, six playoff seasons, the highest ever winning percentage in the league and one Stanley Cup championship, someone from Boston finally won the Hart Trophy: Eddie Shore. He placed 12th in overall points and scored his lowest number of goals (8) to date. However, he was awarded 27 assists (second highest in the league next to Frank Boucher), for 35 points overall. Shore was also fourth overall in penalty minutes with 112.

Boston had the best overall season record in the league, with 58 points and 123 goals for and 88 goals against. Tiny Thompson won the Vezina Trophy for a second time.

Marty Barry tied for seventh in league points this season, with Nels Stewart at ninth. This was George Owens' last season. Under an arrangement with the club, he played only at home and in games that were just a short distance away. Dit Clapper became captain of the team this season.

1932-33 in More Detail

The season started out with Hitch and Shore on defense, with Owen and Percy Galbraith, a converted winger, as spares. Joe Jerwa was sent down to the Boston Cubs.

The Bruins got off to a good start in the season opener in Boston against the defending Stanley Cup champs, the Toronto Maple Leafs, tying them 1-1 in overtime. In the next game in Montreal, they beat the Canadiens 4-0 on November 12, 1932. Four days later Ed Baker, still sports editor of the *Ottawa Citizen*, wrote a column on Hitch:

> Montreal scribes give unlimited credit to Eddie Shore and Lionel Hitchman for the Bruins 4-0 victory over Canadiens in Montreal last Saturday night. Both are credited with sensational performances in keeping the speedy Habitants

in check and holding them goalless. Giving credit where credit is due, Elmer Ferguson, an outstanding hockey critic, says in the *Montreal Herald*:

"With Shore performing these prodigies of defensive skill in emergencies and Thompson even more brilliant, the steady work of the veteran, Lionel Hitchman proved another serious barrier to Canadien hopes. The tall ex-Mountie, starting his eleventh season in the major loop, had his sweeping hook-check working in a fashion that closely approached his best days, and was body-checking hard and fairly, a division in which he knows no superior."

It is refreshing to read that Hitchman body-checked hard and fairly. That seldom appears in the press outside of Boston, although Hitchman is one of the fairest checking defence men ever in the National Hockey League.

In this writer's opinion no other player in the N.H.L. has suffered more through unjust penalties than the big fellow, who as a rookie, was a member of that gallant band of eight players who wore the red, white and black colors at Vancouver in March 1923. On that occasion the Senators defeated Vancouver Maroons and Edmonton Eskimos in turn to win the Stanley Cup.

Lionel Hitchman checks hard 'tis true, but this writer has never seen him body-check an opponent unfairly although on many occasions he was penalized by officials for the fair body-checks.

How come? you may ask. Hitchman is a six-footer, weighs 175 lbs. in condition, and is very powerful. When a lighter opponent comes in combat with Hitch's shoulder, the lighter opponent generally sweeps a portion of the ice with his body. Then hostile crowds yell for Hitch's scalp and there are hockey referees who are influenced by such yells.

Lionel Hitchman is playing his ninth season with the Boston club and his many friends in this city will be pleased to know that he is still playing in his best form.[18]

Late in the third period, after playing a strong game on defense alongside Eddie Shore in Boston's 1-0 win over the Black Hawks in Chicago on December 15, 1932, Hitch suffered a severe head injury. This was game 12 of the season, and two nights earlier in Toronto Hitch was also hit hard on the head in a "mixup" with Charley Conacher of the Maple Leafs.

Boston was now a quarter of the way through the season and was second in the standings with a .625 winning percentage (seven wins, four losses, one tie). Owen was rushed to Detroit to take Hitch's place in game 13. Hitch would be out for another two, both home games. Melville E. Webb Jr., of the *Boston Globe*, noted: "It's a handicap to have Hitchman out."[19]

Hitch played again in game 18 and was slotted for the opening lineup of game 19 against the New York Americans in Boston's first home game of the new year. The *Globe's* Webb noted that "his return will make it possible for Eddie Shore to rest more often." Shore was showing signs of strain, which continued into that game. In the third period in front of 10,000 spectators, "Bill Phillips had bumped Shore at the boards behind which the Bruins' subs were massed. Eddie was so incensed at that that he raced back to the middle of the ice where he bumped everyone he could reach."[20]

The Bruins were jostled out of second place after losing back-to back-games to Toronto and the Canadiens on the road in games 26 and 27, respectively. For game 28, Ross brought in Alex Smith of the Ottawa Senators to take over Hitch's spot on the starting line for the balance of the season and the playoffs. In a letter written by Alex Smith and printed in the *Ottawa Journal* on March 25, he spoke "highly of the encouragement and help given him by Hitchman, whom he has practically displaced as Shore's partner on the Bruin rearguard. The letter on the whole is a splendid commentary on the sportsmanship of 'Hitch' and another evidence of the fine sort of athlete he typifies."[21]

The Canadiens were in Boston for the next game, and Hitch was handed coaching duties, with the team winning 3-2. Boston also won game 29 against the Maple Leafs, putting them in a three-way tie for first place in the American Division with the New York Rangers and

Detroit Red Wings. But they fell back to third place over the next nine games, losing five.

Game 39 was the beginning of a 10-game undefeated streak for Boston. Their win against the Americans on March 9 in game 43 put them in first place and ensured a berth in the playoffs. Late in the first period, Hitch "was struck by the butt end of an opponents stick with such force as to fell him, purely an accident," requiring three stitches near his left eye.[22] This injury did not stop Hitch from playing in the last five games of the season, three wins and two ties, culminating in 25 wins, 15 losses and eight ties for Boston's 1932-33 season.

March 25, 1933 was opening day of the playoffs against Canadian Division leader the Toronto Maple Leafs. That day, notable sports editor of the *Boston Globe* John J. Hallahan passed away. He had covered the Bruins from the beginning. At the Boston Garden the Bruins beat the Maple Leafs in overtime 2-1 on Marty Barry's goal in front of 15,000 cheering fans. It was the first time in Hitch's career in Boston that he hadn't started in a playoff game, but he saw plenty of time. Toronto took the second game with a 1-0 overtime goal, breaking a losing streak in the Boston Garden dating back to February 1929. That goal was earned with Boston down a player, George Owen for tripping.

The series moved to Toronto, and Boston won 2-1 in overtime on a goal by Eddie Shore. Shore, Hitchman, and Owen were credited with supplying "great protection" for goalie Tiny Thompson. Game four, played in front of a record crowd of 14,500, saw Toronto win at home without the assistance of an overtime period and with the superb work of Bill Thoms and Ace Bailey. The series was tied two games each for Boston and Toronto. The fifth and deciding game on April 3 was the longest overtime in Stanley Cup playoff history up to that time with six overtime sessions, 104 minutes and 46 seconds. It ended at 1:50 a.m. on April 4 in front of another capacity crowd at the Maple Leaf Gardens. Toronto defeated Boston 1-0, ending their quest for another Stanley Cup.

The Bruins celebrated their season with a dinner at the Wollaston Golf Club in Milton, Massachusetts, capped off with praise and bonuses for each player for getting the team back into the playoffs.

Enter Koanneeta

Hitch had just finished his eleventh season of pro hockey. It wasn't a secret that his body was starting to break down from all the hits and injuries. Gene Mack wrote an article and sketched a cartoon for the Boston Globe on the leg power of aging athletes. Of Hitch, he said: "Lionel Hitchman, the Bruin's popular defense player, is still valuable in a tight spot because of his heady work in front of the cage, but as an offensive threat he's about through. He can't move those runners as fast as in the old days."

Photo left: Snippet of Gene Mack's cartoon on famous aging athletes including Hitch, Babe Ruth, Jack Dempsey, George Sisler, and Reggie McNamara, Boston Globe, *August 12, 1933, page 6.*

It was time to start planning for the future. In May 1933, Hitch and Tops bought a camp on the shores of Mousam Lake, Maine, that had a lodge and four rental cabins. The camp was called Koanneeta. They knew the area and had friends nearby. Plus, they knew the property as they had taken summer rentals at Koanneeta for the past three years. It reminded them of the grand lodges of Algonquin Park, such as the Highland Inn, but on a smaller scale. This was to be their after-hockey business. They hoped to draw patrons for their new venture from the Boston area just 90 miles away and where they were well known.

Top: Koanneeta, circa 1930. (Photo courtesy of John Chamberlain). Middle: Guests enjoying a day at the camp in 1934 with Hitch's bear (more on that later). Bottom Left: Hitch is second left in this group of dress-up party goers. The parties at Koanneeta were legendary, as recalled by old-timers in the area. Bottom right: Rate card for the camp, circa 1934. (All other photos courtesy of Hitchman private collection.)

Hitch's Last Hurrah

The same nine teams played in 1933-34, the NHL's 17th season. For a third time, the schedule included 48 games.

Division leaders the Detroit Red Wings and Toronto Maple Leafs played in a best-of-five semifinal, with Detroit winning three games to two. The Chicago Black Hawks and Montreal Maroons won their quarterfinals and played in the other semifinal, with Chicago winning 6-2 in a two-game, total-point series. For only the second time, two American Division teams played for the Stanley Cup. Chicago beat Detroit in the best-of-five series, three games to one.

Two Bruins placed in the top 10 for league scoring: Marty Barry finished in fourth place with 39 points (27 goals), and Nels Stewart placed fifth, also with 39 points (22 goals).

This was a tumultuous season for the Boston Bruins. Hitch's steady, calm and positive influence on other players was more essential than ever. His informal leadership was needed this season to quell salary disputes and to traverse the dark days of the Shore "incident."

The effects of the Great Depression were taking a toll on the coffers of the NHL clubs, including Boston. Most player salaries were cut by 9 percent to comply with the new team cap of $65,000, reduced from the previous season's $70,000. Top player allowances were also capped, at $7,500. This was needed because of the smaller crowds and reduced ticket prices of the year before. Three players (Clapper, Barry, Shore) held out for more money and didn't leave with the team for its training camp in Quebec City. "Ross did say just before his train left that Fred Hitchman had agreed to terms and that he would again play a defense position this season."[23]

Shortly after, two of the holdouts followed Hitch and signed their contracts, but not Shore, who stated: "I accepted a contract this Fall that was satisfactory. Shortly after that I was given another contract and it was for $2500 less. Until Boston makes that up I stay here. The next move is up to Ross."[24] While one in four were out of work and on bread lines, it became rather grating that Shore fought so hard to hold on to $2,500, which might have represented a quarter of his yearly contract and the average annual income for two families.

He was suspended by the league for failure to report, missing the first two games of the season before agreeing to his contract. Maybe Shore cared too much about money, and maybe Hitch cared too little. And maybe Hitch cared even less about his own well-being. Boston lost both these games, with Hitch filling in for Shore on right defense next to Alex Smith, taking a serious hit to his head in game two against the Montreal Maroons. With Hitch now out of play, Art Ross brought Art Chapman back up to the Bruins from their farm team, the Cubs. And Shore, with his contract settled, raced to Boston to play in game three, another loss for the Bruins, this time against Detroit 4-2 on November 14, 1933.

Hitch was back on the roster in game four in Montreal for Boston's 2-1 win. And the Boston crowd of 8,000 gave Hitch "one of those welcomes you read about" in the next game at home against the Black Hawks. Boston won 2-0. "Shore, Smith and the welcomed Hitchman got in check after check, and Thompson many a real save."[25]

Going into game 13 on December 12, Boston was in third place in the American Division with 12 points, just one point behind Chicago. They were playing Toronto, who was running away with the Canadian Division. A crowd of 13,000 saved up their money for this game at the Boston Garden. It was the first time Toronto had returned to Boston since last season's playoffs.

The teams were in 1 to 1 deadlock toward the end of the second period, when the big rumpus started. It all began when [Red] Horner had Eddie Shore at the boards near the Bruins' net. And it was a pretty rough little affair. Shore finally broke away and rushed up to Ace Bailey, who was at the Boston blue line, and charged into him, knocking him flat on the ice. Bailey seemed down for the count, but began twisting and writhing while his teammates rushed over to him—even those from the players' box. After driving into Bailey Shore skated away to the Leafs' blue line.

He was standing there when Red Horner came up to him.

It seemed only a matter of a little conversation, but suddenly Horner hit Shore a right-handed blow on the jaw, and Shore, in turn, measured his length on the ice. For a moment it seemed to be a free-for-all fight but it was not. Art Ross and Connie Smythe both rushed onto the playing surface and the officials began separating the players. Meanwhile both Bailey and Shore were on their backs. They finally were carried to the dressing rooms. Here it was found that Shore had received a cut on the back of his head which required seven stitches by Dr Crotty.

Bailey did not regain complete consciousness until he had been in the Cubs' dressing room for several minutes. Frank Selke, business manager of the Leafs, took the injured Toronto player to Audubon Hospital, Dr Linde Gately accompanying. Bailey was rational and appeared not to be seriously hurt.

Meanwhile there had been another fracas out in the players' alley way. Manager Connie Smythe of the Leafs got into a mix-up with a spectator. . . .

Both Shore and Horner received match penalties, the rules requiring the teams to play with only four men each for 20 minutes.[26]

Melville E. Webb of the *Boston Globe* wrote and filed the preceding article right after the game without knowing the full extent of Ace Bailey's injuries. He had suffered a fractured skull and took a turn for the worse. Bailey was operated on twice, given a 50 percent chance of living and remained in critical condition for more than two weeks.

On December 16, both Shore and Horner were suspended indefinitely pending an investigation. That same day the Bruins signed Bert McInenly to fill in for Shore during his suspension. After the investigation, Shore was suspended for 16 games.

In the next game, Hitch scored the first goal for Boston in a 5-4 overtime win against the Americans in New York. They stayed in New York and tied the Rangers 2-2 in overtime before returning to

Boston for the first time after the Bailey incident. With Shore still suspended, Boston beat the Maroons 1-0 in overtime in front of 8,000. Webb reported for the *Globe* on December 20 that between the second and third periods, an announcement was made "that Irvin Bailey's condition had changed from 'poor' to 'fair.' This was roundly cheered. Later the Bruins' management thanked those present for their patronage and stated that the sum of $6642.22 [the gate receipts] would be turned over to Mrs. Bailey."[27]

The Maple Leafs returned to Boston on December 26. They were still in first place in their division, and Boston was in last place in theirs. The game ended in a 2-2 overtime tie. Only 3,000 showed up for the game, and the reality had set in that fans were staying away likely for more than one reason. Hockey had crested as a blood sport, nearly taking the life of Ace Bailey and certainly his career. This was unsettling to many people. The newspapers were inundated with letters to that effect. While they hated the dirtiness or roughness that was ever present in the sport, many also missed Shore's exciting style of play. And one other reason can't be overlooked: People were just hurting financially and had to make choices, and this was an easy one, to stay home.

On January 21, in game 28 in New York, the Bruins lost to the Americans 4-2. Hitch was injured from another hit to the head. Unbeknownst to the Bruins fans, he suited up for his last game at the Boston Garden on January 23 against Cooney Weiland, who was now with the Detroit Red Wings. Meanwhile, the league went about organizing a benefit game between the Toronto Maple Leafs and an all-star team, with proceeds going to Ace Bailey. This was the beginning of what is now known as the NHL All-Star Game. James Norris, owner of the Detroit Red Wings, announced his all-star team picks for this game, to be played on February 14, 1934, in Toronto—left defense: Lionel Hitchman.

However, Hitch's playing days were over. Finally felled by these latest head injuries, Hitch had nothing left to give on the ice. He would have tried, but Adams, Ross and his wife, Tops, were extremely concerned about Hitch's condition, the Bruins would have to go another way. Hitch played his last game for Boston on

January 28, 1934, in New York against the Rangers, the first game back for Eddie Shore after his 16-game suspension, with Boston losing 4-2.

Hitch's retirement was announced the next day, Melville D. Webb Jr., *Boston Globe*, writing:

APPOINTMENT OF HITCHMAN MANAGER OF CUBS ENDS BOSTON PLAYERS LONG MAJOR LEAGUE HOCKEY CAREER

Hockey fans well may gasp in surprise when they perceive the changes in the personnel of the Bruins and Bruin Cubs which have taken place in the past 48 hours; . . . .

The first and most important change ends the brilliant National League career of Fred Hitchman.

"Hitch" has been appointed manager of the Cubs and will assume his duties immediately, leading the junior Bruins of the Canadian-American League against the Philadelphia Arrows tomorrow night at Philadelphia. Hitchman will have complete charge of the Cubs. Joe Gilmore will continue to act in the capacity of trainer for the club, a position which he had coupled with his coaching duties.

Secondly, Myles Lane, first captain, then manager of the Cubs, again has been promoted to the Bruins and will spare on the defense tonight against the Rangers.

Third and last is the acquisition by the senior Bruins of Archie Wilcox. 195-pound defenseman from the Quebec Beavers of the Canadian-American League.

HITCHMAN NOT TO PLAY

Getting back to the personnel changes, the appointment of Hitchman is bound to be a popular one, for the lean, lanky defenseman with his long stick and famous poke check has become sort of an institution to Boston hockey fans. In fact he is the sole surviving member of the old Boston club, having been purchased from Ottawa in [1925]. For nine years "Hitch" has covered left defense for the Bears and has been quite a factor in the successes of the Boston team.

Hitchman managed the Bruins for a brief spell last season during the sickness of Art Ross and filled in quite capably. His duties with the Cubs will be confined strictly to managing the team from the bench.[28]

Boston Globe, *January 30, 1934, page 23.*

The next home game for the Bruins was against the Rangers on January 30. Before the game, the *Boston Globe* wrote: "One familiar figure will be missing as the Bruins take the ice tonight, namely

Lionel Hitchman, who for years has been one of the team's most consistent and brilliant performers. His going to the Cubs marks the passing from the major league stage, at least temporarily, of one of hockey's finest figures." It was the first game Shore was in the lineup at home since his suspension, and a capacity crowd of 15,000 came out to welcome him back. Later the *Globe* reported that a fan, seeing Hitch before the game in street attire, asked him: "What are you going to do tonight?" to which Hitch responded: "I'm going to sit down and enjoy myself."[29]

Boston Globe, *January 31, 1934, page 18.*

Another announcement was made that evening. Percy Galbraith, who had been with the Bruins since 1926 and was the longest in service next to Hitch, was also retiring this season. He would continue to play in some games and was immediately sent on a scouting trip for Ross.

On February 2, it had been decided, and a committee struck: plans to honor the dependable defenseman were announced. "Lionel Hitchman Day will be observed at the Boston Garden on Washington's Birthday, Feb. 22 when the Bruins play Ottawa in a National Hockey League contest, a committee of Hitchman fans announced this morning." And they worked feverishly to give Hitch a great tribute like none seen in Boston Bruins history, staging a mock scrimmage that Hitch was sure to score in and a program full of accolades and gifts.[30]

In preparation for the evening, Art Ross asked Tops what she thought Hitch would like from the Bruins as a parting gift. Without hesitation, she requested that the Bruins retire his No. 3 sweater. When Hitch first came to Boston he wore No. 2 (and 14 for a few games in 1925), but when Eddie Shore arrived and wanted that number, Hitch acquiesced, choosing his birthday number, wearing it for eight years in total, three as captain, one as Stanley Cup champ and one on the winningest team ever. According to Tops, both Ross and Adams thought it was a most fitting gift and would be announced during the ceremony. And that is how Hitch, the last original Bruin, became the first to have his number retired. A fitting gift to a player who gave his all in a remarkable NHL career.

After the curiosity of seeing Shore back in the lineup for the Bruins, the crowds again shriveled to 4,300 on average for the previous three home games. Then in the next home game, 9,000 showed up on February 22, 1934, to see last-place Boston play the Canadian Division's last-place Ottawa Senators. The *Boston Globe's* Sportsman column explains:

> This fast-waning and unsatisfactory hockey season will be marked by a bright spot tonight as the fans honor Lionel Hitchman, veteran defense man with the Bruins for years and recently appointed to manage the Cubs.

Tonight's tribute to Hitchman at the Bruins-Ottawa game at the Garden is well deserved, as no man has worked more earnestly or more competently to put the game on a high plane and bring victory to his team. Not so flashy as some other players, Hitchman was for years a mighty bulwark in the defense of the Bruins.

The Cubs will have to provide whatever Boston is to see in the way of post-season hockey playoffs this year.[31]

J.W. Mooney, *Boston Post*, added:

BIG NIGHT FOR HITCH
A lot of things have been planned to make it an unusual night in local hockey.

Some might feel like shedding a tear watching the lanky Hitch playing his final National league game, and as one woman wrote to the testimonial committee she "had planned to take along an extra handkerchief or two." But there is going to be so much fun packed into the evening that there will be no room for lamentation.

None feel that the tall Hitch is washed up in hockey. He has a lot of good games left in him. But the bosses, Adams and Ross, want Hitch to side step any further battering, he has taken plenty in his day, and they have laid plans to build Hitchman's future, for hockey owes him a lot.[32]

And Bob Dunbar, *Boston Herald*:

That Bruins game, by the way, has not much to offer in a hockey way other than two teams will be out there trying to win. There is no chance for the Bruins or the Ottawa Senators in the National League division races, if a person looks for special importance, but in a sentimental way, the game should be a lure, if for nothing more than an opportunity for Boston enthusiasts to pay their tributes to Lionel Hitchman.

Hitchman goes out of the big league competitive picture tonight and there are many who will see their first game of the year, for they will wish to be on hand for the occasion. To our way of thinking, this is the perfect way to step out, with the plaudits and testimonials of his public, who refuse to forget that he played a prominent part in past Boston successes. He bows himself out in style, not the other way, as a minor leaguer and, finally, not ever that.[33]

Boston Herald, *February 22, 1934, page 29.*

And Arthur Siegel, *Boston Herald*:

"HITCHMAN NIGHT" AT THE GARDEN TO BE FAREWELL FOR "GRAND OLD MAN"

Bruins and Senators Join Fans in Hitchman Tribute Tonight as Star Quits 'Big Time' Ranks

Boston professional hockey departs from its ordered routine of performance without preliminary festivities as former and current enthusiasts unite with the Bruins and the Ottawa Senators in paying tribute to Fred Lionel Hitchman at the Boston Garden tonight.

Occasion to Be "Hitchman Night"

It will be "Hitchman Night" singled out for occasion on which the "grand old man" of the Bruins bows himself out of the major league picture as a player. A month ago named manager of the Bruin Cubs, Hitchman will don his Bruins uniform for the last time, take his position at left defense in the starting array and finish his big league career against the team with whom he started his professional days, the Senators of Ottawa.

"Hitchman Night" was planned by Melrose neighbors of the erstwhile Bruins defenseman. They wished to show him that in his stay of more than a decade in Boston he had come to mean more to them than merely a member of the professional hockey team. Hitchman apparently had played his last major game in New York on Jan. 28, but the Bruins management fell in line with the idea and agreed that it would be only fitting for Hitch to make his big league farewell in the way proposed.

So it is that tonight, preceding the regular game, the Bruins first will present their old-timers' line-up, that is the oldest men, in point of service, with the club. Percy Galbraith will be at left wing, Harry Oliver will be at center, Dit Clapper at right wing, Hitchman at left defense and Eddie Shore at right defense. Tiny Thompson will be in goal, of course. Actually, not one of the players on either club was in major league hockey when Hitchman started with the Senators, or with the Bruins, for that matter.

To Play Until Hitchman Scores

The idea then is to have a mock attack staged, with Hitchman scoring the goal and until Hitchman scores the goal. Then will follow a series of presentations, such as a plaque, his stick, his number 3 jersey and various other gifts, with the Bruins contributing something and, most likely, the Senators honoring him on their own. After that the regular game will begin, with no mockery at all.

The chief feature and the reason that a good turnout is expected however, is that Hitchman is stepping out of the big league with due ceremony. He made hockey history both in Ottawa and in Boston. In Ottawa he was an amateur star who caught the eye of Tommy Gorman, then pilot of the Senators. He was signed an hour before game time one night, walked into the Ottawa dressing room, wore his amateur uniform, which was the same as the pro outfit, and played that night. Later he scored a vital goal against Edmonton in the Stanley Cup series at Vancouver.

Became a Star with the Bruins

. . . he was sold to the Bruins in 1925. Here he gained stardom, the great sweep check stopping attacks cold and his body check breaking up attacks when the sweep could not be used. Under the tutelage of Art Ross he developed and he picked up valuable pointers from his mates. Sprague Cleghorn, for instance, is given credit in some parts for helping him.

Then came the purchase of the Western stars, including Shore, Oliver and Galbraith. Hitchman and Shore formed a great defense partnership, sturdy and rockbound, forming almost perfect protection for their goaler as the Bruins marched to the heights. They were fearless and they were colorful as a pair.

Hitchman rarely sought trouble on the ice, in fact he avoided trouble. Yet there was nothing timid about him. There are the stories of his rollicking nature, about the time he walked into an opposing dressing room after a particularly venomous game, engaged in a general battle and left the room smiling and singing one of the highly colored boating ballads of the Rideau of Ottawa, that famous canoe club.

Then Hitchman, still a young man, but not in a hockey sense, began to feel the toil. He slowed down a bit. The bruises did not depart so quickly and eventually it was decided that Hitch would leave the big league competitive scene. He was made manager of the Cubs. And tonight he pays his final competitive respects to big league hockey.[34]

That afternoon Dit Clapper, Eddie Shore, and Hitch did some trapshooting to blow off steam before the game. Maybe too much steam, as Boston lost to Ottawa that night. But as Webb of the *Boston Globe* explains, Hitch was honored most memorably:

PARTY FOR HITCHMAN
In no very small way the evening was ushered in as an "old-timers" night. Art Ross went through the old birthday book as well as over the original signing dates with the Bruins and then decided to shove the old gang in there pretty much in a bunch.

On the line there was "Dit" Clapper, the all-round lad, who has been with the club since 1928. In the middle was Harry Oliver, who came over from Glengary by purchase in 1926, and then there was "Perk" Galbraith, who landed in Boston as a quasi amateur and has been here ever since.

But the big noise was for that smiling, seldom-ruffled Lionel Hitchman, veteran defensive player extraordinary.
. . .

Shore, of course, was in there too—and the vigorous "Tiny" Thompson. Eddie put a Bruins' number on his back in 1927 and Thompson has been kicking 'em away from Boston strings since [1928].

A Great Act

The boy put on a great act at the start. From the original face-off Hitchman got the puck, rushed in and popped at the goal. He missed. Out came the puck and Hitch popped again, this time scoring in just 15 seconds.

Some frame-up that one. The goal scored, there was no flash on the board—so it was a "phoney"—just a set-up.

The show was then put on, Hitch being drawn from the rank of Bruins at the blue line and made the recipient of much good news. With his father looking on, Lionel received a plaque on which was emblazoned his fine record as a hockey player—all of which was tossed off through the megaphones by Frank Ryan.

While Hitch was looking at the plaque his attention was diverted to a check for $500 from his admiring Boston fans and another $500 check from Pres Charles F. Adams of the Bruins. Art Ross' contribution was a chest of silver which was presented in the dressing room, toward which Hitchman skated, his face wreathed in smiles, following his final National League scoring shot.

It was one sweet tribute to a real boy and a great hockey player who for so many years gave to Boston the best he had—and it was "some best."[35]

The set of silverware given to Hitch that night by Art Ross was a gesture reminiscent of the parting gift Ross' parents received when his father transferred locations for work.[36]

The three newspaper photos are from Tops scrapbook at Library and Archives Canada. I'm uncertain which newspaper all three are from. Both the Boston Globe *and* Boston Herald *carried the middle photo of Hitch receiving the silverware from Art Ross on February 23, 1934.*

Walter Gilhooly of the *Ottawa Journal* had a less sentimental take on the evening:

SMART BOSTON CLUB
When it comes to a matter of keen business dealings one has to hand the palm to the Yankees, and last night the Boston Hockey Club put one over for themselves that would make David Harum look like a yokel going places for a trimming. Crowds have been falling off in Boston. The other night when Detroit Red Wings played there the game drew 1,500 fans. It didn't mean much to Bruins, but it did mean something to Detroit.

Last night the game meant nothing to either Ottawa or Boston. Ordinarily there would not have been as large a crowd as was in the stands for the Red Wings' match, so smart Mr. Adams selected the evening to honor Lionel Hitchman, who is finished as a player with the club and is now manager of the Boston Cubs.

... There were 9,000 fans at the game. Figuring that there would have been the same number as saw Detroit if it had not been Lionel Hitchman night, and averaging the tickets at a dollar each, the Boston club stood to clear about $7,000 for throwing the party. Smart business.[37]

Hitch showed his appreciation to the fans in a letter carried by the local newspapers on February 26:

HITCHMAN EXPRESSES APPRECIATION TO FANS
Fred Hitchman, manager of the Bruins Cubs, who has ended his playing career, has written the following open letter to Boston hockey fans:

"I wish to express to the Boston fans my appreciation of the great honor conferred on me at the Boston Garden, Feb. 22.

"The night bearing my name being prearranged, could not be termed a surprise, but the magnificence of the reception, the gifts and the sendoff left me positively speechless.

"It has been a real pleasure during the past 10 seasons to play before the Boston fans and it is beyond reason to think that any player could fail to respond to their warm-hearted and loyal enthusiasm.

"Now that my playing days are over, the prospect of staying in Boston is very pleasing, and I hope that in the future I will be able to justify the confidence that has been placed in me by Mr Adams and Art Ross in retaining me with the Boston Hockey Club."[38]

Closing out the season in game 48 in New York, the Bruins beat the Americans 9-5 on March 18, 1934. The Associated Press reported: "Lionel Fred Hitchman, former Bruin defense player, who became manager of the Cubs this season, directed the team from the bench in the absence of Manager Art Ross." It was the third season that Hitch had filled in for Ross when he wasn't available—this time as a member of the coaching staff of the Boston Bruins organization.[39]

Picture of Hitch, from 1934. (Hitchman private collection)

Chapter Thirteen

THE COACHING YEARS

Hitch's hockey coaching career began as acting manager of the Boston Bruins during their Stanley Cup Championship season of 1928-29, when in game 43 he piloted the team to a 5-1 win in Detroit. The next year, he and Mickey MacKay were called upon by Bruins owner Charles Adams to take over when manager Art Ross was ordered to take two weeks off, after a brawling incident involving Eddie Shore. And for the last three years of his NHL playing career, he coached the Boston Bruins whenever Ross was not available.

When Hitch hung up his skates after game 30 of the 1933-34 NHL season against the New York Rangers on January 28, 1934, it came as no surprise that he would remain involved with the Boston Bruins franchise in some capacity or another. The longest-serving hockey player in Boston history, the last member of the original team, was made the manager of the Boston Bruins' minor professional farm team, the Boston Cubs of the Canadian-American hockey league, the forerunner of the American Hockey League. The Cubs' president was Weston Adams, the son of Bruins owner Charles Adams. Art Ross was general manager, and now Hitch succeeded Myles Lane as coach. Lane was brought back up to the Bruins as a spare player. It was a time of great flux within the Boston Bruins hierarchy, and rumors were rampant. "Bruins' officials admitted that 'Hitch' was being groomed for the future. Ever since the Shore-Bailey accident, rumors have been rife that Charles F. Adams, owner of the club, would soon retire from hockey and turn the reins over to Art Ross, present manager. In such an event, it is likely that Hitchman would succeed Ross, although Frank Patrick, present managing director of the NHL, has been mentioned for that position."[1]

The Can-Am league, as it was known, was in its eighth season and five teams competed for its championship Henri Fontaine Cup: the Boston Cubs, New Haven Eagles, Philadelphia Arrows, Providence Reds and Quebec Beavers. Boston's representative was formerly known as the Boston Tigers before being bought by the Boston Bruins in February 1931 and renamed the Cubs.

When Hitch took over the team, the Cubs had played 24 of their 41 regular-season games and were tied for first place with the Quebec Beavers with 27 points. Providence was in third place with 25 points, Philadelphia in fourth with 23, and New Haven trailed with 16 points.

Hitch's first game as coach was on January 31, 1934, in Philadelphia against the Arrows. Joe Gilmore, who had shared duties with Lane as the coach, returned to his previous responsibilities as the trainer of the team. The Cubs tied the Arrows that night in front of 4,000 spectators, sending them into sole ownership of first place by one point.

Hitch's first home game as coach of the Boston Cubs was quite a spectacle, in front of a crowd larger than those seen recently at the Bruins home games. It was announced that Hitch would start at left defense to strengthen the team, as the three starting forwards were not available (Tommy Filmore's wife was ill in Detroit, Obs Heximer had an injured ankle, and Frank Jerwa had been called up to the Bruins). Hitch had played in the first game he coached as well and would do so for another two games, but that was it. The Bruins put a stop to it, indicating they didn't want him doing that.[2]

That night, 8,000 came out to see Hitch and his Cubs beat Philadelphia 2-1, giving them a two-point lead ahead of Quebec in the standings. Hitch was presented with an 11-month-old bruin cub as a "lucky token" from D. Leo Dolan on behalf of the New Brunswick (Canada) Guides Association. "Now the Bruins have a bruin for their mascot and the Bruins Cubs have a bruin cub for theirs."[3]

Hitch had become very close with Dolan over his years going to New Brunswick to fish and hunt. The bear cub that Dolan gave Hitch that night stayed with the Hitchman household for two years at their fishing camp, Koanneeta, at Mousam Lake in Maine. His daughter, Gloria, named it "Paprika." Little Paprika became almost as famous as her owner when she got loose in early August and caused quite a stir with the neighbors:

> Reports flew thick and fast that a huge bear with glaring eyes and foaming mouth was seeking whom it might devour. Paprika, all ignorant of the uproar she had caused, was finally treed, with the aid of a hound, and Mr. Hitchman coaxed her down with her favorite delicacy blueberry pie.
>
> Paprika, who has had her first experience of what gossip can do to a lady's reputation, is really most amiable and well-behaved individual. Her most vicious habit is to escape confinement and go to her master's room to beg pie and chocolate. She's very fond of Gloria, daughter of Mr. Hitchman, and likes to play with her and her friends.[4]

Photo right, from August 1934, newspaper unknown

Also adding to Hitch's persona as a woodsman and hunter, the *Boston Globe* ran a lengthy piece in March 1934 on Hitch's skill with a bow and arrow and announced that he would demonstrate this skill at the Boston Garden during a Hunting and Fishing Show the following month:

> Always a sportsman on the ice, it was only natural for 'Hitch' to be one out of hockey. 'Often I have killed with a high-powered rifle,' states Hitch, 'when the game had practically no chance. I felt no exhilaration in those kills. The first feel of a yew bow won me and the romance and history of the sport took hold of me. Like thousands of others, I became an archery 'nut.' ... 'Remember,' pointed out Hitchman, 'there's an element of physical skill and manhood in archery missing from shooting with a gun. ... Take a hunting bow that registers a 90 pound pull, for instance. Many great athletes scarcely can notch it. It requires remarkable strength of arm, fingers and hand.'[5]

Boston Globe, *March 22, 1934, page 20.*

The Boston Bruins operated the Cubs with Hitch as the coach for three years and then folded its operation when the Canadian-American league merged with other leagues to become the AHL.

The 1933-34 Cubs season finished with Providence moving into first place and Boston holding on to second. Philadelphia landed in third place and played Boston in the elimination round. In the first playoff game in Boston, 7,000 fans watched as the Cubs beat Philly 3-1 on March 27. The final game of that series took place in Philadelphia two nights later; the Cubs won 3-2 in a hotly contested battle with six major penalties and two fist fights.

A crowd of 12,000 in Boston watched as the Cubs lost 4-1 to Providence in the opening game of the Fontaine Cup final. The Cubs lost the next two games of the best-of-five series, handing the Can-Am championship to Billy Coutu's Providence team. (Billy, the ousted NHL player formerly of the Bruins back in 1927 and before that with the Canadiens.)

President Charles Adams announced after the Bruins finished last in the division that for the upcoming 1934-35 season, the club would have a new management scheme, putting Art Ross in a noncoaching position for the first time, bringing in Frank Patrick as the Bruins' coach and renaming Hitchman as the Cubs' coach for a second season. Adams stated that "the policy of the club would be to develop promising young players by adding to the Cubs' roster additional talent, mostly amateurs of proven ability who wish to enter professional hockey." He also added that a "fund had been set aside in substantial amounts to purchase professional players of proven ability."[6]

The Cubs joined the Bruins for a three-week training camp in Quebec City in October 1934. While there, the two teams put on a benefit hockey game on October 27, which the Cubs won 6-2. "Joy reigned in Boston Cubs' camp last night, the Canadian-American league club, managed by Lionel Hitchman. . . . Cubs turned on the heat right from the start, Frank Jerwa, of the Cubs' forward line was the outstanding man on the ice, scoring three goals and assisting in a fourth. Phil Besler, former Prince Albert Minto, and his running mate Alex Motter both notched a goal apiece for the Cubs, while the sixth marker came from the stick of 'Nip' Hergesheimer, last year with Winnipeg's Falcon juniors."[7]

The Can-Am League in 1934-35 played 48 games, and the Cubs finished in first place with a 29-13-6 record, 12 points ahead of Quebec in second and 14 points in front of Providence in third. The Providence Reds prevailed in the preliminary round, beating the Quebec Beavers in two straight games in the best-of-three series. They now played Boston for the championship.

Hitch with Gene Carrigan in 1934. From the 1934-35 Boston Cubs Program. (Photo courtesy of Hitchman private collection)

The opening game of the best-of-five final took place on April 2 in Boston in front of 9,600 fans; the Cubs won 1-0, with the only goal in the game from Phil Besler in the first period. The 13 players suiting up for the Cubs, including the starting lineup, were Art Giroux (RW), Gene Carrigan (C), Walter Jackson (LW), Joe Jerwa

(D), Jack Portland (D), Percy Jackson (G) and spares Alex Motter (C), Bob Blake (LW), Phil Hergesheimer (RW), Walter Harnott (LW), Bob McCully (D), Phil Besler (RW) and Milt Halliday (LW). All either spent or would spend time in the NHL, averaging four years each.

The series shifted to Rhode Island, where Boston beat Providence 4-1 in the second game. Back at the Boston Garden on April 7 in front of 10,000 for the third game, the Boston Cubs won 3-1 to sweep the series, becoming the proud owners of the Fontaine Cup. Boston's Joe Jerwa was touted as the star of the series, and "let's tip our hats, too, to Manager Lionel Hitchman. A fine fellow, who knows his hockey."[8]

At a banquet to honor the Fontaine Cup winners, the Boston Cubs, owner Charles Adams announced that Patrick and Ross would continue in their respective roles for next season and that Hitch would be retained as the Cubs' manager for a third season.

The Boston Bruins bounced back in the 1934-35 season, finishing first in their division but losing out to the Toronto Maple Leafs in the semifinal playoff. The Montreal Maroons beat Toronto to win the Stanley Cup. The Maroons were now coached by Tommy Gorman, Hitch's first NHL manager while with the Ottawa Senators, and featured ex-Bruin Dutch Gainor.

By mid-January 1936, the Bruins were in last place in their division for the 1935-36 season, and Art Ross and Frank Patrick were not on speaking terms. At Patrick's urging and by virtue of his contract, Ross was kept away from the daily management of the Bruins for the balance of the season. By the end of the season, the Bruins had pulled up to second place in their division but lost in the quarterfinals to the Toronto Maple Leafs.

Ross found a new outlet for his stress or boredom and tended to spend more time with the Cubs, at the invitation of Hitch, if the newspaper reports are correct.

The Cubs were slow starting this season, with inexperienced amateurs playing against some of the most hardened and seasoned minor pros. But they continued to draw well at the box office, culminating in a season high of 12,000 on February 21, 1936. The game had been promoted as "Ladies Night," and 7,000 showed up to see "Roger 'Broadway' Jenkins, erstwhile Bruin, figure in three goals and lead the junior B's to a thrilling 5-4 triumph over the hapless Springfield Indians at the Garden last night." By then the Cubs were on a winning spree of 10 games in 13 starts, which pulled them out of last place and within two points of a playoff berth.[9]

It was a season that saw several players from the amateur and semi-pro ranks develop their skills and in the next year move up to the Bruins and in short order help them win two Stanley Cups (1939 and 1941). Noteworthy protégés were:

- Woody Dumart, who came from the OHA's Junior Kitchener Greenshirts. He played all 47 games in 1935-36 for the Boston Cubs and 16 years with the Boston Bruins, forming one third of the famous Kraut Line (explained farther on) and winning two Stanley Cups with Boston. He was inducted into the HHOF in 1992.
- Bobby Bauer also came from the Kitchener Greenshirts and played the full season for the Cubs in 1935-36. He was with the Bruins for 10 years, forming another third of the Kraut Line and winning two Stanley Cups. He was inducted into the HHOF in 1996.
- William "Flash" Hollett, from the IHL's Syracuse Stars, played one year with the Boston Cubs and nine years with the Boston Bruins, winning two Stanley Cups. His 1945 league record of 20 regular-season goals by a defenseman stood for 25 years until beaten by Bobby Orr.
- Ray Getliffe, who came from the IHL's London Tecumsehs, played one year with the Boston Cubs and four years with the Boston Bruins. He won the Stanley Cup once with the Bruins (1939) and played six years with the Montreal Canadiens, winning the Stanley Cup a second time in 1944.
- Jack Portland, while not an amateur, was with the Montreal Canadiens for two seasons prior to playing with the Cubs for two seasons under Hitch. He went on to play six seasons with the Boston Bruins, winning the Stanley Cup in 1939.

Over the decades Ross was largely credited with the acquisition and development of these players, but in speaking with Milt Schmidt in 1995, he gave much credit to Hitch, not only in their early professional development but in his own. Schmidt played with both Dumart and Bauer in the junior ranks and first played with Boston in the 1936-37 season. He played 16 seasons with Boston, winning two Stanley Cups, being the 1951 Hart Trophy recipient and a HHOF inductee in 1961. Schmidt then coached the Bruins and later became general manager.

After the 1935-36 season, Frank Patrick, who had coached the Bruins for two seasons, was out and his lifelong friendship with Art Ross came to a sudden halt. Ross at age 51 was back at the helm of the team, where he'd wanted to be all along, and the Boston Bruins created a position for Hitch, the first-ever assistant coach (or manager, the term used in those days):

> After two years devoted exclusively to the front office, Art Ross will resume his old position as active manager of the Bruins this season, it was announced last night [Sept. 14, 1936] by Pres C. F. Adams of the Boston professional hockey interests.
>
> At the same time, Pres Adams revealed that the brand new portfolio of assistant manager has been created for Fred Lionel Hitchman, great defenseman, who piloted the now-defunct Bruin Cubs last season.
>
> Abandonment of the Cubs, along with the taking over of other detail work by the Boston Garden, paves the way for Ross to resume the helm he handed to Frank Patrick two years ago because of ill health and growing duties in the front office as general manager.
>
> Ever since Ross and Patrick had a falling out the middle of last season, it was plain that Patrick would not be back with the B's this year, but, until Pres Adams' announcement last night, it was believed Hitch would be Patrick's successor.

However, with Hitchman in such close contact with him, Ross feels he can return to the active wars as well as swing the general manager's duties.

"Hitch and I worked so well together in our brief term with the Cubs," said Ross, "that we think things will go smoothly under the new arrangements with the Bruins.

"I'll be with the club most of the time," Art continued, "but when I'm unable to be, 'Hitch' will have full charge. It will be great experience for him. He's a little short on experience for a full-fledged manager's job yet.

All Ross would offer in the way of tactical plans was: "We'll return to the style that earned us the reputation of the burly, bruising Bruins."[10]

Boston Globe, *September 15, 1936, page 21.*

The Bruins moved their training camp to Hershey, Pennsylvania, that season. Eddie Shore arrived on time for the first time since he was a rookie, and Hitch had command of the 24 amateurs trying to make their mark. "Whoops! They're at it again. Lionel Hitchman, coach of Boston Bruins, has popped up with the NHL's second 'baby line.' The fans already have had numerous 'kid lines,' as produced by Toronto Maple Leafs and New York Rangers, a 'big S line' and 'green line,' given them by Montreal Maroons, and Leafs' original 'baby line.' The Boston threesome is made up of Milt Schmidt, Bobby Bauer and Porky Dumart."[11] This latest threesome would be known as the Kraut Line in honor of their German heritage and hometown of Kitchener, Ontario (originally Berlin but changed during WWI), and they would become instrumental in the rejuvenation of the Boston Bruins.

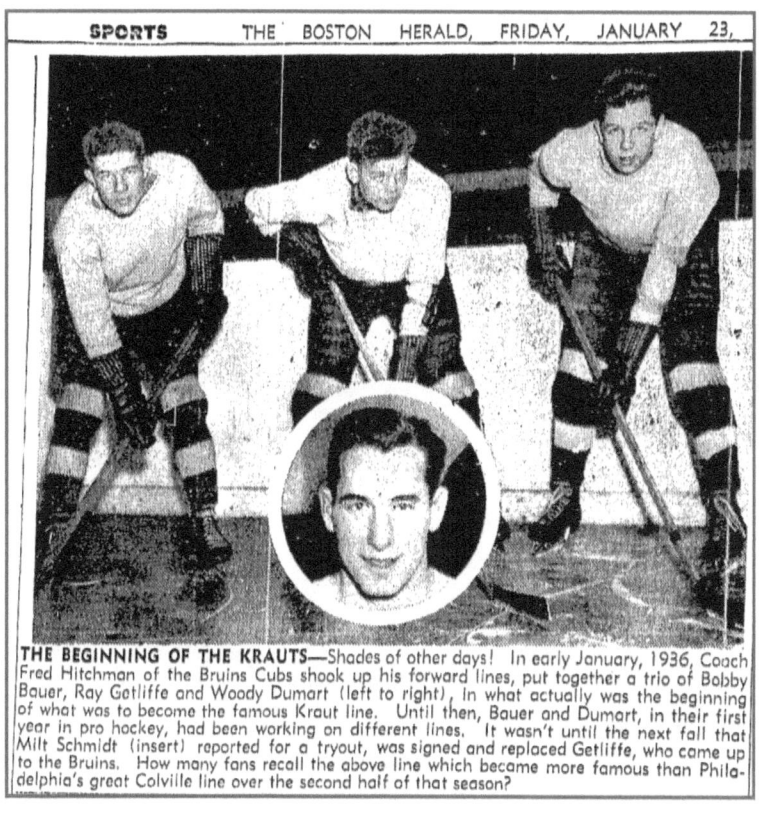

Boston Herald, *January 23, 1942, page 28.*

Hitch stayed in this position for two seasons, primarily responsible for training, player development, scouting and coaching when Art Ross was not available. In season one Hitch coached new player Hooley Smith, someone he was well acquainted with from years of sparring with him both in junior hockey and in the NHL. Hitch was all business, and as done with Sprague Cleghorn more than 10 years earlier, he gave Smith his usual gracious welcome. Hitch was well known around the Eastern Seaboard for the time he clocked in scouting promising young hopefuls, including Jack Crawford, who would star for Boston in 13 seasons and two Stanley

Cup runs, but on one such trip in February 1937, he quipped, "all I saw was three inches of snow in Baltimore."[12]

Also that season, he promoted the new guys, giving them the opportunity to get better known by the locals. On one such occasion, "Fred Hitchman, 'Herbie' Schmidt, 'Porky' Dumart and Ray Getliffe will represent the Boston Bruins at the Watertown High sports program tonight."[13]

Hitch also defended Shore when the scribes suggested his worth to the team was less than in previous seasons. In an interview with Victor O. Jones of the *Boston Globe* on December 23, 1937, Hitch offered:

> 'Everyone these days is saying that Eddie has slowed up or slipped, but as far as I'm concerned, I think Eddie is a far better player this minute than he was when we played the points together back in '29 and '30—the time that you literary birds refer to as the Golden Era of Boston hockey.
>
> 'Why do I think Shore is better now than then? Well, I for one don't think he's slowed up appreciably and he's a much better team man now than he was eight years ago. Shore nowadays plays a type of defensive game that no man has ever attempted before and that I don't think any man except Shore could get away with. If you spend the night some time watching nobody but Eddie, you'll see that his defensive zone covers something like half the rink.
>
> 'Eddie doesn't score as many goals as he used to, but this is because the league is stronger now than it was then and because the other teams have taken to stopping Eddie before he gets started. Anyway I only wish my old dogs would revive long enough to let me join Shore on the team again. Boy we'd be sensational, because with the Shore of today, I'd rush a lot and probably lead the team in scoring.'

Jones agreed with much of what Hitch had to say:

save that part about the league now being stronger and Hitch getting a lot of goals. On the latter point, it is enough to say that Hitch was strictly a scoreless wonder and that even if he never scored a goal, he still was worth a featured spot on any team. I personally don't think the league is stronger now than it was eight years ago, but that's a matter of opinion. In my humble opinion the league now hasn't replaced such men as Hitchman, the Cook brothers, Frank Boucher, Ching Johnson, Frank Clancy, Frank Nighbor, Howie Morenz, Aurel Joliat and others, all in their prime then.[14]

(We'll never know if Hitch could have been a prominent rushing defensive star. Certainly, in his amateur and early days in the NHL he tended in that direction. But as he once quipped when talking about a rival goalie: "I don't even know what he looks like. Art Ross doesn't let me go to the other end of the rink.")[15]

That year Eddie won his fourth Hart Trophy. During Hitch's two seasons with the Bruins as the assistant coach, they placed second and then first in the American Division, earning a playoff berth in both years.

Wanting to get more experience with bench coaching, in the fall of 1938, Hitch took the position of coach of the Springfield Indians in the International Hockey League (the league that formed in the interim between the Can-Am league and the AHL). The Bruins had played Springfield in an exhibition series the season before, and Hitch had the opportunity to show his coaching ability. Springfield owner Lucien Garneau was also familiar with Hitch from the Can-Am league. Garneau had owned the Quebec Beavers, and when that league disbanded, he transferred his franchise to Springfield to resurrect the Springfield Indians (they had initially played from 1926 to 1932 in the Can-Am league before suspending operations).

"Frederick Lionel Hitchman, the old Bruins immortal who has been acting as Art Ross' assistant on the Bruins since the suspension of the Cubs Canam franchise, yesterday was named manager of the

Springfield Indians by Lucien Garneau, owner of the Springfield Canadian American League team. He succeeds George (Buck) Boucher, who had managed the team for three years."[16]

Three weeks after the announcement of Hitch's moving to Springfield, Ross appointed Cooney Weiland to assume Hitch's role with the Bruins, the only difference being that Cooney would continue to play hockey as well.

The Indians set up their training camp in Quebec City in mid-October 1938 to select their final team. Thirteen amateur players were at camp, several from the Ottawa area. In the second week of training, Hitch's leg began to swell and became very sore. He had injured it just prior to leaving for Quebec and thought nothing of it. But now it was more than a distraction. The Associated Press reported: "When the leg began swelling during the week-end, Hitchman entered a hospital. Team officials, however, said tonight the condition of the former Boston Bruin defense stalwart had improved rapidly and it now was expected he would be back in the harness within two days."[17]

Art Ross had heard about the injury before the AP story broke on October 25. When he learned that it had not healed by November 9, he asked Hitch to come to Boston to have it checked out. Upon seeing Hitch's leg, Ross immediately took him to hospital. The papers had reported that Hitch had a deep vein thromboembolism in his leg, but what was not commonly known was that he had also contracted osteomyelitis in a finger and had to have it amputated.

It was now late December and Hitch hadn't been in Springfield since the second game of the season. The team was in last place, and rumors were swirling about the possibility of Hitch being replaced. He was mostly recovered now, and Ross insisted on accompanying him back to Springfield on December 28 to help get resettled.

Hitch dove right in. He immediately went to Philadelphia to scout the competition and then went on to observe his team in Cleveland. What he saw was a team not in condition and immediately started them on an intensive training regimen. On January 18, 1939, the *Evening News* of Harrisburg, Pennsylvania, commented: "Lionel Hitchman, Springfield coach, has returned to the bench after being out with illness for some time and the Indians are now scalping the foe as a 2 to 1 win over Cleveland and a 6 to 1 triumph over New Haven last week would indicate."[18]

But that same day, Springfield Indians owner Lucien Garneau made a brief statement that was carried across the newswire, resulting in this Associated Press article:

> SPRINGFIELD, Mass, Jan. 18 (AP)-The release of Lionel Hitchman, former National League hockey star, as coach of Springfield Indians of the International-American League, was announced tonight by J. Lucien Garneau, president of the club. Garneau declined any comment beyond a flat announcement of Hitchman's release.
>
> Hitchman, once one of the NHL's outstanding players, was forced to miss almost half of the Indians' season because of illness. He was stricken with phlebitis after he joined the club in its Quebec City training camp last November and he found it in last place when he returned to duty about two weeks ago.
>
> Hitchman broke in as an International-American manager in 1934 with Boston Bruins' Cubs, which he led to two consecutive league championships. When that team was disbanded after the 1935-36 season, he returned to Boston Bruins, with whom he played defense for nine years, as assistant manager and coach.[19]

Three days later, Garneau named Johnny Mitchell, "popular international American League hockey referee" as coach.[20] Soon after Hitch's firing, it was also learned that Eddie Shore had been eyeing the franchise. Garneau was in debt and wanted to sell the team, and within a few months, Shore became the new owner and took over as player-coach; he ran the operation for 36 years.

Hitch stayed on in Springfield for the remainder of the 1938-39 season helping the Springfield Braves, who played in the newly formed New England Amateur Hockey League. Four other teams participated including the Boston Junior Olympics, Providence

Marquettes, New Haven Brock-Halls, and Brockingham (MA) Brockvilles. The Braves' coach was Abbie Cox, whom Hitch first knew from Ottawa when Abbie played for the Ottawa Munitions in the senior amateur league there. Abbie played a few games in the NHL with four different teams and played for the Quebec Beavers and Springfield Indians when Hitch was coaching the Boston Cubs.

It was a welcomed offer, and Hitch found he enjoyed the amateur ranks. Shortly after WWII, he was credited with "fathering hockey interest," or maybe resurrecting it, in Berlin, New Hampshire. With the help of a group of local businessmen, he assembled and coached the Berlin Maroons, better known as the Flying Frenchmen. Hitch arranged for teams from Quebec to play the team and then in late March 1947 entered the Maroons in the East National B championship of the Amateur Hockey Association of the United States, where they lost out in the quarterfinals. Their best player, Gilles Dube, received a gold watch and was named outstanding player of the championship. He was also named to the first all-star team, and Maroons right winger John Chambers made the second team. The Maroons would go on to win multiple New England championships in the years to come, and Berlin became known as "Hockey Town USA."[21]

When Hitch relocated to Indian Lake, New York, in 1953, he also coached the local high school team in that beautiful and remote Adirondack enclave.

But at the end of the Springfield Braves' season in 1939, Hitch found his way back to Boston, helping out the Bruins in the front office and organizing a victory tribute for the newly minted Stanley Cup champs. He stayed on in a scouting capacity until after the Bruins won their third Stanley Cup in 1941, before moving completely away from the professional ranks, only to return for the festivities in 1952 to honor the first Stanley Cup winning team of the Boston Bruins.

Chapter Fourteen

LIFE WITHOUT HOCKEY

After the Boston Bruins' 1940-41 Stanley Cup season, Hitch's long and storied association with the club came to an end. In 1941 he also lost his grandfather, John Hitchman, with whom he was very close. In addition, in late 1940, his wife Tops left him, taking their 14-year-old daughter, Gloria, back to Canada. Their relationship began to unravel a few years earlier from the strain of Tops' suffering five miscarriages plus a stillborn son and Hitch's increasing reliance on alcohol to manage the lingering effects of his multiple head and body injuries from his hockey playing days. The Great Depression also contributed to a strain on their financial situation, causing them to give up their beloved Koanneeta lodge in 1939.

Hitch continued to split his time between the Mousam Lake area of Maine and Boston well into the mid-1940s. He had been turned down for active military service during WWII because of his documented multiple concussions, but he got on with the U.S. Coast Guard Auxiliary shortly after taking out his U.S. citizenship in 1942.

His divorce from Tops came through in 1944, and for a short time, he managed a hotel in Berlin, New Hampshire, before getting hired on with a lumber company. He trained for and became an assayer, documenting and surveying forests to determine tree species and their physical measurements, age, overall health, and life expectancy. He spent weeks at a time deep in the mountain ranges of New Hampshire, Maine and New York assessing forests and recommending stands for felling and manufacturing and areas for reforestation. Hitch was happiest and at peace in the quiet setting of the woods, from his earliest introduction to Algonquin Park by

Tops and her parents, his hunting and fishing expeditions throughout New Brunswick and his camp at Mousam Lake in Maine. He was known to quote and keep a copy of Henry David Thoreau's *Walden* with him, espousing the virtues of simple living surrounded by nature. This environment and setting soothed the battle-scarred "titan" of the Boston Bruins.

After Tops left Hitch, she and Gloria went to Montreal for a few years, but when her father died in 1943, they returned to Ottawa to live with her mother. Tops went back to work at the national revenue department, staying until her retirement in 1970. In a letter to Tops in 1963, Cooney Weiland's wife, Gertrude, commented, "But you're still the prettiest one in Canada." To this day, old-timers at Mousam Lake recall her as a beautiful and kind woman. Even after leaving the Bruins "family" she kept in close contact with many of the players' wives as well as with Art Ross and his wife, Muriel.

In the 1940s divorce was considered taboo, and Tops was not only devastated by the demise of her marriage but also humiliated. But these Bruins friends helped her get through. This was also when the Hockey Hall of Fame was being formed, and Art Ross was one of its driving forces. Tops used her influence with Ross to request that Hitch be kept out of it to "minimize any unnecessary publicity about Hitch," as it was making the adjustment for her and Gloria difficult in their new lifestyle. Years later Tops shared this detail with her family, regrettably, citing it as the singular reason that Hitch's name was not brought forth in the early days of this honored membership.

Tops also used her influence to help young players break into hockey. One was Patrick Coburn, an Ottawa neighborhood friend of Gloria's and the younger brother of Gloria's future husband. In an interview for this book, Pat commented, "Tops was a very dear friend to me and helped greatly with my hockey career of 15 years. I went to the Boston Bruins training camp in Quebec City, stayed at the Chateau Frontenac when I was 17. This was a big deal at the time, hardly anyone at this age ever got this kind of opportunity. She knew everybody and had a lot of sway with Art Ross." Pat continued, "and again when I returned from three years in England and Europe, she arranged my career with Detroit."

In 1945 Gloria was skating with the Ice Capades and became very sick. The show was in Detroit, and Tops rushed there to find out what was happening. She didn't like what she saw, and with the help of her old friend Carson Cooper, former Boston Bruins star and then Detroit Red Wings head scout, she brought Gloria home to Ottawa in the middle of the season. "Coop" and Tops became romantically entangled; there was a proposal and a ring, but they never married and remained close friends until his death in 1955. After Hitch, Tops never married again.

Hitch's work took him to upstate New York, where he met and married Edna Rust in 1953. Edna was older than Hitch, a former schoolteacher, and widow. Her first husband, John Daniel Rust, was a Princeton University track star who studied civil engineering and opened his own engineering firm after serving in WWI.

Hitch and Edna had a property in Indian Lake on Route 30 with 110 acres of wooded land, a pond and rental cabins, adjacent to the Cedar River Golf Course. After his retirement from the lumber industry, Hitch took a job with the state of New York as a forest ranger. His post was atop the 70-foot Wakely Mountain Fire Tower, the tallest in the Adirondacks and still in use today. He worked for the State for seven years until shortly before his death.

Hitch with great nieces Penny (left) and Patty (right) at the base of the fire tower on Wakely Mountain, circa 1965. (Photo courtesy of Penny Haskin)

Hitch was taken to hospital on December 4, 1968, after local authorities found him at home unable to get out of bed and coughing up blood. He had not eaten for over two weeks. He died 14 hours later. State officials expressed concern that Hitch had languished in his sick bed without any intervention. An autopsy revealed he had a massive blood clot in his right lung that had been there an estimated three weeks, and a recent clot had formed in his left lung that likely killed him.

Needless to say, Hitch's daughter, Gloria, was devasted to lose her father and horrified at the manner in which he was left to die. The chief of staff of the Glens Falls Hospital where Hitch was taken wrote to Gloria 19 days after Hitch's death, providing her with a detailed description of his condition entering the hospital, adding: "This is the first time I have been aware of your existence or I would have let you know."[1] A social worker expressed concern to Gloria of possible willful neglect on Edna's behalf for not calling the doctor or his daughter when Hitch became ill. Gloria knew that Edna belonged to a religious group that believed illness could be cured with prayer. Gloria feared this was the reason Edna didn't call for the doctor and pressed for an investigation, but it's not certain if one was ever opened.

Four decades later, my partner and I took a trip to Mousam Lake to retrieve some artifacts belonging to Hitch, one of which was that 27-pound salmon, stuffed and mounted, that Hitch caught in the Saint John River in New Brunswick back in 1932. He had donated it to the boys' camp at the lake. The latest owner of the camp had recently died, and his son tracked us down to ensure that Hitch's items were returned to his family. On our way there we stopped in Indian Lake, New York, to visit Hitch's gravesite and to speak with the sexton, who as it turned out knew Hitch and Edna well and as a teenager sometimes accompanied Hitch up the mountain to his station at the tower. He told us that at the time of Hitch's death, Edna was almost completely "senile," and the incident rocked the community. After Hitch's death, the sexton's mother was appointed Edna's trustee as she didn't have any living relatives. Edna was moved into a home and died in 1970.

Hitch's death notice in the local New York newspaper did not get picked up by any other news outlets. It was only after Gloria's announcement in the Ottawa newspapers on December 21 that the hockey world took notice. Here is her announcement:

"HITCHMAN, Frederick Lionel – Suddenly in hospital at Glens Falls, NY on Thursday, Dec 5, 1968, Frederick Lionel Hitchman of Indian Lake, NY, in his 68th year. Son of the late Ida M. and E. Frederick Hitchman. Brother of Dorothy Peterkin, and father of Gloria Coburn, all of Ottawa. Private funeral service was held at North Creek, NY on Saturday, Dec 7. Interment Cedar River Cemetery, Indian Lake."[2]

Sports editors in Ottawa, Boston, and Springfield picked up the story, allocating ample room on their pages to report on Hitch's passing and recount his life in hockey. Bill Westwick of the *Ottawa Journal*, who saw Hitch play both amateur and professional hockey, was the fastest to pull his story together, stating that Hitch "will be recalled by many veteran Ottawa hockey fans, as a former member of the Ottawa Stanley Cup champions who became one of the finest of National Hockey League defencemen." Westwick claimed that it was in Ottawa where Hitch "developed a fine poke check which he used to advantage later as one of the finest of blocking defencemen," and "Hitchman joined the Boston club for the Bruins' first year in the NHL in 1924-25 and later teamed up with Eddie Shore to form one of the finest defensive units in the game. While Shore was also a spectacular puck carrier, Hitchman was characterized by defensive skill."[3]

The *Boston Globe*'s Harold Kaese declared Hitch to be the Boston Bruins' first superstar. "Hitchman was the first top Bruins star, although nobody knew enough to call him a super-star. . . .C. F. Adams bought Hitchman from Ottawa early in the first Bruins season, in January, 1925. He was the only one who lingered." He recounted that Hitch was captain of Boston's first Stanley Cup team and of the "most successful team of all," 1929-30, with its .875

record. Kaese attributed that team's loss in the Stanley Cup final that season to Hitch's having "his jaw broken when hit by a puck Shore was clearing down the ice," on the eve of the playoffs. Referring to the night when Hitch broke his jaw, Kaese continued:

> He played the last two periods, although in agony, went through the play-offs with his jaw protected by a special harness. Two seasons earlier, Win Green had counted 98 stitches taken in Hitchman's face and body, all in one season, the trainer claimed.
> He was a woodsman, had a camp at Emery [Mills], Me. Before he turned pro with the Ottawa Senators, he had been a Royal Mountie for eight months. He quit shooting to hunt with bow and arrow. And he was an all-round athlete—Canadian football, first base in baseball, lacrosse, the ukulele and good enough at golf to win the low net in the players tournament one year at Montreal.
> He boasted of having had only two major penalties while with the Bruins and four fights on the ice—all with his friend, Hooley Smith.

Kaese reported that teammate George Owen remembered Hitch as a "likeable fellow, quiet and mild, but physically very tough and durable." He concluded his article by saying, "Hitchman had two prize mementoes—the sticks he used in his first and last professional games—when he died at Glens Falls, Dec 5, 1968."[4]

The *Springfield Republican* carried this story:

'MR HOCKEY' RECALLS LIONEL HITCHMAN
The tall, slim and bony Lionel Hitchman might have been the most famous defenseman in the early days of the National Hockey League if he weren't teamed with Eddie Shore in the golden days of the Boston Bruins.

Hitchman, the 6-3 youngster who wore No. 3, was overshadowed by the 5-10 solidly built Shore, who wore No. 2.

In any event, both players were great enough to have their numerals retired by the Bruins.

Hitchman died pretty much as he lived and played hockey, virtually unnoticed and with little fanfare.

He died in [Glens] Falls, N. Y. early in December. His death never became public knowledge until the other day.

"That's the only way 'Hitch' would have it," said a saddened Eddie Shore at the coliseum Saturday night while watching the Springfield Kings and Providence Reds game. "He was one of the quietest fellows in the world, never sought recognition."

"As a hockey player, he did his job well and never wanted any acclaim. And that's undoubtedly the way he wanted it in death. He just couldn't stand to have anybody fussing over him."

Yet for all of his mild-mannered ways off the ice, Hitchman was a terror on skates, as Shore remembered his famous old buddy and back-line mate.

"When he hit somebody with that 6-3 frame, the guy went down," Eddie recalled. "I'm glad he was on our side and I didn't have to run up against him."

The latter was quite a tribute to Hitchman's ability to body-check an opponent, as Eddie was regarded as the all-time toughest man on skates.

"When those bones crashed into a rival player's body, they felt like spears all over," Eddie laughed.

After Hitchman retired from hockey in the mid-thirties, he tried coaching. . . . He spent most of his remaining years in the solitude of the wildlife, hunting and fishing.

Although they were diametrical opposites in their personalities and style of play, the spectacular and colorful Shore and the methodical and easy-moving Hitchman blended their talents to form what is regarded as perhaps the best all-round defense pair in the history of the game.

Whenever Shore vacated his side of the ice for one of his free-wheeling rushes, Hitchman stood behind and often held the Bruins fort alone in the rear guard.

Those were the days when the Bruins were mighty Stanley Cup powers, the era of Shore, Hitchman, Tiny Thompson, George Owen, Myles Lane, Dutch Gainor, Harry Oliver, Cooney Weiland and Dit Clapper.

A lot of old Bruin fans still maintain that Hitchman would have been the greatest of the lot, but for the fact that he was playing next to 'Mr Hockey' himself.[5]

After 45 years the *Ottawa Citizen* revealed the name of the lovestruck girl who wrote the poem about Hitch that was published in the *Ottawa Journal* on February 6, 1924: "Now that he has gone, it can be told that at least one Ottawa girl had a 'crush' on the late great hockey star Lionel Hitchman, 'I had loved him, at age [16],' writes Mrs. Lilith Weber [*née* Bennett], 'and I even used to disturb the late Tommy Gorman, his manager, in the wee small hours of the morning to find out how Lionel was, after he was injured in a game.'"[6]

Another girl had loved him too. She married him, had a child with him and "had more fun with him in fifteen years than most people have in a lifetime."[7] Shortly before her death, Tops stood over Hitch's grave in Indian Lake to say her final goodbye.

Chapter Fifteen

LAST WORD ON HITCH

It's true what Eddie Shore said of Hitch, that he never sought the limelight. And while Hitch's contributions were obscured by the brilliant Shore, it seems the notable scribes of the day used enough ink on Hitch to keep his light glowing for decades to come.

Elmer Ferguson, the 1982 Hockey Hall of Fame media honoree and namesake of the Elmer Ferguson Memorial Award, wrote that Hitch in his 10th season in the NHL was still "one of the greatest:"

HITCHMAN ONE OF THE GREATEST
There will be one of hockey's really great defence men - with the accent on "defence" - on the ice tonight in the person of Lionel Hitchman of the Bruins one of the greatest rear-guards in the history of the game. To many qualified hockey judges the long, lean hard hitting ex-Mountie rates ahead of "Ching" Johnson of the New York Rangers, and Johnson has been regarded as one of the best in the business for several years. "Hitch" is strictly a defence player. You can count on the fingers of one hand the number of times Hitchman goes rushing up the ice. The average cash customer, itching for the thrills of flying skates and neatly executed goals, usually overlooks Hitchman in the excitement. Yet he's the type of defenceman that keeps a job year after year while the more spectacular rear-guard is dodging from one club to the other, back to the minors and finally out of hockey altogether. Hitchman is the lone survivor of a club that has harbored more hockey players over a stretch of eight years, than any other professional

unit in the history of the game. His far-reaching poke-check, his fearlessness, and steady play have kept him there.

Over-Shadowed By the Color of Shore

Hitchman has scored only four goals in the last two seasons. He got the four goals and three assists last winter. In 1930-31 he gathered in only two assists. Yet to Manager Art Ross of the Bruins, Hitchman is the greatest hockey player he has ever employed, and one of the greatest he has ever seen in the last 25 years. And Art has seen or played with most of the greats and near-greats of the puckchasing world. Hitchman has become a great defenceman, without blazing a trail to and from the penalty box. Last winter he spent only 36 minutes in the cooler and 40 minutes in 1930-31. Eddie Shore, running mate of Hitchman's and rated as another great defence player, did [98] minutes in the penalty box last winter and 105 the year before. This year he tops the section. But the flamboyant Shore gets the "call" over Hitchman as a defenceman in many quarters because of his sparkling puck-carrying and goal-scoring ability. As a matter of fact, taken strictly on a defensive basis, Hitch rates over Shore, but the color, forcefulness and robust qualities of the Blonde Bullet get more attention.[1]

Its likely Hitch remains shut out of the HHOF because his career stats don't adequately convey his overall importance to the teams he played for. But since Hitch last donned his famous No. 3 Boston sweater, the stewards of Hitch's NHL era, the veteran writers who witnessed that era and the new writers who took over their sports columns, continued to tell Hitch's story well into the 1970s and beyond.

In September 1934 while paying tribute to the late Peter Green, the longtime coach of the Ottawa Senators, former owner Tommy Gorman (1963 HHOF inductee) credited Green with Ottawa's most important player acquisitions, including Hitch. "It was also Petie who took a fancy to Lionel Hitchman. Together we saw Hitchman play for an amateur team in the old Arena on Laurier avenue. 'You go sign that big policeman Tommy, Petie said—and we did it, with the result that Hitchman went to the coast with us and helped win the Stanley Cup in 1923."²

Gorman again, in 1937, offering his condolences on the news of the passing of Eddie Gerard, the captain of that 1923 Stanley Cup team from Ottawa, retold the story of the final game of that championship: "Harry Broadbent scored for Ottawa in the first period and we won the game and the Stanley Cup by 1 to 0, chiefly due to the remarkable defensive play of Frank Nighbor, Frank Clancy, Lionel Hitchman and of course Eddie Gerard."³

In 1941 at the Boston Bruins' preseason press dinner, "14 local hockey writers joined Coach Cooney Weiland, and publicity man Frank Ryan of the Bruins in choosing an 'All-I've Seen' National Hockey League sextet. The team selected included: Tiny Thompson, goal; Eddie Shore and Fred Lionel Hitchman, defense; 'Busher' Jackson and Bill Cook, wings, and the late Howie Morenz, center." In balloting Hitch beat out "such titans as Lionel Conacher, Art Coulter, Ching Johnson, King Clancy and Dit Clapper." All of these players except Hitch have been inducted into the HHOF, as has Cooney Weiland.⁴

In 1943, Art Ross released his first and second all-time, all-star Bruins teams. He named Hitch and Shore as the best defensemen of all time. Clapper and Crawford made the second team for defense. Ross rated Brimsek ahead of Tiny Thompson in goal. The Krauts (Schmidt, Bauer and Dumart) formed the first all-star forward line, with Cowley, Gainor and Wiseman on the second line. Art Ross was inducted into the HHOF in 1949.⁵

Frank "King" Clancy, Hitch's Ottawa teammate who played in the NHL for 16 years and later became coach and an executive with the Toronto Maple Leafs until his death in 1986, gave this assessment of the 1923 Senators in an interview with the Canadian Press in 1943: "Clancy figures his old Senator mates, Clint Benedict, Cy Denneny, Boucher, Lionel Hitchman, Eddie Gerard, Nighbor,

Punch Broadbent and Jack Darragh formed hockey's greatest team." All except Hitch are in the HHOF.[6]

Before heading overseas in 1943 for WWII, Bobby Bauer (1996 HHOF inductee), who played for the Boston Bruins for nine seasons, winning two Stanley Cups, listed his all-time Boston team, all HHOF inductees except Hitch: "Frankie Brimsek in goal with Tiny Thompson as an alternate; Eddie Shore and Lionel Hitchman on defence; Milt Schmidt at centre with Bill Cowley as an alternate and Porky Dumart on left wing, with Dit Clapper on right."[7]

Young players started to be compared to Hitch in the 1940s. Elmer Ferguson noted that Jack Stewart (1964 HHOF inductee) "was a real 'Hitchman' body-checker."[8]

In 1943 Frank Boucher (1958 HHOF inductee), who played professional hockey for 22 seasons and later became coach and general manager of the New York Rangers, said: "the hardest body-checker of them all in his books still is Lionel Hitchman."[9]

In 1944, Mickey Ion, professional hockey referee for more than 30 years, NHL referee-in-chief at the time of his retirement in 1942 and HHOF inductee in 1961, picked 22 players as his all-time greats, divided into three eras. He chose the following players for the 1920-30 era: "Clint Benedict, Eddie Gerard, Sprague Cleghorn, Frank Nighbor, Lionel Hitchman, Newsy Lalonde, Ching Johnson, Duke Keats, Mickey Mackay, Eddie Shore, Howie Morenz, Aurel Joliat, Joe Simpson, Babe Seibert, Lionel Conacher, Frank Foyston, [Pit] Lepine." Only Hitch and Lepine are not HHOF inductees.[10]

Also in 1944, commenting on body-checking, Victor O. Jones of the *Boston Globe* offered: "Hitch was one of the greatest body checkers. . . . Eddie Shore is considered now as the last word in frightfulness, but the fact of the matter is, that in his day, he didn't rate among the league's leading hitters."[11]

In 1945, veteran Bruins fan John J. Hennessy, selected as the Bruins' No. 1 fan by the *Boston Globe*'s Harold Kaese, who "has seen about 500 of the last 503 Bruins home games," was asked for his all-time Bruins team: "Brimsek, goal; Shore and Hitchman, defense; Schmidt, center; Dumart and Clapper wings."[12]

On another subject of player retirements, Kaese commented in 1946 on "Hitchman Night," February 22, 1934: "It was Hitchman who had the most graceful farewell of all Bruins faithfuls. . . . Besides the puck, he was given $500 by the fans, $500 by the Bruins and a silver service set by Ross. His parents were given his jersey and his No. 3 was retired. That's the way for a great hockey player to hang up his skates."[13]

Sportswriter Jerry Nason commented in 1946: "You could be carrying the puck in your teeth and Hitch would steal it from you."[14]

In 1947, Hitch met his daughter in Montreal to watch her friend Pat Coburn play for the Boston Olympics. That was the first time Pat met Hitch, and he offered this impression of the man: "He was an immense presence, he had an effect on you. He was very nice and gentle and loved his little daughter." Scribes from Montreal, Ottawa, and Boston also noted Hitch's presence in the arena and were interested in his impressions:

> FORMER STAR WATCHES GAME
> Lionel Hitchman turned up the other night in Montreal, saw his first game in three or four years and opined that "it was pretty fast." The old Ottawa and Boston defence star favours elimination of the centre red line. He is in favor of letting them pass up to the opposing blue line just as was tried last week in the Rangers-Senator exhibition.
>
> Hitchman thought the game had changed a lot, "but talking of the old days, they would have quite a time getting out from behind that blue line with Nighbor up there forechecking."
>
> Hitchman is all through with hockey, but not a few big league teams would trade players in lots to have Hitch in his prime. When it came to defencemen with the accent on defence Hitch had few peers.[15]

At the beginning of the 1947-48 NHL season, three Montreal sportswriters ranked Hitchman as a "greater defensive player" than Shore.[16]

In 1949, Bill Westwick recalled his conversation with Cooper Smeaton (1961 HHOF inductee) of several years before. "Regarded by practically all in sport as one of the greatest referees in hockey," Smeaton named Hitch ahead of Shore in defense. "Smeaton never attempted to minimize Shore's ability nor his crowd appeal, but neither was he backward in crediting the part Hitchman played as a solid partner making such things possible."[17]

In 1951, the *Boston Daily Record*'s Dave Egan stated: "The only teams of the past quarter of a century that even deserve comparison with the Celtics are the Bruins of Shore and Hitchman and the immortal Sugar Bowl team of Boston College."[18]

A year later, Egan added: "Whatever may be the outcome of the hoe-down between the Bruins and Les Candy-Kids from Canada, it seems safe to say that the Bruins are only a few players and a few years away from the kind of greatness they knew when Eddie Shore and Lionel Hitchman and George Owen were holding the fort."[19]

In November 1952, the "Boston hockey immortals" returned to celebrate the 25th anniversary of the Boston Garden.

Boston Globe, *November 17, 1952, page 15.*

The *Boston Daily Record*'s John Gilhooly commented:

> It was a wondrous spectacle to see these figures from hockey's wax museum come back to life—skating, Hitch

came out gently, travelling on snow-shoes as though the ice had been booby-trapped. It was only a few yards but seemed like a Marathon to this eldering Barrymore of the blades who hasn't skated in a dozen years. He works for a paper mill in Maine, just shy of the Canadian border. Indeed he has worn nothing but lumber jacks garments for 18 months.

"This is the first time I've been in a suit for a year and a half. I haven't worn a tie since then. This tie feels tight like a noose," laughed Hitchman.[20]

On the news that the Boston Garden was sold to an "industrial concern" in March 1953, Dave Egan lamented: "So what's the Arena, in addition to a pile of masonry? It's the memory of a girl of gold named Sonia Henie, making her debut on this continent, the memory of embattled men named Shore and Hitchman, first playing side by side, the memory of Chick Suggs and Honeyboy Finnigan in a battle that is immortal to those who saw it. It's a lot of wonderful things, to a man who has spent so much time there."[21]

Boston Globe writer Tom Fitzgerald wrote in 1953: "Maybe the finest body-checker who ever wore a Bruin uniform was Shore's one-time defense partner, Fred Hitchman. Old Hitch really could rack 'em up, particularly with a precisely-timed hip block.[22]

An executive of the *Montreal Gazette* was visiting Boston in July 1955. He got to talking with a bellhop from his hotel, Joe Hanley, a "veteran hockey fan" who had "missed only 30 National Hockey League games in 30 years. . . . His heroes are Dit Clapper, Lionel Hitchman, Tiny Thompson, Eddie Shore, Dutch Gainor, Cooney Weiland and Milt Schmidt."[23]

Dutch Gainor died in 1962 and was remembered as "one of the slickest performers of his time," and his passing brought out comparisons of Shore and Hitch once more: "They had the great Eddie Shore dominating the league's defencemen, though right alongside him was Ottawa's Lionel Hitchman. 'Hitch' played in the shadows of Shore, but strictly as a defenceman, he was perhaps better than Shore—a tremendous and consistently brilliant blocker."[24]

The *Montreal Gazette*'s Dink Carroll reported in 1969 that the late Dick Irvin, 1958 HHOF inductee as a player and four-time Stanley Cup champ as a coach, once said: "Shore was an exciting player to watch, especially when he was carrying the puck. But he often wound up nowhere. Defensively, the guy he was teamed up with, Lionel Hitchman, was better."[25]

The last quote of this book goes to 1958 HHOF inductee Frank "King" Clancy, Hitch's partner on the "kiddie defense" of the 1923 Stanley Cup final, who in 1971 at a Junior A hockey banquet when introduced to John Coburn, Hitch's grandson, said: "If you are one quarter of the defenceman that Hitch was, you would be really something."

Hitch, the greatest player NOT in the Hockey Hall of Fame.

Frederick Lionel Hitchman
(Photo courtesy of Hitchman Private Collection)

Appendix

Table 1. Summary of Lionel Hitchman's Professional Playing Career

SEASON	TEAM	TEAM RESULTS			HITCH'S VALUE TO TEAM
		Div. / League Rank	Playoff Games	Championships and Trophies	
1922-23	Ottawa	1	Yes	O'Brien Cup winners Stanley Cup winners	• Critical goal during Stanley Cup final • Played seven of eight playoff games, with only three games of NHL regular-season experience, on a team that was reduced to seven players for the playoffs due to injuries
1923-24	Ottawa	1	Yes	O'Brien Cup runners-up	• Played more minutes than any other Ottawa player to a first-place league finish • Tied for first in league assists • Most improved player in the league • Catalyst for improved oversight on league "rough play"
1924-25	Ottawa / Boston	4 / 6	No		• Traded for cash to Boston, as part of an Ottawa management ownership dissolution and payout • Ottawa and Boston then disputed the terms of the transfer and the NHL mediated
1925-26	Boston	4	No	*This was the last year that <50% of teams gained a berth in the playoffs	• Team vice-captain • Three game-winning goals, two in overtime, to pull Boston out of last place and into third • Bruins set league record for improved winning percent over previous season by .328
1926-27	Boston	2	Yes	Stanley Cup runners-up	• Team vice-captain

SEASON	TEAM	TEAM RESULTS			HITCH'S VALUE TO TEAM
		Div. / League Rank	Playoff Games	Championships and Trophies	
					• Starred in playoff series, gaining a reputation as a "money player" • Second highest playoff bonus of $1,400 behind Galbraith ($1,600); Shore and others received $1,000 or less
1927-28	Boston	1	Yes	Prince of Wales Trophy winners Stanley Cup runners-up	• Promoted to team captain partway through the season • Played more minutes than any other player • Considered the most valuable Boston player by sports critics
1928-29	Boston	1	Yes	Prince of Wales Trophy winners Stanley Cup winners	• Team captain of Stanley Cup–winning team • Won every game in playoffs, a record until 1952 • Cemented his reputation of money player—star of playoffs • Cornerstone of Boston's record winning streak • Coached his first game for Bruins (game 43 against Detroit, a 5-1 win)
1929-30	Boston	1	Yes	Prince of Wales Trophy winners Stanley Cup runners-up	• Team captain • Team winning percentage of .875 a record to this day • Hart Trophy runner-up • All-star team (an unofficial managers poll; the league started naming official All-Star Teams the next season)
1930-31	Boston	1	Yes	Prince of Wales Trophy winners	• Team captain
1931-32	Boston	4	No		
1932-33	Boston	1	Yes	Prince of Wales Trophy winners	
1933-34	Boston	4	No		• Retired after game 30 of 48 games • **First sweater retired by Boston, February 22, 1934** • Longest continuous sport number out of circulation in North American sport history

Table 2. Summary of Lionel Hitchman's
Professional Coaching Career

SEASON	TEAM	TEAM RESULTS			HITCHMAN'S VALUE TO TEAM
		Div. / League Rank	Playoff Games	Championships and Trophies	
1928-36	Boston Bruins				Acting manager during the absence of manager Art Ross; Hitch coached over 12 games during this period
1933-34	Boston Cubs	2	Yes	CAHL runners-up	Coach (played four games)
1934-35	Boston Cubs	1	Yes	CAHL winners, Fontaine Cup	Coach
1935-36	Boston Cubs	2	No		Coach
1936-37	Boston Bruins	2	Yes		Assistant coach
1937-38	Boston Bruins	1	Yes	Prince of Wales Trophy winners	Assistant coach
1938-39	Springfield Indians				Coach; did not fulfill contract because of illness

Acknowledgments

I am grateful for the journey that this book became: from reconnecting with family members I hadn't seen in forty years; exploring the lives of those long gone; to meeting relatives I never knew I had. And, it gave me a new appreciation for the history of hockey. There are many to thank.

First, there is my father, Claude Coburn, who shortly before his death asked us to preserve Hitch's hockey legacy. Dad truly loved and respected his father-in-law, Hitch. Sadly, we lost our mother, Gloria way too soon, but in the time we had with her, she told countless stories of growing up with a famous hockey player for a father. Plus, she took great care of her parents' papers, scrapbooks, and mementos which rounded out this story.

My siblings, Claudia, John and Leslie, my amazing "editorial board," provided invaluable recollections, research, feedback, encouragement, and much-needed proofreading.

My daughter Jaclyn Eisenmann added greatly with her early research into Hitch's hockey career.

The first copy of this book goes to Patrick Coburn, my 92-year old uncle, who no longer plays hockey, but still canoes and swims regularly in Skaha Lake. Pat offered many stories on Hitch and my grandmother, Tops, as did the late Boston Bruin Milt Schmidt.

Tammy McLaughlin, my long-lost skating buddy, cousin, and the daughter of Hitch's youngest sister, Dorothy, provided many beautiful early pictures of the Hitchman clan. So, did newly discovered relatives, Laurie Trudel, Penny Haskin, and Patty Gordanier.

Catherine Gagnon and Leon Jensen, thank you for reviewing the book and for the extra help with the military stuff. The same goes to Adam Findlay who brought clarity to many hockey aspects of the book.

In Toronto, Mary Lou Harrison, administrator, St. Anne's Anglican Church showed tremendous enthusiasm for the church activities of Hitch's parents from the turn of the twentieth century. Richard Nosov, former principal of Oakwood Collegiate, took great interest in the history of Hitch, a former "notable" student of a bygone era.

Julie Clawson, the town clerk of Indian Lake, NY, was very helpful in guiding me to discover more on Hitch's life there.

Special thanks to John and Nancy Chamberlain, current owners of Hitch's beloved Koanneeta, who helped advance this story.

Scott Melnyk, photo archivist and collections coordinator, RCMP Heritage Branch, and, Chris Johnstone, museum curator, Ontario Provincial Police helped track down Hitch's policing career.

The libraries! I found immeasurable value from Library and Archives Canada, and the Ottawa, Toronto, Boston and Sarasota libraries. Also, I gained insight into the inner workings of the Ottawa Senators from documents at the Queen's University Archives. The Boston Sports Museum provided added encouragement for this project.

Karen Wonoski, the alumni coordinator for the Boston Bruins, was very helpful in putting me in touch with staff and past members of the team.

Samantha Chianta, archivist & collections registrar at the D. K. (Doc) Seaman Hockey Resource Centre of the Hockey Hall of Fame was generous with her knowledge and time.

To help with the research, I joined the Society for International Hockey Research and found great resources and a welcoming community of like-minded researchers. The NHL was also helpful, and I relied heavily on their stats with thanks to Benny Ercolani for the work he does there.

My copy editor, Patricia MacDonald of Powerplay Editing, who specializes in sports books with a keen interest in hockey provided great value.

Hockey writers and historians Brian McFarlane and Eric Zweig gave generously of their knowledge and encouragement.

Finally, and most importantly, thanks to my partner, Andre Gagnon who has given me more than a quarter-century of love. He read multiple drafts, provided helpful critiques and has put up with my single-mindedness for this project.

Chapter Notes

Introduction: Three Tries for No. 3
1. Toronto Maple Leafs had retired Irvine "Ace" Bailey's No. 6 eight days before Hitch's No. 3 was permanently retired by the Boston Bruins. Bailey requested that it be taken out of retirement for Ron Ellis in 1968.
2. Letter to Gloria Coburn from Lefty Reid, June 27, 1973.
3. Bill Westwick, "Carnage on the Ice," *Ottawa Journal*, Sept. 22, 1969, 15.
4. Brian McFarlane, "A Dreadful Incident: Green Versus Maki," http://www.ithappenedinhockey.com/2011/01/a-dreadful-incident-green-versus-maki/. Accessed May 7, 2018.
5. Elmer Ferguson Memorial Award, https://www.hhof.com/html/leg_writers.shtml. Accessed May 10, 2018.
6. https://www.hhof.com/LegendsOfHockey/jsp/LegendsMember.jsp?mem=b196302&type=Builder&page=bio&list=ByName. Accessed May 10, 2018.
7. Brian McFarlane, *The Bruins, Original Six* (Toronto: Stoddard, 1999), 20-21.

Chapter 1: Toronto By Way of England
1. GB Historical GIS / University of Portsmouth, Wellesbourne Mountford Tn/CP through time | Population Statistics | Total Population, A Vision of Britain through Time. URL: http://www.visionofbritain.org.uk/unit/10321682/cube/TOT_POP. Accessed: July 5, 2018.
2. https://en.wikipedia.org/wiki/Wellesbourne. Accessed July 7, 2018
3. https://en.wikipedia.org/wiki/Ironmongery. Accessed July 5, 2018; http://www.worldthroughthelens.com/family-history/old-occupations.php. Accessed July 5, 2018.
4. https://en.wikipedia.org/wiki/History_of_education_in_England [22]. Accessed July 4, 2018.
5. https://en.wikipedia.org/wiki/Second_Industrial_Revolution. Accessed July 4, 2018.
6. Lucille H. Campey, *Seeking a Better Future: The English Pioneers of Ontario and Quebec* (Toronto: Dundurn Press, 2012), chapter 1.
7. https://en.wikipedia.org/wiki/National_Agricultural_Labourers_Union [policies]. Accessed July 4, 2018.
8. Campey, *Seeking a Better Future*, chapter 9.
9. Campey, *Seeking a Better Future*, chapter 1.
10. Campey, *Seeking a Better Future*, chapter 1.

11. Library and Archives Canada, Immigration Records, Passenger Lists 1865-1922. "In some of the earlier manifests, personal information is omitted for wives, minor children, groups of labourers and first and second class passengers." https://www.bac-lac.gc.ca/eng/discover/immigration/immigration-records/passenger-lists/passenger-lists-1865-1922/Pages/list.aspx?ShipName=parisian&Year=1888&ArrivalPort=montreal&. Accessed July 22, 2018.
12. "Federation to be Formed of Men's Associations," *Globe* (Toronto), April 1, 1913, 9.

Chapter 2: The War Years

1. https://www.warmuseum.ca. Accessed Aug. 6, 2018; https://en.wikipedia.org/wiki/Belgium_in_World_War_I. Accessed Aug. 6, 2018.
2. https://www.thecanadianencyclopedia.ca/en/article/first-world-war-wwi/. Accessed Aug. 8, 2018.
3. https://www.warmuseum.ca/firstworldwar/history/after-the-war/legacy/the-cost-of-canadas-war/. Accessed Aug. 12, 2018.
4. 1919 city directory.
5. https://medicine.utoronto.ca/magazine/article/old-school-remembering-first-war. Accessed Aug. 16, 2018.
6. "Purse of Gold for Solider," *Toronto Daily Star*, April 13, 1915.
7. "University Hospital has Over 450 Patients Daily," *Toronto Globe*, Dec. 25, 1915, 21.
8. Michael Neiberg in http://greatwarproject.org/2016/09/12/salonika-the-most-forgotten-front/. Accessed Aug. 6, 2018.
9. "Cricketers' Response to Country's Call," *Toronto Daily Star*, Jan. 18, 1916.
10. https://www.veterans.gc.ca/eng/remembrance/medals-decorations/details/209. Accessed Jan. 22, 2019.
11. https://en.wikipedia.org/wiki/Wartime_Elections_Act. Accessed Aug. 6, 2018.
12. "Beaches League had a Successful Season: Thirty Seven Teams Competed in Various Series during Past Winter," *Globe* (Toronto), Mar. 31, 1916, 11.
13. "Three Hundred from the Beaches League," *Globe* (Toronto), Nov. 30, 1916.
14. Brett Popplewell, "When Half the City Took Ill," *Toronto Star*, May 2, 2009.

Chapter 3: Getting on With Life

1. "Oakwood Juniors Win from U.T.S. Seconds," *Globe* (Toronto), Nov. 21, 1918, 10.

2. "Oakwood Collegiate to Honor Brave Dead," *Globe* (Toronto), Nov. 30, 1918, 8; "Oakwood Collegiate Has Great Success in Its Campaign," *Globe* (Toronto), Dec. 3, 1918, 9.
3. "Goodyear Win Senior Title; Beaches Juveniles Lose," *Globe* (Toronto), March 26, 1919, 14.
4. "Olympic Men Reach Home," *Globe* (Toronto), July 12, 1919, 8.
5. "Oakwood Wins Senior Honors," *Globe* (Toronto), Nov. 22, 1919, 20.
6. "William Marsden Coach of Famed Hockey Club Dies," *Ottawa Journal*, Sept. 23, 1960, 20.
7. "William Marsden Coach of Famed Hockey Club Dies," *Ottawa Journal*, Sept. 23, 1960, 20.
8. "Aura Lee Had Whole Raft of Juniors Out," *Toronto Daily Star*, Nov. 27, 1919, 27.
9. https://en.wikipedia.org/wiki/Lou_Marsh. Accessed July 21, 2018.
10. "First Hockey Game on Saturday Night," *Toronto Daily Star*, Dec. 7, 1920, 22.
11. Lou E. Marsh, "Varsity Beat Aura Lee in Overtime," *Toronto Daily Star*, Dec. 16, 1920, 27.
12. "Bankers Away to Good Start," *Globe* (Toronto), Jan. 4, 1921, 12.
13. "Win by Aura Lee May Decide Group," *Globe* (Toronto), Jan. 29, 1921, 8.
14. "Aura Lee Ready for Next Round," *Globe* (Toronto), Feb. 7, 1921, 8.
15. "Aura Lee Juniors Tie at Bowmanville," *Toronto Daily Star*, Feb. 10, 1921, 20.
16. "Fans in Bowmanville Confident of Victory," *Globe* (Toronto), Feb. 7, 1921, 8.
17. "Aura Lee Junior Team Ready for Next Round," *Globe* (Toronto), Feb. 14, 1921, 9.
18. "Cornwall Juniors Trounce Aura Lee," *Globe* (Toronto), Feb. 17, 1921, 22.
19. "Cornwall Wins Round 9 to 4," *Globe* (Toronto), Feb. 19, 1921, 8.
20. "Contant Brothers, Both Ineligible, Aura Lee, Queen's and Belleville Juniors, Therefore, Get Another Chance," *Globe* (Toronto), Feb. 24, 1921, 10.
21. "Classic City Players Out," *Globe* (Toronto), Feb. 22, 1921, 12.
22. "Aura Lee Juniors Put Belleville Out," *Globe* (Toronto), Feb. 28, 1921, 10; "Aura Lee Juniors Down, Queen's Winning 2-0," *Globe* (Toronto), March 1, 1921, 10.
23. "Players Expelled in North Country," *Globe* (Toronto), March 21, 1921, 12.
24. "Men's Association Honors Fred Hitchman," *Toronto Daily Star*, April 25, 1921, 18.

Chapter 4: The Capital of Hockey
1. Sixth Census of Canada, 1921, Volumes I, III and IV.
2. Scott Melnyk, photo archivist and collections coordinator, RCMP Musical Ride and Heritage Branch, Ottawa, ON.

3. "Canada's Capital Heartily Greets 'Victor of Vimy'; Rousing Ovation Given New Governor-General and Lady Byng Today," *Ottawa Journal*, Aug. 12, 1921, 1.
4. "City Rugby Teams are Hard at Work," Citizen (Ottawa)*, Sep. 10, 1921, 10. "Burghs City League Champions Defeat Rideaus in Overtime Game," *Ottawa Journal*, Nov. 14, 1921, 14; "New Edinburghs Capture City Title By a Sensational 8-7 Victory Over Rideau Club," *Citizen* (Ottawa), Nov. 14, 1921, 10.
5. "Seven Senior Hockey Teams Toronto League," *Ottawa Journal*, Dec. 16, 1921, 18.
6. "Ottawa Circuit Ready for Action," *Ottawa Journal*, Nov. 22, 1921, 12; "Capital League Teams are Strong, New Edinburghs Sign Up [Hitchman]," *Ottawa Journal*, Dec. 6, 1921, 12.
7. "Capital Hockeyists Keep Up Pace," *Ottawa Journal*, Dec. 17, 1921, 23. "Burghs Had Brains Hitting on High When They Signed Lionel Hitchman," *Ottawa Journal*, Dec. 20, 1921, 15; "Gunners and Canadiens Magnets for Fans at Arena League Opener," *Ottawa Journal*, Dec. 22, 1921, 22; "Capital League Games Tonight," *Ottawa Journal*, Dec. 23, 1921, 15; "Fans Focus Attention on Burghs; Canadiens Are Also in Spotlight," *Ottawa Journal*, Jan. 3, 1922, 17.
8. "Interior and RCMP Meet in First Game," *Ottawa Journal*, Dec. 8, 1921, 15.
9. "Is Honorary President," *Ottawa Journal*, Dec. 15, 1921, 17.
10. "Fans Focus Attention on Burghs," *Ottawa Journal*, Jan. 3, 1922, 17.
11. "Both Leagues Are Putting on Doubleheaders This Evening," *Citizen* (Ottawa), Jan. 6, 1922, 8.
12. "To Leave RCMP Out of New Department," *Ottawa Journal*, Apr. 7, 1922, 5.
13. E.S. Jackson, "Cricket Notes," *Toronto Star*, May 18, 1922, 23.
14. "Reduce R.C.M.P. from 1,600 to 1,200 in Month," *Ottawa Journal*, Jun. 22, 1922, 1.
15. "Random Notes on Current Sports," *Toronto Star*, Jul. 20, 1922, 20.
16. "Cornwall Colts Play the Gunners, Game has Bearing on Championship," *Ottawa Journal*, Aug. 5, 1922, 20.
17. "Paddlers' Good Work." *Mail and Empire* (Toronto), Sept. 8, 1922.
18. "Parkdales Hold a Line-up Practice," *Toronto Star*, Sep. 12, 1922, 8.
19. Michael Barnes, *Killer in the Bush: The Great Fires of Northeastern Ontario* (Erin, ON: Boston Mills Press, 1987), 63-67.
20. "Rugby Ramblings," *Citizen* (Ottawa), Oct. 20, 1922, 10.

Chapter 5: Turning?
1. "Burghs Out to Revive Old Glory Meet St. Pats in First Contest," *Ottawa Journal*, Dec. 12, 1921, 19.

2. "St. Pats Spill Dope and Trim New Edinburgh Team By 3 to 2," *Citizen* (Ottawa), Dec. 23, 1921, 10; "Gunners Trounce New Edinburghs 6-2," *Ottawa Journal*, Jan. 4, 1923, 15.
3. "Surprises Galore in Arena Games," *Ottawa Journal*, Jan. 18, 1923, 17; "Gunners Stop New Edinburgh and Hand Honors to St. Pats," *Citizen* (Ottawa), Jan. 18, 1923, 11.
4. "Ottawa Line-Up Uncertain for Tomorrow Night's Match," *Citizen* (Ottawa), Jan. 30, 1923, 11.
5. "Toronto St. Patricks Arrive, Battle Senators Here Tonight," *Citizen* (Ottawa), Jan. 31, 1923, 15.
6. "Thursday Senators Retain Command in National Hockey League by Defeating St. Patricks 2 to 1," *Citizen* (Ottawa), Feb. 1, 1923, 18.
7. "Senators Beaten in Montreal Under Peculiar Circumstances," *Citizen* (Ottawa), Feb. 5, 1923, 11.
8. "Eddie Gerard Likely to Play Against Canadiens," *Citizen* (Ottawa), Feb. 7, 1923, 16.
9. "Ottawa Leads in Race for Pennant," *Ottawa Journal*, Feb. 8, 1923, 14.
10. "Burghs and St. Brigids Are Now Tied for First Position," *Citizen* (Ottawa), Feb. 10, 1923, 12; "St. Pats Defeated by New Edinburgh," *Ottawa Journal*, Feb. 10, 1923, 13.
11. "National Hockey League Race Has Three Contending Teams," *Citizen* (Ottawa), Feb. 13, 1923, 11.
12. "Canadiens Here Tomorrow for Battle With Senators," *Citizen* (Ottawa), Feb. 16, 1923, 11.
13. "Stormy Meeting of Group 2 Delegates," *Citizen* (Ottawa), Feb. 19, 1923, 13.
14. "Gunners Beaten in Replay Game by 4-1," *Citizen* (Ottawa), Feb. 20, 1923, 10.
15. "New Edinburghs Eliminate Saints After Gruelling Overtime Game, 1-0," *Ottawa Journal*, Feb. 21, 1923, 13.
16. "Burghs and St. Pats Play 90 Minutes of Scoreless Hockey," *Citizen* (Ottawa), Feb. 26, 1923, 8.
17. "Hamilton Stands Between Ottawa and a Sure Playoff," *Citizen* (Ottawa), Feb. 24, 1923, 13.
18. "Burgs Win Second Half Flag; Same Teams at Arena Tonight," *Citizen* (Ottawa), Feb. 27, 1923, 10.
19. "St. Pats Win Capital Champions in Hard Game," *Ottawa Journal*, Feb. 28, 1923, 14-15.
20. "St. Pats Finally Eliminate Burghs by One Goal to Nil," "Hitchman May be With Ottawa Team," *Citizen* (Ottawa), Feb. 28, 1923, 10.

Chapter 6: 32 Days to the Stanley Cup
1. Data compiled from *NHL.com*. Accessed November 3, 2017.

2. "Lionel Hitchman Makes Auspicious Debut on Defence," *Ottawa Journal*, March 1, 1923, 16.
3. Brian Devlin, "From Another Angle," *Citizen* (Ottawa), March 3, 1923, 21.
4. "N.H.L. Teams Nearing the Wire: Senators in Montreal Tonight," *Citizen* (Ottawa), March 3, 1923, 13.
5. "Hitchman Resigns from Ontario Police," *Citizen* (Ottawa), March 5, 1923, 11
6. "Newcomer Made Good," *Gazette* (Montreal)*, March 5, 1923, 16.
7. "Hitchman's Gameness Proven," *Montreal Herald*, March 5, 1923 quoted in the *Citizen* (Ottawa), March 5, 1923, 2.
8. "Canadiens Defeat Senators After Grueling Struggle 1-0," *Citizen* (Ottawa), March 5, 1923, 11.
9. "Ottawa Plays Off Against Montreal: Irish Finish Season With Win, But Canadiens Beat Hamilton," *Globe* (Toronto), March 6, 1923, 8; "Hitchman Good," *Toronto Daily Star*, March 6, 1923, 10.
10. "Enormous Crowd for Tonight's Match," *Citizen* (Ottawa), March 7, 1923, 11.
11. "Senators and Canadiens Meet in First Game Play-Off Series Montreal Arena This Evening," *Citizen* (Ottawa), March 7, 1923, 11.
12. "Ottawa Hockey Team Shut Out Canadiens in First Game 2 to 0 in Unusually Rough Battle, Habitants, Outplayed on Their Own Ice, Resort to Deliberate Fouling," *Citizen* (Ottawa), March 8, 1923, 10.
13. "Wild Scenes in Hockey Battle Won by Ottawa, Hitchman Suffers from Concussion," *Gazette* (Montreal), March 8, 1923, 16.
14. "Ottawa Hockey Team Shut Out Canadiens in First Game 2 to 0 in Unusually Rough Battle, Habitants, Outplayed on Their Own Ice, Resort to Deliberate Fouling," *Citizen* (Ottawa), March 8, 1923, 10.
15. "Dandurand Has Suspended Two of His Players," *Ottawa Journal*, March 8, 1923, 1.
16. "Canadians to Play Return Game Without 'Peg' Cleghorn and [Coutu]," *Ottawa Journal*, March 9, 1923, 9.
17. "Lionel Hitchman Is Very Much Alive," *Citizen* (Ottawa), March 9, 1923, 11.
18. "Champions Leave Tonight for Coast to Defend Stanley Cup," *Citizen* (Ottawa), March 10, 1923, 11.
19. "Ottawas Leave on Long Jaunt to Coast Billy Boucher Will Replace Darragh," *Ottawa Journal*, March 12, 1923, 15.
20. Ed Baker, "Senators Depart in Quest of Professional Hockey Title," *Citizen* (Ottawa), March 12, 1923, 9.
21. Basil O'Meara, "Calgary Next Stop and Team in Fine Shape," *Ottawa Journal*, March13, 1923, 1.
22. Basil O'Meara, "Maroons Favorites for the First Game," *Ottawa Journal*, March 16, 1923, 17.

23. Basil O'Meara, "Ottawa Takes the First Game: Score Is 1 to 0 at the Finish; Broadbent Scores Lone Goal," *Ottawa Journal*, March 17, 1923, 1 & 4.
24. Tommy Gorman, "Senators Won the First Game of Series with Vancouver by Sheer, Nerve, Pluck and Determination," *Citizen* (Ottawa), March 17, 1923, 1.
25. Basil O'Meara, "Ottawa Loses Second Game Maroons Score Four to One the Boucher Boys Staring," *Ottawa Journal*, March 20, 1923, 14.
26. Basil O'Meara, "Misfortune Still Trails Senators Ottawa Stars Badly Battered Up," *Ottawa Journal*, March 21, 1923, 14.
27. Ed Baker, "Senators Determined to Beat Maroons in Third Game Friday," *Citizen* (Ottawa), March 21, 1923, 11.
28. Ed Baker, "Ottawas Further Weakened by Accident to Harry Helman"; Tommy Gorman, "Gorman Appeals to Trustee W.M. Foran for Boucher Ruling"; "Trustees Are Adamant," *Citizen* (Ottawa), March 22, 1923, 11.
29. http://ericzweig.com/2018/02/26/whats-the-deal-on-trade-deadline-day/, accessed Jan. 27, 2019.
30. Ed Baker, "Despite Unusual Handicaps Senators Hope for Victory"; Brian Devlin, "From Another Angle," *Citizen* (Ottawa), March 22, 1923, 11.
31. Basil O'Meara, "Frank Patrick Refuses to Relent Bars Boucher From World's Series," *Ottawa Journal*, March 23, 1923, 17.
32. Ed Baker, "Crippled Ottawas Battle to Great Victory Over Vancouver Maroons and Now Lead in Worlds Hockey Series," *Citizen* (Ottawa), March 24, 1923, 10.
33. Basil O'Meara, "Ottawa Takes Needed Game by Score Five Goals to One; Eddie Gerard a Casualty," *Ottawa Journal*, March 27, 1923, 16 & 19.
34. Canadian Press, "Ottawa Beats Edmonton 2 to 1 in First Stanley Cup Contest," *Citizen* (Ottawa), March 30, 1923, 11.
35. Tommy Gorman, "Eskimos Were Victims of 'Ottawa Spirit,'" *Citizen* (Ottawa), March 30, 1923, 1.
36. Basil O'Meara, "Senators Take First Game," *Ottawa Journal*, March 30, 1923, 14 & 17.
37. Ed Baker, "Senators' Whirlwind Finish Leaves Eskimos Gasping," *Citizen* (Ottawa), March 30, 1923, 10.
38. Canadian Press, "Ottawas Win the Stanley Cup," *Ottawa Journal*, April 2, 1923, 14.
39. Basil O'Meara, "Ottawa Should Be Proud of Senators, Greatest Team in Years," *Ottawa Journal*, April 2, 1923, 14.
40. Basil O'Meara, "Senators Are on Way Home with Famous Stanley Cup Win Final with Lone Goal," *Ottawa Journal*, April 2, 1923, 15.
41. Canadian Press, "Ottawas Win the Stanley Cup," *Ottawa Journal*, April 2, 1923, 14.
42. "City to Welcome Home World Champions," *Ottawa Journal*, April 2, 1923, 1.

43. Andy Lytle, "Greatest Team of All Time," *Ottawa Journal*, April 2, 1923, 14.
44. Ed Baker, "Ottawa Senators Are World's Hockey Champions," *Citizen* (Ottawa), April 2, 1923, 10.
45. Basil O'Meara, "World's Champions Speeding Home," *Ottawa Journal*, April 3, 1923, 14.
46. "Ottawa Players Get $700 Each," *Ottawa Journal*, April 2, 1923, 2.
47. Basil O'Meara, "Senators Leave Vancouver Amid Thundering Cheers," *Ottawa Journal*, April 3, 1923, 14; Basil O'Meara, "Curtain Descends on Hockey Season," *Ottawa Journal*, April 9, 1923, 14.
48. Basil O'Meara, "Pass Through 'Peg with Only Short Stay," *Ottawa Journal*, April 4, 1923, 1; Ed Baker, "Edmonton Players Did Not Attend Senators Departure," *Citizen* (Ottawa), April 3, 1923, 11; Basil O'Meara, "George Boucher Has an Injured Foot," *Ottawa Journal*, April 5, 1923, 14.
49. "Pembroke Gave Boys a Hearty Welcome," *Ottawa Journal*, April 6, 1923, 1.
50. "Immense Crowd of Admirers Acclaim Conquerors of West on Triumph Return Home," *Ottawa Journal*, April 6, 1923, 1.
51. "Cheering Thousands Welcome Home World Champion Hockey Team from Victorious Struggle in Far West," *Citizen* (Ottawa), April 6, 1923, 1.
52. "Ottawa Players Are All of One Opinion," *Citizen* (Ottawa), April 7, 1923, 10.
53. "Ottawa Citizens Pay Great Tribute to Stanley Cup Holders at Banquet," *Ottawa Journal*, April 10, 1923, 15.

Chapter 7: The Ottawa Adonis
1. "Champion Senators All Set for West," *Citizen* (Ottawa), Nov. 15, 1923, 6.
2. W.J. Findlay, "Regina Sweeps Through Senators," *Ottawa Journal*, Nov. 20, 1923, 15.
3. "Ottawa System Winner Because Nighbor There," *Ottawa Journal*, April 2, 1923, 1.
4. "Ottawas Win Second Game but Lose Out on Round to Regina Capitals," *Ottawa Journal*, Nov. 26, 1923, 12; "Regina Champions Pro. Hockey Series," *Citizen* (Ottawa), Nov. 27, 1923 11.
5. "Edmonton Defeat Ottawa in Opener," *Ottawa Journal*, Dec. 3, 1923, 12.
6. "Hitchman Hero of Game with Winning Goal in Third Period," *Ottawa Journal*, Dec. 4, 1923, 14.
7. "St. Pats, Tigers and Canucks Infuse Many New Faces into Early Workouts," *Ottawa Journal*, Dec. 7, 1923, 18.
8. "N.H.L. Clubs All Strengthen for Season Which Opens Dec. 15," *Citizen* (Ottawa), Dec. 7, 1923 11.
9. "Hitchman Pairs Off with Buck Boucher," *Ottawa Journal*, Dec. 11, 1923, 12.

10. "National Hockey: Ottawa 3, Hamilton 2," *Ottawa Journal*, Dec. 16, 1923, 16.
11. "Champion Senators Win First National League Game Beating Hamilton Tigers 3-2," *Citizen* (Ottawa), Dec. 17, 1923 11.
12. "Ottawa's World Champions Take Clear Lead in N.H.L. Race With 5-2 Victory Over St. Pats," *Citizen* (Ottawa), Dec. 20, 1923, 11.
13. "Ottawas Beat Canadiens in Strenuous Hockey Game Which Went Overtime, by 3-2," *Citizen* (Ottawa), Dec. 20, 1923, 9; "Denneny Breaks Up Overtime Game Rolls in Long Shot in Extra Session," *Ottawa Journal*, Dec. 27, 1923, 12 & 13.
14. "Subless Senators Have to Win Game Away From Home to Even Up for Loss," *Ottawa Journal*, Jan. 1, 1924, 8.
15. "Senators Win at Toronto: 4-3," *Ottawa Journal*, Jan. 3, 1924, 14 & 15; "St. Patrick's Bow to Pace-Setters," *Globe* (Toronto), Jan. 3, 1924, 8; "St. Pats Trying to Strengthen for Game With Champs Tonight," *Citizen* (Ottawa), Jan. 5, 1924, 11.
16. "Ottawas Make Show of St. Patricks," *Ottawa Journal*, Jan. 7, 1924, 10.
17. "Ottawas and Canadiens Play Again," *Ottawa Journal*, Jan. 7, 1924, 10.
18. "World Champion Senators Show Great Resourcefulness Beating Canadiens by 2 to 1," *Citizen* (Ottawa), Jan. 10, 1924, 9.
19. "Ottawas Come from Behind to Trim Tigers in Hamilton," *Citizen* (Ottawa), Jan. 14, 1924, 11.
20. "Ottawas Lose to Canadiens in Overtime Struggle by 2-1," *Citizen* (Ottawa), Jan. 14, 1924, 11; "Canadiens Hoping to Better Position," *Ottawa Journal*, January 18, 1924, 15.
21. "Champions Win Thrilling Overtime Game; Score 2 to 1," *Ottawa Journal*, January 21, 1924, 10 & 11.
22. "Ottawa Captured Thrilling Battle from Canadiens," *Gazette* (Montreal), Jan. 22, 1924, 18.
23. "Denneny and Broadbent Unable to Journey Westward," *Citizen* (Ottawa), Jan. 23, 1924, 11.
24. "Ottawas' Officers Are Very Indignant," *Citizen* (Ottawa), Jan. 23, 1924, 11.
25. "Ottawa Sweeps to Victory," *Ottawa Journal*, Jan. 24, 1924, 12.
26. "World Champion Senators Establish New Record in N.H.L.," *Citizen* (Ottawa), Jan. 25, 1924, 11.
27. "Senators on Trail of New Record," *Ottawa Journal*, Jan. 25, 1924, 16.
28. "Ottawa Hockey Ass'n Protest Fails at Special N.H.L. Meeting," *Citizen* (Ottawa), Jan. 28, 1924, 11.
29. P.J. Jones, "Senators Again Lose to Hamilton," *Ottawa Journal*, Jan. 28, 1924, 10.
30. "Toronto St. Pats and Senators Meet in Auditorium Tonight," *Citizen* (Ottawa), Jan. 30, 1924, 11.

31. "Senators Play Tag with St. Patricks; Visitors Put Up a Poor Exhibition," *Ottawa Journal*, Jan. 31, 1924, 12 & 13.
32. "Nighbor Ordered to Rest Up and Will Be Out of Canadien Game Saturday," *Ottawa Journal*, Feb. 1, 1924, 12; "Ottawa Hockey Association Ask for Special N.H.L. Meeting," *Citizen* (Ottawa), Feb. 2, 1924, 11.
33. Ed Baker, "Canadiens Defeat Ottawas in Thrilling Match by 1 to 0," *Citizen* (Ottawa), Feb. 4, 1924, 11.
34. "Sprague Cleghorn Is Suspended by President Calder," *Gazette* (Montreal), Feb. 4, 1924, 16; "To Appeal Calder's Decision; Dandurand Will Take Action Over Case Sprague Cleghorn," *Ottawa Journal*, Feb. 4, 1924, 1 & 2.
35. "Canadiens and Ottawas Rate Evenly Though Minus Their Defence Aces," *Ottawa Journal*, Feb. 5, 1924, 10.
36. Phillip McCann, "Sport Jabs and Counters," *Citizen* (Ottawa), Feb. 5, 1924, 11.
37. "Oh You Lionel," *Ottawa Journal*, Feb. 6, 1924, 10.
38. "Social and Personal Activities," *Citizen* (Ottawa), Feb. 6, 1924, 13.
39. "9,600 Witnessed Ottawa Victory Over Canadiens," *Gazette* (Montreal), Feb. 7, 1924, 14; "Ottawas Lengthen Lead in National League Race Beating Canadians by 4 to 0. Record Attendance for Hockey Match in Capital Set by Ten Thousand Fans," *Citizen* (Ottawa), Feb. 7, 1924, 11.
40. "Nighbor Goes Hunting and Brings Back Tiger Pelt Handing On Stick," *Ottawa Journal*, Feb. 11, 1924, 12; "Hockey Record Established When Ottawas Beat Tigers 1-0 in Game Free From Penalties," *Citizen* (Ottawa), Feb. 11, 1924, 11.
41. "Pres. Frank Ahearn Explains Position," *Citizen* (Ottawa), Feb. 13, 1924, 11.
42. "Some Sloppy Hockey Saturday," *Ottawa Journal*, Feb. 18, 1924, 12.
43. "Killing the Game," *Gazette* (Montreal), Feb. 20, 1924, 12.
44. "At Home: Senators 1, Canadiens 0," *Ottawa Journal*, Feb. 25, 1924, 10.
45. "Senators Easy Winners Over Tigers," *Ottawa Journal*, Feb. 28, 1924, 14.
46. "Ottawas Hit Toronto Trail for Final with St. Patricks," *Citizen* (Ottawa), March 5, 1924, 11.
47. NHL.com. Accessed Sept. 2, 2018.
48. Ed Baker, "Canadiens Win First Play-Off Game 1-0 on Slushy Surface in Mount Royal Arena," *Citizen* (Ottawa), March 10, 1924, 11.
49. "11,650 Present When Ottawas Are Defeated," *Ottawa Journal*, March 12, 1924, 1; "Canadiens Are Champions, Win Hard Fought Contest Before Record NHL Crowd," *Ottawa Journal*, March 12, 1924, 12; Canadian Press, "Team Play Lacking," *Gazette* (Montreal), March 12, 1924, 16; "Canadiens Win N.H.L. Title by Defeating Ottawas 4 to 2 Winning Round by 3 Goals," *Citizen* (Ottawa), March 12, 1924, 11.
50. "Manager Gorman Happy and Praises His Team," *Ottawa Journal*, March 12, 1924, 1.
51. "Vive, Les Canadiens!," *Ottawa Journal*, March 13, 1924, 6.

52. "Manager Gorman Hits Back in Defence of Ottawa Players," *Citizen* (Ottawa), March 15, 1924, 13.
53. "Duggan Has Sold One Franchise," *Ottawa Journal*, March 19, 1924, 15.
54. Mayo Clinic, https://www.mayoclinic.org/diseases-conditions/peritonitis/symptoms-causes/syc-20376247. Accessed May 15, 2018.
55. "Streets Are Lined with Mourners as J.P. Darragh, Idol of Sportdom Is Borne to Beechwood Cemetery," *Ottawa Journal*, July 2, 1924, 11; "Burial of Darragh Silenced Ottawans," *Gazette* (Montreal), July 2, 1924, 13.

Chapter 8: In Transition

1. "Manager Gorman Hits Back in Defence of Ottawa Players," *Citizen* (Ottawa), March 15, 1924, 13.
2. "Takes Action Against Ottawa Hockey Club," *Ottawa Journal*, June 7, 1924, 13;
   "Ottawa Hockey Club on C. Benedict's Suit," *Ottawa Journal*, June 9, 1924, 1.
3. "Defence Statement of Senators to Clint Benedict's Claim for Payment of $800 Makes Charges," *Citizen* (Ottawa), Sept. 25, 1924, 1 & 3; "Benedict Denies Any Misconduct Under Contract," *Citizen* (Ottawa), Sept. 26, 1924, 1; "Ex-Goaler Denies Statement That He Was Unfit to Fulfill Terms of Contract with Team," *Ottawa Journal*, Sept. 26, 1924, 1.
4. "Did Not Withdraw His Action or Accept $300 as Balance of Salary," *Citizen* (Ottawa), Oct. 11, 1924, 11; "Ottawa Club," *Ottawa Journal*, Sept. 25, 1924, 6.
5. "Listening In on the Sports Line," *Ottawa Journal*, Oct. 4, 1924, 24.
6. "New Clubs in Pro Hockey Loop," *Ottawa Journal*, Oct. 13, 1924, 12.
7. "Ottawas Give Tigers Hockey Lesson Put on Polished Display to Win 5-1," *Ottawa Journal*, Nov. 27, 1924, 16.
8. "Grist from the Sport Mill by 'Baz'," *Ottawa Journal*, Nov. 28, 1924, 15.
9. Canadian Press, "Hamilton's N.H.L. Team Wins from Ottawa Senators 5 to 3," *Citizen* (Ottawa), Dec. 1, 1924, 11.
10. "L. Hitchman Suffers Slight Concussion," *Ottawa Journal*, Dec. 4, 1924, 1.
11. Ed Baker, "Montreal's New N.H.L Team Defeats Ottawa Senators 3-1," *Citizen* (Ottawa), Dec. 8, 1924, 11.
12. "Offering Price to Mr. Ahearn," *Ottawa Journal*, Dec. 15, 1924, 17.
13. "Four Horsemen to Pit Their Skill Against Craft of Three Musketeers," *Ottawa Journal*, Jan. 7, 1925, 12.
14. "Third Place Deadlock to Be Broken When Maroons and Senators Clash," *Ottawa Journal*, Jan. 9, 1925, 12.
15. "Bruins Will Buy but Not Borrow Players," *Boston Globe*, Jan. 10, 1925, 8; "Boston Refuses to Accept Offer of Hitchman on Loan," *Gazette* (Montreal), Jan. 10, 1925, 18; "Notes and Comment," *Ottawa Journal*, Jan. 10, 1925, 10.

16. "Boston Surprised Canadiens, Taking Overtime Tilt 3-2," *Gazette* (Montreal), Jan. 12, 1925, 16.
17. "Mr. T. Gorman Out of Hockey," *Ottawa Journal*, Jan. 26, 1925, 12.
18. Minute Book of NHL, Jan. 25, 1925; "T.P. Gorman Starts Action for $5,000," *Ottawa Journal*, Dec. 15, 1925, 1.
19. "Ottawa Barely Defeats Bruins," *Boston Globe*, Jan. 18, 1925, A19.
20. "St. Pats Trim Bruins in Erratic Game; Boston Leads for Awhile but Lose Out," *Ottawa Journal*, Jan. 26, 1925, 12.
21. "Joliat's Flashy Goal Gives Canadiens Win by 3-2 Score," "A Disgraceful Hockey Episode," "Stop Rough Hockey Is League Ukase," *Ottawa Journal*, Jan. 26, 1925, 12.
22. "Bruins Trail Canadiens, 5-1," *Boston Herald*, Feb. 15, 1925, B1-B2.
23. "Hub Team at Arena," *Boston Post*, Feb. 18, 1925.
24. "Boston Bruins Pull Big Surprise, Outplay Hamilton Tigers – Win 2-0," *Ottawa Journal*, March 9, 1925, 11.
25. "Bruins Hold Whip Hand Over N.H.L. Play-off in Ottawa Game Tonight," *Boston Herald*, March 9, 1925, 11.
26. "George Boucher Won't Play Tonight Senator Mix With Old Time Friends," *Ottawa Journal*, Dec. 6, 1924, 15.
27. "Senators Away to Early Lead, Win 4-1," *Boston Globe*, March 10, 1925, 12; "Victory Avails Senators Little as Canadiens Cop Also to Land in Playoff," *Boston Herald*, March 10, 1925, 21.
28. "Lady Byng Has Presented Cup for Pro. Sport," *Ottawa Journal*, March 9, 1925, 10.
29. "Grist from the Sport Mill, That Hamilton Strike," *Ottawa Journal*, March 17, 1925, 12; "King Clancy Hurt in Game at Boston," *Ottawa Journal*, March 12, 1925, 12.

Chapter 9: Ramping Up

1925-26: Clutch Player
1. NHL Official Rule Book 1925-26.
2. https://en.wikipedia.org/wiki/1925%E2%80%9326_NHL_season. Accessed July 24, 2018; NHL.com. Accessed July 24, 2018.
3. "Burgs Here Tonight," *Boston Globe*, March 12, 1926, 22.
4. Stanley Woodward, "Cooper's Goal in First Period Gives Bruin 1-0 Win Over Ottawa," *Boston Herald*, March 7, 1926, 4.
5. John J. Hallahan, "Pro Hockey Title Is Likely to be Taken Away From Canada," *Boston Globe*, Nov. 30, 1925, 17.
6. "Canadiens Downed Boston on Morenz' Goal in Overtime," *Gazette* (Montreal), Dec. 21, 1925, 22.
7. Stanley Woodward, "Boston Shuts Out Pittsburgh, Its Greatest Hockey Rival, 3 to 0," *Boston Herald*, Jan. 6, 1926, 30.
8. "Senators Lose Close Game, Goal Umpire Is Overruled," *Ottawa Journal*, Feb. 5, 1926, 16.

9. "Bruins' Wizardry Turns Back Pirates'," *Boston Globe*, Feb. 17, 1926, 13.
10. John J. Hallahan, "Rossmen Face 3 Hard Games," *Boston Globe*, Feb. 17, 1926, 19.
11. Stanley Woodward, "Hitchman Again Gives Bruins Overtime Win; St. Pats Losing, 2 to 1," *Boston Herald*, Feb. 23, 1926, 17.
12. Stanley Woodward, "Cooper's Goal in First Period Gives Bruins 1-0 Win Over Ottawa," *Boston Herald*, March 7, 1926, B4.
13. Stanley Woodward, "Hitchman's Poke Check Rivals Nighbor's," *Boston Herald*, Jan. 6, 1926, 30.

1926-27: The Gang's Mostly Here
1. "Bruins Fast Hitting Stride," *Boston Globe*, Nov. 10, 1926, A25.
2. John J. Hallahan, "Bruins and Blackhawks Ready for First Clash," *Boston Globe*, March 28, 1927, 10.
3. Stanley Woodward, "Adams Distributes $10,000 in Bonuses at Bruins Lunch," *Boston Herald*, April 15, 1927, 27.
4. John J. Hallahan, "New Players Add Strength," *Boston Globe*, Nov. 17, 1926, A20.
5. "Bruins May Recall New Haven 'Hands'," *Boston Herald*, Nov. 26, 1926, 23.
6. Stanley Woodward, "Bruins Break Losing Streak, Walloping Detroit Cougars, 7 to 2 Despite Sick Goalie," *Boston Herald*, Dec. 15, 1926, 27.
7. "Free-for-All Jam Takes Place as Bruins Defeat Montreal Maroons by 2 to 1," *Boston Herald*, Dec. 24, 1926, 11.
8. John J. Hallahan, "Curb on Wild Doings in Hockey Demanded," *Boston Globe*, Dec. 27, 1926, 10.
9. Stanley Woodward, "Bruins Gain Tie for Lead in Their Division of League by Beating Americans, 2-1," *Boston Herald*, Dec. 29, 1926, 12.
10. John J. Hallahan, "Maroons Beat Bruins, 3 to 0," *Boston Sunday Globe*, Jan. 9, 1927, 1 & 23.
11. Associated Press, "Bruins Defeated at Ottawa, 5-4," *Boston Sunday Globe*, Jan. 16, 1927, 22.
12. John J. Hallahan, "Winkler to Defend Bruin Goal Tonight," *Boston Globe*, Jan. 18, 1927, 18; Stanley Woodward, "[Fredrickson] Scores Four Goals as Revamped Bruins Throttle N.Y. Rangers, 7-3," *Boston Herald*, Jan. 19, 1927, 15.
13. Stanley Woodward, "Bruins Give Pirates Lesson in Hockey and Stop Their Winning Streak, 3 Goals to 1," *Boston Herald*, Jan. 26, 1927, 17.
14. "Bruins for First Time Beat St Pats," *Boston Globe*, Feb. 2, 1927, 12.
15. John J. Hallahan, "Roughness in Hockey Big Handicap to Game," *Boston Globe*, Feb. 7, 1927, 10.
16. Associated Press, "Bruins Defeat Maroons, 3-2," *Boston Herald*, Feb. 13, 1927, B1.

17. John J. Hallahan, "Bruins Shut Out Blackhawks, 3-0," *Boston Globe*, Feb. 16, 1927, 21.
18. David F. Egan, "Bruins Shut Out Americans, 5 to 0," *Boston Globe*, March 6, 1927, 21.
19. Associated Press, "Bruins Nose Out Hawks, 2-1, in Overtime Session Jammed with Thrills and Penalties," *Boston Herald*, March 16, 1927, 15.
20. "Bruins Practically Cinch Place in Final Play-off by Whaling Blackhawks, 6 to 1," *Boston Herald*, March 30, 1927, 16.
21. Stanley Woodward, "Bottle Tops, Paper and Coins Scatter Ice as Rangers and Bruins Play to Scoreless Tie," *Boston Herald*, April 3, 1927, B4.
22. John J. Hallahan, "Bruins and Rangers in Scoreless Clash," *Boston Globe*, April 3, 1927, B1.
23. Stanley Woodward, "Board Checks," *Boston Herald*, April 6, 1927, 25.
24. Associated Press, "Bruins and Blackhawks to Open Series March 29," *Boston Globe*, March 15, 1927, 18.
25. John J. Hallahan, "No Goal Scored in 80 Minutes," *Boston Globe*, April 8, 1927, 1 & 33.
26. John J. Hallahan, "Ottawa Battleground in Closing Hockey Clashes," *Boston Globe*, April 11, 1927, 8.
27. Stanley Woodward, "Third Hockey Game Tied, 1-1," *Boston Herald*, April 12, 1927, 33; "Bruins Hold the Senators to 1-1 Tie," *Toronto Daily Star*, April 12, 1927, 12.
28. Stanley Woodward, "Ottawa Wins World Hockey Title, 3 to 1; Game Ends in Riot," *Boston Herald*, April 14, 1927, 1.
29. J.W. Mooney, "Head Guards for Bruins Tomorrow," *Boston Post*, March 24, 1930 (Dsc 2304); Associated Press, "Expel Billy Coutu From Hockey League," *Boston Herald*, April 15, 1927, 1.

1927-28: Prince of Wales
1. "The Newest Sport," *Boston Herald*, April 4, 1928, 26.
2. "Scoring Honors to Canadian Division," *Boston Globe*, March 26, 1928, 8.
3. Steward Richardson and Richard Leblanc, *Dit Clapper and the Rise of the Boston Bruins* (PACTS Management Inc.), 43.
4. "Bruins and Rangers Battle to 1-1 Tie in Rough Contest Before 17,000 at Garden - Hitchman Shines for the Bruins," *Boston Herald*, Nov. 28, 1927, 13.
5. "King Clancy – Geo. Boucher Turn Defeat into a Victory with Sizzling Long-Shots," *Citizen* (Ottawa), Dec. 5, 1927, 11-12.
6. Stanley Woodward, "New York Americans Hand Bruins First Setback of Season in Overtime, 4 to 3," *Boston Herald*, Nov. 27, 1927, 26.
7. John J. Hallahan, "Boucher Still Leads League Goal Scorers," *Boston Globe*, Dec. 14, 1927, 26.
8. John J. Hallahan, "Bruins Beaten By Their Rough Work," *Boston Globe*, Dec. 14, 1927, 25.

9. Stanley Woodward, "Oliver's Goal, Three Minutes From End, Gives Bruins 1-0 Edge Over Ottawa Senators," *Boston Herald*, Dec. 21, 1927, 15.
10. "Bruins Shut Out Rangers Here, 2-0," *Boston Globe*, Dec. 28, 1927, 12.
11. Associated Press, "Hitchman Shines as Bruins Win, 3-2," *Boston Globe*, Jan. 2, 1928, 13; "[Fredrickson's] Goal Beats N.Y. Americans, 3-2, After Hitchman Twice Ties Score, Hitchman Hero of Great Game," *Boston Herald*, Jan. 2, 1928, 19.
12. "Contest Teeming with Action Promised When Bruising Team From Hub Clash With Senators - Shore Wins Bad Man Title of League - Hitchman Is Star Boston Attraction," *Ottawa Journal*, Jan. 14, 1928, 26.
13. Stanley Woodward, "Les Canadiens Get Two-Goal Jump at Very Start of Game and Defeat Bruins, 3 to 1," *Boston Herald*, Jan. 18, 1928, 14.
14. "Bruins-Canadiens' Clash Ends 1 to 1," *Boston Globe*, Feb. 12, 1928, 22.
15. Stanley Woodward, "Bruins Defeat Rangers, 2-0; Lead Division, Hitchman Goliath in Defensive Checking," *Boston Herald*, Feb. 20, 1928, 1.
16. Associated Press, "Montreal Maroons Win From Bruins," *Boston Globe*, Feb. 26, 1928, A20.
17. Stanley Woodward, "Hitchman's Counter in Final Minute of Play Gives Bruins 2-1 Victory Over Maroons," *Boston Herald*, Feb. 29, 1928, 12.
18. John J. Hallahan, "Unique Goal by Bruins Defeats Ottawa Six, 1-0," *Boston Globe*, March 7, 1928, 12.
19. John J. Hallahan, "Bruins Hold Lead by Tying Rangers 3-3," *Boston Globe*, March 11, 1928, 19.
20. John J. Hallahan, "Boucher and Oliver Count Early in Third Period in New York as 17,000 Watch Tie Game," *Boston Globe*, April 2, 1928, 1 & 9.
21. "New Yorkers' Remarkable Defence Frustrates Hub Team's Attempts to Score till Last Minutes," *Boston Post*, April 4, 1928; John J. Hallahan, "Rangers Beat Bruins, 4 to 1," *Boston Globe*, April 4, 1928, 1 & 15.

Chapter 10: Stanley Cup Champs
1. Bob Dunbar, "By Bob Dunbar," *Boston Herald*, Nov. 3, 1928, 18.
2. "Bruins Start West to Meet Cougars Tonight," *Boston Globe*, Nov. 22, 1928, 23.
3. "Hitchman Will Not Play Until Tuesday," *Boston Herald*, Dec. 7, 1928, 32.
4. Stanley Woodward, "Board Checks," *Boston Herald*, Dec. 12, 1928, 35; Dec. 13, 1928, 32.
5. Associated Press, "Maple Leaf Team Shuts Out Bruins," *Boston Globe*, Dec. 16, 1928, 30.
6. John J. Hallahan, "Ross Not at All Disturbed Over Bruins' Losing Streak," *Boston Globe*, Dec. 17, 1928, 20.
7. John J. Hallahan, "Bruins Apparently Still in Quest of Goal-Scoring Punch," *Boston Globe*, Dec. 26, 1928, 27.
8. Carl Warton, "Owen Should Shine in Pro Hockey," *Boston Herald*, Jan. 13, 1929, Magazine Section 2.

9. John J. Hallahan, "Eddie Shore Starring, Too," *Boston Globe*, Jan. 14, 1929, 20.
10. Stanley Woodward, "Bruins Score Seventh Win in a Row by 4-1 Triumph Over N.Y. Rangers at Garden; Hitchman and Owen Get into the Swing," *Boston Herald*, Jan. 16, 1929, 24; Stanley Woodward, "Bruins Play Detroit Without Eddie Shore," *Boston Herald*, Jan. 17, 1929, 30.
11. John J. Hallahan, "Americans Shut Out Bruins 1-0," *Boston Globe*, Feb. 6, 1929, 14.
12. Elmer F. Ferguson, "Maroons, in Fighting Form, Out-Crash Bruins to Win and Uncover Fin Attack," *Montreal Herald*, Feb. 10, 1929.
13. Associated Press, "Bruins Shut Out Blackhawks 3-0," *Boston Globe*, Feb. 17, 1929, 55; John J. Hallahan, "Bruins Shut Out Maroons Here 1-0," *Boston Globe*, Feb. 27, 1929, 22.
14. Associated Press, "Boston Winners Over Pittsburgh," *Boston Globe*, March 18, 1929, 18.
15. John J. Hallahan, "Bruins Win Final League Game, 3-1," *Boston Globe*, March 17, 1929, 28.
16. Brian McFarlane, *The Bruins* (Toronto: Stoddart, 1999), 21.
17. Stanley Woodward, "Board Checks," *Boston Herald*, March 21, 1929, 35.
18. W.E. Mullins, "Hitchman Is a 'Than-Whomer' as 'Money-Player of Hockey'; Garden Accommodates Only One-Third of Hopeful Bruin Fans," *Boston Herald*, March 20, 1929, 35.
19. J.W. Mooney, "Bruins Win Score 1-0," *Boston Post*, March 20, 1929.
20. A. Linde Fowler, "Little Fellow Plays Big Part as Bruins Win," *Boston Evening Transcript*, March 20, 1929.
21. Stanley Woodward, "Bruins Defeat Canadiens, 1-0 in Second Game," *Boston Herald*, March 22, 1929, 1; John J. Hallahan, "Weiland Again Wins Game for Bruins, 1-0," *Boston Globe*, March 22, 1929, 31.
22. J. W. Mooney, "Canadiens Are Beaten Again 1 to 0," *Boston Post*, March 22, 1929.
23. Elmer F. Ferguson, "Bruins' Man-Power Blasts Canadiens From Finals Again," *Montreal Herald*, March 24, 1929.
24. Sportsman, "Live Tips and Topics," *Boston Globe*, March 25, 1929, 11.
25. Peter F. Kelley, "Guessing on Date. Hundreds Greet Team," *Boston Record*, March 25, 1929.
26. John J. Hallahan, "Fans Give Bruins Big Welcome Home," *Boston Globe*, March 25, 1929, 11; Stanley Woodward, "Board Checks," *Boston Herald*, March 25, 1929, 15.
27. John J. Hallahan, "Bruins Defeat Rangers in Stanley Cup Game 2-0," *Boston Globe*, March 29, 1929, 30; George MaGuire, Canadian Press, "Hitchman Star of Boston Win," *Ottawa Journal*, March 29, 1929, 23.
28. Hugh S. Fullerton, Jr., Associated Press (in Tops' scrapbook, not certain from which paper), March 31, 1929; Canadian Press, "Boston Man Power

Too Much for Rangers Who Are Beaten Through Crafty Line Playing," *Ottawa Journal*, March 30, 1929, 40.
29. Ed Baker, "Boston Finally Wins Stanley Cup," *Citizen* (Ottawa), March 30, 1929, 15.
30. Brian McFarlane, *The Bruins* (Toronto: Stoddart, 1999), 11.
31. A. Linde Fowler, "Bruins Receive Gold and Praise in Final Act," *Boston Transcript*, April 3, 1929.
32. "Bruin Players Hold Banquet," *Boston Herald*, April 3, 1929, 37.

Chapter 11: Greatest Team, Greatest Defenseman
1. NHL.com. Accessed Nov. 20, 2018.
2. Walter Trumbull, the North American Newspaper Alliance, "Hammond Returns from Round Trip, *Evening Citizen* (Ottawa), Dec. 20, 1929, 12.
3. Ross Cameron, "The Sports Racket," *Winnipeg Evening Tribune*, Jan. 9, 1930, 12.
4. A. Linde Fowler, "Hitchman Says There May Be a Real Thrill When They Win 30 in a Row," *Boston Transcript*, Jan. 6, 1930.
5. Baz O'Meara, "Brilliant Display Marred at Finish," *Montreal Daily Star*, Nov. 25, 1929.
6. Elmer Ferguson, "Shore Battered but Heroic as He Leads Bruins to Win in Sanguinary Ice Battle," *Montreal Herald*, Nov. 25, 1929; "Sport Facts and Fancies," *Ottawa Journal*, Nov. 26, 1929, 17.
7. Elmer Ferguson, "Shore Battered but Heroic as He Leads Bruins to Win in Sanguinary Ice Battle," *Montreal Herald*, Nov. 25, 1929.
8. A. Linde Fowler, "Bruins Sustain Worst Defeat in Two Seasons," *Boston Transcript*, Nov. 27, 1929.
9. Associated Press, "Bruins Brilliant Beating Pirates, 6-2," *Boston Globe*, Dec. 1, 1929, A24.
10. "Ottawas Yield a 3-2 Decision to Boston Bruins Last Night Before a Crowded House," *Ottawa Journal*, Dec. 13, 1929, 32; Ed Baker, "Mixing the Bitter with the Sweet," *Citizen* (Ottawa), Dec. 13, 1929, 14.
11. John J. Hallahan, "Bruins Thrill Fans in 6-to-2 Triumph," *Boston Globe*, Dec. 18, 1929, 22.
12. John J. Hallahan, "Bruins Thrill Fans in 6-to-2 Triumph." *Boston Globe*, Dec. 18, 1929, 22.
13. John J. Hallahan, "Blackhawks Added to Bruins' Victims," *Boston Globe*, Dec. 22, 1929, A26; Hallahan, "Fast Travelling Bruins Too Good for Rivals," *Globe*, Dec. 23, 1929, 17.
14. Elmer Ferguson, "Bruin Machine Smothers Canadien Speed as Champs Win Their Tenth Straight," *Montreal Herald*, Dec. 30, 1929.
15. J.W. Mooney, "Bruins Tie Mark for Straight Wins," *Boston Post*, Jan. 2, 1930.
16. "Bruins Set Record," *Montreal Star*, Jan. 6, 1930.

17. Ross Cameron, "The Sports Racket," *Winnipeg Evening Tribune*, Jan. 9, 1930, 12.
18. Henry J. Disken, "Joliat Canada Star Says Hard to Pass Hub Ace," *Boston Advertiser*, Jan. 10, 1930.
19. Ed Baker, "Short Shots on Sport," *Evening Citizen* (Ottawa), Jan. 15, 1930, 11.
20. J.W. Mooney, "Blackhawks Outclassed by Champs," *Boston Post*, Jan. 22, 1930.
21. A. Linde Fowler, "Hitchman Shines," *Boston Transcript*, Jan. 22, 1930.
22. The Falcon, "Unsung Heroes of the National Hockey Circuit," *Toronto Star Weekly*, Jan. 25, 1930.
23. Baz O'Meara, "The Passing Sport Show," *Montreal Star*, Jan. 27, 1930; Elmer Ferguson, "Bottle and Penny Tossers Hurt Chance of Canadiens as Bruins Win Torrid Game," *Montreal Herald*, Jan. 27, 1930.
24. Stanley Woodward, "Board Checks," *Boston Herald*, Jan. 30, 1930, 22.
25. John Kieran, *New York Times*, Feb. 4, 1930.
26. John J. Hallahan, "Fists Fly as Bruins Crush Cougars, 3-1," *Boston Globe*, Feb. 5, 1930, 24.
27. "Bruins Manager Sent Away on a Vacation," *Boston Globe*, Feb. 6, 1930, 13.
28. C.W. MacQueen, "Boston Rallies in Third Period," *Toronto Mail and Empire*, Feb. 17, 1930.
29. "Boston's Last Period Rush Overtook Leafs' Early Lead," *Toronto Telegraph*, Feb. 17, 1930.
30. Baz O'Meara, "Boston Simply Have to Go Through the Motions," *Montreal Star*, Feb. 17, 1930.
31. Elmer Ferguson, Mr. Hitchman, the Unsung Hero," *Montreal Herald*, Feb. 20, 1930.
32. John J. Hallahan, "Canadiens May Top Maroons," *Boston Globe*, Feb. 24, 1930, 18.
33. "Bruins Defeat Ottawa, 2-1, on Weiland's Goal," *Boston Herald*, March 2, 1930, 22.
34. Henry J. Disken, "Favors Bruins' Captain and Defense Star to Outscore Individual National League Stars," *Boston Advertiser*, March 2, 1930.
35. Peter F. Kelley, "Loss of Hitchman Severe Blow to Bruins," *Boston Record*, March 3, 1930.
36. Ralph Clifford, "The Bruins Suffered a Smashing Blow," *Boston Traveler*, March 4, 1930.
37. John J. Hallahan, "Bruins Crippled by Hitchman's Injury," *Boston Globe*, March 4, 1930, 14.
38. Associated Press, "First Bruins Loss in 18 Games, 3-2," *Boston Globe*, March 14, 1930, 34.
39. J.W. Mooney, "Great Home Record," *Boston Post*, March 19, 1929.

40. Elmer Ferguson, "One Hundred and Five Minutes, and Thirty-Five Seconds!," *Montreal Herald*, March 21, 1921.
41. Stanley Woodward, "Bruin Defeat Montreal, 2-1, After 45 Minutes of Overtime," *Boston Herald*, March 21, 1930, 32.
42. John J. Hallahan, "Bruins Make It Two Straight," *Boston Globe*, March 23. 1930, A1 & 21.
43. J. W. Mooney, "Head Guards for Bruins Tomorrow," *Boston Post*, March 24, 1930.
44. Elmer Ferguson, "The Colorful Canadiens Loom Today," *Montreal Herald*, March 24, 1930.
45. Laurence G. Hanscom, "Tamest of Lions When at Home," *Boston Globe*, March 23, 1930.
46. John J. Hallahan, "Bruins Out to End Big Series Tonight," *Boston Globe*, March 25, 1930, 13.
47. Victor O. Jones, "Sidelights of the Third Bruins-Maroons Clash," *Boston Globe*, March 26, 1930, 17.
48. Stanley Woodward, "Maroons Beat Bruins, 1-0, in Overtime Game," *Boston Herald*, March 26, 1930, 1.
49. Baz O'Meara, "Bruins Were Breaking Down Under Pressure," *Montreal Star*, March 26, 1930.
50. Stanley Woodward, "Barry Scores Two Goals and Assists in Third as Bruins Rout Maroons at Garden, 5-1," *Boston Herald*, March 28, 1930, 36.
51. Elmer Ferguson, "Another Hockey Miracle Can Be Credited to Canadiens Today," *Montreal Herald*, April 2, 1930.
52. Peter F. Kelley, "Hitchman in Lead to Get Hart Trophy," *Boston Record*, April 2, 1930.
53. Ralph Clifford, "Bruins Given Five of Six Places on All-League Team," *Boston Traveler*, April 2, 1930.
54. Elmer Ferguson, "Canadiens Were Great in Victory," *Montreal Herald*, April 4, 1930.
55. John J. Hallahan, "Canadiens Repeat, Winning the Title," *Boston Globe*, April 5, 1930.
56. Baz O'Meara, "Today's Hero–Write Your Own Ticket!," *Montreal Star*, April 4, 1930.
57. Bob Dunbar, "Manager Art Ross of the Bruins," *Boston Herald*, May 7, 1930, 35.

Chapter 12: Waning
1. "Lionel Hitchman Big Cog in St Geroge's Showing," *Boston Globe*, Jul. 14, 1930, 19.
2. "Second Front Line to Start Against Bruins," *Detroit Free Press*, Nov. 23, 1930, 16.
3. Canadian Press, "Canadiens Down Bruins, McCaffrey Breaks Tie," *Ottawa Journal*, Dec. 1, 1930, 21.

4. Arthur Siegel, "Bruins Stop Maroons, 2-1," *Boston Herald*, Dec. 10, 1930, 33.
5. John J. Hallahan, "Owen's Goal Gives Bruins Victory, 2-1," *Boston Globe*, Feb. 11, 1931, 23.
6. Arthur Siegel, "Aged Fred Hitchman (He's 28), Faces Sixth Play-Off Series," *Boston Herald*, March 8, 1931, 21.
7. J.W. Mooney, "Veterans of Play-Offs Among the Bruins," *Boston Post*, March 23, 1931.
8. Bill Grimes, "They Shall Not Pass," *Boston American*, March 23, 1931.
9. J.W. Mooney, "Bruins Win First Game of Playoff," *Boston Post*, March 25, 1931.
10. Arthur Siegel, "Canadiens Win from Bruins, 1-0," *Boston Herald*, March 27, 1931.
11. Elmer Ferguson, "It Must Be Just an Old Boston Custom," *Montreal Herald*, March 31, 1931.
12. Arthur Siegel, "Canadiens Win Final Game, 3-2," *Boston Herald*, April 2, 1931, 34.
13. "Suggested Sale of Hitchman," *Boston Herald*, April 2, 1931, 34.
14. "Adams Denies Hitchman Will Go to Detroit," *Boston Herald*, April 2, 1931, 34.
15. "To Wed Hockey Star," *Vancouver Sun*, April 11, 1931, 16; "Clapper-Pratt Nuptials," *Vancouver Sun*, April 28, 1931, 8.
16. "Issues Denial," *Ottawa Journal*, Sept. 16, 1931, 17; Associated Press, "Hitchman Not for Sale, Says Ross," *Boston Globe*, Sept. 17, 1931, 11.
17. Associated Press, "Bruins and Falcons Battle to 1-1 Draw," *Boston Globe*, March 18, 1932, 41.
18. Ed Baker, "Short Shots on Sport," *Citizen* (Ottawa), Nov. 16, 1932, 12.
19. Melville E. Webb Jr., "Bruins Play Two Games on Garden Ice This Week," *Boston Globe*, Dec. 19, 1932, 11.
20. Melville E. Webb, "Bruins Play Amerks Again Here Tonight," *Boston Globe*, Jan. 3, 1933, 9; Webb, "Bruins in 0-0 Tie Lose Some Ground," *Globe*, Jan. 4, 1933, 9.
21. "Lauds Hitch and Shore," *Ottawa Journal*, March 25, 1933, 18.
22. "Bruins on Big End of 4 to 2 Score," *Boston Globe*, March 10, 1933, 21.
23. Sportsman, "Barry and Clapper Bruin Holdouts," *Boston Globe*, Oct. 20, 1933, 31.
24. Associated Press, "Ross Puts It Up to Frank Calder," *Boston Globe*, Nov. 5, 1933, A24.
25. Melville E. Webb, "Bruins Win From Blackhawks 2-0," *Boston Globe*, Nov. 22, 1933, 20.
26. Melville E. Webb, "Hockey Stars Fight, Two Knocked Cold," *Boston Globe*, Dec. 13, 1933, 1 & 22.
27. Melville E. Webb, "Bruins Score Only Goal in Overtime," *Boston Globe*, Dec. 20, 1933, 23.

28. Melville E. Webb, "Bruins Buy Wilcox to Pair With Shore," *Boston Globe*, Jan. 30, 1934, 23.
29. Sportsman, "Live Tips and Topics," *Boston Globe*, Jan. 30, 1934, 22; "Welcoming Eddie Back," *Boston Globe*, Jan. 31, 1934, 19.
30. Victor O. Jones, "Cracked Ice," *Boston Globe*, Feb. 2, 1934, 20.
31. Sportsman, "Live Tips and Topics," *Boston Globe*, Feb. 22, 1934, 16.
32. J.W. Mooney, "Big Night for Hitch," *Boston Post*, Feb. 22, 1934.
33. "By Bob Dunbar," *Boston Herald*, Feb. 22, 1934, 26.
34. Arthur Siegel, "Bruins and Senators Join Fans in Hitchman Tribute Tonight as Star Quits 'Big Time' Ranks," *Boston Herald*, Feb. 22, 1934, 29.
35. Melville E. Webb, "Boston Bruins Lose to Ottawa by 3 to 1," *Boston Globe*, Feb. 23, 1934, 21.
36. Eric Zweig, *Art Ross: The Hockey Legend Who Built the Bruins,* (Toronto, Dundurn Press, 2015), 26.
37. "In the Realm of Sport by Walter Gilhooly," *Ottawa Journal*, Feb. 23, 1934, 16.
38. "Hitchman Expresses Appreciation to Fans," *Boston Globe*, Feb. 26, 1934, 9.
39. Associated Press, "Bruins Close Season With 9 to 5 victory," *Boston Globe*, March 19, 1934, 8.

Chapter 13: The Coaching Years
1. Associated Press, "Hitchman of Bruins Sent to Hub Cubs," *Springfield Republican* (MA), Jan. 30, 1934, 11.
2. Victor O. Jones, "Hitchman Plays With Team," *Boston Globe*, Feb. 3, 1934, 8.
3. Hy Hurwitz, "Cubs Beat Arrows and Take the Lead," *Boston Globe*, Feb. 4, 1934.
4. "Paprika' Found What Harm Gossip Can Cause," Paper unknown, found in Canada Archives and Library, Aug. 11, 1934.
5. "Fred Hitchman to Perform With his Bow and Arrow," *Boston Globe*, March 22, 1934, 20.
6. "New Management for the Bruins," *Boston Globe*, April 7, 1934, 7.
7. "Boston Cubs Upset Bruins," *Winnipeg Tribune*, Oct. 29, 1934, 15.
8. Sportsman, "Live Tips and Topics," *Boston Globe*, April 8, 1935, 11.
9. Gerry Moore, "Bruin Cubs Crawl Nearer Third Place," *Boston Globe*, Feb. 21, 1936, 19.
10. Gerry Moore, "Art Ross Again to Pilot Bruins," *Boston Globe*, Sept. 15, 1936, 22.
11. "At the NHL Training Camps," *Winnipeg Tribune*, Oct. 29, 1937, 22.
12. Jack Maunder, "Another Angle," *Ottawa Journal*, Nov. 6, 1940, 21; Paul V. Craigue, "Notes of the Game," *Boston Globe*, Feb. 10, 1937, 19.

13. "Bruins on Watertown High Sports Program," *Boston Globe*, March 5, 1937, 32.
14. Victor O. Jones, "Cracked Ice," *Boston Globe*, Dec. 24, 1937, 9.
15. Vern DeGeer, "Good Morning," *Montreal Gazette*, April 1, 1965, 18.
16. Lionel Hitchman to Manage Springfield Indians Hockey Team," *Boston Globe*, Sept. 3, 1938, 6.
17. "Coach Hitchman May Resume Work Tomorrow," *Boston Globe*, Oct. 26, 1938, 8.
18. "Bears Priming for Springfield," *Evening News* (Harrisburg, PA), Jan. 18, 1939, 12.
19. Associated Press, "Hitchman Let Out as Indians' Coach, Former N.H.L. Defence Star Has Been Victimized by Illness for Most of Season," *Gazette* (Montreal), Jan. 19, 1939, 18.
20. Associated Press, "Mitchell Takes Hitchman's Job," *Boston Globe*, Jan. 20, 1939, 19.
21. "Hitch Fathers Hockey Interest in Berlin, NH," *Boston Globe*, Feb. 28, 1947, 26; "Lake Placid Belts Junpics, 11-4, in A.H.A. Final," *Boston Globe*, March 30, 1947, 31. https://www.facebook.com/berlinmaroons/. Accessed Nov. 2, 2018.

Chapter 14: Life Without Hockey
1. Letter to Gloria Coburn from E.Y. Clarke, M.D., Chief of Staff, Glens Falls Hospital, Dec. 23, 1968.
2. Hitchman death notice, *Ottawa Journal*, Dec. 20, 1968, 31.
3. Bill Westwick, "Former Ottawa and Boston Star Lionel Hitchman Dies," *Ottawa Journal*, Dec. 21, 1968, 16.
4. Harold Kaese, "Hitchman First B's Super Star," *Boston Globe*, Feb. 6, 1969, 28.
5. Sam Pompei, "'Mr. Hockey' Recalls Lionel Hitchman," *Springfield Sunday Republican*, Jan. 19, 1969, 8.
6. Win Mills, "Debunking a Poet's Cocktail," *Citizen* (Ottawa), Jan. 30, 1969, 33.
7. Tops to her grandson, circa 1965.

Chapter 15: Last Word on Hitch
1. Elmer Ferguson, "Hitchman One of the Greatest," *Montreal Herald*, circa 1932-33 NHL season (from National Archives).
2. "Hockey Leaders Pay Fine Tribute to Peter [Green]," *Ottawa Journal*, Sept. 24, 1934, 17.
3. "Sportsmen Pay Tribute to Eddie Gerard," *Ottawa Journal*, Aug. 7, 1937, 24.
4. "All-I've-Seen" Team Picked by Hockey Writers," *Boston Globe*, Jan. 8, 1941, 6.

5. Fred Knight, "Ross' Ice System Rivals Football's Rockne, Warner," *Boston Traveler*, Feb. 17, 1943, 23; Harold Kaese, "Cracked Ice," *Boston Globe*, Feb. 18, 1943, 10.
6. Charles Edwards, Canadian Press, "King Clancy Says Frank Nighbor Greatest of All Hockey Players," *Ottawa Journal*, Jan. 25, 1943, 17.
7. Bill Westwick, "The Realm of Sport," *Ottawa Journal*, June 18, 1943, 18.
8. Charles Edwards, Canadian Press, "Senior Grid Season Opens Next Saturday," *Calgary Herald*, Sept. 11, 1943, 15.
9. Harold Kaese, "Boston-N.Y. Ice Rivalry Hits Peak," *Boston Globe*, Dec. 10, 1943, 22.
10. Canadian Press, "Ion Selects Four Former Ottawa Stars on All-Time Team," *Ottawa Journal*, April 8, 1944, 20.
11. Victor O. Jones, "Mourn Passing of Body-Check," *Boston Globe*, March 5, 1944, 22.
12. Harold Kaese, "Hennessy No. 1 B's Fan, but He Holds Only Thin Edge Over Les Wilmot," *Boston Globe*, March 15, 1945, 8.
13. Harold Kaese, "Krauts Fadeout Proves War Not an Interruption but Full Stop for Athletes," *Boston Globe*, Feb. 26, 1946, 11.
14. Jerry Nason, "Hurryup Henderson Herewith Nominated Bruin of the Year," *Boston Globe*, March 14, 1946, 22.
15. "Former Star Watches Game," *Ottawa Journal*, Feb. 6, 1947, 18.
16. D.A.L. MacDonald, "Sports on Parade," *Montreal Gazette*, Oct. 11, 1947, 19.
17. Bill Westwick, "The Realm of Sport," *Ottawa Journal*, Jan. 1, 1949, 18.
18. Dave Egan, "The Colonel Predicts," *Boston Daily Record*, Dec. 5, 1951, 21.
19. Dave Egan, "The Colonel Predicts," *Boston Daily Record*, March 25, 1952, 18.
20. John Gilhooly, "Schedules Ruin Hockey – Mantha," *Boston Daily Record*, Nov. 18, 1952, 23.
21. Dave Egan, "It's the Memories of Wonderful Things," *Boston Daily Record*, March 18, 1953, 20.
22. Tom Fitzgerald, "Shades of Shore and Hitch," *Boston Globe*, Oct. 22, 1953, 13.
23. Vern DeGeer, "Those Australians Are Back," *Gazette* (Montreal), July 28, 1955, 19.
24. Bill Westwick, "He Helped Form Starry Boston Array," *Ottawa Journal*, Jan. 18, 1962, 15.
25. Dink Carroll, "Playing the Field," *Gazette* (Montreal), Feb. 11, 1969, 30.

*The *Montreal Gazette* and *Ottawa Citizen* are divisions of the Postmedia Network.

Bibliography

Barnes, Michael. *Killer in the Bush: The Great Fires of Northeastern Ontario*. Erin, ON: Boston Mills Press, 1987.

Cameron, Steve. *Hockey Hall of Fame Treasures*. Richmond Hill, ON: Firefly Books, 2011.

Campey, Lucille H. *Seeking a Better Future: The English Pioneers of Ontario and Quebec*. Toronto: Dundurn Press, 2012.

Coleman, Charles, L. *The Trail of the Stanley Cup*. Montreal: National Hockey League, 1966.

Diamond, Dan. *Hockey Hall of Fame: The Official History of the Game's Honour Roll*. Toronto: Doubleday, 1996.

_____. *Total Hockey: The Official Encyclopedia of the National Hockey League, 1st and 2d editions*. New York: Total Sports, 1998 and 2000.

Finnigan, Joan. *Old Scores, New Goals: The Story of the Ottawa Senators*. Kingston, ON: Quarry Press, 1992.

Fischler, Stan. *Boston Bruins: Greatest Moments and Players*. New York: Skyhorse Publishing, Inc, 2012.

Fitsell, J.W. *Hockey's Captains, Colonels and Kings*. Erin, ON: Boston Mills Press, 1987.

Hiam, C. Michael. *Eddie Shore and That Old Time Hockey*. Toronto: McClelland & Stewart, 2010.

Kitchen, Paul. *Win, Tie, or Wrangle: The Inside Story of the Old Ottawa Senators—1883-1935*. Manotick, ON: Penumbra Press, 2008.

Kullas, Kris. *Accessed Denied: Forgotten & Future Heroes of Hockey's Hall of Fame*. Timmins, ON: Frosted Forest Northern Ontario Publishing, 2011.

McAuley, Jim. *The Ottawa Sports Book*. Burnstown, ON: General Store Publishing House, 1987.

McFarlane, Brian. *The Bruins: Brian McFarlane's Original Six*. Toronto: Stoddart Publishing Co. Ltd., 1999.

———. *Clancy: The King's Story*. Toronto: ECW Press, 1997.

Richardson, Stewart and Richard Leblanc. *Dit: Dit Clapper and the Rise of the Boston Bruins*. PACTS Management Inc., 2012.

Vantour, Kevin. *The Bruins Book*. Toronto: ECW Press, 1997.

Zweig, Eric. *Art Ross: The Hockey Legend Who Built the Bruins*. Toronto: Dundurn

Index

Abel, Clarence (Taffy), 192, 220
Adams, Charles, F., 145, 158, 168, 188, 205, 331, 338
  first season, Boston Bruins 137, 142
  Hitch, 132, 177, 252, 254, 265, 269-270, 275-279, 283, 285, 287, 299
  Ross, Art, 223, 283, 285, 287
  WHL player contracts, 155, 158
Adams, Vernon, 146
Adams, Weston, 279
adonis, 90, 101, 113
Ahearn, Frank, 107, 114-117, 122, 130, 133-134, 328-329
Algonquin Park, see Myers cabin
All-American, 5
Allan Cup, 38, 47, 51, 58, 63, 127,
Allan Line Steamship Co., 17
All-star team(s), 10, 222, 241, 265, 294, 305, *314*
amateur sports, 59-60
American Hockey Association, AHA, 156, 170
Ancaster, On, 18
Anglican(s), 18, 20, 27, 43-44, 325
Applegath, Harold, 35-36, 39
archery, 21, 53, 282
Archibald, Ed, Captain, 48
Arena Gardens (Toronto), 40, 224, 323
Art Ross: The Hockey Legend Who Built the Bruins, Eric Zweig, 11, 339
assayer, 295
Associated Press, (AP), 174, 189, 194, 203, 234, 252, 254, 278, 292-293, 331-336, 338-340
Atkinson, Archie, 78
Aura Lee, 21, 32-42, 47-49, 52, 54, 72, 104, 126, 129, 149, 177, 201, 321
Bailey, Irvine (Ace), 188, 259, 263-265, 279, 319

Baker, Ed, 79, 83, 90, 94, 96, 203, 212, 218, 256, 324-326, 328-329, 335-336, 338
barber, 18
Barry, Martin (Marty), 213, 215, 217, 224, 230, 239, 243, 247, 253-254, 256, 259, 262, 337-338
Basingstoke, Kent, 32
Bauer, Bobby, 286-288, 305-306
Beaches Hockey League, 25, 27-28, 31, 33, 42, 320-321. See also Toronto Hockey League
Beatty, Cliff, 34
Bell, Billy (referee), 173,
Belleville (Jr. OHA hockey team), 41, 321
Belmont, MA 179, 201
Benedict, Clint, 125-127, 129, 180, 305-306, 329
  1922-23 season, 57, 60, 68, 75, 82, 84, 88-89, 94, 96
  1923-24 season, 98, 105, 110, 115, 118-120, 122
Benson, Bobby, 133, 135-136
Berlin Maroons, 294
Berlin, NH, 294-295, 340
Besler, Phil, 283-285
Beveridge, Bill, 222
Black Hawks (Blackhawks), 190, 194, 246-248, 253, 258, 262-263
  1926-27 season, 155, 159, 162-163
  1929-30 season, 207, 213-214, 219, 234, 243
  chapter notes, 331-332, 334-336
Blake, Bob, 285
body check, 9, 107, 150, 157, 160, 168, 179, 247, 251, 257, 273, 301, 306, 309, 341
  1923-24 season, 71, 88, 90
  1928-29 season, 193, 200

1929-30 season, 209, 213, 221, 227-229, 235, 238, 240
Booth, J.R., 48, 114
Booth, Lois, 114-115
Boston American, 137, 187, 250, 338
Boston Americans, 146
Boston Arena, 134-135, 140, 146, 151, 156, 160-161, 163, 174, 330
Boston Advertiser, 137, 155, 216, 230-231, 336
Boston Bruins, 1-3, 5, 11, 57, 62, 296, 299-300, 305
 1924-25 season, 127-128, 130, 132-140, 142
 1925-26 season, 143-155
 1926-27 season, 155-169
 1927-28 season, 169-184
 1928-29 season, 185-206
 1929-30 season, 207-244
 1930-31 season, 245-253
 1931-32 season, 253-255
 1932-33 season, 255-261
 1933-34 season, 262-278
 Hitch's coaching years, 279-280, 283, 285-289, 294
 appendix, *313-315*
 chapter notes, 330, 332, 335, 339
Boston Celtics, 308
Boston College, 146, 308
Boston Cubs, 229, 256, 263-264, 266-270, 272, 274, 277-280, 283-288, 291, 293-294, *315*, 339
Boston Garden, 1, 3, 8, 187, 192, 269, 272, 277, 282, 285, 287, 308-309
 Last Hurrah, 3-4, 6
Boston Globe, 299, 306, 308-309
 1924-25 season, 136-137
 1925-26 season, 144, 147, 151, 154
 1926-27 season, 157, 159, 161-162, 166
 1927-28 season, 173, 183
 1928-29 season, 190, 196, 199-202
 1929-30 season, 210, 213, 222-223, 233, 235, 237-238, 241
 1930-31 season, 245, 248
 1932-33 season, 255, 258-260
 1933-34 season, 264, 266-269, 274, 276
 Hitch's coaching years, 281-282, 288, 290
 chapter notes, 329-341
Boston Herald, 135, 137, 145, 164, 167-168, 174, 247, 249, 251-252
 1928-29 season, 189, 191-192, 196-199
 1929-30 season, 215, 221, 230, 235, 238-239, 243
 1933-34 season, 270, 271, 276, 289
 chapter notes, 330-335, 337-339
Boston Junior Olympics, 293, 299
Boston police, 179, 188, 223
Boston Post, 137, 148, 154, 175, 249-250, 270
 1928-29 season, 182-183, 198-199
 1929-30 season, 214, 218, 234, 236
 chapter notes, 330, 332-339
Boston Record, 137, 201-202, 232, 240
 chapter notes, 334, 336-337
Boston Tigers, 170, 280
Boston Transcript, 137, 198, 210, 212, 219, 334-336
Boston Traveler, 137, 146, 232, 241
 chapter notes, 336-337, 341
Boucher, Billy, 107-108, 115, 160, 163, 324
 1922-23 season, 71, 74, 78-82, 84-85, 94
Boucher, Frank, 82, 207, 209, 230, 242, 256, 291, 306
Boucher, George (Buck), 129, 138, 168-169, 181, 292
 1922-23 season, 57, 59, 61, 68, 70, 73-74, 82, 88, 94, 96
 1923-24, 98-99, 101-103, 105, 110, 112, 119-120, 122
 chapter notes, 326, 330
Bowmanville (OHA, Jr. hockey team), 39-40, 321
Boyd, Hank, 253-254
brazier, 15
Briden, Archie, 156, 160
Brimsek, Frank, 305-306
Bristol (PA) Courier/Bucks County Courier Times, 248
Broadbent, Harry (Punch), 10, 305-306
 1922-23 season, 57, 68, 75, 82, 87-88, 91, 94, 96
 1923-24 season, 98, 105-111, 117-118, 120, 122

1924-25 season, 126-127, 129
  chapter notes, 325, 327
Brockingham (MA) Brockvilles, 294
Brown, George V., 145
Bruins, The, Brian McFarlane, 4, 195, 204, 319, 334-335
Burch, Billy, 103, 135
Burghs, rugby. *See* New Edinburghs, rugby
Burke, Bertie, 61, 63-64, 78
Burnett, Grey, 64
Burns, Hal, 130
Byng, Evelyn, Lady, 45, 49, 61-62, 78, 102, 141, 235, 240, 242, 322, 330
Byng, Julian, Lord, 45, 49, 61-62, 78, 99, 102
Cahill, Charles, 156
Calder, Frank, 166, 235, 240
  1922-23 season, 60, 71, 76-77
  1923-24 season, 99, 107-109, 111-113, 116
  1924-25 season, 127, 141-142
  chapter notes, 328, 338
Calgary Tigers (prairie league), 81, 122, 128, 133, 329
Campbell, Earl (Spiff), 99-100, 103-105, 108-111, 114, 129
Campey, Lucille, 17, 319
Canadian Amateur Hockey Association, CAHA, 46, 63
Canadian Press, 90, 120, 247, 252, 305
  1928-29 season, 202-203
  chapter notes, 319, 325, 328-329, 334, 337, 341
Can-Am Hockey League, 170, 207, 266, 279-280, 283-284, 291-292
capital of hockey, 42-43, 45-47, 59
Capital Senior Hockey League (Capital League or Group 2), 46, 49, 51, 57-58, 61-64, 67, 322-323
Carleton, Floyd, 243
Carrigan, Gene, 284
Carroll, Dink, 310, 341
Carson, Bill, Dr., 38, 51, 187, 193, 195, 203-204, 213, 215, 244
Cayuga St, 43
Cedar River Cemetery, 299
Cedar River Golf Course, 297
Census, 17, 18, 321

Chabot, Lorne, 164, 182
Chamberlain, John, 7-8, 261
Chamberlain, Nancy, 8
Chambers, John, 294
Chapman, Art, 243, 250, 253-254, 263
Christ Church Cathedral, 44
Christian Science Monitor, 137
Church of England, 17-18
City directory, Toronto, 17-18, 320
Civil Service League (senior amateur hockey), 46, 49
CKAC, Montreal, 145
Clancy, Frank (King), 38, 168, 291, 305, 310
  1922-23 season, 59, 63, 68, 72, 75, 82-83, 86-89, 94, 96
  1923-24 season, 98-99, 101-106, 108-113-115, 117-119, 122
  1924-25 season, 128-130, 140
  1927-28 season, 172-173
  1929-30 season, 209, 213, 216, 218, 242-243
  chapter notes, 330, 332, 341
Clancy, Tom, 86
Clapper, Aubrey (Dit), 170-171, 247, 253-254, 256, 262, 272, 274, 302, 305-306, 309
  1928-29 season, 186-187, 189-192, 194-195, 202, 204
  1929-30 season, 209, 213, 215, 224, 243-245
  chapter notes, 342, 338
Clapper, Loraine (Honey, *née* Pratt), 253
Clark, Patrick (Nobby), 170
Cleghorn, Odie, 71, 74, 105
Cleghorn, Sprague, 10, 138, 186, 211, 228, 229, 273, 289, 306
  1922-23 season, 60-61, 71, 74, 76-78
  1922-24 season, 105-109, 112-113-116
  1925-26 season, 144-145, 147. 149-150, 153-154
  1926-27 season, 156-159, 161-163, 166-167
  1927-28 season, 170-171, 179-180
  chapter notes, 324, 328
Cleghorn, Sprague, Mrs., 155
Clifford, Ralph, 137, 232, 241, 336-337
Clinton Iowa, 18
Coburn, Claude, 3

Coburn, Claudia, 2
Coburn, Gloria (*née* Hitchman), 1, 2-3, 13, 156, 177, 230, 237, 276, 281, 295-299, 319, 340
Coburn, John, 2-6, 8-9, 11, 310
Coburn, Leslie (Les), 2, 7-8
Coburn, Patrick (Pat), 296
Collingwood (Jr. OHA hockey team), 41
Conacher, Charlie, 258
Conacher, Lionel, 21, 33-34, 151-152, 160, 163, 175, 195, 305-306
Connell, Alex, 128-129, 153, 171, 212, 254
Connor, Harry, 170, 172, 174, 181, 244
Contant brothers, 40-41, 321
Cook, Alexander (Bud), 253
Cook, Bill, 305, 174, 209, 291
Cook, Frederick (Bun), 164, 291
Cook, John, 41
Cooper, Carson, 138, 140, 153, 156, 158, 160, 189-190, 291, 330-331
Cornwall (Jr. OHA hockey team), 40-41, 321
Cornwall lacrosse team, 52, 322
Cottrell, Leslie, 276
Coutu, Billy, 211, 228-229, 283, 324, 332
  1922-23 season, 61, 71, 74, 76-78
  1923-24 season, 107, 118
  1926-27 season, 156-158, 162-163, 169
Cowley, Bill, 305-306
Cox, Abbie, 294
Coyne, Bob 167, 181
Crawford, Jack, 289, 305
Cricket, 20-21, 25, 32-33, 44, 51-52, 243, 320, 322
Crotty, Dr., 256
Dandurand, Leo, 76-77, 108, 112-113, 140, 324, 328
Darragh, Harold, 59-60, 242
Darragh, Jack, 59, 69, 74, 78-79, 98-99, 102-104, 106, 109-110, 122-123, 126, 306, 324, 329
De La Salle (Jr. OHA hockey team), 40-41
Deacoff, (first name unknown), 34
Death, Edith, Jane 18
Dempsey, Jack, 260
Denneny, Corbett, 82, 86-119

Denneny, Cy, 128-129, 140, 153, 186, 204, 211, 228, 305, 327
  1922-23 season, 68, 73-76, 78-85, 87, 92, 94, 96
  1923-24 season, 98, 100, 104-111, 115, 118, 120, 122
Department of National Revenue, 50
Department of Soldiers' Civil Re-establishment, 42
Detroit Cougars, 155, 158, 170, 172, 192-193, 195, 222, 246, 331, 333, 336. *See also* Detroit Falcons and Detroit Red Wings
Detroit Falcons, 246, 253-255, 238. *See also* Detroit Cougars, Detroit Reg Wings
Detroit Free Press, 247, 337
Detroit Red Wings, 208, 255, 259, 262, 265, 277, 297. *See also* Detroit Cougars and Detroit Falcons
Devlin, Brian, 69, 324-325
Dey Arena, 46, 61-65, 78, 305, 322-324, 328
Dey, Ted, 79, 85, 91-92, 94, 96
Dignano, E.F., 276
Dinsmore, Charles, 29, 34-35, 38-40, 129
Disken, Henry, 216, 218, 230, 336
Dolan, Cosy, 79, 94, 96
Dolan, D. Leo, 280
Dr. Hand, 75
Dube, Gilles, 294
Dumart, Woody (Porky), 286-288, 290, 305-306
Dunbar, Bob, 243, 270, 333, 337, 339
Dundas St, 18-20
Duquesne Garden, 146
Dutton, Norman (Red), 160, 162, 195
Dye, Babe, 33
dynamite line, 186, 209
Eastern Canada Lacrosse League, 52
Edmonton Eskimos, 82, 85-89, 91, 97, 99-102, 126, 160, 257, 273, 325-326
Egan, Dave, 308-309, 332, 341
Elmer Ferguson Memorial Award, 303. *See also* Ferguson, Elmer
Emery Mills, ME, 300
emigrate, immigrate, immigration, 16, 17, 320
English origin, 43

Erik, Prince of Denmark, 114
Ferguson, Elmer, 9, 12, 251, 257, 303, 306. *See also* Elmer Ferguson Memorial Award
   1922-23 season, 71
   1928-29 season, 193, 200,
   1929-30 season, 210-211, 214, 220-221, 225, 235-236, 240-242
   chapter notes, 319, 334-338, 340
Filmore, Tommy, 280
Findlay, W.J., 98, 326
Finnigan, Frank, 103, 118, 122, 126, 129, 213
First World War, *see* WWI
Fitzgerald, Tom, 309, 341
Fleet Center, 3
Flying Frenchmen, 294
football (American), 21, 48, 53-55, 58, 60, 69, 73, 86, 191, 238, 300
Foran, William, 84, 325
Forbes, Vern, 33, 139
forest ranger, 1, 297
Fort Erie, ON, 194, 224
Foster, Harry (Yip), 254
Fowler, Lynde, A., 137, 198, 210, 212, 219, 334-336
Foyston, Frank, 38, 306
Fredrickson, Frank, 156, 160, 163, 170, 173-174, 182, 186, 190-191, 331, 333
French, 24, 43, 197
Gainor, Norman (Dutch), 285, 302, 305, 309
   1927-28 season, 170, 173
   1928-29 season, 186-187, 190, 194-195, 199, 202, 204, 206
   1929-30 season, 209, 213, 215, 233, 243-244
Galbraith, Percy, 253-254, 256, 268, 272-274, *314*
   1926-27 season, 156, 158, 162
   1927-28 season, 170, 173-174, 182
   1928-29 season, 186-187, 190, 192, 195, 204
   1929-30 season, 210, 215, 243-244
Gallagher and Shean, 93
Gardiner, Chuck, 242
Gardiner, Herb, 217
Garneau, Lucien, 291-293
gas stove maker, 18

Gately, Linde, Dr., 264
Gerard, Eddie, 305-306, 340
   1922-23 season, 57, 60-61, 68-70, 72, 74-75, 79, 83, 85-88, 90, 93-97
   1923-24 season, 99, 101-102-103, 107, 109, 121
Giafranchi, Ferdinand (Ferd), 8
Giafranchi, Lul, 8
Gilhooly, John, 308, 341
Gilhooly, Walter, 277, 339
Gill, Dave, 37, 48, 58, 78, 134
Gilmore, Joe, 266, 280
Giroux, Art, 284
Gladstone Public School, 18
Glens Falls Hospital, 298-299, 340
Goodfellow, Ebbie, 222-223, 254
Gordanier, Patty (*née* Yurlowsky), 297
Gordon, Fred
Gorman, Ed, 127-129, 130
Gorman, Tommy, 11, 242, 255, 273, 285, 302, 304-305
   1922-23 season, 59, 62, 67-68, 71, 76, 78-79, 81-82, 84-87, 89-90, 93-94, 96
   1923-24 season, 99, 101-104, 106-107, 109-111, 113-114, 116, 120-122
   1924-25 season, 125, 130, 132-134
   chapter notes, 325, 328-329
Governor General of Canada. *See* Bing, Julian, Lord
Grace Church, 21
Graham, Leith, 103
Great Britain, 21, 23-24, 43
Great Depression, 1, 246, 253, 262, 295
Great Fire of 1922, 54-55, 177, 322
green line, 288
Green, Peter (Petie), 59, 79, 90, 98, 129-130, 134, 305, 340
Green, Redvers (Red), 103, 173, 186
Green, Ted, 4-5, 319
Green, Win, 204, 215, 300
Grey Cup, 53-54
Grimes, Bill, 137, 250, 338
Grosvenor St, 43
Group of Seven, 20
Hainsworth, George, 156, 189, 197-199
Hallahan, John, J., 152, 173, 248, 259, 330-337
   1926-27 season, 157, 159, 161, 166
   1928-29 season, 190, 196, 199, 201-

350 | HITCH

202
1929-30 season, 213-214, 222, 233-235, 237, 241
Halliday, Milt, 285
Hambly, Percy, 76
Hamilton Herald, 110
Hamilton Spectator, 118,
Hamilton Tigers (NHL hockey team), 143
   1922-23 season, 61-63, 65, 67-68, 70
   1923-24 season, 102-103, 109, 118
   1924-25 season, 135, 139-141
   chapter notes, 326-328, 330
Hanley, Joe, 309
Harnott, Walter, 285
Harrington, Leland (Hago), 156, 170
Harrington, Leland, Mrs., 155
Hart Trophy, 9, 110, 119-120, 141, 189, 246, 255-256, 287, 291, *314*, 337
   1929-30 season, 226, 230, 232, 235, 240-242
Hart, Cecil, 121, 126
Hartt's Island pool, 246
Haskin, Penny (*née* Yurkowsky), 297
Hay, George, 162, 242
Helman, Harry, 68, 83-86, 91, 94, 96, 98, 103-105, 110-111, 122, 325
Helman, Hitchman Fitzgerald, 68
helmets, headgear, 4, 236-237
Henri Fontaine Cup, 280, 283, 285, *315*
Herbert(s), Jimmy (Sailor), 133, 153, 156, 159-160, 163, 169-174, 177, 183, 189-190
Hergesheimer, Phil (Nip), 284-285
Hewitt, Foster, 35
Hewitt, William, 35, 104
Heximer, Orville (Obs), 280
Himes, Norman, 242
Hitch's Last Hurrah, 262-278
Hitch's NHL playing career, 1, 11, 45, 269, 279, 285, 291, 303, 305, *313-314*
Hitchman private collection, 13, 22, 34, 44, 50, 83, 92, 123, 204, 244, 261, 284, 311
Hitchman, Amelia (*née* Cahill), 14, 16, 17-18
Hitchman, Amy, 14, 16
Hitchman, Caroline (*née* Stockley), 14, 15

Hitchman, Caroline (Carrie), 14, 16
Hitchman, E.F. (Edward Frederick), 14, 16-21, 24-27, 31-33, 43-44, 51, 198, 201, 205, 275, 276
Hitchman, Edna (*née* Rust), 1, 2, 297-298
Hitchman, Edward, 14, 15
Hitchman, Elizabeth Fanny, 14, 18, 32
Hitchman, Fanny (Hitch's great aunt), 14, 16
Hitchman, Florence Blanche (*née* Myers). *See* Hitchman, Tops, Topsy
Hitchman, Ida Dorothy (Dot), 14, 20, 27, 42, 44, 48, 142, 153-154, 166, 299
Hitchman, Ida May (*née* Thuresson), 18-20, 27, 44, 276
Hitchman, John, 14, 15-20, 27, 118, 294
Hitchman, Mary Florence, 14, 20, 27, 42
Hitchman, Road, 7
Hitchman, Tops, Topsy, 33, 155, 237, 245, 253, 260, 265, 269, 276, 295-297, 302
   girlfriend to Hitch, 50-53, 113
   Introduction, 1, 3-4, 6, 8, 13
   marriage, 123
   chapter notes, 334, 340
Hitchman, William (Hitch's great uncle), 14, 16
Hitchman, William Henry (Hitch's uncle), 14, 16-17, 19
Hockey Hall of Fame (HHOF), 2, 3-6, 8-12, 57, 60-61, 68, 294, 296, 303-306, 310, 319
   eligibility, 5
   inductee, 3, 9, 61, 287, 304, 306, 308, 310
   public submission, 5-6, 11
hockey sweater(s), 1, 2, 34, 65, 98, 102, 269, 304, *314*. *See also* retired number
Hockey Town USA, 294
Hockey Year Book 1923, 96
Holmes, Bill, 38
Hopewell Public School, 44, 47
Houston, J. W., 18
Hub, 134
Hughes, James, 222-223
Hunting and Fishing Show, 282
Hutton, Bill, 215
Ice Capades, 297
Indian Lake, 1, 294, 297-299, 302

Index | 351

insurance agent, 18, 25, 177
Interior (civil service amateur hockey team), 49, 322
International Hockey League (IHL), 286, 291
Irish, 18, 43, 72, 82, 104, 324
ironmongery grocer, 15
Ironstone, Joe, 122, 125
Irvin, Dick, 162, 265, 310
Jackson building, 48
Jackson, Harvey (Busher), 305
Jackson, Percy, 285
Jackson, Stan, 139, 224-225
Jackson, Walter, 284
Jenkins, Roger, 286
Jerwa, Frank, 253-254, 280, 283
Jerwa, Joe, 253, 256, 284-285
John Hammond, Col., 10, 209, 335
Johnson, Ivan (Ching), 10, 164, 174, 214, 217, 291, 303, 305-306
Joliat, Aurel, 10, 41, 73, 78, 107-108, 118, 138, 216, 230, 291, 306, 330, 336
Jones, P.J., 110, 327
Jones, Victor, O., 238, 290, 306, 337, 339-341
Juhnke, Admiral, 115
Junior A hockey, 13, 310
Kaese, Harold, 299-300, 306-307, 340-341
Keats, Duke, 87-88, 90, 156, 160, 306
Kelley, Peter, F.,137, 201, 232, 240, 336-337
Kelly, Dan, 4
Kennebunkport, 6
Kilrea, Hec, 172, 230, 241-243
King, Mackenzie, 49
Kirby, Chauncy, 95
Kitchener Greenshirts (Jr. OHA team), 286
kitty-bar-the-door, 98, 108,
Klein, Lloyd (Dutch), 186-187, 194-195, 204-205
Knights of Columbus (Ottawa senior amateur hockey team), 46
Koanneeta, 6-8, 12, 260-261, 281, 295
kraut line, 3, 286, 288, 305, 341
laborer, 15-18
Ladies Ontario Hockey Association, 142, 154, 166

Lady Evelyn Public School, 50
Laflamme, Jerry, 115, 140, 168-169
Lalonde, Edouard (Newsy), 306
Lamb, Joe, 213, 255
Lane, Myles, 187, 193-195, 204, 206, 266, 279-280, 302
Larochelle, Wildor, 240
Lauder, Martin (Marty), 170
Leduc, Albert (Battleship), 198, 201, 240
Lepine, Alfred (Pit), 38, 240, 251, 306
LeSueur, Percy, 118
Library and Archives Canada, 20, 276, 320
London Tecumsehs (IHL hockey team), 286
London, England, 16, 32
Lou Marsh Trophy, 35. *See also* Marsh, Lou
Lyons, Ron, 243
Lytle, Andy, 90, 326
Mack, Gene, 260
MacKay, Mickey, 38, 82, 93, 279, 306
  1928-29 season, 186-187, 190, 192, 194-195, 204
  1929-30 season, 212, 215, 223-224, 229, 244
MacKenzie, Kenny, 87, 101
MacQueen, C.W., 224, 336
Madawaska River, *see* Myers cabin
Madison Square Garden, 144
MaGuire, George, 202, 334
Maine (state), 6, 260, 273, 295-296, 309
Maki, Wayne, 4-5
Mallinson, George, 222, 240
Malone, Joe, 10
Mantha, Georges, 250
Mantha, Sylvio, 197, 200, 216-217, 230, 250
manufacturing, 18, 43, 134, 295
Marsden, Bill, 21, 32-36, 321
Marsh, Lou, 129, 148, 157, 229, 321. *See also* Lou Marsh Trophy
  1922-23 season, 72-77
  1923-24 season, 99, 105
  amateur referee, 34-35, 37-38
Mathews Arena, *see* Boston Arena
McCann, Philip, 113, 328
McCully, Bob, 285
McCurry, Dune, 151

McFarlane, Brian, 4, 12, 195, 204, 319, 334-335. *See also Bruins, The*
McGuire, Joe, 96
McInenly, Bert, 264
McKay, Robert, 38
McLaughlin, Tammy, 19, 27, 80
McNamara, Reggie, 260
McNeil, Guy, 229
McRoberts Ave, 19
McVeigh, Charley, 162
Meeking, Harry, 160
Meighen, Arthur, Prime Minister, 45, 49
Melrose, MA, 245, 272
Memorial Cup, 33, 41-42
MID (mentions in dispatch), 26
Milks, Hib, 38
Miller, Joe, 58, 64, 78
Minneapolis Millers, 186
Mitchell, Herb,138-139,
Mitchell, Johnny, 293, 340
Montagnards (Ottawa senior amateur hockey team), 46, 51, 127
Montreal Canadiens, 9, 38, 246-247, 249-251, 254, 256, 258, 283, 286
   1922-23 season, 60-62, 67, 70, 72-74, 76-79, 96
   1923-24 season, 103, 107-109, 112, 120, 122
   1924-25 season, 125-126, 129, 132-134, 138-142
   1925-26 season, 143-144, 149-150
   1926-27 season, 155-156, 158, 160-161
   1927-28 season, 170, 173-174, 178-179
   1928-29 season, 185, 187, 189, 195-196, 200-201, 203
   1929-30 season, 208, 213-214, 216, 221, 228-229, 234-235, 240-241
   chapter notes, 322-324, 327-328, 330, 333-334, 336-338
Montreal Forum, 126, 170, 210
Montreal Gazette, 70, 75, 106, 115, 117, 120, 132-133, 150, 309-310, 340-341
Montreal Herald, 9, 71, 140, 193, 251, 257
   1929-30 season, 200, 210, 214, 221, 225, 235, 240
   chapter notes, 324, 334-338, 340
Montreal Maroons, 35, 38, 248, 255, 262-263, 265, 285, 288
   1924-25 season, 127, 129, 132, 134, 137, 139
   1925-26 season, 143-144, 147-148, 153
   1926-27 season, 155, 158-160, 162
   1927-28 season, 169, 178, 180
   1928-29 season, 189, 191-195
   1929-30 season, 207, 210-215, 225-226, 232, 234-239, 242
   chapter notes, 329, 331, 333-334, 336-338
Montreal police, 76
Montreal Star, 113, 210, 215, 221, 225, 238, 234, 335-337
Mooney, J. W. (Doc), 137, 175, 198, 214, 218, 234, 236, 249-250, 270, 332, 334-339
Moore, Alfie, 35, 41
Moose Athletic Club, 38-39
Morenz, Howie, 106-107, 128-129, 198-199, 230, 235, 242, 251, 291. 305-306, 330
Morris, Bernie, 133
Morrison, Scotty, 5
Morse, Webster, 137
Motter, Alex, 283, 285
Moulds, Shirley, 165
Mount Royal Arena, 70, 73, 107-108, 111, 211, 228
Mousam, Lake, 260, 281, 295-296, 298
Muchmore Public School, 50
Mullins, W.E., 198, 334
Munitions (Ottawa senior amateur hockey team), 46, 294
munitions factory, 27
Munro, Duncan (Dunc), 226
Murdock, Murray, 164
Myers cabin, 52-53, 123, 245, 253, 260, 295
Myers, Lillie May (*née* McRae), 50
Myers, Warren, 50
Myers, Willis Ford, 50
Nason, Jerry, 307, 341
National Agricultural Union, 16
National Hockey League, *see* NHL
New Brunswick (Canada) Guides Association, 280
New Edinburghs (Burghs) (Ottawa senior amateur hockey team), 46-51, 57-58, 61-64, 67, 78, 99, 134, 146, 322-323

New Edinburghs (Burghs), rugby, 45, 47, 322
New England Amateur Hockey League, 293,
New Haven Brock-Halls, 294
New Haven Eagles, 171, 207, 280, 293
New York Americans (Amerks), 38, 254-255, 258-259
  1925-26 season, 143
  1926-27 season, 155, 159, 163
  1927-28 season, 172-174, 179
  1928-29 season, 188-189, 193-195
  1929-30 season, 214, 218, 225, 234
  1933-34 season, 264-265, 278
  chapter notes, 331-334, 338
New York Herald Tribune, 247, 255
New York Islanders, 208
New York Rangers, 10, 38, 279, 288, 303, 306-307, 331-335
  1926-27 season, 155, 158-160, 163-166
  1927-28 season, 169, 172-175, 179-183
  1928-29 season, 187-195, 201-203
  1929-30 season, 207, 209, 213, 215, 222-223, 229, 232, 234, 242
  1930-31 season, 247, 253
  1932-33 season, 255, 259
  1933-34 season, 264, 266-267
New York Times, 10, 222, 336
NHA (National Hockey Association), 28, 144, 156
NHL, National Hockey League, 1, 5, 8, 11, 28, 37, 45-46, 280, 299-300, 305, 307, 309
  1922-23 season, 60-62, 67-68, 71-74, 76-78, 81, 91
  1923-24 season, 97, 107-108, 109-111, 117, 120, 125
  1924-25 season, 126-128, 134, 141-142
  1925-26 season, 143-144, 151
  1926-27 season, 155-156, 158-159, 166, 169
  1927-28 season, 169-170, 175
  1928-29 season, 185, 188, 191, 203
  1929-30 season, 207-208, 214-216, 218, 233, 235, 240-242
  1930-31 season, 246, 249-250
  1931-32 season, 253
  1932-33 season, 255, 257
  1933-34 season, 262
  All-Star game and picks, 10, 241, 265
  complaints and disputes, 107, 109-111, 134, 141-142
  fines and suspensions, 5, 76-77, 144, 169
  Golf Tournament, 245
  records and firsts, 109, 119-120, 144, 165, 188, 208, 214, 235
  referee(s), 9, 34, 60, 72, 306
  rules, 143, 166
  special meetings, 109-111, 127
  chapter notes, 323, 328, 330, 332, 335, 339-340
Nighbor, Frank, 153, 181, 291, 305-307
  1922-23 season, 58-60, 68, 72, 79, 82, 84, 87-90, 93-94, 96
  1923-24 season, 97-98, 104-105, 107-111, 115, 118-120, 122
  1924-25 season, 125, 127-128, 141
  chapter notes, 326, 328, 331, 341
No. 4 Canadian General Hospital, *see also* University of Toronto Hospital, 25-27, 32
NOHA (North Ontario Hockey Association), 41-42
Norris, James, 265
North American Figure Skating Championships, 63
North Cambridge, 191
Northern Ontario, 54
Northwestern University, 134
O'Brien Cup, 67, 78, 95, 141, 144, 169, 195, *313*
O'Meara, Basil (Baz), 128
  1922-23 season, 79, 82-83, 88-89, 92, 94, 96
  1929-30 season, 210, 221, 225, 238, 242
  chapter notes, 324-326, 335-337
O'Neil, Tom, 57
Oakwood Collegiate, 29, 31-32, 320-321
OHA (Ontario Hockey Association), 28, 32-35, 38-42, 286
  eligibility, 41
Oliver, Harry, 247, 253-254, 257, 272-274, 302, 333
  1926-27 season, 156, 165-166, 168-169
  1927-28 season, 170-171, 174, 182-183
  1928-29 season, 186-188, 190, 192,

194-195, 203-204, 206
  1929-30 season, 210, 212, 215, 217, 235, 243-244
Olympic, ocean liner, 31
Olympics, 1924, 38
Ontario Provincial Police, Ontario police, 54, 57, 69-70, 177, 324
Orr, Bobby, 3, 286
Ottawa Alerts, 142, 153, 165
Ottawa Amateur City Hockey League (City League or Group 1), 46, 51, 58-59, 121, 177, 322
Ottawa and District Amateur Hockey Association, 46
Ottawa and District Ladies' Hockey Association, 153
Ottawa Auditorium (the Aud), 97, 99-100, 102-104, 115, 122, 327
Ottawa Citizen, 47, 55, 59, 64, 256, 302
  1922-23 season, 59, 61, 64, 67, 69, 71, 75-79, 82, 84, 90, 94-95
  1923-24 season, 106-108, 111-114, 119-121, 131-132,
  1924-25 season, 125, 131-132
  1929-30 season, 203-204, 212-213, 218
  amateur hockey, 55, 59, 64, 67, 75, 77
  rugby 45, 47, 55, 69
  Weber, Lilith (*née* Bennett), 302
  chapter notes, 322-329, 332, 335-336, 338, 340
Ottawa Football Club, 69
Ottawa Gunners (senior amateur hockey team), 46, 51, 57-59, 62-63, 322-323
Ottawa Gunners lacrosse team, 52-53, 57, 322
Ottawa Hockey Club, 64, 69, 90, 115, 133, 329
Ottawa Journal, 10, 151, 175, 212, 242, 258, 277, 299, 302
  1922-23 season, 52, 64, 79, 82-83, 86, 89-92, 94
  1923-24 season, 100, 103, 113, 120-121
  1924-25 season, 128, 132, 134
  amateur hockey, 45, 48, 64
  chapter notes, 319, 321-330, 333-335, 337-341
Ottawa Lansdowne Park, 44
Ottawa police, 5, 61, 93-94
Ottawa Rowing Club, 153, 165-166
Ottawa Senators
  1922-23 season, 1, 11, 49, 57-63, 67-96, 228-229, 300, 304-305
  1923-24 season, 97-123, 125
  1924-25 season, 38, 122, 125-134, 140
  1925-26 season, 143-144, 146, 148
  1926-27 season, 155, 160, 165
  1927-28 season, 172-173, 177
  1928-29 season, 186
  1929-30 season, 212, 218
  1932-33 season, 255, 258
  1933-34 season, 1, 269-270, 272
  1934-35 season, 285
  chapter notes, 324-329, 333
Ottawa Silver Band, 93-94
Ottawa Silver Seven, 57, 95
Ottawa South, 43
Ottawa University (senior amateur hockey team), 46
Ottawas, *see* Ottawa Senators
Owen, George, 300, 302, 308, 333-334, 338
  1928-29 season, 186-187, 191-195, 204, 206
  1929-30 season, 209-210, 215, 221, 224, 237, 239, 243-244
  1930-31 season, 246-247, 250-251
  1931-32 season, 253-254
  1932-33 season, 256, 258-259
Pacific Coast Hockey Association, Pacific Coast League, coast league, 67, 79-80-81, 90-91 126, 153, 186, 229
Paprika, 280-281, 339
Parisan, SS, 17
Parkdale (area of Toronto), 19-20
Parkdale Canoe Club, Jr. OHA hockey, 38-39, 41, 126
Parkdale Canoe Club, rugby, 53-55, 330
Parkdale Cricket, 21, 26, 32
Parnell, Walter, 53
Patrick, Frank, 80-82, 84-85, 91, 93, 126, 229, 243, 279, 283, 285, 287
Patrick, Lester, 37, 93
peritonitis, 18, 122, 329
Pettinger, Eric, 186
Philadelphia Arrows, 266, 280, 283, 292
Philadelphia Flyers, 208
Philadelphia Quakers, 246, 253

Phillips, Bill, 239, 258
Pittsburgh Pirates, 189, 194, 212, 221, 246, 331, 335
  1925-26 season, 143-144, 150-153
  1926-27 season, 155, 157-158, 163
Pittsburgh Yellow Jackets, 143
Plant, Frank, 78, 94, 99
points percentage, 1, 119, 142, 144, 246, 256, 258, *314*
poke-check, 58, 64, 115, 150-153, 156, 158, 161, 200, 266, 299, 304, 331
  1929-30 season, 203, 209, 214, 217, 236
Portland, Jack, 285-286
Prince of Wales Trophy, 144, 169, 171, 188, 193-194, *314-315*
Pringle, B., 96
Prospect Cemetery, 18, 29
Providence Marquettes, 294
Providence Reds, 280, 283-285, 301
public administration jobs, 44
Pulford, Harvey, 60-61, 70, 95-96
Quebec Beavers, 266, 280, 284, 291, 294
Queen's University (Jr. OHA hockey team), 41
Queen's University rugby, 53
Querrie, Charlie, 76, 111-112, 116
Raft, George, 243
ragging, 73, 76, 143
Randall, Ken, 108, 110
RCMP (Royal Canadian Mounted Police), Northwest Mounted Police, 44-45, 47, 49-51, 54, 80, 138, 148-149, 177, 226
  cricket team, 51-52
  hockey team, 49, 80
  N Division, 44, 50-51
  chapter notes, 321-322
Red Sox, 201
Regina Capitals, 82, 97-99, 126, 326
Regina Victorias, 51
Reid, Maurice (Lefty), 2
Reise, Leo, 163
retired number, 1, 3. *See also* hockey sweater(s)
Richfields, 243
Rickard, George (Tex), 192
Rideau Canoe Club. *See also* Rideaus 274

Rideau Rink, 46, 63
Rideaus (Rideau Canoe Club), rugby, 45, 47, 48, 322
Riverdale high school, 32
Riverdale Rugby Club, 35
Roach, John Ross, 33-35, 104, 201, 203
Roberts, Mauri, 156
Rock Lake. *See* Myers cabin
Rodden, Eddie, 34, 186-187
Rodden, Mike, 53, 105, 119
Rogerson, Charles, 42
Roman Catholics, 43
Romeril, Alex, 194
Rookie of the Year, 256
Ross, Art, 8, 144, 246, 263-264, 276, 285, 299
  1924-25 season, 126, 133, 137
  1926-27 season, 156, 160, 168
  1927-28 season, 170, 179-180
  1928-29 season, 186, 198, 204-205
  1929-30 season, 211, 215, 237, 243-244
  Hamilton Tigers manager, 62, 68,
  Hitch's coaching career, 195, 223, 229, 267, 278-279, 283, 287, 289, 291-392, *315*
  Hitch's contribution to the Bruins, 1, 149, 158, 176, 248-249, 254, 273, 291, 304-305
  ..Hitch's 1924-25 season, 133, 135, 139
  Hitch's 1928-29 season, 190, 195
  Hitch's 1929-30 season, 215-216, 219, 223, 229, 243
  Hitch's retirement, 267, 269, 273-276, 278
  referee, 102-103, 106-107, 110-112, 115
  chapter notes, 337, 339
Ross, Art, Jr., 215
Ross, J.K.L., 159
Ross, John, 215
Ross, Muriel (Art's wife), 296
Rover, 28
Royal Bank of Canada, 35
Royal Canadiens (Ottawa senior amateur hockey team), 46, 49, 58, 62
Royal Connaught Hotel, Hamilton, ON, 66
Royal Rooters, 146, 237

rugby, 21, 29, 31-35, 45, 47-48, 52-55, 58, 60, 69, 73, 86, 90, 191, 210, 300, 322, 341
Runge, Paul, 254
Rust, John Daniel (Edna's first husband), 297
Ruth, Babe, 260
Ryan, Frank, 1, 146, 275, 305
Saint John River, 246, 298
Salonika, 26, 330
Samuel 'Horseshoes' Webber, 63, 79, 93-94, 102
Saskatoon Crescents, 99, 126
Saskatoon Sheiks, 170
Savard, Capt. (Montreal police), 75-76
Schmidt, Milt, 3-4, 6, 287-288, 290, 305-306, 309
Schroeder, Leo, 58, 63
Seattle Metropolitans, 169
Second World War. *See* WWII
Seibert, Babe, 306
seven-man hockey, 28-29
Shakespeare, William, 15, 205, 253
Shapleigh, Maine, 6
Shay, Norm, 133
Shore, Eddie, 8-10, 279, 288, 290, 293, 299-310, *314*
   1926-27 season, 156-161, 166-168
   1927-28 season, 170-176, 179-183
   1928-29 season, 186-187, 189-193, 195, 199-201, 204
   1929-30 season, 209-230, 234, 236-240, 243-244
   1930-31 season, 246-247, 251-252
   1931-32 season, 253-254
   1932-33 season, 256-260
   1933-34 season, 262-266, 268-270, 273-274
   chapter notes, 333-334, 339, 341
Shortell, Joseph, Dr., 215, 232
Siegel, Arthur, 247-249, 251, 271, 338-339
Simcoe South, 18
Simpson, Joe, 87, 306
Sinden, Harry, 5-6
Sisler, George, 260
six-man hockey, 29
Smeaton, Cooper, 9-10, 60, 70, 72-73, 75-76, 106, 308

Smith, Alex, 181, 258, 263
Smith, Alf, 57
Smith, Art, 221
Smith, Brian, 3, 57
Smith, Des, 57
Smith, Eileen (*née* Carroll), 57
Smith, Frank Donald (founder, Beaches Hockey League), 28
Smith, Gary (Suitcase), 57
Smith, Hooley (Reginald), 38, 289, 300
   1924-25 season, 126-127, 129, 140-141
   1927-28 season, 168-170
   1928-29 season, 191, 194-195
   1929-30 season, 235-238
Smith, Rodger, 57, 59, 62-63, 151-152
Smylie, Rod, Dr., 104-105, 110
Smythe, Conn, 156, 264
Snowden, Inez (*née* Giafranchi), 8
Sons of England Benevolent Society, 20
SPA (Sportsmen's Patriotic Association), 33, 35
Spanish flu, 29, 30-31, 46, 72
Spring, Jesse, 103
Springfield Braves, 293-294
Springfield Indians, 286, 291-294, *315, 340*
Springfield Kings, 301
Springfield Republican, 300
SQMS (staff quartermaster sergeant), 26, 27
St. Anne's (Saint Anne's) Anglican Church, 20, 26, 32, 42
   men's association, 21, 32
St. Barnabas, 18
St. Brigids (Ottawa senior amateur hockey team), 46, 58, 63, 68, 323
St. Brigids rugby team, 55
St. Louis (NHL hockey team), 4
St. Patricks (St. Pats), (Ottawa senior amateur hockey team), 46, 49, 58, 61, 63-64. 322-323
Stanley Cup, 72, 122, 144, 153, 156-157, 165, 167-170, 182, 253, 262, 285, *313-314*
   1922-23 Season, 67, 84-86, 89-91, 96
   1928-29 season, 185, 196, 199-201, 203-205
   1929-30 season, 240-242
   1930-31 season, 246, 250-251

1932-33 season, 257, 259
Hitch's eligibility in 1923, 81-82, 85
trustee, 10, 60, 84, 325
chapter notes, 323-326, 334-335, 336
Statford-upon-Avon, 15
Steeves, William Henry, 50
Stevens, Phil, Mrs., 155
Stewart, Charlie, Dr. (Doc), 133, 139, 147, 151, 156, 160
Stewart, Charlie, Mrs., 155
Stewart, Jack, 306
Stewart, Nels, 148, 159, 230, 238-239, 242, 255-256, 262
Stratford Midgets (OHA Jr. hockey team), 33, 41-42
Stuart, Bill (Red), 108, 138-139, 147, 156, 159
Stubbs, Dave, 8-9
Sugar Bowl, 308
Sunnyside Av, 123
super six, 110, 130,
sweep check, 164, 167, 199, 233, 247-248, 273
TCC (Toronto Canoe Club), 35
Td Garden, 3
team captain, 143
  Clapper, 256
  Cleghorn, S, 161, 170-171
  Gerard, 57, 68, 86, 93-95, 305
  Hitch, 1, 12, 186, 205, 219, 246, 250, 252, 269, 299, *314*, 336
  Lane, 266, 269
  Nighbor, 115
  Owen, 253
Tecumseth, 18
Thompson, Cecil (Tiny), 248, 251, 253-254, 256-257, 259, 263, 272, 274, 302, 305-306, 309
  1928-29 season, 186-188, 190, 195, 197, 200-204
  1929-30 season, 209, 212, 215, 222, 224, 230, 238, 240, 243-244
Thoms, Bill, 259
Thoreau, Henry David, 296. See also *Walden*
Thuresson, Mary Ann (mother of Ida Hitchman), 18-20, 27
Thuresson, Susan (sister of Ida Hitchman), 19-20

Thuresson, Thomas (father of Ida Hitchman), 18-19
Tilton, Ralph, 40
Toronto (city), 17, 18, 20-21, 26, 28-31, 38, 43-44, 46
Toronto Arenas, 46
Toronto Argonauts, 53
Toronto federation of church men's association, 21
Toronto Globe, 26, 29, 38-39, 72, 320
Toronto Granites, 38, 51, 126
Toronto Hockey League (Greater), 28, 42, 177. See also Beaches Hockey League
Toronto Mail and Empire, 224, 336
Toronto Maple Leafs, 156, 170, 248, 253, 255-256, 259, 262-265, 285, 288, 305, 319, 336. See also Toronto St. Patricks
  1928-29 season, 185, 187, 190, 192-193, 201
  1929-30 season, 210, 223-224
Toronto Parkdale Canoe Club senior rugby team, 38, 53
Toronto Pats (ladies hockey), 166
Toronto St. Patricks (St. Pats), 143, 152, 154-156. See also Toronto Maple Leafs
  1922-23 season, 59-61, 67, 72, 76, 85
  1923-24 season, 104, 108-109, 112, 116
  1924-25 season, 134, 137, 141
  chapter notes, 323, 325-328, 330-331
Toronto Star, Toronto Daily Star,
  E.F. Hitchman, 26, 31-32
  Aura Lees, 34-37
  Boston Bruins, 37, 157, 167, 220
  lacrosse, 52
  Ottawa Senators, 72, 104
  rugby, 54
  chapter notes, 320-322, 332, 336
Toronto Telegraph, 224, 336
Toronto west, 43
Touhey, Bill, 253
Touhey, Willis, 64
Train(s), 32, 39-40, 45, 52, 63, 70, 78-81, 92-94, 97, 124, 240, 242-243, 258, 262
training camp, 5, 186, 262, 283, 288, 292-293, 296, 339
Trapp, Robert, 87, 100
Trottier, Dave, 236, 239

358 | HITCH

Trumbull, Walter 10, 209, 335
U.S. Amateur Hockey Association, 143
unemployment, 16-17
Union Station, Ottawa, 45, 78, 93-94
University of Toronto Hospital, 25-27. *See also* No. 4 Canadian General Hospital
University of Toronto Varsity Arena, 166
University of Toronto Varsity Blues (men's hockey), 34-37, 321
US Coast Guard Auxiliary, 295
Valdemar, Prince of Denmark, 114
Vancouver Maroons, 80-82, 85-86, 88, 90-91, 126, 257, 325-326
Vancouver Province, 90
Varsity Arena (Toronto), 166
Vezina Trophy, 57, 156, 209, 256. *See also* Georges Vezina
Vezina, Georges, 10, 156. *See also* Vezina Trophy
vice-team captain, 145, 147, 171, 182, *313*
Victor of Vimy, 45, 322
Victoria Cougars, 93, 126, 142, 144
Victorias (Ottawa senior amateur hockey team), 46, 51
Viggo, Prince of Denmark, 114
Voss, Carl, 256
Wakely Mountain Fire Tower, 297
Walden, Henry David Thoreau, 296
Walsh, James (Flat), 239
Walters, William, 36
Warton, Carl, 191, 333
Watson, Harry, 33
Watters, Henry, 105
WBZ, Boston, 145
Webb, Melville, E., 258, 264-266, 274, 338-339
Weber, Lilith, (*née* Bennett), 113, 302
Weiland, Gertrude, 296
Weiland, Ralph (Cooney), 170, 247, 253-255, 265, 292, 302, 305, 309, 334, 336
 1928-29 season, 186-187, 190, 192, 194-200, 202, 204
 1929-30 season, 209, 212-213, 215, 217, 222, 230, 235, 240, 242-244

Wellesbourne, 15-16, 319
Wesley, Dr. 76
Western Canada Hockey League (prairie), WHL, 47, 67, 81-82, 99, 126, 144
Westwick, Bill, 10, 299, 308, 319, 340-341
Wilcox, Archie, 266, 339
Williams, Victor, General, 70
Winkler, Hal, 87-88, 160, 163, 170-171, 174, 176, 180, 182, 186, 195, 331
Winnipeg Falcons (jr hockey team), 42, 284
Winnipeg Free Press, 98
Winnipeg Tribune, 215, 335-336, 339
Winnipeg, 80, 93, 97-99
Wollaston Golf Club, 260
Wood, William, 187
Woodward, Stanley, 164, 167-168, 247
 1924-25 season, 135, 137
 1928-29 season, 189, 192, 196, 197-198, 201
 1929-30 season, 221, 235
 chapter notes, 238-239, 330-334, 336-337
Worters, Roy, 42, 151, 161, 188-189
WWI, 23-24, 26-27, 33, 45, 289, 297, 320
 Canada's role, 24
 E.F. Hitchman's role, 24-27
 Toronto's role, 24
WWII, 26, 208, 294-295-296, 306
Wychwood hockey, 27, 31, 34, 36, 47, 177
Wychwood, 91, Ave, 34
X-ray, 189, 231-232
Young Men's Hebrew Association, 48
Zweig, Eric, see also *Art Ross: The Hockey Legend Who Built the Bruins*, 11, 325, 329